The Politics of Work–Family Policies

The work–family policies of Sweden and France are often held up as models for other nations to follow, yet political structures and resources can present obstacles to fundamental change that must be taken into account. Patricia Boling argues that we need to think realistically about how to create political and policy change in this vital area. She evaluates policy approaches in the US, France, Germany and Japan, analyzing their policy histories, power resources and political institutions to explain their approaches, and to propose realistic trajectories toward change. Arguing that much of the story lies in the way that job markets are structured, Boling shows that when women have reasonable chances of resuming their careers after giving birth, they are more likely to have children than in countries where even brief breaks put an end to a career, or where motherhood restricts them to part-time work.

PATRICIA BOLING is an associate professor in the Department of Political Science at Purdue University in the United States. She is interested in how issues housed in the private sphere of the family get translated into negotiable political issues, and has written a book about the politics of intimate life, edited a book on new reproductive technologies, and authored various articles and chapters related to public–private distinctions and work–family policies. Having lived in Japan for three years, her research agenda has considered various practices that mostly occur in the intimacy of family that raise issues of justice and equality both in Japan and around the world.

The Politics of Work–Family Policies

Comparing Japan, France, Germany and the United States

Patricia Boling

CAMBRIDGE
UNIVERSITY PRESS

University Printing House, Cambridge CB2 8BS, United Kingdom

Cambridge University Press is part of the University of Cambridge.

It furthers the University's mission by disseminating knowledge in the pursuit of education, learning and research at the highest international levels of excellence.

www.cambridge.org
Information on this title: www.cambridge.org/9781107098121

First published 2015

A catalogue record for this publication is available from the British Library

Library of Congress Cataloguing in Publication data
Boling, Patricia, 1953–
The politics of work–family policies : comparing Japan, France, Germany and the
United States / Patricia Boling.
    pages   cm
Includes bibliographical references and index.
ISBN 978-1-107-09812-1 (hardback)
1. Work and family.   2. Work and family – Government policy.   3. Family policy.
I. Title.
HD4904.25.B65   2015
306.3′6 – dc23   2014046183

ISBN 978-1-107-09812-1 Hardback

Contents

Figures

Tables

Interviewees

Amino Takehiro (interviews, October 19, 1999; November 11, 1999). Professor, Shakai Fukushi-gakka (School of Social Welfare), Sophia University, Tokyo.

Atoh Makoto (interviews, October 29, 1996; October 5, 1999; June 2, 2008). In 1996 and 1999, he was Director-General of the National Institute of Population Problems, part of the NIPSSR (国立社会保障・人口問題研究所). In 2008 Atoh had retired from the NIPSSR and had a research affiliation with the Faculty of Human Sciences at Waseda University in Tokyo.

Bothfeld, Silke (interview, July 12, 2004). Researcher affiliated with the Social Science Research Institute, Berlin [WZB, Wissenschaftszentrum Berlin].

Brin, Hubert (interview, July 18, 2005). President of the National Union of Family Associations (President de l'Union Nationale des Associations Familiales), Paris.

Calman, Leslie, and Lisalyn Jacobs (interview, August 4, 2004). Calman: Senior Vice President and Director, Family Initiatives, Legal Momentum, Washington, DC; Jacobs: Vice-President for Goverment Relations, Legal Momentum, Washington, DC (Legal Momentum used to be called the NOW Legal Defense Fund).

Coleman, Liv (interview, April 4, 2011).

Daniel, Yasmine (interview, August 3, 2004). Director of Early Childhood Development, Children's Defense Fund, Washington, DC.

Fagnani, Jeanne (interviews, June 1, 1999; June 11, 2003). Researcher with MATISSE-CNRS and adviser to the French National Family Funds (Directrice de recherche au CNRS, MATISSE – Université de Paris 1, Conseillère à la CNAF, Caisse national d'allocations familiales).

Golin, Stacie (interview, June 27, 2003). Study Director, Institute for Women's Policy Research, Washington, DC.

Goto Eiji (interview, February 26, 1997). Director, Department of Research and Investigation, The Foundation for Children's Future (Kodomo Mirai Zaidan).

Grant, Jodi (interview, July 26, 2003). National Partnership for Women & Families.

Greenberg, Mark (interview, August 5, 2004). Director of Policy, Center for Law and Social Policy, Washington, DC.

Hartman, Heidi, and Barbara Gault (interview, August 4, 2004). Hartman: Director of the Institute for Women's Policy Research, Washington, DC; Gault: Associate Director of the Institute for Women's Policy Research, Washington, DC.

Helmke, Hans Joachim (interview, July 14, 2004). Assistant Secretary – Director of the Office in charge of Child Support payments at the German Family Ministry (Ministerialrat, Leiter des Referats 205, Kindergeld, BMFSFJ).

Hihara Tomomi (interviews, November 15, 1999; June 2, 2011). In 1999 Hihara was a mid-level bureaucrat in the Children and Family Bureau Childcare Office at Japan's Ministry of Health and Welfare (厚生省児童家庭局保育課). In 2011, she was a principal researcher at the Institute for Health Economics and Policy in Tokyo.

Honda Hajime (interview, January 18, 2001). Director, Child-Rearing Promotion Division at Japan's Ministry of Health, Labor and Welfare (厚生労働省雇用均等児童家庭局育成環境課長 課長).

Horie Izumi (interview, November 13, 1999). Member, Public Employees' Union, Daycare Teachers' Union (Hobosan kumiai).

Kamohara Motomichi (interview, January 21, 2001). Head, Child Allowances room, Childrearing Environment Section, Equal Employment – Child Family Division at Japan's Ministry of Health, Labor and Welfare (厚生労働省雇用均等・児童家庭局育成環境課, 児童手当管理室長).

Kobayashi Kazuhiro (interview, December 20, 1999). Section head of the Child and Family Planning Section at Japan's Ministry of Health and Welfare (厚生省児童家庭局企画課長).

Kornbluh, Karen (interview, June 26, 2003). Director, Work & Family Program, New America Foundation, Washington, DC.

Kull, Silke (interview, July 16, 2004). Research Assistant at the WZB, Social Science Research Institute, Berlin.

Letablier, Marie-Thérèse, and Olivier Büttner (interview, May 23, 2003). Letablier: researcher at the Center for Study of Employment (Centre d'études de l'emploi, Noisy-le-Grand). Büttner: research assistant on Letablier's team.

Manabe (interview, November 21, 1996). Deputy Director, Policy Planning and Evaluation Division, Minister's Secretariat at Japan's Ministry of Health and Welfare.

Martin, Claude (interview, June 5, 2003). Researcher and sociologist, University of Rennes (Université de Rennes).

Muraki Atsuko (interview, January 22, 2001). Director of the Equal Employment Policy Division at Japan's Ministry of Health, Labor and Welfare (厚生労働省雇用均等・児童家庭局 雇用均等政策課長).

Naumann, Ingela (interview, June 30, 2004). Naumann was the graduate student who assisted me with German translation, summer 2004. In addition to helping me with translation, she also gave me significant help with substantive explanations of family policy issues.

Nishizawa Hideaki (interview, June 13, 2008). Bureaucrat with the Children and Families General Affairs Section at Japan's Ministry of Health, Labor and Welfare (厚生労働省児童家庭局総務課).

Okazaki Tomiko (interview, June 1, 2011). Member of Japan's House of Councilors from Miyagi (Democratic Party of Japan).

Périvier, Hélène (interviews, June 6, 2003; July 13, 2005). Researcher, French Observatory for Economic Concerns (Observatoire français des conjonctures économiques, Fondation nationale des sciences politiques, Paris).

Rolston, Howard L. (interview, June 26, 2003). Director of Planning, Research and Evaluation, Administration of Children, Youth and Families, at the US Department of Health and Human Services.

Saimura Jun (interview, November 12, 1999). Researcher, Japan Children and Family Research Institute (日本子ども家庭総合研究所).

Shimizu Michio (interview, November 20, 1999). Head of the Daycare Section at Japan's Ministry of Health and Welfare (厚生省児童家庭局保育課長).

Shimbo Yukio (interview, February 20, 1997). Chief, Family Welfare Division, Children and Families Bureau at Japan's Ministry of Health and Welfare.

Shimomura Toshifumi (interview, June 12, 2008). Deputy Director for the Declining Fertility / Aging Society Countermeasures Office in Japan's Cabinet Office Social Policy General Headquarters (内閣府共生社会政策統括官少子高齢化対策第一担当参事括官).

Strobel Pierre, (interviews, May 28, 2003; July 12, 2005). Director of MIRE (Research arm of DREES, the Research, Studies, Assessment and Statistics Directorate) for the French Ministry of Social Affairs, Labor and Solidarity (Mission Recherche [MIRE], Direction de la recherche, des études, de l'évaluation et des statistiques, Ministère des affaires sociales, du travail et de la solidarité).

Struck, Jutta (interview, July 19, 2004). Assistant Secretary – Director of the Office in charge of Child Rearing and Paid Maternity Leave at the German Family Ministry (Ministerialrätin, Leiterin des Referats 204, Bundeserziehungsgeldgesetz, Mutterschutzgesetz, Bundesministerium für Familie, Senioren, Frauen und Jugend [BMFSFJ]).

Tanaka Shigeki (interview, June 12, 2008). Deputy Director for the Declining Fertility Countermeasures Office in Japan's Cabinet Office Social Policy General Headquarters (内閣府共生社会政策統括官少子化対策第一担当参事括官).

Toulemon, Laurent (interviews, May 27, 1999; June 5, 2003; July 10, 2005). In 2003 and 2005 Toulemon was a researcher at INED, the French National Institute for Demographic Studies (Institut national d'études démographiques).

Tsukasaki Yūko (interview, June 12, 2008). She was head of the Gender Equality Promotion Division at the Cabinet Office Gender Equality Bureau (,内閣府男女共同参画局推進課長). (Note: this was a joint interview with four people, Tsukasaki, Tanaka, Shimomura and Yoshino, each of whom is cited separately here – citation in text is "Tsukasaki, 2008.")

Tsukasaki Yūko (interview, May 25, 2011). Section head for the Work–Childrearing Section of the Work–Family Harmonization Office at Japan's Ministry of Health and Welfare (塚崎 裕子,厚生労働省 雇用均等・児童家庭局 職業家庭両立課長).

Tvedt, Karen, et al. (interview, June 25, 2003). Policy and Research Director, Child Care Bureau, at the United States Department of Health and Human Services. Several others attended this meeting along with Tvedt, although without speaking or interacting with me: a career HHS bureaucrat named Shannon Christian (Associate Director, Child Care Bureau), Ron Filewich, Shannon Rutacil and an intern named Ngozi Onunaku.

Ulrich, Ralf E. (interview, July 13, 2004). Researcher at the Institute for Population Research (Institut für Bevölkerungsforschung und Sozialpolitik), University of Bielefeld.

Villac, Michel (interview, May 27, 2003). Chief of the Project on Upgrading Information for the Health System at the French Ministry for Health, Family and Handicapped Persons (Chef de la MISS – Mission pour l'informatisation du système de santé, Ministère de la santé, de la famille et des personnes handicapées).

Von Bassewitz, Martina (interview, July 5, 2005). Assistant Secretary – Director of the Office in charge of International Affairs and Planning at the German Family

Ministry (Ministerialrätin, Leiterin des Referats 201, Grundsatz- und internationale Angelegenheiten, Planung, BMFSFJ).

von Keyserlingk, Ulrike (interview, July 14, 2004). Assistant Secretary – Director of the Office in charge of Promoting Local Family Support Networks at the German Family Ministry (Ministerialrätin, Leiterin des Referats 206, Lokale Bündnisse und Engagement für Familien, BMFSFJ).

Wersig, Maria (interview, July 19, 2004). Wersig was pursuing graduate studies in law, at Freie Universität in Berlin.

Wiesner, Reinhard (interview, July 19, 2004). Assistant Secretary – Director of the Office in charge of Child and Youth Health at the German Family Ministry (Ministerialrat, Leiter des Referats 511, Kinder- und Jugendhilfe, BMFSFJ).

Yamamoto Mami (October 25, 1999). Researcher, Japan Children and Family Research Institute (Kodomo katei sougou kenkyujo, 子ども家庭総合研究所).

Yoshino Hideo (interview, June 12, 2008). Member of the Survey Analysis section in Japan's Cabinet Office Social Policy General Headquarters (内閣府男女共同参画局調査分析).

Preface

The idea of comparing several countries with respect to how well they support working parents occurred to me at a point in my life when I was immersed in establishing an academic career and raising three small children. Because my children were born before I had tenure, I got to experience how parents manage to find and pay for childcare on a shoestring budget, and to do so in both Japan and the United States. The experience ignited my desire to understand why some countries are more willing and able to support working parents than others.[1]

My first two children were born while I was in grad school, and the third a couple of years later. During the run up to completing my dissertation, my older daughter attended the University of California Berkeley childcare centers for two years, and the other two children attended these excellent centers (and ones run by the nearby city of Albany) for a stretch in the late 1980s. Once cut loose from the Berkeley umbilical cord, I found myself working to find adequate care in ordinary American cities that would fit my schedule and budget. The options were not wonderful: for a time, one of my kids attended a commercial, for-profit center whose caregivers had little training or interest in being teachers. For a few months, the next-door neighbor watched the two older kids after school until I got home from work. I relied on several different "family home care" arrangements, in which I took the kids to a provider's home where she took care of them along with several other children. After muddling along with these arrangements, we eventually worked our way to the top of the waiting list for one of the best early childhood programs in our city, which was a happy location for my youngest child for a year or so. At a later stage, I hired students from the university I taught at to be at home with the kids after school a few days a week. A dual-academic household, my husband and I did our best to arrange

---

[1] At the outset, I acknowledge that the work–family issues I address here are those facing families with children, leaving out the practices and policy lacunae that make work and family difficult for other kinds of families. Of course, other kinds of families – childless ones, single person, empty nest, same-sex partners with or without children – face problems reconciling work and family life too. I take part of my focus here to be on low-fertility issues and concerns about encouraging people to have more babies, so this book addresses the work–family problems facing families that are raising children.

complementary schedules and to use the flexibility we had as professors to minimize both the amount of paid care we needed and the amount of time the children spent as "latch key" kids.

Unexpectedly, a high point to this busy period of trying to keep two academic careers on track and raise three young children was a 2½-year stay in Tokyo in the late 1980s. At the start of this period, our daughters were 4½ and 2 years old; our son was born in Tokyo. We sent all of them to childcare centers (*hoikuen*) in Fuchu-shi (about 30 minutes west of central Tokyo on a fast commuter train), utilizing three different private centers in all, one unlicensed and two licensed ones. All three of them attended a large licensed center in Higashi Fuchu for more than a year; the oldest child graduated from this center and attended first grade and after-school care – *gakudō kurabu* – for 9 months.

We learned a lot about Japanese childcare from this experience. One thing was absolutely obvious: a low-income family could find much better, more affordable care for their children in Japan than in the USA. In Japan, teachers were well trained; many had special skills (e.g., they could lead singing or crafts or teach children to play musical instruments); they thought being a day care teacher was a good job, and stayed in their positions for long periods of time; and they were treated by parents and children with respect and warmth. We were charged nominal amounts for full-time childcare, based on our family income; despite the fact that we were resident foreigners, the national, prefectural and city governments provided substantial subsidies.

The contrast with our experiences in the United States was remarkable: at home, the Flex Spending account and tax credits we got to help pay for childcare were tiny compared to the total cost, and we were hard pressed to find adequate care that we could afford on a modest income. In each new community we moved to, we had to figure out what providers were available and how good they were. Over and over we had to make tradeoffs, settling for a caregiver who was kind but not trained, or picking a home care mother in the neighborhood who was convenient but apt to park kids in front of the television set, or scrimping on other expenditures in order to be able to afford a better childcare center. Except for our experience with UC Berkeley's exceptionally well-run, professional childcare centers, we never encountered affordable, high-quality childcare in the USA that matched the childcare provided in licensed facilities in Japan.[2] Nor does the USA offer monthly family allowance payments or paid maternity or parental leaves, both standard features of many countries' policies to support working parents.

---

[2] These centers were run as a service to enable students at UC Berkeley to concentrate on their studies; they only provided about 25 hours a week of care, and they required 2 hours of parent participation per child per week. The teachers were well trained, compassionate, experienced, and thoughtful.

After my experience of dealing with caring for my children in a country with quite different work–family reconciliation policies, it struck me that it would be interesting and important to understand why different countries take such divergent approaches to supporting working parents. Why does the United States, despite being the largest and most productive economy in the world, mostly leave matters related to caring for babies and children up to individuals and families, despite the fact that many parents struggle to pay for their children's care or to take a few months off from work without pay? Why did the "few child crisis" and work–family issues become a prominent part of Japan's public discourse by the mid-1990s, and what impact did this sense of crisis have on efforts to improve childcare and parental leave policies?

Initially, the goal of the project was to understand Japanese and American work–family reconciliation policies in comparative perspective, in part because Japan was not a case that many scholars doing comparative work had addressed with care.[3] Eventually I decided to include France and Germany, conservative European welfare states that spend much more than the United States or Japan on family support policies. France has developed a variety of childcare and early childhood education programs that insure affordable care for many infants and toddlers and most preschoolers, while Germany sends more ambivalent messages to working mothers, spending heavily on policies that encourage male breadwinner families, and only recently developing short well-paid parental and paternity leaves. It still does much less to support childcare than France. Both share Japan's concern with supporting fertility; indeed, in recent years Germany has been ranked with Japan among the lowest low-fertility countries in the world. Adding them to the comparison made sense, especially given the attention Japanese policy makers pay to both these countries' approaches to work–family issues.

Managing life as a dual-career academic couple with three small children living in Japan and the United States gave rise to the problems and insights that led me to write this book, and led me to do comparative research on policy making. Although the road has been a long one, I'm glad my experiences led me to take this approach.

---

[3] Esping-Andersen has written about Japan as a hybrid and as one of the "familialistic" welfare states like Italy, Spain and Greece (1997, 1999), but without much familiarity with Japanese policy history or its welfare state; Kasza (2006) has addressed Japan's approach to social welfare in comparative context, but without much focus on work–family policies; Gelb (2003) writes generally about women's movements and rights in Japan and the United States, as does Kobayashi in her 2004 study of state feminism in Japan, but neither focuses closely on policy processes or family support policies.

Acknowledgements

I got a good start on this project in Tokyo as a Fulbright Fellow in 1999, returning for short visits in 2000 and 2001, and receiving a grant from the Japan–US Friendship Commission that enabled me to travel to Berlin, Paris and Washington DC to conduct interviews with scholars, demographers, bureaucrats and activists. The project hit some weedy stretches in the early 2000s due to family upheavals and ill health which made it hard to focus on writing for a stretch. I am grateful to the many friends and colleagues who expressed confidence that I would figure out what I wanted to say about the interesting case study material I had accumulated. Sometimes it takes a community to provide the varieties of support that one needs to see one's work through to completion, and this book is certainly such an instance.

I have accumulated many debts over the years in pursuing this project, and I am happy to acknowledge all of the various forms of support I have received with it. I received generous support from several institutions, including a Fulbright research fellowship to study in Japan in late 1999, a grant from the Social Science Research Council to fund a follow-up trip in 2000, two Northeast Asia Council travel grants funded through the Association for Asian Studies, a grant from the Japan–US Friendship Commission that permitted travel to multiple countries, and an invitation from an incisive young scholar named Sawako Shirahase to spend a stretch as a visiting scholar at the NIPSSR in Tokyo (Japanese names are given in Western order throughout).

Shirahase was extremely helpful in making introductions and accompanying me on interviews at the Ministry of Health, Labor and Welfare. Several others were kind enough to introduce me to appropriate policy makers and officials, through a variety of avenues: an old friend, Takehiko Yanaka, introduced me to Diet members who were kind enough to speak with me. The director of NIPSSR, Makoto Atoh, helped me contact scholars interested in policies to counter low fertility and demographers, and the head of international studies at NIPSSR in the 1990s, Hiroshi Kojima, suggested numerous important studies and sources of data for me to read in Japanese, English and French, and introduced me to scholars of demography in France and Germany. Both have stayed in touch over a lengthy period, and I have enjoyed developing warm friendships with them.

I have had repeated conversations about work–family policies with leading feminist scholar Mari Osawa of the Social Science Research Institute (Shaken) at Tokyo University, who was kind enough to introduce me to Yūko Tsukasaki of the Gender Equality Bureau in the Prime Minister's Cabinet Office.

My research network in France, Germany and the United States is not as elaborated as the one I developed in Japan, but I am happy to express my thanks to several scholars who talked with me generously and helped me establish contacts in France and Germany. I was invited for a stay as a visiting international scholar at the National Institute for Demographic Studies (INED) in Paris by Laurent Toulemon, who also generously facilitated introductions to various members of the French work–family research community, including several government officials. Marie Thérèse Letablier, Jeanne Fagnani and Hélène Périvier, three feminist scholars interested in work–family policy issues, were generous with their time and resources, and helped me figure out the connections between the mainstream "welfare elite" and feminists who were somewhat more critical of government policies. A fifth French informant, Pierre Strobel, was generous with his insightful explanations of how French policy making worked. I was fortunate to be invited to spend several weeks as a visiting scholar at the WZB (the Wissenschaft Zentrum Berlin, Social Science Research Institute) in 2004, which was an excellent opportunity to present work and interact with other scholars interested in labor market and family support issues, including Günther Schmid and Jacqueline O'Reilly.

My language abilities for conducting this four-country project were adequate but not spectacular, and I would like to thank several graduate students who worked as interpreters, translators and facilitators in my conversations in Germany and Japan. Ingela Naumann assisted me in half a dozen interviews at the German Family Ministry (Bundesministerium für Familie, Senioren, Frauen und Jugend). In Japan, I worked with Chikako Kashiwazaki, Aya Ezawa and Kimiko Osawa, all of whom were immensely helpful in making sure I didn't get lost in difficult explanations, insuring that my interlocutors understood me and I them, and translating and cleaning up questions that I sent ahead of time to people I interviewed. I have a special debt of appreciation to Glenda Roberts, an anthropologist of work–family issues in Japan and a good friend, who for a time collaborated with me in doing interviews with representatives of day care teachers' unions, a representative of the national private childcare association, the president of a pro-childcare parents' organization, the staff at an *eki-gata hoikuen* (a childcare center near a train station), bureaucrats at the Ministry of Health and Welfare, representatives of the Foundation for Children's Future, and in discussions with various academics. Glenda and I make different sense of the world, but she was patient and generous in helping me learn the lay of the land in the policy area that I had chosen to study in Japan.

Another form of intellectual sustenance has been through formal and informal academic meetings and symposia. I thank John Campbell for including me in two such events he organized at the University of Michigan: a 2001 conference on "Change, Continuity, and Context: Japanese Law in the Twenty-First Century," and a 2002 symposium, "The Way Some Japanese Live Now," both held at the University of Michigan Law School. Frances Rosenbluth of Yale University kindly invited me to participate in two workshops, in 2001 and 2002, on "The Political Economy of Childcare and Female Employment in Japan, the US, and Europe," which were great opportunities for a variety of scholars to discuss the work–family policies and roles of women in the workforce that were in the process of changing in Japan. In 2008 I was invited to give a paper at a conference on "Fertility and Social Stratification in Japan and Germany" organized by the Deutsches Institut für Japanstudien (DIJ, German Institute for Japan Studies) in Tokyo; both at that conference and in other conversations with scholars from the DIJ, I have found it valuable to talk with people who share my interest in Japan–Germany comparisons.

Less formal interactions at conference panels, especially at the Association for Asian Studies yearly conferences, the Midwest Japan Seminar sessions where I got to know Susan Long, Laura Miller, Lou Perez, Gregory Kasza and others, and political science conferences like the Midwest Political Science Association and the American Political Science Association, have also been frequent sources of stimulation and chances to get feedback on ideas and arguments. I especially want to thank a community of scholars that includes Mark Tilton, Ito Peng, Priscilla Lambert, Jiyeoun Song, Liv Coleman, Mary Brinton, Leonard Schoppa, Deborah Milly, Margarita Estevez-Abe, Heidi Gottfried, Karen Shire, David Leheny, Glenda Roberts and Kimberly Morgan for rich, varied conversations over the years. An extremely interesting group of scholars whom I have gotten to know through the International Political Science Association's Research Council (RC) 19 on Gender Politics and Policy includes Sonya Michel, Rianne Mahon, Ann Orloff and Ito Peng, and their discussions of social policy and gender (published and in person) have been a source of insight and an impetus to rethink my own positions. I appreciate the opportunities I have had to participate in RC19 conferences in Toronto and Paris.

My colleagues at Purdue University, where I have had the good fortune to teach for the last twenty-plus years, have been a constant source of intellectual camaraderie, instigation and friendship. I especially appreciate the Workshop on Public Policy and Political Theory, where I have presented parts of my book on several occasions. Workshop organizers Leigh Raymond and Laurel Weldon have been great interlocutors, reading my work with care and giving me useful critiques and responses on several occasions. Participants in the workshop and various other colleagues include Dwayne Woods, Aaron Hoffman, Ann Clark,

Will McLauchlan, Rosie Clawson, Mark Tilton, Daniel Aldrich, Keith Shimko, Bert Rockman, Sally Hastings, Patsy Schweickart and Berenice Carroll. Many have been generous with their time, reading parts of the book and giving me comments on it, and I cannot thank them enough for the effort and intelligence they put into this.

I also want to thank various people associated with Cambridge University Press who helped guide this book from a sprawling manuscript into its present form: first, the two anonymous reviewers who provided me with extremely helpful suggestions for recasting the argument of the book, including a detailed roadmap for how to reorganize my thinking. Second, thank you to Lucy Rhymer, the editor with whom I had my earliest contact and whose faith in the project was crucial. Third, a big thank you to Leigh Muller, the copy editor who worked tirelessly on tidying up my language and chasing down discrepancies across eight chapters. The book is a better piece of work because of all of you.

I would also like to thank the graduate students with whom I have worked over the last few years who have really had a hand in discussing ideas and shaping arguments that have influenced the development of this book. In the process of teaching a graduate seminar on comparative social policy, I have tried out my approach on a handful of students who have given me very useful responses: Katie Cahill, Cheryl O'Brien, Holly Gastineau-Grimes, Rachel Walker, Andy Tuholski, Fernando Tormos and Summer Forester. Tom Klein worked as my RA, reading works on the French welfare state, as did Hiroaki Watanabe on Japan. A third RA, Rachel Walker, worked to put together a clean version of the sprawling bibliography for this book, and read each chapter with an eye toward encouraging me to write lively, accessible, clear prose. A fourth, Bob Kulzick, helped me obtain publishers' permissions and clean up several tables.

My friends and family have been terrific in all kinds of ways, helping me stay focused without getting too obsessed. A special thanks to Eric Waltenburg for initiating years of running and being my friend through many seasons, and to Leigh Raymond who has likewise logged many a mile with me. I want to thank my husband Howard for his balance, good humor and love through the long process of writing this book. Finally, I want to thank my children, Ellen, Clio and Andy, who in crucial ways have shared this project with me from its inception. It is for them and their children that I undertook this project. My hope is that my book might push our country to emulate some of the lessons that France, Germany and Japan have to teach, improving the kinds of care available to all children, not just those whose parents can afford nannies and excellent, select nurseries and schools.

Of course, any errors of fact or interpretation are my own.

1 Why work–family policies matter, and how best to study them

This book has had a long gestation period: I began thinking about comparing different countries' approaches to supporting working families when my children were babies, and I completed it a year after the birth of my first grandchild. I wish I could say that the situation for working mothers and fathers in the United States is much better now than it was when I started, but it really hasn't changed very much. Families still muddle along, trying to make time to stay home and recover and get to know their babies and doing their best to find decent affordable care for their children without much help from the government. Unless there is a family member who can care for the children, the quality of care their children receive is still largely proportional to the size of their pocketbooks.

Even though many Americans feel that our country has failed to provide high-quality care to all of our children, and President Obama has tried to place universal early childhood education on the domestic agenda,[1] we still rely on a market system that employs low-wage workers to do caregiving work and reproduces inequality with every generation. Why has it been so hard to reform work–family reconciliation policies in the United States? Do all countries have such a hard time reforming their family support policies, or is the difficulty related to something particular about the institutions, policy repertoires and power holders in the US?

A Japanese woman might ask similar questions about her country's inability to provide adequate policies to support young people as they seek to marry and establish families. Why do young people have such difficulty finding decent jobs that would allow them to start a family? Why do parents who live in cities have to wait so long to get their children into licensed childcare centers?

---

[1] He brought this issue up in his State of the Union speeches in 2013, 2014 and 2015; the response to his attempt to put universal pre-kindergarten schooling on the domestic policy agenda in 2013 has been tepid. Senator Tom Harkin of Iowa, joined by twenty-five co-sponsors, introduced the "Strong Start for America's Children Act" (S. 1697, HR 3461) to the Senate on November 13, 2013 (Govtrack, 2013). Chances of such a Bill being passed by the Republican-controlled Senate and House of Representatives are minuscule.

1

Why can't women go back to work after they take a year of parental leave without being harassed by resentful co-workers? Why do mothers still earn 60 percent less than men? Under these circumstances, it is not surprising that the total fertility rate (the average number of children a woman has over the course of her life) has fallen steadily over the last forty years in Japan. But even though supporting working mothers is a high-priority domestic issue, the national government continues to have trouble ascertaining and carrying out policies that effectively ease work–family conflicts.

I could go on spinning out such scenarios. But the point is that for many countries, enacting workable, generous work–family policies is a challenge, even in those that have high percentages of working women, adequate resources, and are acutely concerned about reproducing well-educated, hardworking citizens to help them manage the bills for their aging baby boomers. This book has grown out of my puzzlement over what makes many countries so recalcitrant about passing work–family support policies.

I aim to provide insight into this puzzle by comparing the development of work–family policies in France, Germany, Japan and the United States. Of the four, France stands out for having developed several programs that support high-quality affordable care for infants, free universal preschool edcucation, paid parental and maternity leaves, short work hours and generous family allowances. Germany and Japan face rapidly aging populations and economic problems related to having fewer workers and higher costs for supporting retired people. Both have male-breadwinner, intensive-mothering family patterns, and mothers in both countries have a hard time retaining continuous full-time jobs. In response to lowest-low fertility rates,[2] both initiated policy changes in recent years, albeit with rather different levels of investment and degrees of success. The last, the United States, has a number of tax policies and means-tested programs to help families with early childhood education and care (ECEC), and a twelve-week job-protected unpaid family leave. It invests the least of the four in policies to support working families, leaving it up to families to purchase care for their children in the private market and to save up in order to be able to take a few months off around a birth or adoption. Sparse leave policies and a flexible labor market contribute to women taking short breaks for childrearing – but also to relatively low opportunity costs (that is, the net pay, raises and retirement benefits that a woman loses because of taking time off from work to raise children) for mothering. American women are more successful than their French, German or Japanese sisters in breaking through the glass ceiling into management-level positions.

[2] I use "lowest-low" to refer to countries with total fertility rates (TFRs) at or below 1.4, that is, with extremely low TFRs. Both Japan and Germany had TFRs of 1.39 in 2010 (OECD, 2013m).

Because they take quite different approaches to supporting working mothers, these countries make for interesting and useful comparisons. They present revealing contrasts with respect to cultural attitudes toward gender roles, the structure of their labor markets, their political institutions and constellations of power resources, and the historical trajectories of their work–family policies.

Having introduced my project, the rest of this chapter goes on to make the case that we should care about how well different states support working mothers, and to review the most important issues, debates and approaches that have arisen over twenty-five years of discussion among sociologists and political scientists about how best to compare welfare states and work–family support policies.

Much of the comparative work on work–family policies takes the approach that "we should be more like Sweden," which is understandable: Sweden, France and a few others have adopted generously funded, well-designed policies that do a lot to help working parents and their children. There's a lot to admire there, and I think it makes sense to treat such policies as exemplary. But this is just a starting point; a realistic, pragmatic consideration of how best to support working families must go beyond a discussion of which countries have the best work–family support policies, and consider what is politically feasible in different countries, given their respective histories and political economies. Even if we were all to agree that social democratic countries have developed the most effective, generous family support policies in the world, that doesn't mean that other countries can simply take a cutting off their plants, graft it to native stock, and expect it to flourish in quite different political soils.

Luckily a great deal of interesting work has been done that can help us figure out what a sound approach to thinking comparatively about work–family policies and welfare states needs to do. I draw on the evolving discussion of states, families, markets, the political economy of work–family policies, and historical approaches to policy making to explain what such an approach would involve. I conclude by explaining my research design and choice of countries, and setting out the terrain of the rest of the book.

Why should we care?

Work–family policies matter because they enable children to get a good start in life. In wealthy post-industrial countries today, most mothers and fathers work for pay outside the home, even when their children are small. In the absence of state-provided childcare centers or substantial state support, many parents make do with untrained or overburdened care providers because high- quality care is unavailable or too expensive. Finding ways to insure high-quality care for all children is important because the first few years of verbal and emotional interaction provide them with the basic personal and intellectual skills they take into elementary school. Children who have not received good care don't do as well, intellectually or emotionally. Children are a nation's future, and insuring they are well cared for ought to be considered a public good (Esping-Andersen, 2009; Gornick and Meyers, 2003).

Further, policies that reduce the tensions between working for pay and working without pay to raise children and do other care work are crucial to achieving gender justice. Women still take primary responsibility for childrearing and housework in most countries, a division of labor that is reinforced by public policies. For example, workplaces that expect workers to put in ten or twenty hours above the standard workweek, pension systems that grant generous survivor's benefits, dependent spouse payments that put a ceiling on how much a woman can earn for the "main" earner to qualify, tax systems that reward disparate earnings between spouses through income averaging or joint taxation are common policies that perpetuate traditional gendered divisions of labor (Osawa, 2007b). But even though family commitments mainly fall on their shoulders, most women in wealthy post-industrial countries work for pay, and many aspire to hold demanding jobs or to pursue professional careers. Work–family policies that make it easier to work while raising small children, and that encourage men to take on some of the childrearing and housework burden, help promote equality in the workplace and at home (Orloff, 2009a, 328–9).

Gøsta Esping-Andersen puts this concern with gender equality a little differently when he writes about the "incomplete revolution," that is, the lag between changes in public life that have brought large numbers of women into the paid workforce and the development of policies to lighten the burden of producing the next generation. Evidence of this lag can be found in the quickly declining fertility rates of many post-industrial countries in Europe and Asia, as women who are pressed to choose between kids and careers increasingly opt to have fewer or no children. Esping-Andersen sees the fact that people are having fewer children than they desire and investing too little in the quality of those few children as evidence of widespread disequilibria that are facing modern societies and leading to rapid population aging in many countries (Esping-Andersen, 2009, 3). In his view, declining fertility is a reasonable response to the state's failure to support gender equality.

We might take the fact that large numbers of young people are deciding not to form families or have children as evidence that social conditions make it difficult to raise children. The evidence of falling fertility rates is an important wake up-call: either states can make those choices easier, or they can face rapid depopulation and aging (Esping-Andersen, 2009; Rosenbluth, 2007). As an editorial in the *Japan Times* put it,

The resistance to having children is, in part, a plea for serious improvements in the conditions of daily life . . . Few people in any country would consider bringing up a child under stressful conditions . . . Before more young people will again feel confident in investing the time, money and effort needed to raise a child, they must be assured of help. More flexible working conditions, better child care options, affordable education and community support networks need to be assured. (published on the occasion of Children's Day, *Japan Times*, May 10, 2011)

To be sure, long-term changes have been driving down fertility rates since the mid-1960s. More women have been going on to tertiary education, gaining degrees and skills that allow them to get better-paid jobs, and traditional families – in which women do most of the unpaid care work in the home and men are the breadwinners, marriages are stable and women can anticipate relying on their husbands' incomes without having to work themselves – are giving way to more diverse ones as out-of-wedlock birth and divorce rates increase and female-headed households and families where all parents work for pay become more common.

Understanding declining fertility rates is important for "getting" the contemporary discourse about work–family policies. When women face steep opportunity costs for interrupting their careers to have babies, they tend to have fewer babies (Harris, 2006). From a macro level, this is neither surprising nor bad, given the rising world population and the severe strains this puts on ecosystems and resource consumption. If people in wealthy countries have fewer babies, surely this will relieve some of the global population pressure. But from the point of view of states that are facing rapidly aging and shrinking populations, declining fertility poses problems of declining productivity and intergenerational inequity as fewer working people are asked to contribute more to social security funds to pay for services for swelling ranks of oldsters.

In other words, declining fertility is a symptom of strain and disequilibrium, a wake-up call showing that governments need to do more to support working mothers if they want young women to keep on having enough babies to stave off rapid population aging. But supporting work–family reconciliation policies also matters from the point of view of overall social equality. States that rely on markets to provide care services without providing government subsidies are counting on the availability of a large cohort of workers who will provide care for low pay.[3] But those who are getting paid the least also have children

---

[3] Care providers include those who care for babies and children, the ill and elderly, but also those who clean, shop and cook or care for the lawn and garden, those who support household work in establishments outside the home, like laundries, fast food restaurants or places that make take-out food. In a different vein, willingness to work for low pay may be related to forms of coercion that drive workers to take jobs: for example, American women receiving Temporary Aid to Needy Families – means-tested assistance – are required to find jobs to support themselves and their children, and must accept jobs for which they are qualified, even if they pay very little. Similarly, immigrants to the US and other countries may agree to work for low wages if the employer is not too picky about their visa or green card status. I address this issue more fully in Chapter 7. For a good discussion of coercion and care work in the United States, see Glenn, 2012.

who need to be taken care of, and their care solutions may be quite limited by lack of resources.[4] This can result in children who do not receive excellent care or a great start in life. When countries provide affordable high-quality care to all children, they help to equalize the chances that all children will be cared for well, talked and read to, and given a start that sets them up to flourish emotionally and intellectually.

In short, the problems that drive this research project – the reason we should care about work–family policies – revolve around questions of child welfare, justice and equality. Good support for working parents helps men and women share responsibility for care work, and helps women pursue paid, productive work outside the household (which many regard as the sine qua non of full citizenship – see, for example Schultz, 2000). Well-designed work–family policies address child welfare by guaranteeing all children a good start in life, regardless of whether they are born into low- or high-earning families, and help address income inequality, poverty and social mobility. Further, some low-fertility countries consider these policies crucial to making childbearing attractive to their young people and working for pay more attractive for mothers, as a strategy to address shrinking working-age populations. I propose several metrics for gauging how well work–family policies work in Chapter 7, which compares data on five welfare states (our basic four plus Sweden) to evaluate the effectiveness of their work–family policies. But for now, I hope that I have convinced my readers that work–family policies are important. The two basic goals of this study are to enhance our understanding of which policies work best, and to provide an assessment of the political and institutional limitations on policy change. We need to understand which policies work best, but paying attention to what stymies change is a crucial part of the story too. Scholars, activists and policy makers who want to bring about better policies in their own countries need to confront the historical, institutional and ideological barriers to passing and enforcing exemplary policies. Otherwise, the project of comparing work–family policies is in danger of turning into a fantasy that all countries can be like Sweden or France.

The utopian strain

Indeed, an important strand in comparative studies of work–family policies and welfare regimes has taken this utopian turn. Work in this vein compares states that have excellent work–family policies (like Sweden and France) with states

---

[4] The lowest-paid workers spend a higher proportion of their paychecks on care than do the middle class and wealthy. See Immervoll and Barber, 2006, 15, 22, 53–8; and Gornick and Meyers, 2003, Table 7.8. One of the consequences of better-off women relying on low-paid women to do their care work is that the children of middle-class and of poor families get very different starts in life.

that do not, then argues that the latter should adopt the exemplary policies of the former. This strategy is not confined to books that focus on the United States; one also sees it in work comparing Japan to other countries and in more broadly comparative studies done under OECD (Organisation for Economic Co-operation and Development) auspices (Crittenden, 2001; Mahon, 2002; Gornick and Meyers, 2003; OECD, 2003, 2007a; Sleebos, 2003; Bettio and Plantenga, 2004; Stone, 2007; Yamaguchi and Higuchi, 2008; Sato and Takeishi, 2008; Gornick and Meyers, 2009; Yamaguchi, 2009; Gerson, 2010). The approach is so common and widely read that it merits some reflection.

For example, Janet Gornick and Marcia Meyers compare the United States with eleven other countries (four Scandinavian social democratic welfare states, five continental conservative ones, plus Canada and the United Kingdom), noting how they vary with respect to the length of the standard work week; regulation of part-time work and overtime; maternity, parental and paternity leaves; the availability and quality of childcare and early childhood education; and the standard school-day and school-year in the state school system (Gornick and Meyers, 2003).[5] The comparisons are hardly startling – the United States has, after all, long been known as a laggard in this area – but they are clearly and strikingly presented. What is surprising is the implicit exhortation – "We can do better! Look at all these other wealthy postindustrial countries that do a much better job than the United States!" – without much consideration of the political processes that lead different countries to adopt particular policy approaches.[6] No doubt other wealthy countries do a better job of supporting working parents than the US, but those examples are not very pertinent or helpful. Such policy approaches – universal benefits funded by high taxing, welfare states that have substantial middle-class support through dominant left-leaning parties and powerful labor unions – are unlikely to be supported in a fragmented state with strongly pro-business interests, weak organized labor and a middle-of-the-road party regularly trading office with a staunchly small-state, fiscally conservative right-wing one. The approach leaves one wanting to understand why policy approaches that work well in France or Sweden cannot easily be transported to Japan or the United States.

This is a common problem: often work in a utopian vein focuses on exemplary policies that other welfare states have adopted without considering why

---

[5] A later edited volume, *Gender Equality*, which Gornick and Meyers produced in collaboration with Erik Olin Wright, part of the "Real Utopias" series, makes explicit the utopian themes of the 2003 book (Gornick and Meyers, 2009). Several of the chapters authored by other people in the *Gender Equality* book articulate critiques of, and suggestions about the political obstacles to enacting, the policies that Gornick and Meyers favor. See, for example, contributions by Morgan (2009b), Orloff (2009b) and Ferree (2009).

[6] Their last chapter rebuts several common objections to their policy prescriptions, but it comes across as a bit defensive and dismissive, rather than as a full consideration of the roadblocks to change in the US (Gornick and Meyers, 2003).

different tools and approaches evolve in different countries. At the end of the day, such approaches are unsatisfying, because they ignore several crucial and unavoidable questions and problems. We should and will consider the question, "What are the best practices that any country committed to justice and equality and a good start in life would want to adopt?" But this book is also dedicated to answering the questions, "What gets in the way of adopting such best practices? What do we need to know about a state's political and policy making processes that set the horizons for what policies can be imagined, introduced to its policy agenda, passed into law and enforced with reasonable vigilance?" I argue here that politics matters: passing generous work–family policies requires political support, including strategic alliances among left political parties, organized labor, women's groups, pro-child and anti-poverty groups that are not easy to accomplish everywhere. Political institutions, policy making regimes, veto players and historical factors that political scientists treat as part of path dependency matter for what can be accomplished.

Change and stasis are both parts of this project: we need to consider what conditions favor change. Sometimes a focusing event or change in the configuration of political processes can set the scene for a shift in course. But continuity and incrementalism are also powerful forces that shape policies, and the pull of inertia and the investment of powerful groups in established ways of doing policy are challenges to adopting new approaches, especially ones that represent profound changes. Utopian aspirations are important for giving us a new sense of possibility and actual blueprints for policies that have worked elsewhere, but we have to be strategic in thinking about the best way to build support for new policy departures, and identifying the likely sticking points and how to work past them. We have some hard thinking to do about what, practically speaking, can be done in particular national contexts in order to improve the chances of "best practices" becoming viable policy options.

I have made the case that a comparative study of the politics of work–family policy making is an important addition to work in this area, because comparative insights are crucial for understanding processes of policy change, figuring out the avenues of change that are likely to work in particular national contexts and because so many comparative discussions of care policies neglect these questions. The next section of this chapter reviews work on welfare regimes and work–family policies that has helped me better understand what leads to success in developing work–family support policies. I address several typologies of welfare states, and then turn to multi-level analyses, historical institutionalism and explanations that attend to values.

Welfare state typologies

An explosion of comparative work on welfare states and welfare policies was ignited by Gøsta Esping-Andersen's 1990 book, *The Three Worlds of Welfare*

Capitalism. Esping-Andersen set out three different regime types: social democratic, continental conservative and liberal. He categorized them on the basis of the distinctive policy approaches they take to providing social welfare; the degree to which they decommodify workers (enabling them not to work when sick, disabled, aged, etc.); the role played by powerful political groups (e.g., political parties, labor unions, employer groups); deeply rooted cultural, religious and political values; and the historical roots and development of their typical policy trajectories. The typology still provides a starting point for most cross-national studies of social welfare policy (for work in this vein, see Huber and Stephens, 2001; Pierson, 2001; Korpi, 2000).

This approach has set the terms for comparative work for a generation, producing much work that has piggy-backed on the "three worlds" typology and eliciting lively debates. Feminist scholars have been especially critical, pointing out that Esping-Andersen's attention to policies that reduce workers' dependence on the market made male workers the central focus. They attacked him for falsely assuming that the experiences of the worker were gender-neutral and universal, having nothing to say about the kinds of social insecurity to which women are typically subject, and overlooking the importance of unpaid care work as a social good that both is undervalued and interferes with women's ability to "commodify" themselves by becoming wage workers (Lewis, 1992, 1998; Orloff, 1993, 1996; Sainsbury, 1994; O'Connor, 1996). In welfare systems that provide benefits to full-time workers via social insurance that pays for pensions, health care, unemployment, disability, etc., one's claim to-full citizenship comes from being a worker, and women typically receive coverage as wives, mothers or survivors. Furthermore, welfare benefits geared toward meeting the needs of women in poverty tend to be means-tested and less politically popular than social benefits that accrue to male workers.

Critics developed numerous typologies of their own, based on how well welfare regimes accommodate women's participation in the paid workforce, where states lay on a continuum from male-breadwinner to dual-breadwinner regimes (Lewis, 1992; Sainsbury, 1994), and how well states were able to "defamilialize" women, that is, free them from dependence on husbands or their role as family members (Orloff, 1993; Lister, 1997; Saraceno, 1997). A more recent typology distinguishes male-breadwinner, market-oriented and work–life balance "livelihood security systems" (Osawa, 2007a, 2007b). Most of these new typologies shift focus from the degree to which different welfare states decommodify workers, to how well they enable women to access paid work or to be free of economic dependence on marriage. I think Esping-Andersen's version continues to be the touchstone for many conversations because it "has the virtue of everyone understanding exactly what the three clusters are, even if they disagree on what is most significant in their characterization" (Orloff, 2009a). Indeed, many of those who articulate new typologies end up with groups that resemble his three clusters.

Typologies aim to provide clear, intellectually convenient ways of articulating family resemblances among welfare states and regimes. I find the three worlds approach useful, and use it to organize some of my comparisons here. But I have also learned a lot from what I call "multiple-level approaches" that attempt to explain how domestic life, the organization of the labor market, the provision of social security, tax systems and fringe benefits from employers operate together to reinforce gendered divisions of labor. Below I review several multi-level approaches, and explain why they are valuable.

Multiple-level approaches

One such study examines social policy in four liberal welfare states, Australia, Canada, the United Kingdom and the United States, focusing on families, markets and states as providers of welfare. Examining how states interact with familial and market approaches to providing welfare and supporting working parents in countries that take broadly similar stances, the authors attribute differences in policy approaches to the influence of women's movements (O'Connor, Orloff and Shaver, 1999).

Echoing some of the feminist critiques of Esping-Andersen, the authors note that women's responsibilities in private life continue to affect their ability to participate equally in public life as workers and citizens:

the role of families – really, women in families – in providing care has been neglected in mainstream accounts of welfare provision. We agree that what goes on in the "private" sphere of families – notably the gender division of domestic labour and care-giving, but also sexual and reproductive relations – is actually quite consequential for men's and women's performance in the public spheres of (paid) work and politics. (O'Connor, Orloff and Shaver, 1999, 14)

Even though women in all four of these countries have entered the paid workforce in large numbers, the fact that the only "public services and supports for combining paid and unpaid work" are means-tested has made "class differences . . . quite significant for women workers' material situations and the relative ease or difficulty of organising everyday life" (O'Connor, Orloff and Shaver, 1999, 14).[7] Those class differences represent a crucial problem of intragender wage gaps and social inequality facing liberal market economies.

Two things are valuable about this study of social policies in liberal welfare states. First is its focus on the distinctive roles that states, markets and families

[7] Many others have remarked on the gap between public assertions of rights and continued female responsibility for care in the private sphere (for example, Kittay, 1999; Williams, 2000; Folbre, 2001; Abramovitz and Morgen, 2006), underlining the contradiction between public discourses about the rights and opportunities of women in the workplace, civil society and politics, and the reality of women's continued responsibility for care work in all kinds of regimes.

play in providing for social welfare in these states, which informs my understanding of the American preference for providing care through the family
and the market. This is somewhat different from the mixture of state provision
and support of childcare, leaves and cash transfers combined with reliance on
women's unpaid work in the domestic sphere that one sees in France, Germany
and Japan. Indeed, the sense of demographic crisis due to falling fertility
rates in Germany and Japan is leading policy makers to re-think subsidiarity –
the notion that individuals in need should exhaust their private and familial
resources before seeking assistance from the state – as a central tenet of family
policy, and to move toward more reliance on public provision of care services.
Although the four countries I study rely in different ways on the state, market
and family as loci of welfare provision, the spatial metaphor of overlapping
and interconnected spheres is a useful one for thinking about women's roles as
mothers, workers and citizens.

Second, I appreciate the attention here to differences in policy approaches and
the influence of women's movements. Especially useful is the effort to explain
the impact of gender equity movements in the context of an array of political
forces (e.g., right-wing and anti-feminist groups and parties, strong or weak
labor mobilization) and institutional and historical constraints and legacies,
such as unitary vs. federal structures of government, fragmentation vs. centralization, and varied industrial relations frameworks (O'Connor, Orloff and
Shaver, 1999, 202–3). While I do not focus as strongly on women's movements,
I appreciate the model offered here of how to attend to political, institutional
and historical constraints on political change.

A second work that offers a rich multiple-level approach to comparing welfare state development is Heidi Gottfried and Jacqueline O'Reilly's comparison of industrial relations, the family and social welfare policies in Japan and
Germany. They regard these two countries as variations on the strong male-
breadwinner welfare regime, noting that both have pursued developmental
industrial policies aimed at sustaining high-growth economies, but now face
the striking reluctance of young women to have babies, as evidenced by their
lowest-low fertility rates (Gottfried and O'Reilly, 2002, 31). Even though both
states have begun to adopt policies more favorable to working mothers and to
move toward gender equality, both continue to rely on income tax and pension
policies that reinforce traditional gender arrangements, especially reliance on
women's unpaid care for children and elderly family members (Gottfried and
O'Reilly, 2002, 47).

Tracking social policy, labor market participation and fertility behaviors,
Gottfried and O'Reilly examine the dynamic relationship among formal policies and private, familial practices of care and decisions about having babies.
They discuss change and continuity on three levels at once, the evolution of
gender equality and welfare policies, gender inequality in the labor market,

and reluctance to have children. They conclude that Germany and Japan are both experiencing serious dislocations as labor shortages and women's rising educational qualifications combine to push women to seek well-paid jobs, but women are still pressured and encouraged by gender ideologies and tax policies to be hands-on mothers and to take low paid part-time jobs (Gottfried and O'Reilly, 2002, 30–1).

This essay makes clear several things that Japan and Germany have in common:

1. The continued salience of norms about intensive mothering that are reinforced in daily interactions and gender role expectations, and by tax and benefit policies that encourage male breadwinner – stay-at-home mother / secondary earner divisions of labor;
2. The simultaneous adoption of more progressive work–family policies that aim to help women get and keep get jobs;
3. A sense of contradiction or disequilibrium that is resulting in sharply falling fertility rates as women feel they must choose between having careers and having children.

The deep similarities between Germany and Japan that this perceptive article takes note of helped direct me toward this rich and useful comparison.

Building on these works that examine how social welfare policies, market structures and gender ideologies connect, a third approach combines work on varieties of capitalism with insights from the "gendering the welfare state" literature, a shorthand for the feminist responses to Esping-Andersen's three worlds paradigm which we discussed above (Estevez-Abe, 2007, 63). Work on the varieties of capitalism attends to specific ways that labor and capital markets are structured, and the importance of such differences for the design and function of social welfare measures. A crucial distinction among capitalist economies is between "coordinated market economies" (CMEs) and "liberal market economies" (LMEs). CMEs are governed by corporatist bodies that represent organized labor and big business, and they are more likely to have regulations and benefits that protect workers in the event of market downturns. LMEs are more laissez-faire, less regulated, prize general skills and generally have little or no role for organized labor in terms of influencing worker protections. LMEs roughly map onto the liberal welfare states (they include the English-speaking countries and Switzerland), and CMEs map onto the social democratic and conservative welfare states (both the continental and Asian varieties), including France, Germany and Japan. In addition, some CMEs adopt sector-specific skills regimes, others firm-specific ones, and this is also important for distinguishing among different "varieties of capitalism."

Two scholars of comparative politics who specialize in Japan, Margarita Estevez-Abe and Frances Rosenbluth, articulate a new frame for thinking about the connections among labor markets, low-fertility countries and welfare states and the work–family policies they pursue.[8] Because I find their approach illuminating, I set out their core arguments.

Estevez-Abe spends some time puzzling over which country has more gender equality, Sweden or the United States. Contrary to most people's expectations, she claims that liberal countries, even though they provide little support for working mothers, perform well on various gender-equality scores (Estevez-Abe, 2007, 65). The reasons for this have to do with the ready availability of childcare in both the liberal and the Nordic social democratic states, which is essential if countries are to have high Female Labor Force Participation (FLFP) rates. It doesn't matter whether childcare is provided by the state or purchased in the market. Both social democratic and liberal welfare states have achieved high FLFP rates, one through the public provision of childcare, the other through widely available cheap private care services (Estevez-Abe, 2007, 68; also see Castles, 2003). Furthermore, liberal market economics are able to provide ample childcare services precisely because their unregulated labor markets and high levels of wage dispersion produce plenty of cheap, low-skill service jobs, making market-based personal services available to working mothers. A manifestation of this is large intra-gender wage gaps in liberal market economies, which I will address in Chapter 7 (Estevez-Abe, 2007, 69, 81–2).

Not only do liberal and Scandinavian countries both have plentiful childcare which enables high FLFP rates, but Scandinavia has high levels of occupational segregation and gender pay gaps because so many women are employed in the public sector (especially in caregiving jobs).[9] Gender segregation is not as marked in liberal welfare states, where women are more likely to advance to managerial positions than their Scandinavian counterparts, in part because of the existence of equal opportunity and affirmative action laws and labor standards that mitigate gender discrimination with respect to employment patterns (Estevez-Abe, 2007, 68–9). Not only are women in LMEs not tracked into public-sector jobs, but mobile, lightly regulated economies allow women more access to management-level positions. Estevez-Abe's overarching point is that labor markets contribute to facilitating or worsening gender equality in key ways.

---

[8] Their contributions to the edited volume *The Political Economy of Japan's Low Fertility* (Rosenbluth, 2007) provide a strong theoretical core for a collection of essays that traverses a variety of topics related to Japanese work–family policies, labor force participation and low fertility.

[9] In 7, I compare gender equality data for Sweden with those for France, Germany, Japan and the United States (see Table 7.6). Out of those five countries, Sweden's gender pay gap is the lowest. However, gender gaps vary within the Scandinavian countries, with Denmark and Norway doing better than Sweden, Finland and Iceland. The gender gap figures vary across the LMEs too, with Ireland and New Zealand doing much better than Australia, Canada, the UK or the United States. See OECD, 2012.

Estevez-Abe and Rosenbluth both focus on explaining the situation in Japan, a lowest-low-fertility country that has been ramping up its work–family programs to encourage young people to have more babies. Fundamental to their arguments is the notion that occupational segregation and gender gaps are related to skills regimes. The three skills regimes, general, industry-specific and firm-specific, vary in terms of how portable the skills are, where people are trained, and atrophy rates. Although general skills and industry-specific ones are acquired differently (the first through school-based or vocational training, the second through vocational schools or apprenticeship programs, often resulting in degrees or certificates), both are portable: if a worker takes time off and then re-enters the job market, her skills will still be valuable. In contrast, firm-specific skills are only acquired through on-the-job training, and they are neither certified nor portable. They require the highest degree of employer cost and commitment because the employer pays for and provides skill acquisition. Because women are much more likely than men to interrupt their work lives in order to raise children, firm-specific skills regimes are biased against them. From the firm's point of view, it makes sense to assume that women are a bad risk as regards investing a lot of resources in teaching them firm-specific skills, and not to hire them, since a woman who quits a job at a given firm has wasted the money the firm spent training her (Estevez-Abe, 2007, 70–2).

The more limited the portability of her skills, the more vulnerable the worker is if she should be fired. Welfare states can mitigate this danger by making layoffs costly or by providing wage subsidies for retention of redundant workers, thus sending signals to workers and employers that their investments in firm-specific skills will be safeguarded. This helps us begin to see the institutional complementarities between welfare programs and the distinctive skills regimes that they help sustain. When neither labor regulations nor the welfare state do much to overcome bias against women with respect to firm-specific skills, they in fact exacerbate occupational segregation.

Given the likelihood of discrimination against women on the grounds that they are likely to interrupt their careers to have children, Estevez-Abe thinks statutory maternity leaves "are almost equivalent to what generous unemployment benefits are to men": they protect mothers from being fired and from loss of income (Estevez-Abe, 2008, 74). But the design of leave programs and the mix of work–family policies matter, as we will see in the discussion of different countries' policies in Chapters 3 through 6. For example, long leaves that encourage women to take a lot of time off can exacerbate skill loss, whereas plentiful childcare promotes a woman's attachment to employment by helping her return to work quickly (Estevez-Abe, 2008, 72–5). And the burden of replacing a woman who is on leave is especially onerous when companies rely on workers with a high degree of firm-specific skills, since they cannot easily hire outsiders. In such regimes, the work of the woman on leave tends to be shared among colleagues, creating resentment and disincentives to granting women maternity or childrearing leaves, and to women taking such leaves if they are worried about their long-term relationships with their colleagues. This issue is not so fraught when workers have general or vocational skills, making it easier to hire replacements.

Rosenbluth also thinks that firm-specific skills increase statistical discrimination against women, since it is fair to assume that they will in general be less committed workers than men (Rosenbluth, 2007, 9). A consequence of this is that women are more likely to work for smaller firms than larger ones, where their particular skills and education may win out over the suspicion that they are more likely to quit than male workers. But small and medium-sized companies in Japan generally pay less than larger firms, and they are less likely to abide by government policies requiring paid childrearing leaves, so the fact that they hire more women and inspire more loyalty from female workers may be offset by their reluctance to grant women job-protected time off for childrearing.

Contrasting the predilection of Japanese firms for firm-specific skills with the situation in general skills-based LMEs like the US, the UK, Australia and Canada, Rosenbluth notes that the LMEs have higher female labor participation rates and fertility rates because "employers have less reason to discourage women from work. Employers are not investing in a woman's firm-specific skills, so her career interruptions on account of childrearing represent less of a cost to the firm" (Rosenbluth, 2007, 17). Clearly, labor markets where firm-specific skills are the coin of the realm discount a woman's wages to a greater extent for interrupting "her career path for childbearing and family work" than LMEs where more portable general skills are valued. In the former, the tradeoffs between having children and pursuing a career are starker, because one's best hope for a good career is to get and keep a regular track job. Any interruption means one can never go back. In the latter, women have greater security and leverage in seeking employment elsewhere should they take time off, be fired or grow dissatisfied with a job (Rosenbluth, 2007, 15).

Countries can enact policies that make it easier for women to enter the labor market on an equal footing with men, even in a firm- or sector-specific skills economy. But doing so requires the government to make up for the advantage that men enjoy in the private sector by disproportionately hiring women in secure public-sector jobs, heavily subsidizing the costs of childcare, or both. Not all countries try to level the playing field, of course. Rosenbluth observes that Sweden deals with this issue by hiring women to public-sector jobs, while countries with moderately strong labor movements, such as Germany, most of non-Scandinavian Europe, and Japan, have labor practices and regulations that keep jobs secure for core male union workers by relegating women and immigrants to less secure jobs (Rosenbluth, 2007, 19).

Rosenbluth generalizes from this rich analysis of skills regimes to argue that Japan's low-fertility crisis is related to "the relative inaccessibility of Japan's labor market to women." The point of analyzing skills regimes is to be able to explain why cross-national differences in labor market institutions are decisive for understanding gender inequality, fertility behaviors, and the design and efficacy of work–family policies in advanced post-industrial economies. If we only look at explicit work–family policies such as leave laws or childcare systems, that will not tell the full story about the workplace-related pressures that shape women's choices regarding jobs and taking breaks to have children. Attending to skills regimes is crucial to the arguments that I make later in this book about the importance of labor market constraints and opportunities for understanding why states adopt particular work–family policy regimes, and why their work–family policies sometimes misfire.

What I have called "multiple-level approaches" vary in terms of their focuses and theoretical ambition, but they all invite us to think about women's decisions regarding work and babies in the context of overlapping spheres: families, markets and states; gender ideologies that reinforce male-breadwinner arrangements and intensive mothering; and labor markets and skills regimes that are more or less tolerant of interruptions. They all endeavor to show how intimate life in the family (where women care for children and old people, and young people decide to form families) is related to the organization of the labor market, the provision of work–family policies through the market or the state, and the social security system.

Historical institutionalist approaches

Attending to policy history and specifically to how institutional starting points shape subsequent policy options and developments is central to how I understand policy making processes. Jacob Hacker does a good job of explaining how vested interests grow up alongside policy approaches and institutions (Hacker, 2002). He offers detailed historical examples and intelligent explanations of the political logic of path-dependent change. Policies mobilize attentive, interested beneficiaries, as well as third parties who stand to benefit from having those policies maintained or strengthened, or who will lose out if they are abandoned. To take one of Hacker's examples, in addition to lenders and home owners, an entire real estate industry – real estate brokers and agents, title insurance providers, housing inspectors and contractors – grew up around US tax policies that encourage people to own and sell homes. It might make sense to abandon the mortgage interest tax write-off, which provides a substantial subsidy to middle-class and wealthy homeowners but does little to help those who rent their homes or apartments. But changing this tax deduction is next to impossible given the enormous power of the groups that will fight to defend it.

Many American policy scholars take path dependency seriously, arguing that policy development is shaped by early and strategic choices made in a given area of regulation or policy.[10] A number of scholars have taken a historical institutionalist approach to work–family policies, including several studies of American policy developments.[11] I mention historical institutionalist approaches here because I think this is a useful way to understand why the origins of policies have important consequences in shaping powerful interest groups and institutional processes that exert significant influence over policy change and innovation later on (Pierson, 2004). Path dependency is a useful way to explain work–family policy development in all the countries we shall study here, as I hope to demonstrate.

Values

Several comparative scholars treat social or cultural values as important in explaining policy outcomes. For example, one study uses religious values and the power of religious groups as the fulcrum for understanding the development of childcare and early childhood education programs in four countries, demonstrating how religious-cultural debates about women's roles as primary caregivers and reluctance to have the state intervene in the family have significantly shaped policy developments in France, Sweden, the Netherlands and the United States (Morgan, 2006).

Several scholars focus on norms about intensive mothering and good housewifery, some connecting these to religious beliefs. Francis Castles and Gøsta Esping-Andersen both note that the lowest-low-fertility Mediterranean rim countries – Spain, Greece and Italy – are Catholic and embrace family values, while high-fertility countries like France, Sweden and the United States have high rates of cohabitation, divorce and extramarital births (Castles 2003, 214; Esping-Andersen, 1991, 51). Evidently Catholicism plays a role in supporting traditional gender roles, as several Catholic countries still expect mothers to stay home with children, and have poorly developed childcare and labor markets that exclude women (Esping-Andersen, 1991). Esping-Andersen writes that "the 'familialistic' social policy typical of countries in which Catholicism

---

[10] Theda Skocpol's work on the origins of maternalist social policy and veterans' benefits in the United States (1992), and comparative studies by Sven Steinmo on taxation policies (1993), Ellen Immergut on health policy (1992), and Kathleen Thelen on skills acquisition (2004) are good examples.

[11] These include Sonya Michel's careful history of childcare policy in the United States (2002), Anya Bernstein's study of the passage of the Family and Medical Leave Act (2001), Suzanne Mettler's work on New Deal social policy and the GI Bill (1998 and 2005), Mimi Abramovitz and Sandra Morgen's work on tax policy (2006), and Kimberly Morgan's comparative study of childcare policy (2006).

remains culturally salient makes it extremely difficult for women to combine work and family, leading to lower rates of fertility than in countries where the obstacles are less daunting" (Esping-Andersen, 1999, quoted in Castles, 2003, 214). Brewster and Rindfuss also argue that expectations of intensive maternal involvement with children's care and education lead to lengthy interruptions of work for mothers, citing Ireland, Japan and Germany as countries where such norms are still prevalent (2000). In the same vein, Suzuki argues that one of the reasons that Japan has such low fertility is that almost nobody has children outside of wedlock. If the problem is that people are not getting married in the first place, he questions whether improving childcare and parental leaves will have much impact on fertility rates (Suzuki, 2006).

Sociologists, demographers and political scientists have all suggested that Japan and the lowest-low-fertility countries of southern Europe, Italy, Spain and Greece, form a cluster of familialistic welfare states that have gender and family norms grounded in the religious values of Confucianism in Japan and Catholicism in Europe (Esping-Andersen, 1997, 1999; Castles, 2003; Brewster and Rindfuss, 2000; Caldwell and Schindlmayr, 2003; Newman, 2008). Because welfare states in these countries have been reluctant to "displace the traditional familial welfare function," they are confronting tensions as women become better educated and want to work outside the home in order to gain greater economic independence. As women's career and earning potential increases, "the opportunity cost of having to care full time for babies or for frail elderly relatives" rises. If welfare states fail to provide alternatives, "families will respond in either of two ways. One, wives will remain at home to care for children and parents. If they are educated, this implies a massive waste of human capital. Two, women will nonetheless pursue careers, but given the associated difficulties of forming families, they will delay and reduce fertility" (Esping-Andersen, 1997, 186). Thus, high opportunity costs help explain the extraordinarily low total fertility rates in familialist countries.

Expectations about women's unpaid care work matter for understanding fertility behaviors. Cross-national data on the amount of time women and men spend on housework and childrearing reveal telling differences between countries in the lowest-low fertility group and high-fertility countries like the US or France, with women in the former spending more time on care work, less time working for pay, and receiving less help from their husbands with household work and childrearing.

Some scholars have focused on factors that undermine such traditional values. One study notes that women's higher educational attainment and labor force participation often lead women to value autonomy and financial independence, and to have a broader array of goals they want from life than just raising children. According to data from the World Values Survey, younger women have less traditional views about women's roles within families than do older ones, or than men. In countries where such norms are emerging, we are likely to find higher average ages at first birth, higher FLFP rates, more diverse family forms and relatively high fertility rates, while countries where traditional values persist are likely to have lower fertility rates (D'Addio and Mira d'Ercole, 2006, 15–16, and n. 14).

Research pointing to the persistence of traditional cultural values, especially the tendency of many lowest-low-fertility countries to subscribe to traditional gender expectations about intensive mothering and male breadwinning, can help us understand the barriers to adopting and implementing work–family policies in familialistic welfare regimes. I return to this point when I take up the importance of cultural and ideological barriers to policy change in Chapter 8.

Summing up: what the literature teaches us, research design and a map of the book

We cannot understand low-fertility crises or family support policies without thinking about the organization of labor markets. Labor markets cover a wide range of features: skills regimes, hiring practices, standard work hours, regulations and practices concerning overtime, treatment of part-time and flexible workers, minimum wages, paid vacations, maternity and parental leaves, unemployment rates and compensation, and anti-discrimination laws. Mobile labor markets that value general skills are more welcoming to mothers than coordinated market economies that prize firm-specific skills. In the former, workers have more portable skills (like college degrees or vocational licenses), which makes the costs of interrupting their careers cheaper both for them and for their employers. Such labor markets can also provide a functional equivalent to publicly supported childcare systems, since affordable childcare is readily available in laxly regulated economies in which there are lots of people who will do care work for low wages (Esping-Andersen, 1999, 56–7; Estévez-Abe, 2007, 82). In firm-specific skills regimes, on the other hand, workers who interrupt their careers (like women who have children) create expenses and problems for their employers, and are often sidelined from (or never hired for) career-track jobs. Simply put, many policies relevant to working parents are in the realm of industrial relations or workplace governance.

We also need to think about political economy from the point of view of powerful political interests. Both business and organized labor are major voices in political decision making in all of the countries I study here, and figure into any approach that takes power resources seriously, along with major political parties and well-organized groups with a stake in work–family policies – such as service providers, feminists and anti-feminists, religious groups, children's rights advocates, experts, think tanks and relevant bureaucrats and policy specialists[12] – and groups that advocate for family-friendly policies.

We shall take up other political considerations as well, especially ones related to the institutional structures that govern policy making – for example parliamentary vs. presidential systems, majoritarian winner-take-all electoral competitions vs. proportional representation ones, federal vs. unitary governments. How many veto points there are in the legislative process has a lot to do with the institutional competence of the government, that is, its ability to pass and enforce new policies. In federal systems, one must attend to the interaction between the national and sub-national governments, the ambit of power and authority of each, the role of local experimentation and innovation (or stonewalling and resistance), and so on.

Of course, no policy maker inherits a blank slate, and where and how countries start down the road of supporting families limits their range of motion farther down the road. Policy choices have consequences, in terms both of those who stand to benefit or lose from a policy change, and of the committees, advisers, ministries and agencies that have developed expertise and budgetary control over the policy area. Recognizing path dependency as a characteristic of policy development is crucial for understanding how policy making choices are constrained by paths already taken. This goes for policy repertoires that are familiar and convenient, as well as policy approaches that seem so foreign they are never even considered. Attending to the path-dependent character of work–family policy development can help us understand why market solutions and tax payments have dominated policy discourse in the United States, why France assumes the necessity of high-quality and universal care for children, why Germany balks at providing full-time childcare and after-school care, and why Japan's policies are often underfunded and laxly enforced.

To put this a little differently, policy choices give rise to political opportunity structures. Policy scholars need to pay attention to what Schattschneider (1960) called the "mobilization of bias," that is, the interests that are mobilized into political processes and institutions, and those that are shut out. This is a matter of figuring out which groups are politically powerful, and where and how they are likely to wield their power.

I close this chapter with a brief discussion of my research design, then set out the argumentative structure of the book. This book compares the development of work–family reconciliation policies in four post-industrial wealthy countries. I draw on a variety of cross-national comparative data related to demographic variables, labor markets and work–family policies, much of them from the Organisation for Economic Cooperation and Development (OECD), but also

---

[12] In France, Germany and Japan, government-affiliated and government-funded think tanks, and ones affiliated with policy-relevant actors and institutions, are quite common.

from Eurostat, the International Labor Organization and national government sources. In addition, I conducted several dozen interviews with elite government sources (legislators, bureaucrats, experts in demography, economics, statistics, child welfare, work–family issues, academics, activists and representatives of interest groups or service providers) in each country. In these conversations, I aimed for insight into the political structure of the policy making process and the aims of work–family reforms. Many were generous with their time, and helped me better understand the processes of agenda setting, deliberation and consultation, compromise, policy enactment and implementation.

A small-N qualitative study that provides an in-depth comparison of four countries' work–family policies can accomplish many things. First, it can convey a great deal of information about the substance of these countries' policies. Second, it can provide insight into the political constraints and opportunities that shape different countries' efforts to pass work–family policies. This is particularly so because these countries support working mothers in quite different ways. Some have managed to take advantage of crises, moments of political change or focusing events to innovate and start something new; others have failed to do so. Third, it can help us move toward a more general understanding of the institutional and political resources that account for policy success and failure in this area. At the end of the day, we should better understand the possibilities for policy innovation, not just in France, Germany, Japan and the United States, but in countries that share values, market arrangements and political institutions with them.

A word about why I chose to study these four countries: my choice was shaped by my initial desire to understand why Japan was able to provide far better childcare services to modest-earning families than the United States. As a low-spending welfare state which has both pursued deregulation and privatization in many of its family policies and developed subsidized, high-quality childcare and paid maternity, parental and paternity leaves, Japan seemed to fit somewhere between the United States and the European conservative continental welfare states.

I decided to study France and Germany because, like Japan, they are conservative welfare states that treat low fertility as an important public problem. That said, France is clearly the success story among these three, having achieved a high and steady TFR of 1.99 and developed well-articulated, generous leave, family allowance and ECEC policies. Germany and Japan are among the lowest-low-fertility countries of the world, both with TFRs of 1.39 in 2010. Germany has well-designed parental leaves, generous family allowances and tax breaks for married couples, but a paucity of full-day childcare. Japan also has high-quality state-supported childcare, paid maternity, parental and paternity leaves and cash family allowances, but it spends much less than Germany or France to support these policies. It has a small welfare state and it relies heavily on private employment-based benefits as a source of social welfare.

As a liberal welfare state that relies heavily on market provision of childcare services and offers little financial or state support for work–family policies, the United States doesn't fit with the other three very neatly. But it is part of the comparison for a number of reasons. First, my interest in doing this study was fueled by my experience of having my children attend schools and childcare centers in Japan, Germany and the United States when they were small, and by my outrage that the United States does so little to support children and working mothers. I hope that the US can learn from other countries' approaches to work–family policies. Second, the American approach to work–family issues has been influential in other countries, especially Japan. As a low-spending welfare state which has pursued deregulation and privatization in many of its family policies, Japan has borrowed from the American play book as well as the French and German ones. For those who want to understand Japan, it makes sense to study it alongside France and Germany on the one side, and the United States on the other. Third, despite the paucity of policies to support working families, the United States has a TFR of 1.93, one of the highest total fertility rates of the post-industrial OECD nations. The American labor market has high percentages of women in professional and management-level positions, and strong, well-enforced anti-discrimination laws. Contrasting the United States with the other three countries invites us to consider differences in the organization of the labor market and in the compass of government responsibility for work–family policies

My overarching goal here is to understand why welfare states develop quite different responses and approaches to supporting working mothers. But the young mother struggling to care for kids on a shoestring and launch a career still has a voice here. I would like to make policy recommendations that stand a chance of improving work–family policies *and* being successful. I want to understand what courses of action are possible in the United States, France, Germany, Japan and elsewhere to make it easier for all adults to experience the fundamental human pleasures and responsibilities of raising children and working at jobs that pay the bills. An adequate answer does not simply exhort the United States to adopt a set of big spending policies like Sweden's or France's, but attends to the policy repertoires that have gained currency and been workable, and to the conditions that have maximized activists' chances to have an impact on policy.

Here is a map of where the argument goes from here. Chapter 2 reviews comparative data on fertility rates, workforce participation patterns, labor-friendly regulations, and existing work–family policies. It provides context for considering the approaches these four countries have taken, and identifying countries whose workforces and policy approaches resemble them. Chapter 3 examines the evolution of work–family policy making in France, asking where the policies came from, who supported them, and what is distinctive about the politics of work–family policy making there. Chapter 4 does the same for Germany, and Chapter 5 examines work–family policy making in Japan, focusing on the politics of the Angel Plans and other programs to address low fertility that Japan has pursued since the mid-1990s. Chapter 6 examines the evolution of work–family policies in the United States. Chapter 7 evaluates work–family policies in our four countries plus Sweden, aiming to answer the question "What works best?" Chapter 8 builds on research from the country chapters to offer a comparative analysis of the reasons why countries choose the policy tools and approaches they do. I divide barriers to adopting ideal policies into five broad themes: the political economy of work–family policies, institutional competence, policy repertoires, path dependency and cultural and ideological values. I conclude by suggesting some politically feasible approaches that could provide children and parents better work–family reconciliation policies in each of our four countries, and by drawing some more general lessons from the study of the politics of work–family policy in France, Germany, Japan and the United States.

Writing this chapter has felt a little bit like an army hauling out its siege engines and getting them in place to lay siege to a fortress. Now let us see where all of the arguments and perspectives surveyed here get us as we start to think about the politics of work–family policy making.

2   Demographic and policy trends in OECD countries

In this chapter I discuss the tensions between women's increased labor force participation and continued responsibility for most of the unpaid work of raising children and taking care of the home. Countries manage these tensions in different ways: some make it easy for workers to leave and re-enter the labor force; others provide generous work–family policies that help mothers care for their children while working; and others reinforce traditional male-breadwinner, female-secondary-worker roles while steering women toward part-time jobs that are compatible with intensive mothering. My aim here is to call attention to several distinctive patterns in how states and labor markets deal with working mothers, and to offer some preliminary explanations for these groupings. I consider differing attitudes toward and expectations about women as mothers and workers, how working mothers are treated in the labor force, and the generosity and structure of their work–family reconciliation policies.

After a brief discussion of the move toward lower fertility rates and population aging, I examine patterns of female labor force participation, indicators that afford insight into how labor markets are structured, and data on work–family reconciliation policies.

Taking the long view: demographic indicators

Some very large forces are at work that are changing when and whether people marry, when women give birth to their first babies, women's attachment to paid work, and the need and demand for policies to support working parents. Understanding them is useful in order to provide context for the discussion of policy developments in four countries that follows.

In most wealthy post-industrial societies, fertility rates have been falling for about a century, with a brief interlude after World War II when economic prospects looked up and most of these countries went through a baby boom. Several broad social and economic changes account for this long-term move toward falling fertility. Until the late nineteenth century, children were regarded as net contributors to household economies that revolved around farming and skilled crafts. But as work moved away from farms and out of households into factories and white-collar workplaces, children gradually came to be regarded as a luxury item requiring significant investments in education.

Universal compulsory public education was established in most wealthy industrial countries by the early twentieth century, and by the late twentieth century large numbers of women had gained access to higher education, increasing the value of their skills and pulling them into paid work. By 2005, substantially greater proportions of women than men were attending colleges and universities in most Organisation for Economic Cooperation and Development (hereafter OECD) countries (OECD, 2008a).[1]

Other significant changes were afoot: the development of safe, dependable forms of contraception and access to legal abortions, allowing women to control conception and decide on the timing and number of children they wanted to have. In the late 1960s, second-wave women's movements pushed for reproductive choice, gender equality and women's political and social rights. The labor market shifted in fundamental ways as many OECD countries shed good manufacturing jobs, and the real wages of male workers fell as manufacturing moved to countries with cheaper labor costs. Families began to depend on mothers' as well as fathers' salaries in order to earn enough to maintain middle-class lifestyles, and post-industrial economies created more service sector jobs that attracted women workers. As women's education and skills increased, so did their opportunity costs, affecting calculations about when and whether to have children – and if so, how many. As a consequence of these manifold changes, women's workforce participation rates have increased substantially since 1980 across the OECD countries.

These economic changes triggered profound social changes in families, as women were no longer as dependent on their spouses for economic support, and began to think about maintaining their own earning potential and to reconsider traditional divisions of labor which assumed that women were primary caregivers, dependent on their husbands' earning to support them. Divorce became more common, along with single parent households, blended families and new attitudes toward marriage, which was no longer regarded as a permanent commitment that reinforced reciprocal obligations between spouses. Out-of-wedlock births became common in many advanced post-industrial countries,[2] and family formation now occurs several years later than it used to, as one can see in Figures 2.1 and 2.2, which show average ages at first childbirth and changes in age at first birth since 1970. Although age at first birth has risen across the board, the countries where age at first birth rose most

---

[1] I refer to OECD countries as a shorthand for designating a group that is mostly composed of wealthy, post-industrial countries.

[2] For example, most of the Nordic countries, the United States, the UK, New Zealand and France all have high percentages of out-of-wedlock births (OECD, 2012f).

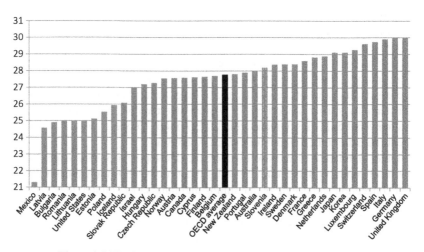

Figure 2.1 Women's age at first childbirth in 2009
Source: OECD, 2012b.

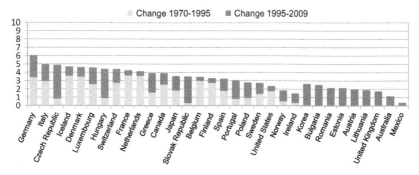

Figure 2.2 Increases in age at first birth, from 1970 to 1995 and 1995 to 2009
Source: OECD, 2012b.

dramatically between 1995 and 2009 are mostly low-fertility countries from the former Eastern bloc, plus Germany, Italy, Greece, Portugal, Spain, Japan and Korea.

Even though people are having fewer children and waiting longer to have them, most people still want to become parents. When surveys ask young people what their ideal number of children would be, they respond they would like to have between two and three children, a figure that has been steady in most wealthy countries for decades.[3] Although most parents think raising

---

[3] Why is this desire to have children so durable? Decisions to form families and have children are viewed by many as central to living a fulfilling human life. In raising children, people develop

children is a rewarding and fulfilling experience, childrearing is not simply a self-regarding goal or good. Children are not like pets, a hobby or pastime that parents indulge in because of the satisfaction it gives them: my dog will never pay into social security or shovel the snow off our streets (Crittenden, 2001, 234). Parents are raising the next generation of citizens who will take on jobs, do necessary work, contribute to the tax coffers and keep society going. Childrearing is work that many societies recognize as a public good and try to support.

Gratifying as it is to raise children, people refrain from or postpone having children when they perceive tradeoffs between childrearing and other satisfying experiences (autonomy, travel, professional accomplishment) or when they are pessimistic about their economic outlook. Without a stable job that promises future promotions and raises, many young people feel they cannot afford a house or apartment suitable for raising children, and do not want to take a chance on bringing a child into a difficult financial environment (Newman, 2008).

The collective decisions to postpone childbearing and to have fewer children are a cause for public concern in several post-industrial countries where substantially lower fertility rates and healthier, longer-lived populations are creating a bulge at the top of the population pyramid (see Figure 2.3). In rapidly aging societies, dependency ratios (the ratio of dependent children and elderly adults to employed adults) are creating generational inequities as fewer working-age people are saddled with paying for services and pensions for the elderly. Such demographic changes are producing new needs and demands to reform policies to support old people and working mothers. Some of these lowest-low-fertility countries, including Germany and Japan, consider low fertility and population aging a crisis that demands a policy response.

In order to understand better this crisis and how it relates to family policy debates, let us examine the data on total fertility rates (TFRs). TFRs provide a window into how young people in the aggregate weigh the fundamental human satisfactions of work, childrearing and marriage, as opposed to their responses to surveys asking them about the ideal number of babies they would like to have. They can help us think about women's reasons for having fewer or no children, including familialistic or traditional assumptions about women's responsibility for unpaid care work, how hospitable the labor force is to working mothers, and anemic work–family policies.

Table 2.1 shows TFR figures for twenty-seven OECD countries since 1970, sorted by regime type (drawing on Esping-Andersen's three worlds of welfare

the capacity to care for and love someone else and learn to foster their children's capacities of curiosity, attachment, trust and intelligence. The relationship between parents and children is unique, important and lifelong (Senior, 2014).

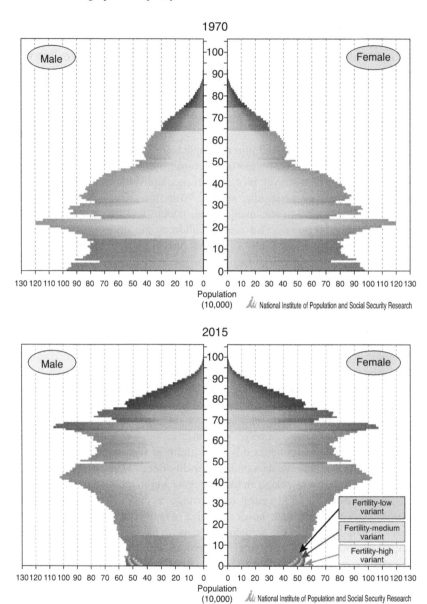

Figure 2.3 Population pyramids for Japan, 1970 and 2015
Source: NIPSSR, Japan, 2014.

Table 2.1 *Total fertility rates: number of children born to women aged 15 to 49*

Country	1970	1980	1990	2000	2010	2012	Tempo- & parity-adjusted TFR, 2008
Low fertility (Med, East Asia, former Eastern bloc)							
Czech Republic	1.91	2.10	1.89	1.14	1.49	1.45	1.81
Greece	2.40	2.23	1.40	1.26	1.51	1.34	1.66
Hungary	1.97	1.92	1.84	1.33	1.26	1.34	1.66
Italy	2.43	1.68	1.36	1.26	1.41	1.43	1.51
Japan	2.13	1.75	1.54	1.36	1.39	1.40	1.47
Korea	4.53	2.82	1.57	1.47	1.23	1.30	n/a
Poland	2.20	2.28	1.99	1.37	1.38	1.29	1.60
Portugal	2.83	2.18	1.56	1.56	1.37	1.28	1.61
Spain	2.90	2.22	1.36	1.23	1.38	1.32	1.54
						1.35 avg.	
Continental conservative							
Austria	2.29	1.65	1.46	1.36	1.44	1.43	1.67
Belgium	2.25	1.68	1.62	1.67	1.87	1.79	1.93
France	2.48	1.95	1.78	1.87	1.99	1.99	2.12
Germany	2.03	1.56	1.45	1.38	1.39	1.38	1.68
Luxembourg	1.98	1.50	1.62	1.78	1.63	1.57	2.05
Netherlands	2.57	1.60	1.62	1.72	1.80	1.72	1.83
Switzerland	2.10	1.55	1.59	1.50	1.54	1.53	1.69
						1.63 avg.	
Nordic social democratic							
Denmark	1.95	1.55	1.67	1.77	1.88	1.73	1.98
Finland	1.83	1.63	1.79	1.73	1.87	1.80	1.91
Iceland	2.81	2.48	2.31	2.08	2.20	2.03	2.41
Norway	2.50	1.72	1.93	1.85	1.95	1.85	2.08
Sweden	1.94	1.68	2.14	1.55	1.98	1.91	1.97
						1.86 avg.	
Liberal							
Australia	2.86	1.89	1.90	1.76	1.89	1.90	n/a
Canada	2.33	1.68	1.71	1.49	1.67	1.60	n/a
Ireland	3.87	3.23	2.12	1.90	2.07	2.01	2.10
New Zealand	3.17	2.03	2.18	1.98	2.15	2.00	n/a
United Kingdom	2.43	1.90	1.83	1.64	1.98	1.92	2.12
United States	2.48	1.84	2.08	2.06	1.93	1.90	2.14
						1.88 avg.	

Italicized countries had high net immigration between 2004 and 2008. Note that the 2012 averages are based on the author's calculation from country averages rather than aggregate population figures.

Source: OECD, 2013m. The last column and the information on migration rates are from the Vienna Institute of Demography, 2013.

capitalism typology, 1990) with an additional category of lowest-low-fertility states. The lowest-low-fertility countries come from disparate cultural and political milieux, the Mediterranean Rim, former Eastern bloc countries, and two Asian countries, Korea and Japan – and it might make sense to include very-low-fertility conservative welfare states like Germany and Austria here too. By treating low fertility as a problem that needs to be explained, this chapter tries to identify a few of the reasons why some wealthy countries are holding their own with respect to population stability, while others have fallen far below replacement levels of fertility.

We can see that TFRs have fallen substantially and quickly across most OECD countries since 1970, a moment when all of them had close to or above replacement-level TFRs. But they have not fallen uniformly, nor did all countries start at the same level. Most of the liberal countries have sustained close to replacement level fertility, as have the Nordic countries. Fertility rates in the conservative countries plunged in the 1970s, and since then have crept steadily downward to a current average TFR of 1.63. The low-fertility countries break into two groups, the Eastern Bloc countries which did not show profound drops in fertility until after the collapse of the Soviet Union and communist governments throughout the region in 1989, and the "early population decline" countries that have had TFRs below 1.6 since 1990, Greece, Italy, Japan, Korea, Portugal and Spain (note that Austria and Germany fit this pattern too).

The last column of Table 2.1 gives tempo- and parity-adjusted TFRs for 2008, which are based on calculations about delay in having children vs. actual declines in fertility (see Bongaarts and Sobotka, 2012, for a theoretical explanation of this adjustment). If we accept the argument that some of the apparent decline in TFRs is temporal, and that we can expect to see TFR figures rebound somewhat, we see the low-fertility group of countries split into three groups: the hard-core low-fertility ones, Japan, Korea,[4] Italy and Spain (with adjusted TFRs between 1.47 and 1.54); Poland and Portugal, which recover to TFRs of about 1.6; and Greece, the eastern bloc countries (Czech Republic, Hungary) and Austria and Germany, which rebound to the 1.66 to 1.81 level.

I have also indicated five countries among those in the table that had quite high immigration rates over the 2004–8 period – Italy, Spain, France, the United Kingdom and the United States – because it is reasonable to expect that high rates of immigration will lead to higher TFRs, as immigrants are generally assumed to have higher fertility rates than native-born women. This appears to be the case in France and the two English-speaking countries, but not in Italy

---

[4] The dataset with tempo- and parity-adjusted TFRs did not include Korea, but I am guessing that it will follow the Japanese pattern pretty closely.

and Spain, which have very low TFRs for both the raw 2012 TFR figures and the tempo-adjusted ones for 2008.

What explains the rapid declines in total fertility in some parts of the OECD world, and relative stability in others? There are three possible explanations. First, low fertility is rooted in labor market structures and opportunities. Fertility declines both in labor markets with very high unemployment rates, especially for young workers, and when there are dual labor markets that treat female workers as shock absorbers for economic boom and bust cycles (because they can be easily hired and fired and are apt to work in low-paid irregular positions).

A second possibility is that women in low-fertility countries are delaying or forgoing having children because of familialistic cultural values that support intensive-mothering and male-breadwinner employment patterns, as opposed to the greater commitment to gender equality and openness to immigration seen in liberal and northern European countries. It appears that religion might also be a factor in supporting rather traditional social mores, as Mediterranean Rim countries plus Austria and Germany have large Catholic or Eastern Orthodox populations, and Confucianism could play a similar role in Korea and Japan (Esping-Andersen, 1997).

A third explanation is that low fertility is related to underdeveloped work–family reconciliation policies, leaving women in low-fertility countries with too little support to help them deal with work–family conflicts. This explanation fits with the approach of comparative family policy scholars who suggest that falling fertility and aging populations can be reversed if states pass appropriate work–family policies (Thévenon, 2013; OECD, 2007a). But the logic of this connection seems questionable, both because some countries maintain their populations without making much effort to support working mothers (like the United States), and because others *have* made serious efforts to improve their work–family support policies without making a dint in the population problem (like Japan and Germany).

The rest of this chapter considers these arguments for why some countries appear to be in demographic free fall, while others are quite stable. In the following section, I consider indicators related to participation in workforce and household work and discrimination against women and mothers, making a prima facie case that labor market structures and the opportunity costs of having children contribute to the low-fertility aging population problem. Then I examine work–family support policies in OECD countries, and come back at the end of the chapter to arguments that labor market structures, cultural attitudes about the division of labor between men and women, and policies that support working mothers make for environments that are more or less congenial to raising children while working.

Labor market organization and women's work

It used to be a truism that, when women have fewer children, female labor force participation (FLFP) rates will be higher, since women with fewer childrearing responsibilities have more time available to work. But the correlation between total fertility and FLFP rates shifted from negative to positive in the mid-1980s (Brewster and Rindfuss, 2000, 278): now FLFP rates are higher in countries with higher fertility rates. This is apparent when we look at Table 2.2: the lowest FLFP rates in 2008 were for the low-fertility countries, and the highest were in the two high-fertility groups – the social democratic and liberal countries.

It is worth pausing a moment to reflect on why the FLFP rate in the Netherlands was so much higher than in the other continental countries. Most Dutch women (and men) work part-time, and they are encouraged to do so by policies that insure that part-time workers receive pay and benefits proportional to those received by full-time workers. The approach of insuring that part-time jobs are not marginalized attracts many to a more humane part-time schedule that leaves them able to pursue other activities, including childrearing and household work, as well as leisure activities and community and volunteer work.

Ease in finding and keeping good jobs is key to understanding countries' differing fertility rates. High unemployment rates among young people act as a damper on fertility rates, as difficulty finding decent jobs leads young people to delay family formation and first births until they are more financially secure (Adsera, 2004, 27). Women who are worried about finding positions in a tough job market often delay having babies because they are afraid to worsen their employment prospects by getting pregnant in such circumstances (Castles 2003, 214). Indeed, one of the reasons that fertility and female labor force participation are now positively correlated may be that women feel more secure about having children if they are able to work and support themselves, because the increased risk of unemployment and divorce have undermined the male-breadwinner model. With many families relying on two earners, some believe strong employment prospects for women are a precondition for family formation (D'Addio and Mira d'Ercole, 2006; Castles, 2003, 219).

Turning to workforce participation rates for childless women compared to those with one or more children (see Table 2.3), we see that mothers are more likely to continue to work in some regimes than others. In the social democratic and conservative countries most mothers continue to work after their first child is born, except in Germany and Switzerland. In the liberal countries, women are more likely to stop working, except in the USA and Canada, which resemble the continental pattern of a slight reduction in FLFP upon the birth of a first child. The low-fertility countries are a mixed bag. In Japan, as in the Czech Republic and Hungary, there is a marked drop off in first-time mothers working, as we shall see in Chapter 5. But the western European countries

Table 2.2 *Female Labor Force Participation rates by country, 1980–2008 (total number of women working divided by total women between ages of 15 and 64)*

Country	1980	1990	2000	2008
Low fertility (Med, East Asia, former Eastern bloc)				
Czech Republic	(X)	69.1	56.9	57.58
Greece	33.0	43.6	41.28	49.02
Hungary	(NA)	(NA)	49.64	50.57
Italy	39.6	45.9	39.55	47.21
Japan	54.8	60.4	56.75	59.74
Korea	(NA)	51.3	50.05	53.19
Poland	(NA)	(NA)	48.91	52.38
Portugal	54.3	62.9	60.55	62.49
Spain	32.2	41.2	41.98	55.74
				55.22 avg.
Continental conservative				
Austria	48.7	55.4	59.40	65.77
Belgium	47.0	52.4	51.88	55.73
France	54.4	57.6	54.33	60.09
Germany	52.8	57.4	58.13	64.32
Luxembourg	39.9	50.7	50.04	55.76
Netherlands	35.5	53.1	62.71	70.24
Switzerland	54.1	56.2	57.80	61.40
				61.90 avg.
Nordic social democratic				
Denmark	(NA)	78.5	72.07	74.41
Finland	70.1	72.9	64.47	69.01
Iceland	(NA)	65.6	80.99	80.31
Norway	62.3	71.2	73.97	75.44
Sweden	74.1	80.5	72.24	73.20
				74.47 avg.
Liberal				
Australia	52.7	62.9	61.44	66.71
Canada	57.8	67.8	65.64	70.12
Ireland	36.3	38.9	53.30	60.51
New Zealand	44.6	62.9	63.50	69.00
United Kingdom	58.3	65.5	65.55	66.87
United States	59.7	68.8	67.79	65.50
				66.45 avg.

Source: OECD, 2008b.

in this category – Greece, Italy, Portugal and Spain – resemble the conservative countries. Most countries see a steep decline in women's workforce participation with the birth of second and subsequent children, the exception being Sweden. The reasons for this are related to the availability of affordable

Table 2.3 *Employment rates of women by presence of children, 2003*

	Employment rates by group (%)			
	All women	Women w/o children	One child	Two or more children
Low fertility (Med, East Asia, former Eastern bloc)				
Czech Republic	73.5	83.6	69.9	55.6
Greece	56.6	56.1	54.4	47.4
Hungary	67.4	74.6	67.0	48.3
Italy	54.9	57.2	54.5	45.7
Japan	64.4	**	**	**
Korea	56.8	**	**	**
Poland	62.1	**	**	**
Portugal	74.2	72.3	78.6	74.9
Spain	56.5	56.1	54.4	47.4
Continental conservative				
Austria	76.7	79.5	79.9	67.6
Belgium	67.7	70.4	71.2	65.3
France	71.6	76.1	77.0	61.6
Germany	72.0	77.6	70.3	56.5
Luxembourg	64.5	71.2	67.6	51.2
Netherlands	74.0	76.8	73.8	68.6
Switzerland	77.2	84.3	75.5	65.5
Nordic social democratic				
Denmark	78.9	78.5	88.1	77.2
Finland	78.9	79.2	78.5	73.5
Iceland	85.7	89.1	89.3	80.8
Norway	79.7	82.9	83.3	78.0
Sweden	81.7	81.9	80.6	81.8
Liberal				
Australia	68.6	68.4	60.1	56.2
Canada	75.7	76.5	74.9	68.2
Ireland	65.1	65.8	51.0	40.8
New Zealand	72.0	80.7	66.9	58.9
United Kingdom	74.1	81.6	72.4	61.8
United States	72.0	78.6	75.6	64.7

** – Data n/a
Source: OECD, 2005b.

childcare (see Thévenon, 2013, and the tables comparing work–family policies later in this chapter) and expectations about intensive mothering, especially the idea that mothers ought to stay home for a few years with their babies until they are three years old.

We can see from Table 2.4 that women make up a large majority of part-time workers in the OECD countries, although, of course, not all women are part-time workers. The two groups with the highest percentages of women who work part-time are the continental and liberal countries, where close to a third of all women workers are part-time.

Part-time work is often an attractive option for mothers of young children who prefer to spend more time with their children when they are small; indeed, some countries have set up parental leave programs that permit mothers to work part-time and still receive partial paid leave. Further, shorter hours and greater flexibility can be helpful for women who do not have access to or cannot afford to pay for full-time childcare (D'Addio and Mira d'Ercole, 2005, 34). This is common both in continental states that do not offer much formal care for infants and toddlers and in liberal market economies where childcare services are provided through the market and are therefore costly. Part-time work is also popular in countries like Germany where the official school day is short and there is little after-school care. Worthy of note again is the Netherlands, where part-time jobs pay well and childcare is set up to accommodate part-time work schedules.

That said, many women work part-time because they cannot find anything better. In such circumstances, they are likely to take jobs that pay badly, do not come with benefits, afford fewer promotions and raises, and may require them to work irregular hours (e.g., evenings, weekends, or split shifts to cover peak demand in retail businesses). Table 2.5 gives the percentages of women in involuntary part-time positions since 1990. The countries that have persistently high percentages of women in such jobs include four of the LMEs, Australia, Canada, Ireland, New Zealand, plus three countries with lowest-low fertility rates: Italy, Japan and Spain.

Clearly, the meaning of part-time work has to do with specific labor market practices and rules. Sometimes such jobs are defined as low-skill, low-pay work, an off-ramp from more competitive, better-paid full-time positions that circumvents the expectations and rewards accorded to full-time workers. In many labor markets short and flexible schedules are not very desirable, as they are often associated with variable, unpredictable hours rather than regular shifts. But in countries where parents can cut back their hours until their children reach a certain age, as in Sweden, part-time work paid at the same hourly rate as usual is a boon.[5]

---

[5] For workers whose talents and skills give them bargaining power, it may be possible to ask for and even insist on flexible and short hours. But research on professional positions in the United States suggests that requesting flexible and part-time schedules can mark a worker as difficult. See Stone (2007) for a study of professional women who asked to cut back their hours and were subtly – or not so subtly – marginalized in their professions.

Table 2.4 *Percentage of women who work part-time, and percentage of part-time workers who are female, 2007*

	% of women who work part-time	women as % of all part-time workers
Low fertility (Med, East Asia, former Eastern bloc)		
Czech Republic	5.9	72.3
Greece	13.6	67.9
Hungary	4.2	68.6
Italy	29.9	78.6
Japan	32.6	71.5
Korea	12.5	58.9
Poland	15.0	67.0
Portugal	14.3	66.1
Spain	20.9	79.8
Avg.	16.5	
Continental conservative		
Austria	31.5	83.5
Belgium	32.9	81.3
France	23.1	80.4
Germany	39.2	80.7
Luxembourg	28.8	93.1
Netherlands	59.7	(NA)
Switzerland	45.6	81.3
Avg.	37.3	
Nordic social democratic		
Denmark	23.9	62.8
Finland	15.5	63.7
Iceland	25.4	72.7
Norway	31.6	72.0
Sweden	19.7	65.0
Avg.	23.2	
Liberal		
Australia	38.5	71.6
Canada	25.2	68.0
Ireland	35.6	79.6
New Zealand	34.7	72.6
United Kingdom	38.6	77.4
United States	17.9	68.4
Avg.	31.7	

Source: OECD, 2013f.

Table 2.5 *Percentage of women, aged 25–54, employed in involuntary part-time employment*

Involuntary part-time workers are part-timers because they could not find a full-time job.

Country	1990	1995	2000	2005	2008	2009	2010	2011
Low fertility (Med, East Asia, former Eastern bloc)								
Czech Republic	N/A	N/A	1.01	0.97	0.75	0.86	1.19	1.12
Greece	1.54	1.99	2.59	3.68	3.60	4.35	4.47	4.77
Hungary	N/A	0.86	0.59	0.59	0.68	1.08	1.29	2.02
Italy	1.71	3.05	4.14	7.71	8.85	10.17	11.33	12.61
Japan	2.41	2.32	3.42	7.85	8.19	10.24	9.52	9.44
Poland	N/A	N/A	N/A	2.87	1.44	1.39	1.58	1.83
Portugal	1.81	2.28	3.70	3.68	4.41	3.82	4.23	5.22
Spain	3.04	3.04	3.40	6.56	7.07	9.54	10.39	11.51
Continental conservative								
Austria	N/A	0.92	1.96	2.69	2.61	2.50	2.61	2.33
Belgium	5.97	6.90	5.77	4.76	4.18	3.41	3.27	2.92
France	N/A	7.33	4.67	5.70	6.04	6.08	6.23	5.68
Germany	1.42	2.20	3.25	6.26	6.78	6.45	6.34	4.89
Luxembourg	0.99	1.10	1.16	3.14	1.87	2.10	2.04	2.36
Netherlands	11.04	2.53	1.82	2.05	1.55	2.08	2.02	2.74
Nordic social democratic								
Denmark	3.22	3.76	2.46	3.42	2.19	2.42	2.51	2.90
Finland	N/A	N/A	5.28	4.50	4.24	4.25	4.49	4.47
Iceland	N/A	3.95	2.01	N/A	N/A	N/A	N/A	N/A
Norway	5.28	6.24	1.98	2.73	1.74	1.75	1.80	1.78
Sweden	N/A	N/A	4.90	3.63	3.42	3.63	3.18	3.01
Liberal								
Australia	N/A	N/A	N/A	8.59	8.00	9.33	8.97	9.13
Canada	4.96	7.84	6.11	6.13	5.31	6.39	6.66	6.49
Ireland	2.79	3.76	2.83	N/A	1.10	4.23	6.27	8.06
New Zealand	6.78	7.94	7.62	5.11	5.29	6.23	5.59	5.72
United Kingdom	1.82	3.77	2.26	1.87	N/A	3.04	3.41	4.22
United States	N/A	N/A	0.84	1.15	1.13	1.71	2.11	2.10
OECD countries	**2.84**	**2.86**	**2.52**	**3.45**	**3.50**	**4.13**	**4.29**	**4.23**

Source: OECD, 2013g.

The high incidence of involuntary part-time jobs in four LMEs may be related to the fact that their labor markets are not regulated as stringently as those in CMEs (for example, they may have low minimum wages). But it makes a difference whether workers understand part-time work to be a life sentence that will consign them to low-paid jobs forever, or whether they see

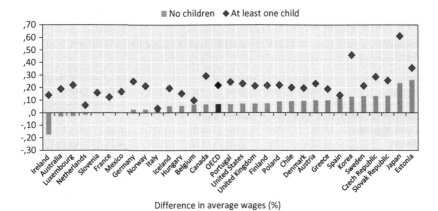

Figure 2.4 The gender pay gap for mothers and non-mothers vs. men for workers, 25–44
Source: OECD, 2012c, 170.

such jobs as an interlude that may meet particular short-term needs. Dual labor markets that are structured around "insiders" who are well-paid, receive good benefits, are promoted and have job security, and "outsiders" who are badly paid, receive few or no benefits, are unlikely to be promoted or given raises, and are typically vulnerable to layoffs during economic downturns, are likely to slot outsiders into the permanent part-timer category. In such labor markets, women, and especially mothers, tend to find it tough to crack the "insider" barrier and are likely to be stuck in bad jobs, raising the opportunity costs of having children considerably and leading to lower fertility rates.[6] Countries where male-dominated labor unions have an important voice in protecting certain job categories and setting labor market rules, and ones that prize firm-specific skills, are likely to exclude women, and especially mothers, from insider jobs. CMEs where large numbers of women work in involuntary part-time jobs – Germany, Italy, Japan, Greece, Portugal and Spain – practice this kind of exclusion. Several other countries appear to have dual labor markets, judging from those that have large maternal and gender wage gaps (Poland, Austria, Greece, Korea, the Czech and Slovak republics – see Figure 2.4).

Gender and maternal pay gaps suggest labor markets that discriminate against women and mothers. As we can see in Figure 2.4, about a third of the countries listed here have little or no gender gap: childless women and men are paid equally. But, except for the Netherlands and Italy, all of them have sizeable

---

[6] If women's inability to find good jobs depresses fertility rates in some of these countries, *men's* inability to find anything better than part-time, temporary or contract work has an even more strongly negative impact on marriage and fertility (Adsera, 2004, 34; Brinton, 2010).

maternal wage gaps, which contribute to what we ordinarily call the "gender gap" – that is, the gap in pay between women and men.[7] This suggests that the interruptions that go along with childrearing may push women into lower-paid jobs,[8] and it certainly suggests that the mommy pay gap represents a significant part of the opportunity cost that women pay for having children. Japan and Korea stand out for having enormous mother–male wage gaps: Japanese mothers only earn 39 percent as much as men do, and Korean mothers earn 54 percent as much. Two-thirds of the countries in Figure 2.4 have maternal wage gaps above 20 percent. Standing out on the other side are Italy, the Netherlands, Belgium and France with maternal wage gaps of less than 12 percent.

What accounts for wage gaps in different countries, and what can they tell us about labor force conditions that affect women's decisions about work? High degrees of pay stratification are frequently found in: (1) dual labor markets with big discrepancies in the wages and treatment of core and peripheral workers, especially on the basis of sex; or (2) liberal market economies with weak organized labor, weak regulations and low minimum wages. When gender wage gaps are small, it may reflect the effect of non-discrimination laws or ones that mandate comparable pay for jobs of comparable worth, and high minimum wages, not to mention better-organized and more effective action by labor unions, women's sections of labor unions, and women's movements.

Looking at Table 2.6, we see that lightly regulated LMEs account for five out of the ten countries with the highest percentages of low-paid workers, and the rest are low-fertility countries, the same pattern we saw with women in involuntary part-time work.

Although LMEs have many low-paid workers and significant wage inequalities, there may be a silver lining to the poverty and inequality that pervade them. Lightly regulated LMEs have flexible, mobile labor markets that have relatively low unemployment rates and readily allow workers to re-enter the job market after taking a break (say, to raise children). CMEs on the other hand are more highly regulated and typically have more guarantees of job security and high wages. This leads to greater income equality, but also to higher unemployment rates. High unemployment among young people is associated with postponing births and having fewer children, so that where "unemployment risk goes up,

---

[7] Indeed, gender-based hiring and pay discrimination are probably related to discrimination against women as (potential) mothers, since Human Resources (HR) directors often assume that most women are likely to become mothers at some point and to interrupt their work lives to raise children, requiring time off and other accommodations that make them more troublesome and expensive to their employers. This is especially so in labor markets that seek workers with firm-specific skills, as we noted in Chapter 1.

[8] Parenting interruptions hurt earning potential whether the parent taking time off to raise children is a man or a woman. But in fact women are almost always the ones who take parental leaves and interrupt their career development.

Table 2.6 *Low-wage incidence (percentage of all workers earning less than 67 percent of median earnings)*

Country	1995	2005
Korea	22.9	25.4
US	25.2	24.0
Poland	17.3	23.5
Canada	22.0	22.2
UK	20.0	20.7
Ireland	20.4	17.6
Hungary	19.9	(N/A)
Spain	15.2	16.2
Japan	15.4	16.1
Australia	13.8	15.9
Germany	11.1	15.8
NZ	14.9	11.5
Sweden	5.7	6.4

Source: OECD, 2007b, 268.

fertility declines" (Adsera, 2004, 19–20; see also Hall and Soskice, 2001, and Estevez-Abe, 2007). The ability of LMEs to create jobs, and the ease with which people can move from one position to another, have a positive effect on people's willingness to have children, even though many of those jobs pay badly and most LMEs have high levels of inequality.

Before turning to work–family policies, I consider two final aspects of labor market organization: standard work hours and vacation days (see Table 2.7), and the degree to which men and women share the unpaid work of childrearing and other domestic work (see Figure 2.5). Work and vacation hours are a crucial complement to explicit work–family policies; if workers are only required to work 7 or 7½ hours a day, it is easier to manage childcare and after-school care for their children. And when parents can take off a month or five weeks of leave during their children's summer vacation, they have less trouble accommodating care needs. Conversely, countries with longer working hours (especially ones with work cultures that frequently demand overtime work or quasi-mandatory socializing) make work–family tensions harsher, and put pressure on secondary earners (usually mothers) to work part-time in order to have time to spend with their kids and take care of the unpaid work of feeding, clothing and sheltering family members. The organization of work and school schedules is germane to work–family conflicts, and can be an important way in which countries support working parents.

Table 2.7 *Standard hours per week and vacation days (sum of official holidays and mandated paid vacation)*

Country	Regular work week	Paid vacation days per year*
Low fertility (Med, East Asia, former Eastern bloc)		
Czech Republic	38.0	28
Greece	40.0	30
Hungary	40.0	26
Italy	40.0	30
Japan	40.0	25
Korea	40.0	20
Poland	40.0	31
Portugal	38.3	34
Spain	38.5	33
		28.6 avg.
Continental conservative		
Austria	38.8	35
Belgium	38.0	28
France	35.0	36
Germany	37.0	29
Luxembourg	39.0	35
Netherlands	37.0	28
Switzerland	41.5	20
		30.1 avg.
Nordic social democratic		
Denmark	37.0	34
Finland	37.5	36
Iceland	42.0	24
Norway	37.5	29
Sweden	40.0	34
		31.4 avg.
Liberal		
Australia	38	28
Canada	40	20
Ireland	39	29
New Zealand	40	20
United Kingdom	37.2	28
United States	40	10
		22.5 avg.

* These vary with seniority in some countries. Iceland data are from European Employment Services, 2007; those for New Zealand are from the NZ Ministry of Business, Innovation & Employment, 2013; South Swiss data are from the Swiss Federal Statistical Office, 2011.

Source: OECD, 2007a, 178.

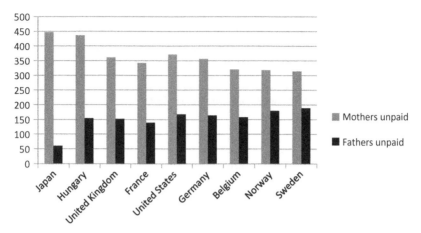

Figure 2.5 Mothers' and fathers' contributions to unpaid care and household work (for parents of at least one child under age six, in minutes per day) *Source*: Tamiya and Shikata, 2010, 153. The figures are for housework + childcare done by mothers vs. housework + childcare done by fathers.

As we can see in Table 2.7, most European countries have adopted standard work hours in the 35- to 38-hour range, while most of the English-speaking and low-fertility countries still treat 40 hours as the standard work week. Both the conservative and social democratic countries average just over six weeks of vacation time each year, a shade more than the low-fertility countries, and significantly longer than the liberal countries.

Figures for official work hours don't tell the whole story, since in some countries many work overtime or moonlight in order to earn enough to support their families, accumulating a lot more than the mandated hours. Nor do official paid days off necessarily mean that workers take all the vacation time to which they are entitled; not using all of one's vacation time is commonplace in Japan for example, and not unheard of among white-collar workers in the USA.

Figure 2.5 draws on time use survey data to show how much time husbands and wives spend doing the unpaid work of childrearing and housework. Japanese women spend 7½ hours a day doing unpaid work at home, to their husbands' 1 hour a day. Although none of the other countries in the chart are as lopsided as Japan, women in most countries put in two to three times as many hours on unpaid care work as men. The most egalitarian divisions of unpaid labor are in Norway and Sweden. To the extent that the work of keeping a household running and caring for children has commonly been regarded as a familial responsibility and therefore beyond the purview of the state, these disparities give us some insight into why women in housework- and mothering-intensive cultures might be less willing to undertake childrearing than those in more gender-egalitarian ones.

Thus far we have examined data that can help us understand why women are having fewer babies in most of the OECD countries, and very few indeed in the lowest-low-fertility ones. The comparative data on workforce participation, part-time work, gender and maternal gaps, and responsibility for unpaid care work suggest that women are having fewer children because they find themselves caught between mixed messages or expectations. Parents used to assume that their daughters would marry and find a husband to support them. But now they invest in helping them accumulate the human capital they need to be able to get a good job and flourish in the work world. In most OECD countries, more girls than boys go to college. The message of this kind of investment in human capital seems to be "go forth and earn."

But even though young women are being told "You're smart, take your education seriously and be independent, find a career you care about and flourish in it," they are still more likely to work part-time than men are, and to spend more time than men doing unpaid household and childrearing work. Disproportionately, women work part-time and at jobs that don't pay well, often in service sector positions. In some countries, there are huge mommy penalties. If the first message is "Be more like a man," the second is "Be more like a woman." The bind faced by working mothers is worst in the countries with dual labor markets, where discrimination against women and especially mothers bars them from career-track jobs that pay well and come with promotions, raises and benefits. The bind is ameliorated in countries where the opportunity cost of taking time off to raise children is not so steep, either because the market recognizes that mothers can be excellent workers and rewards them on the basis of skills or merit, or because there are good work–family reconciliation policies that help them get back to work and care for their children. These two approaches are at the heart of the two basic variants of high-fertility, demographic success stories: the liberal countries and the social democratic ones.

When labor markets make it relatively easy for women to return to work after giving birth, they keep the opportunity costs of having children low and encourage higher fertility. But some labor markets, like Japan's, exacerbate opportunity costs by making it impossible for anyone who takes a substantial break from working to return to a regular full-time job (Yu, 2002). Others, like Germany's, make it difficult for mothers to return to work full-time because there are few spaces available for babies and toddlers in childcare, and because disapproval of working mothers is still widespread. Both the organization of the labor market and work–family reconciliation policies are critical to understanding how women's labor force participation and childbearing decisions are related. Women's decisions to take time off from work to raise children undermine their career investments. This clash in roles between paid worker

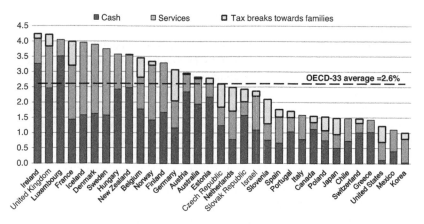

Figure 2.6 Spending on families via cash, services and tax measures as percentage of Gross Demographic Product (GDP), 2009

Notes
- Public support accounted here only concerns public support that is exclusively for families (e.g. child payments and allowances, parental leave benefits and childcare support). Spending recorded in other social policy areas such as health and housing support also assists families, but not exclusively, and is not included here.
- Data on tax breaks for families is not available for Greece and Hungary.
Source: OECD, 2013b.

and unpaid nurturer affects women's decisions about how to balance work and family throughout the OECD world. Increasingly, women are deciding to work throughout their lives, and to have fewer children.

Although I have alluded to the impact of work–family policies on fertility behaviors, we have not yet examined those policies from a comparative perspective. Let us turn to them now.

Work–family policies

Countries use a variety of policies to support working parents: family allowances and tax breaks; maternity, parental and paternity leaves; and childcare and preschool programs. I present recent data on these policies in order to get the lay of the land; we will take a closer look at these measures in Sweden, France, Germany, Japan and the United States in Chapter 7 when I assess which work–family policies work best.

I begin with figures on overall levels of support for family benefits. Figure 2.6 provides recent data on the amount that OECD countries spend on family benefits, combining cash transfers, in-kind services and tax expenditures. Surprisingly, the three highest spenders are France, the United Kingdom and Hungary – one continental, one liberal and one low-fertility country. But they are followed by the countries one might expect to spend generously to support work–family policies, the social democratic countries plus Belgium, Luxembourg, Germany – and also Australia. At the low-spending end of the spectrum are Switzerland (generally a residual low-spending welfare state), Canada, Italy, Portugal, Japan, Greece, the USA, Mexico, Chile and Korea.

The percentage of GDP different countries spend on family support benefits is a rather gross measurement of commitment to supporting families, so we turn next to different kinds of leave and early childhood education and care (ECEC) policies. Table 2.8 summarizes data on maternity, parental and paternity leaves. The United States stands out as the only country that does not offer any kind of paid leave, although in truth none of the liberal countries except Canada offer much in terms of fully reimbursed leave time (see column 7 of Table 2.8), nor do Switzerland, Spain, Iceland or Greece.

Most countries offer better reimbursement rates for maternity than for parental leave. All the continental countries offer 14–16 weeks of maternity leave paid at 100 percent of usual wages except for Belgium and Switzerland. The length of maternity leaves varies more in the other groups than among the conservative countries, and they are generally not paid as well either, especially in the liberal countries. Notice that Ireland and the United Kingdom offer paid maternity leaves in the 1-year range, and several low-fertility countries have maternity leaves in the 5- to 6-month range.

Six countries offer three years of parental leave (Czech Republic, Hungary, Poland, Spain, France and Finland), all at very modest rates of reimbursement that are consistent with flat-rate paid leaves, except for Hungary, which pays 51 percent. Four of the six countries allowing long low-paid leave are low-fertility ones; the other two continental and social democratic. Paternity leaves are common in all the sets of countries except the liberal ones, although they are best-developed in the social democratic countries.

Leave policies aim to help parents take time off from work for the birth or adoption of a child, but they are controversial. Too long, and they are attacked for encouraging women to take long breaks from working, which causes their skills to atrophy and keeps them stuck in low-pay jobs (D'Addio and Mira d'Ercole, 2005, 50, 59; Afsa, 1998; Fagnani, 1998). Too focused on elite high-earning women, like Germany's 2007 parental leave law, and they are attacked for exacerbating class and ethnic divisions (Henninger et al., 2008). And others note that paid leaves can create disincentives to hiring female workers in the first place, leading to higher female unemployment rates, greater difficulty getting good jobs, and lower pay for women workers (Mandel and Semyonov, 2005).

Table 2.8 *Maternity, parental and paternity leaves, 2011 (duration is in weeks unless otherwise noted)*

Country	Maternity Leave (1)	% rate of allowance (2)	Paternity leave (3)	Parental and prolonged period of leave (4)	% rate of allowance (5)	Parental leave (unpaid) (6)	Maternity and parental paid leave (full-rate equivalent) (7)	Maximum length of leave for women (1)+(4)
Low fertility (Med, East Asia, former Eastern bloc)								
Czech Republic	28.0	68.9	N/A	156.0	25.3	87.4	58.7	184.0
Greece	17.0	100.0	0.4 @ 100	14.0	0	30.3	17.0	31.0
Hungary	24.0	70.0	1.0 @ 100	156.0	51.0	76.7	96.4	180.0
Italy	20.0	80.0	N/A	24.0	30.0	18.2	23.2	44.0
Japan	14.0	67.0	8.0 @ 50	52.0	50.0	12.8	35.2	66.0
Korea	12.8	100.0	0.4 @ 100	45.6	21.2	35.9	22.5	58.4
Poland	24.0	75.0	2.0 @ 100	156.0	12.4	134.9	37.4	180.0
Portugal	12.5	100.0	6.0 @ 100	9.0	100.0	13.0	21.5	21.5
Spain	16.0	100.0	3.0 @ 100	15.06	0	144.0	16.0	172.0
Continental conservative								
Austria	16.0	100.0	0.4 @ 100	104.0	40.0	84.7	57.6	120.0
Belgium	15.0	76.9	2.0 @ 62.3	12.0	91.7	10.2	22.5	27.0
France	16.0	100.0	2.0 @ 100	156.0	18.9	118.2	45.5	172.0
Germany	14.0	100.0	8.0 @ 67.4	52.0	67.0	107.4	48.8	66.0
Luxembourg	16.0	100.0	0.4 @ 100	24.0	42.9	13.9	26.3	40.0
Netherlands	16.0	100.0	0.4 @ 100	26.0	18.8	20.7	20.9	42.0
Switzerland	14.0	80.0	N/A	N/A	N/A	0	11.2	14.0

Nordic social democratic								
Denmark	18.0	53.3	2.0 @ 55	32	53.4	22.8	26.7	50.0
Finland	17.5	66.9	7.0 @ 70	156.0	21.0	119.7	44.5	173.5
Iceland	13.0	64.6	13.0 @ 64.6	26.0	32.3	15.6	16.8	39.0
Norway	9.0	100.0	14.0 @ 85.7	88.0	32.7	59.4	37.8	97.0
Sweden	10.0	80.0	10.0 @ 80	60.0	64.3	20.6	46.6	70.0
Liberal								
Australia	6.06	42.9	N/A	52.0	0	52.0	2.6	58.1
Canada	15.0	55.0	N/A	37.0	52.0	15.8	27.5	52.0
Ireland	48.0	22.5	14 (unpaid)	14.0	0	14.0	10.8	62.0
New Zealand	14.0	50.0	N/A	52.0	0	38.0	7.0	66.0
United Kingdom	52.0	24.4	2.0 @ 20	13.0	0	13.0	12.7	65.0
United States	12.0	0	N/A	N/A	N/A	N/A	0	12.0

Source: OECD, 2013j; source for Japan's maternity leave reimbursement is JMC, 2014.

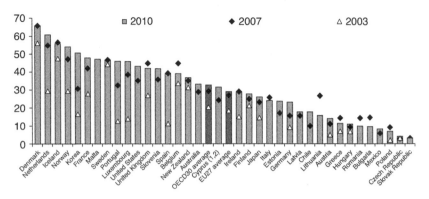

Figure 2.7 Average enrollment of children under three in formal childcare (2010)
Source: OECD, 2013d.

Childcare policies have been embraced more enthusiastically, as many believe that abundant, affordable childcare does the most to enable women to return to paid work promptly, minimizing atrophy in their job skills and helping avoid female job ghettoization and gender discrimination in hiring (Castles, 2003; Mandel and Semyonov, 2005).

Countries support childcare in widely differing ways, including provision of care through government-run childcare centers, government-licensed and supported private centers, employer-provided centers, and private market-based provision, with the government sometimes providing financial support to parents through tax expenditures or subsidies. Governments commonly regulate aspects of childcare, for example by setting base-level health and safety requirements for facilities; wages and benefits, and education and training requirements, for teachers; child-to-teacher ratios; and sliding scales for parent contributions based on family income or need.

Enrollment rates for young children in childcare vary tremendously, as the graph in Figure 2.7 illustrates. Of children under the age of three in Denmark, 66 percent are in formal care, compared to virtually none in the Czech and Slovak republics. Eastern European countries (from Austria and Germany eastward) are well represented among countries with less than 20 percent enrollment in childcare for children under three, along with Mexico, Chile and Greece. At the other end of the curve, all the social democratic countries (except Finland), along with the Netherlands, Belgium, Portugal, France, the UK, Luxembourg, New Zealand and South Korea, have 38 percent or more of children under the age of three in formal care, though children in the Netherlands and the UK mostly attend part-time (see Table 2.9 below).

Table 2.9 *Percentage of children in formal
childcare and preschool/childcare by age (2010)*

	Ages <3	Ages 3–5
Low fertility (Med, East Asia, former eastern bloc)		
Czech Republic	2	N/A
Greece	16	48
Hungary	9	87
Italy	29	96
Japan	28	90
Korea	38	40
Poland	8	60
Portugal	47	84
Spain	37	99
Continental conservative		
Austria	12	82
Belgium	48	99
France	42	100
Germany	18	94
Luxembourg	39	87
Netherlands	56*	67
Switzerland	N/A	47
Nordic social democratic		
Denmark	66	94
Finland	29	56
Iceland	55	96
Norway	51	96
Sweden	47	93
Liberal		
Australia	29*	53
Canada	24	47
Ireland	31	49
New Zealand	38	94
United Kingdom	41*	93
United States	31	67

* indicates preponderance of part-time care
Source: OECD, 2013l.

Enrollment of children between the ages of three and five is predominantly
for preschool or kindergarten programs that last 3 or 4 hours a day, although
the figures in Table 2.9 combine childcare and kindergarten enrollments. Some
preschool programs are set up to accommodate working parents, and provide
"add-on" care to cover hours beyond the normal school day, summer vacation, etc. Most of Europe sends upwards of 80 percent of preschool-age children to preschool or childcare programs, except the Czech Republic, Greece,

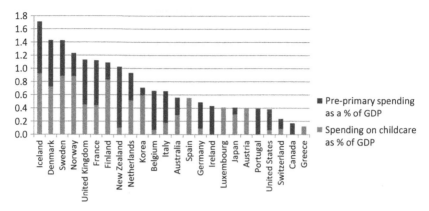

Figure 2.8 Public expenditure on childcare and early education services as percentage of GDP (2009)
Source: OECD, 2013k. (The data for Spain are not sorted into childcare and kindergarten.)

Poland, the Netherlands, Switzerland and Finland. Preschool is also less common in Korea and four of the liberal countries, Australia, Canada, Ireland and the US.

As we can see from Figure 2.8, the social democratic countries generously support childcare, as does the Netherlands. Korea, Luxembourg, Japan, Austria and Greece put most or all of their more modest budgets into supporting childcare, leaving parents to pay fees for preschool (which may explain why attendance rates are rather low in Korean and Greek preschools). Several continental countries – France, Belgium, Italy, Germany – support preschool more generously than childcare, as do most of the liberal countries and Portugal.

Why do enrollment rates in formal childcare and preschool vary so much across different OECD countries? Various explanations are plausible: low attendance for children under age three could be related to a strong preference among mothers to stay at home with their children for a few years, leading to lack of demand. Or there may be insufficient spaces in childcare and preschool to meet existing demand (this fits Germany and Japan, as we shall see). In countries that depend heavily on market provision of services paid for by families with little or no government support, the high out-of-pocket cost that families have to pay for ECEC may be prohibitive, as in the liberal countries and Switzerland.

Figure 2.9 indicates the net cost of full-time childcare for two children for a two-earner family earning 167 percent of average wages. The impact of leaving it to families to pay for these services is severe: families in all of the

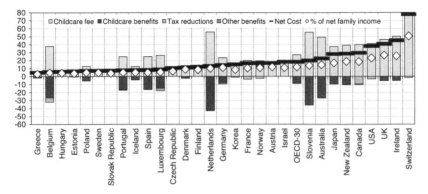

Figure 2.9 Net childcare costs for a dual-earner family earning 167 percent of the average wage with two children in full-time care (2008)
Note: Y axis is childcare-related costs and benefits as a percentage of average worker salaries for the specified family type.
Source: OECD, 2013e.

liberal countries, plus Japan and Switzerland, must spend between 15 and 50 percent of their net income on childcare services. Treating childrearing as a private responsibility that the state need not significantly subsidize puts a huge burden on families, especially working-class ones. From the point of view of all children getting a good start in life, which is important to insuring a modicum of social equality, the liberal welfare states are not doing very well.

If one's primary concern is which work–family policies will encourage young people to have more babies, what matters is the availability of childcare, not how it's provided. Thus Francis Castles has argued that it doesn't matter whether childcare is provided by the government, through government-subsidized private centers, or purchased on the market with families paying 100 percent of fees, as long as the supply is abundant (Castles, 2003, 219). But from the perspective of families that don't earn high salaries, having to foot the bill for childcare is onerous. Market systems are responsive to competition and cues about how much families can afford to pay, and private childcare providers will cut corners (hire less-qualified people, train them less and pay them less) in order to keep costs low if that is what they have to do to meet the demand for affordable services. Surely these cost and quality dynamics make a difference. Paying childcare workers higher salaries in order to attract well-trained and experienced people and avoid high turnover is a wage justice issue for this feminized workforce, and crucial to assuring that children receive high-quality care and teaching. We return to these issues in Chapter 7.

Work–family policies are flourishing in most of the social democratic welfare states.[9] All except Finland are at or near the top of the comparative scales for financial support of family benefits, public support for childcare, and the percentages of children enrolled in formal childcare and preschool. They offer well-designed leave policies, including generous paternity leaves.

The conservative countries are not uniform with respect to how they support childrearing families: France, Belgium, the Netherlands and Luxembourg strongly support family policies, and have large percentages of children in childcare and preschool. Austria and Germany also spend a lot on family benefits, but not to support childcare. Neither these two nor Switzerland (which is the lowest spender on work–family and ECEC policies among the conservative countries) has very many children under three attending childcare, which in the case of Switzerland may be due to the fact that parents have to pay so much to purchase such care. Only a few have well-developed paternity leaves (Germany has eight weeks at 67 percent, France and Belgium each offer two weeks paid at 100 percent and 62 percent respectively, and the rest offer two paid "daddy days" or nothing). Parental leaves vary in design from a short well-paid twelve-week leave in Belgium, to a three-year flat-rate paid leave in France for parents of second and subsequent children. Germany recently adopted a one-year leave paid at two-thirds of usual wages, Austria has a two-year leave paid at 40 percent of usual wages, and the rest offer shorter leaves reimbursed at lower rates.

Most of the low-fertility countries are frugal spenders when it comes to their support for cash benefits and childcare, with the exceptions of Hungary and the Czech Republic.[10] They all offer paid maternity leaves, and most offer paid parental and paternity leaves as well. Noteworthy among them with respect to parental leaves is Japan, which offers fifty-two weeks of parental leave paid at 50 percent of usual wages: not so different from Germany and the Nordic countries.[11] These countries are not generous supporters of childcare and preschool, and they vary considerably with respect to enrollment rates of

---

[9] Finland lags behind the other social democratic countries with respect to: (1) its spending on family benefits; (2) providing a three-year flat-rate paid parental leave rather than a short well-paid one; (3) spending less to support ECEC; and (4) lower enrollments of Finnish children in formal childcare and preschool.

[10] Hungary and the Czech Republic spend 3.3 percent and 2.5 percent of their GDPs respectively on family benefits, making Hungary the third-highest overall spender on work–family policies and putting the Czech Republic solidly above the 2.2 percent average spending level for the thirty-three OECD countries listed in Figure 2.6.

[11] The others range widely with respect to parental leaves. Several low-fertility countries have adopted paternity leaves, with Portugal the leader with its six-week, 100% paid leave, followed by Japan (eight weeks at 50%), Spain (three weeks at 100%), Poland (two weeks at 100%), and the rest with shorter ones (the Czech Republic and Italy as yet have no paternity leave).

children under the age of three in formal childcare services, from 38 percent of Korean toddlers to just 2 percent of Czechs.

As we noted earlier, the liberal countries are not big supporters of leave policies in any form; leaves are much less generous than those in the other three groups. There seems to be a strong expectation that workers will take little or no time off when a baby is born or adopted, or that families will finance longer periods out of the labor market on their own. Strong employer resistance to laws that require them to hold jobs open for new mothers appears to be the reason why leaves are so poorly developed in these countries. Like the conservative and low-fertility groups, the liberal countries are heterogeneous. The United States comes in near the bottom of countries surveyed for its support of family benefits and its public support for ECEC, and the United Kingdom comes in near the top. Attendance rates for childcare for children under three range from 24 percent in Canada to 41 percent in the UK, but childcare is mostly part-time in both the UK and Australia. The liberal countries all rely on private provision of childcare services, making it burdensome for many families to pay for childcare: they cluster at the top of the range for the percentage of net family income required to pay for such care.

A new rubric for sorting work–family policy regimes

Putting together the demographic markers and data about labor market regimes with the work–family support policies, I identify four groups with respect to how friendly to working mothers countries are. First are high-fertility CMEs with good work–family policies; second are high-fertility LMEs with under-developed work–family policies; third are "hard core" low-fertility countries; and last is a residual category that includes most of the conservative countries, the Eastern bloc and Greece, which have in-between TFRs (in the 1.65–1.83 range for tempo- and parity-adjusted TFRs).[12]

The first group is made up of the high-fertility countries that have developed and found the political wherewithal to fund excellent work–family reconcili-ation policies along just about every dimension: cash transfers, childcare and preschool, and generous, well-designed leave policies which include policies that encourage men to spend several weeks at home with babies. This group includes Sweden, Denmark, Norway, Iceland, France and Belgium. These countries generally anticipate and reinforce dual-earner families, in which both men and women participate in paid work throughout their lifetimes (Gornick

---

[12] Luxembourg does not cleanly fall into any of these groups: it is a tiny (500,000 people), wealthy country which is 87 percent Catholic. The Vienna Institute of Demography projects it will have a tempo- and parity-adjusted TFR of 2.05, quite a bit higher than its TFR figures since 1980, which have varied between 1.5 and 1.8.

and Meyers, 2009 identify a similar "dual earner" category). Many have CMEs that track women workers into public-sector jobs (especially Sweden), or into secondary- earner jobs (e.g., France). Such tracking often results in gender wage gaps that reflect the fact that women are not competing for the best, highest-paid private sector jobs, though this is mitigated in countries that require employers to pay comparable wages for jobs of comparable worth.

The second group includes the high-fertility countries that do not have well-developed work–family policies, the liberal countries. They do not generously support leave policies, cash transfers or ECEC, relying instead on market provision for abundant childcare. On the other hand, their labor markets value general skills, keep women's opportunity costs low by facilitating easy exits and entries, and have been a focus for feminist efforts to promote anti-discrimination laws and consciousness of the "glass ceiling." The LMEs generate a lot of badly paid jobs, but one of the consequences of this is that many families can afford to hire someone to provide childcare and other forms of care, including food preparation, housework and yard maintenance. Australia, Canada, Ireland, New Zealand, the United Kingdom and the United States belong here.

The third group is composed of low-fertility countries that still mostly expect men to be breadwinners and women to engage in intensive mothering, and have generated work–family policies that are less generous and less well designed than the first group's. The countries in this group are CMEs with dual labor markets that tend to exact high opportunity costs for women who take time off for childrearing, so that a step off the career track is devastating for advancement and lifetime wages and benefits. The percentage of women who work in part-time jobs, and in *unwanted* part-time jobs, is high for this group, and the overall trend here is toward high gender and maternal wage gaps (but not universally: Italy does not have a high gender gap). I include the hard- and medium-core low-fertility countries (see explanation of tempo- and parity-adjusted TFRs following Table 2.1): Italy, Japan, Korea, Poland, Portugal and Spain.

This group offers a variety of parental leaves, from long unpaid or low-paid ones to shorter better-reimbursed ones. One, Japan, has recently changed its parental leave policies to encourage women to take short breaks and return to work, and to encourage men to take time off while their children are small. These countries do not offer much support for childcare and preschool, and do not have very high childcare enrollments among children under three.

The residual group here is composed of conservative countries (except for France and Belgium, which I put with the high-fertility CMEs), Austria, Germany, Luxembourg, the Netherlands and Switzerland, plus the Eastern bloc countries and Greece. All these conservative countries except Luxembourg speak Germanic languages (Switzerland is mixed) and pursue rather conservative social values, at least when it comes to encouraging mothers to work full-time for pay (recall from Table 2.4 the high proportion of women who work part-time in all four of these countries, mostly voluntarily).[13] The other moderately low-fertility countries, Greece and the Eastern bloc, are harder to categorize. After the abrupt jolt of the end of communist systems in 1989, the economies of eastern European countries seem to be slowly recovering, producing more jobs that will improve the outlook for young people considering having babies. Likewise, as the Greek economy recovers from harsh debt-cutting measures enforced by the rest of the EU countries (especially Germany) after the 2008 recession and creates more and better-paid jobs, its demographic prospects should improve. Most of this in-between group are reluctant to spend much on ECEC and have relatively low enrollments for infants and preschool-age children in formal care. They do better with other kinds of supports, such as income tax and cash payments that benefit married couples or children. Several of these countries have labor markets where male-dominated labor unions exert a lot of influence over labor market regulations and are not overly concerned with accommodating women workers.

I have argued that the drivers of fertility among the wealthy OECD countries are the working-mother-friendliness of labor market structures, work–family reconciliation policies and values, all working synergistically and in combination. The rest of this study draws on a close-up examination of four countries, looking at how institutional forces and political histories explain their approaches to work–family policy making. Those countries happen to be the four largest economies among the advanced wealthy democracies of the world, and they represent extremes that can serve as ideal types. Thus France is the most generous and interventionist of the big economies. Germany is also interventionist and generous in many ways, but it is the archetype perhaps of a generous social welfare spender that embraces rather conservative social values (so there is lots of spending to support married couples that approximate the male breadwinner, non-working wife pattern, but very little to support childcare), along with a rigid union-constrained labor market. Japan is much less generous and more traditional and "hidebound" than the other rich democracies, with respect to both family structures and labor market organization; it suggests the contours of a distinctive Asian conservative welfare state. And the United States is the extreme, quintessential residual welfare state and liberal market economy, reliant on markets and families to provide most forms of care.

---

[13] The Netherlands stands out in this group for its creative labor market adaptation to traditional gender norms: it has mandated good wages and benefits for part-time workers, alleviating the need for a lot of full-time day spaces in childcare centers or preschool. Large proportions of men as well as women work part-time in the Netherlands, permitting fathers to spend more time with their families, and families to be able to sustain themselves on two good part-time jobs.

3   Familialist policies in France

This chapter examines the historical roots of France's concern with encouraging large families in the nineteenth century, and traces connections between these beginnings and contemporary approaches to family policy. Focusing on policy developments since the 1970s, I explain the politics of the policy making process and examine dissenting voices and critiques of work–family policies. My aim here is to understand why France has developed the constellation of work–family policies it has, drawing on my reading of primary and secondary sources and interviews with those familiar with the policy process.

Historical beginnings

The desire to bolster France's total fertility rate has inspired active support for families with children since the late nineteenth century, as the French state regarded a healthy fertility rate as essential to being able to fend off invasions, maintain its territorial integrity, and fight wars. Having children was viewed as both a patriotic duty and a public good that the state should support, and redistributing wealth from childless families to those with children was seen as a key approach to supporting childrearing families (Pedersen, 1993, 361). Demographic concerns played a crucial influence in shaping early French family support policies, and demographers were routinely appointed to councils that were formed in the 1920 and 1930s to deliberate about family support policies, where they influenced public debates and policy making (Pedersen, 1993, 370; also see Gauthier, 1996). Although concern about territorial integrity and fighting wars no longer seems urgent, France's concern with maintaining its total fertility at close to replacement levels continues to be an important motivation for insuring that families and children are well supported (McIntosh, 1983; Gauthier, 1996; Toulemon et al., 2008; Martin, 2010).

France has not been particularly fussy or doctrinaire about the roles mothers adopt: stay-at-home mothers, ones who take breaks to stay home with small children before returning to paid work, and mothers who return to work full-time soon after giving birth have all been supported via leave, childcare, family allowance and tax policies. This is in contrast to the approach taken in countries like Germany, Austria and the Netherlands, which have long been predicated on a male-breadwinner/female-caregiver system, with policies and cultural values that support traditional gender roles and reinforce the expectation that mothers should stay at home with young children, and only work part-time (if at all), in order to accommodate their care duties.

Early decisions about how the state supported workers with families and early childhood education set up institutional lines of authority that are still germane. For example, the Caisses d'allocations familiales (CAF, the Family Allowance Funds) began as social welfare funds created voluntarily by employers in the 1910s to help compensate working fathers who were hard pressed to support their families on regular wages (Pedersen, 1993, 227ff.). One of the reasons for setting up the *caisses* and paying fathers higher wages was to put a damper on union organizing by offering pay supplements to help men who were supporting large families, while keeping overall wages low; another was to encourage higher birth rates via horizontal redistribution of wealth. In 1932, the French government passed a law requiring all employers to join a fund (*caisse*), which Pedersen views as the single most important piece of legislation France passed in the interwar period. This measure both established the basis for extending family support allowances, and reconciled business interests with pronatalist demands for family policy. Pedersen regards the law as "a peculiarly French type of contract, with the legislature, the Ministry of Labor, and the employers . . . each receiving a significant share of institutional power, to the exclusion of the CGT" (the Confédération générale du travail, a major communist-affiliated labor federation – Pedersen, 1993, 372). One of the policy legacies of the origins of the CAF as an anti-union measure is that family policy is still considered rather conservative, associated with pronatalism, big families and the Catholic Church, and seen as not very receptive to organized labor or feminist influences.

In 1939 the Daladier government created the High Committee on Population (Haut conseil de la population), a group of pronatalist experts who were charged with drafting a coherent population growth policy. The Committee's deliberations resulted in adoption of the Family Code (Code de la famille) in 1940, which was applied piecemeal after the beginning of World War II (Pedersen, 1993, 386–7). Government policies throughout the 1930s and 1940s favored households with large families and reinforced the idea of stay-at-home mothers (French women did not gain the right to vote until 1945). The MRP, Mouvement republicaine populaire, a political party with Catholic sympathies that favored large families, was very influential in shaping family policies in the 1940s and 1950s, and for a time during the postwar period, ministers in charge of family policy were commonly recruited from the MRP (Lenoir, 1991, 144–5). The legacy of familialist policies, demographic expertise and early institutions color government deliberations over family policy measures to this day.

Groups actively involved in crafting family-friendly policies date back to the interwar period and include the National Union of Family Associations (Union nationale des associations familiales, or UNAF, a federation of mostly Catholic pro-family groups), the CAF, the National Family Allowance Fund (the Caisse national d'allocations familiales, or CNAF) and the National Institute of Demographic Studies (INED, the Institut national des études demographiques).

In addition to the participation by such experts, groups and institutions, opposition to the Catholic Church was a crucial influence on the development of early childhood education and care policies. Secular republicans in the nineteenth century identified the Catholic Church with regressive, right-wing, royalist tendencies, and wanted to curtail its influence over daily life by shifting the provision of education and care for young children from parochial schools to the state. The state accomplished this by setting up the *écoles maternelles* in 1881 as part of the public education system under the supervision of the Ministry of Education, in one fell swoop removing provision of preschool and kindergarten care from church auspices and establishing a state monopoly over these services (Morgan, 2002; Toulemon *et al.*, 2008, 538). Now, 135 years later, the *écoles maternelles* are the linchpin of France's varied ECEC services, since they are universally available and free for children aged two and a half and older, and often offer add-on services that provide care before and after school and during school vacations.

The CAF and the Family Code guaranteed the institutional legitimacy of pronatalist policies and established the funding mechanisms – payroll taxes and employer contributions – that still pay for most family policies. Contributions from employers and employees fund policies mandated under national law, and are administered by the decentralized CAF. The CAF also play an important role in decision making about particular spending decisions and policy proposals, in conjunction with relevant government ministries and agencies, peak business and labor groups, and the UNAF, which is required by law to participate in family policy deliberations (Commaille *et al.*, 2002; Morgan, 2002). The CAF, which still have ties to particular industries and localities, provide an arena for discussion about how to collect and allocate contributions, and contribute to the relatively dispersed and localized nature of the policy making process.

Indeed, attempts to create a centralized social insurance fund in the mid-1940s were defeated by pressure from the CAF – which saw a single national fund as a financial threat – and from the Catholic Church and Church-affiliated family associations, which regarded centralization as a threat to the autonomy of the family benefit system (Ashford, 1991, 38). Although the socialists had hoped social insurance would become a powerful, centralized "palace" (to borrow Ashford's turn of phrase), instead it remained a number of smaller, separate "pavilions" (Ashford, 1991, 38). The ability of the existing funds, the Church and family associations to resist efforts to centralize social security funds, and to maintain a dispersed approach to social policy, illustrates how early policy decisions have influenced policy developments down the road. The influence of these groups was fostered both by the early private arrangements in the 1910s and 1920s and by the 1932 law requiring all employers to join a fund. This made them powerful enough to stave off calls for centralization and retain institutional arrangements that favored their continued influence.

Postwar developments: the golden age of family policy

After World War II, two policies were put in place that guided France's approach to supporting families. One was tax deductions for families, the *quotient familiale*, adopted in late 1945, which allows families to reduce the amount of tax they pay according to the number of dependent children in the family, and permits family allowances and indirect income from Social Security to be exempted from taxation (Lenoir, 1991, 157–8). The *quotient familiale* aimed to encourage a robust fertility rate by redistributing wealth from families with no or few children to families with more children. Because it benefits childrearing families whether they are wealthy or poor, it has been attacked by leftists for not encouraging vertical redistribution (i.e., from wealthy to poor – Fagnani, 2006).

The government also broadened the system of family benefits in 1946 to make family allowances, single-income allowances and maternity allowances payable through the CAF; to extend family allowances to nonworking families; and to allow payments to all families with one income, regardless of the nationality of the parents (Lenoir, 1991, 157). The *quotient familiale* guaranteed political support from center and right parties, and the second set of changes made family allowances more generous and comprehensive for a variety of families, including ones with traditional stay-at-home mothers. The 2014 amounts for the child benefit or family allowance payments are listed below in Table 3.1; the pronatalist policy design is evident in the fact that child benefit payments start with the second child.

France's standard of living was so low after World War II that the country launched ambitious family support measures, with family benefits reaching nearly 40 percent of total social security spending in 1946. The 1940s through the early 1960s marked the height of the MRP, which briefly showed promise of developing into a viable Christian Democratic party. The MRP helped push spending on family support policies to their highest levels ever: the period from the late 1940s to the mid-1950s was the peak period for family policy in France (Lenoir, 1991, 153–4, 159–61). But despite this surge of power and popularity, the MRP was not able to sustain high levels of popular support: by 1960, the proportion of social spending for family policy had declined to 29 percent, and by 1962 the MRP only received 5 percent of the vote (Lenoir, 1991, 166).

Table 3.1 *Family allowances*

Benefit type	% BMAF (€403.79 in 2014)	Monthly amounts in euros	Means-tested	Subject to the CRDS
Child benefit				
- 2 children	32	129.21	No	Yes
- 3 children	73	294.76	No	Yes
- for each additional child	41	165.55	No	Yes
- increase for each child between 11 and 16	9	36.34	No	Yes
- increase for each child over 16	16	64.61	No	Yes
Flat-rate allowance	20	81.70	No	Yes
Family income supplement	41.65	164.53	Yes	Yes
Family support allowance				
- full rate	30	121.14	No	Yes
- partial rate	22.5	90.85	No	Yes

Source: CLEISS, 2014 (BMAF, Base mensuelle de calcul des allocations familiales, is the monthly family benefit base; CRDS, Contribution pour le remboursement de la dette sociale, is a social tax paid by employees at the rate of 0.5% on their earnings).

Despite the decline in the power of the MRP, groups that supported large families, pronatalism and policies to support stay-at-home mothers (many of them affiliated with the Catholic Church) continued to influence French family policy.

The period from 1945 to 1965 has been characterized as the "golden age of French family policy," fueled by strong familialism, defense of the male-breadwinner family, and universalism. Family benefits were generous and universal, with several policies that aimed to compensate parents for the cost of children (Martin, 2010, 412). For a number of reasons – a working-age population inadequate to satisfy labor demands for production and defense, too few people paying taxes to support the general costs of the nation, and the fact that the burden of supporting the elderly was becoming too heavy for the young – mid-twentieth-century politicians and experts reached a consensus on natalist objectives. Debate was not particularly heated or partisan, and family support legislation usually passed unanimously. Reflecting the surge in familialist and pronatal influence, the 1950s and 1960s saw the lowest French FLFP rates in the twentieth century (Toulemon *et al.*, 2008; Strobel, 2004, 60).[1]

---

[1] Coontz, 1992, points out that FLFP rates ebbed in the United States at the same time.

The 1970s to the present: the evolution of French family policies

By the early 1970s, French women were entering the workforce in large numbers. A broad range of groups – organized labor, the national council of French employers, feminists, well-placed civil servants – supported women's right to work and work–family reconciliation policies (Lenoir, 1991, 152–5). As the French women's movement emerged in the late 1960s and 1970s, it brought issues related to reproductive choice and mothers' right to work into public policy debates: contraception was legalized in late 1969, and abortion in 1975 (Martin, 2010, 412). A number of reforms occurred under Giscard d'Estaing (1974–81): a 72 percent increase in spaces in *crèches* (nursery schools for babies under the age of three that charge sliding-scale fees depending on the family's income) in the late 1970s; passage in 1977 of a law giving mothers a two-year maternity leave;[2] establishment of benefits for single parents (the API, Allocation de parent isolé); passage of a law prohibiting discrimination on the basis of sex, pregnancy or marital status; and measures guaranteeing social security pensions to mothers who raised two or more children (Jenson and Sineau, 2001, 91–3; Lenoir, 1991). Yet even while feminists were pushing for passage of such measures, pronatalist policies encouraging families to have three or more children were also being adopted as public concern about falling fertility rates increased. Due in part to the on-going influence of pronatalists, tensions between progressive and feminist groups and familialist and pronatalist ones have marked French family policies since the early 1970s. Even though France's current total fertility rate is higher than that of most OECD countries, demographic concerns still resurface regularly in public debate, and some advocates continue to argue for policies to sustain high fertility at the expense of policies that aim at greater gender equality, despite the fact that two-thirds of French women work outside the home (Strobel, 2004, 59).

As demand for spaces for infants in childcare centers increased, the women's movement and the Left were able to push the national government to spend more money subsidizing the construction of new *crèches*, a move that began under the Pompidou government (1969–74) and continued under Giscard d'Estaing and Mitterand (1981–95).[3] The rate of increase of spaces in *crèches* peaked at 72 percent under Giscard in the 1970s, slowed to 44 percent between 1981 and 1988 and fell to 29 percent between 1988 and 1995. Although Mitterand's socialist government initially proposed big increases in spending for childcare, he backed away from his campaign promises to expand family support services

---

[2] The leave was unpaid and only applied to women who had worked for at least one year for a large (over 200 employees) company.

[3] Pompidou was a leader of the UDR (Union for the Defense of the Republic), a Gaullist party; Giscard, a leader of the Union for French Democracy, another center-right party; Mitterand was a socialist.

when a financial crisis in the early 1980s pushed his government to adopt austerity measures. Altogether the Mitterand government created an additional 89,000 spaces in *crèches*; this was far short of the 300,000 that he had promised and of what was needed to meet increasing demand (Jenson and Sineau, 2001, 95).

The failure to meet the projected number of childcare spaces in *crèches* infuriated feminist supporters, and the Mitterand government made matters worse with them by moving to privatize childcare and encouraging women to take time off from work to raise their children. Two programs aimed to encourage private provision of childcare: the Allocation de garde d'enfant à domicile, AGED (payment to care for a child at home, a program to subsidize hiring nannies), in 1985; and the Aide à la famille pour l'emploi d'une assistante maternelle agréée, AFEAMA (aid to families to help pay for a home-care mother – a woman who watches children in her own home), in 1990. Under these programs, the government provided subsidies to cover the social wages of a nanny or home-care mother, respectively (Letablier, 2008, 39). The idea behind passing them was to provide more childcare spaces quickly by encouraging private approaches to providing care for children too young for *école maternelle*, a cheaper approach than increasing the number of spaces in *crèches*. AGED and AFEAMA saved the government money by avoiding construction and personnel costs. They also created jobs for women to work as nannies or home care mothers, thus alleviating high unemployment rates, especially among women who were not well educated. But these policies signaled a step away from supporting *crèches*, the most affordable way for hard-pressed working families to care for infants and toddlers and a far more redistributive policy (Jenson and Sineau, 2001, 105–6). The AGED and AFEAMA programs were touted using a rhetoric of "choice" that appealed to a liberal, pro-market sensibility. Because they were more flexible than center-based care they were attractive to mothers who increasingly were required to work non-standard hours (Fagnani and Letablier, 2005). But the cost of private provision often exceeds what families of modest means can afford: only 1 percent of children under age three are cared for by nannies (Toulemon *et al.*, 2008, 359), and even AFEAMA is out of reach of families of modest means (Périvier, 2003). Despite their advantages in terms of providing jobs for female caregivers and places for children, with relatively low government expenditures, AGED and AFEAMA have been criticized because they encourage women to take low-paid, gender-ghettoized jobs, and because both programs are out of reach for poor families.

The Mitterand government also passed a paid parental leave, the Allocation parentale d'education (APE), in January 1985. It allowed either parent to take a leave to care for a child under the age of three if the child was the third or subsequent child in the family, and the parent had been employed for twenty-four of the past thirty-six months. The APE paid a flat-rate stipend well below the level of the minimum wage for up to two years. Georgina Dufoix, Mitterand's minister for family policy, responded to criticisms that the law would weaken women's attachment to the labor force and consign them to badly paid dead-end jobs by acknowledging that "'The child-rearing allowance is proportionally more interesting for low-income earners and might be more attractive to them. This effect is not something worth criticizing, to the extent that the jobs they hold are often the least rewarding'" (Dufoix, quoted in Jenson and Sineau, 2001, 100).

Falling fertility rates and the influence of the French National Institute of Demographic Studies, INED, helped shape a revision of the APE in 1986 that made it easier to qualify for the parental leave, and extended pay to three years (Jenson and Sineau, 2001, 101). The law was again extended in 1994 to include families giving birth to second children, to relax work requirements so the leave would cover parents who had worked two out of the last five years, to allow parents to combine paid parental leave with part-time work, and to increase the value of the benefit. The impact of these changes was immediate, with the FLFP rate for mothers with two or more children dropping from 69 percent to 53 percent and the number of beneficiaries of the APE tripling (Morgan, 2003, 156).

Mitterand drew sharp criticism for reneging on campaign promises to support women's right to work and to expand *crèche*-based care, and for passing measures that expanded private forms of childcare and established paid parental leaves. Jenson and Sineau comment that he:

accepted without any apology that family policy would support population policy and demographic goals . . . One can conclude that, for a variety of reasons, Francois Mitterrand, like his predecessor [Giscard d'Estaing], came to accept that dualism is inevitable. Some mothers would pursue their working lives without interruption, whereas others would swell the ranks of contingent and part time workers. Mitterrand's justification for this breach in women's right to full labour force participation is no different from that of Giscard. Free choice for mothers was the fundamental principle. The result was, for Mitterand as for Giscard, that defence of individual liberty overshadowed any threats to republican equality that the new childcare programs might imply. (2001, 110)

Although Jenson and Sineau excoriate Mitterand for introducing family policies that curtailed the expansion of *crèches* and pushed women into marginal, low-paid work, they note the presence of a "consensus on the right and the left about the need to encourage a higher birth rate" which led the state to spend more on childcare even in times of economic austerity. They write: "The legitimacy of this financing is rarely, if ever, in dispute. A neo-liberalism implying that the French state ought to get out of the business of paying for childcare never had much purchase" (Jenson and Sineau, 2001, 111). Despite the fact that feminists and the Left were deeply disappointed in Mitterand for not pursuing feminist policies after campaigning on promises to do so, support at the national level for work–family policies continued under his leadership.

Looking at France's current maternity, parental and paternity leaves and childcare support policies, mothers receive sixteen weeks of maternity leave paid at 100 percent of earnings up to a ceiling of €2,885 per month. Maternity leaves are funded through health insurance that is paid for by contributions from employers and employees. Since 2001, fathers receive eleven days of paternity leave, compensated the same way as the maternity leave (Fagnani and Boyer, 2012). Even though many believe that encouraging men to take paid leaves is important for insuring gender equality in the workplace (Martin interview, 2003; Strobel interview, 2003), France has not moved to extend paid paternity leave beyond eleven days, in contrast to Portugal, Germany, Finland, Iceland, Norway and Sweden, which provide six weeks or longer of well-paid paternity leaves. Such measures aim to encourage fathers to share the work of raising children. If fathers also take substantial childrearing breaks, it is more difficult for employers to assume that childrearing is the responsibility of mothers and discriminate against women workers on that account.[4]

The parental leave law initiated under Mitterand in 1985 and expanded in 1986 and 1994 was folded into the 2004 Young Children's Benefit Program (PAJE, Prestation d'accueil du jeune enfant). The crucial change in the PAJE was to give first-time parents six months of paid leave, adding to the already-existing three years of paid leave for parents with two or more children (Badinter, 2004).[5] The current monthly parental leave payments are €575.68, and parents who work part-time receive pro-rated payments depending on the number of hours they work each week (see Table 3.2 below). Alternatively, families with three or more children can opt to receive the Complément optionnel de libre choix d'activité (COLCA) if one parent stops working entirely for a year. In this case, the family receives €823.25 per month for twelve months. In addition, the parental leave law guarantees that a man or woman taking the leave will be able to return to his or her job at the end of the leave period (Fagnani and Boyer, 2012). (For a summary of French work–family policies, see Table 3.3 below.)

Although the French paid parental leave policies are written in gender-neutral language, 98 percent of those taking these leaves are women. As with gender-neutral parental leave policies elsewhere, women typically take time off to stay home with infants and men continue to work full-time. There are a number of reasons for this, including women's need or desire to recuperate postpartum,

[4] Japan has eight weeks of paternity leave paid at 50 percent, which I will discuss more fully in Chapter 5. The other countries discussed here reimburse at 65 percent or more, a threshold that Japan doesn't meet.

[5] The PAJE set up the Supplement for Free Choice of Activity (the Complément libre choix d'activité, CLCA) to add six months of paid leave for first-time parents.

Table 3.2 *Birth grants, parental leave payments, support for privately arranged childcare*

Benefit type	% of BMAF – €403.79	Monthly Amounts in euros	Means-tested	Subject to the CRDS
Early childcare benefits (PAJE)				
- Birth grant	229.75	927.71	Yes	Yes
- Adoption grant	459.50	1855.41	Yes	Yes
- Basic allowance	45.95	185.54	Yes	Yes
Supplement for Free Choice of Activity (Complément libre choix d'activité)				
For families that do not receive the basic allowance				
• Full rate	142.57	575.68	No	Yes
• Employment ≤ 50%	108.41	437.75	No	Yes
• Employment > 50% and ≤ 80%	81.98	331.03	No	Yes
For families that receive the basic allowance				
• Full rate	96.62	390.14	No	Yes
• Employment ≤ 50%	62.46	252.21	No	Yes
• Employment > 50% and ≤ 80%	36.03	145.49	No	Yes
Complément optionnel de libre choix d'activité (COLCA): 12-month parental leave without working				
For families that receive the basic allowance	637.71	157.93	No	Yes
For families that do not receive the basic allowance	823.25	203.88	No	Yes
Supplement for free choice of childcare				
• If income is less than €21,000	114.04	460.48	Yes	Yes
• If income is between €21,000 and €46,888	71.91	290.37	Yes	Yes
• If income more than €46,888	43.13	174.20	No	Yes
- Association or company – child aged 0 to 3				
- Childminder				
• If income is less than €21,000	172.57	698.82	Yes	Yes
• If income is between €21,000 and €46,888	143.81	580.00	Yes	Yes
• If income more than €46,888	115.05	464.56	No	Yes
- Home childcarer				
• If income is less than €21,000	208.53	823.78	Yes	Yes
• If income is between €21,000 and €46,888	179.76	710.12	Yes	Yes
• If income more than €46,888	151.00	596.51	No	Yes

Source: CLEISS, 2014.

dominant gender norms that make mothering the expectation, and the fact that husbands generally earn more money than their wives. As a matter of policy design, long leaves which pay a modest fixed amount are more attractive to relatively low-paid workers than they are to higher-earning men and women,

Table 3.3 *Summary of French work–family reconciliation policies*

Family allowances
Only for families with 2 or more children
With 2 children, family receives €129.99 per month
Each subsequent child adds €166.55 per month
Parents receive payments till children's 20th birthday

Income taxes
Quotient familiale: tax rate is lower the more dependants are claimed

Childrearing leaves
Maternity leave is 16 weeks at 100% of pay
Parental leave for first child is 6 months at €575.68 per month
Parental leave for second and subsequent children is 3 years at €575.68 per month
Parents can also opt for 1 year at €823.25 per month
Paternity leave is 11 days at 100% pay

Childcare and early childhood education
Wages of home care mothers and nannies are subsidized
Childcare: 42% of children under 3 in formal care in 2008
École maternelle (ages 3–5): 100% of children 3–5 enrolled

Source: CLEISS, 2014; OECD, 2013l.

who pay high opportunity costs in terms of lost wages and forgone future wages and promotions for taking time off to stay home with children. Many criticize France's paid parental leave laws for encouraging women to take long, repeated, low-paid leaves, arguing that such behaviors result in them getting stuck in low paid, dead-end jobs (Afsa, 1998; Badinter, 2004; Périvier, 2004; and, generally, Revue de l'OFCE, 2004).

Five of the other countries listed in Table 2.8 offer three years of low-paid or unpaid leave (Czech Republic, Hungary, Poland, Spain and Finland). In contrast, a handful offer short well-paid leaves – Portugal gives nine weeks paid at 100%; Belgium, twelve at 92%; Germany, fifty-two at 67%, and Sweden gives sixty weeks at 64% – in order to encourage high-earning women to give birth, and to keep childrearing breaks relatively short so that the periods of detachment from the workforce are brief and the impact on women's earnings and promotions minimized. A few others – Italy, Japan, Korea, the Netherlands, Luxembourg, Denmark, Iceland and Canada – offer between six and twelve months of low-paid leave.

In addition to leave policies, France offers a variety of childcare options. The Supplement for Free Choice of Childcare (Complément de libre choix du mode de garde) covers the costs of the social security contributions the parent is obliged to pay as employer of a childminder, either a home care mother (*assistante maternelle*) who watches children in her own home, or a nanny who watches children in the parents' home. Rates differ according to whether the parents arrange care on their own or work through a care provision company. Unlike the other payments in Table 3.2, this Supplement also varies by income.

In addition to cash allowances for families with two or more children, paid parental leaves, and subsidies to help pay for individualized forms of childcare, France also operates a system of *crèches*. Taking all of its childcare arrangements into account, France provides spaces for about 50 percent of children under the age of three in some form of childcare or preschool. Of all children three and under, 28 percent are cared for by *assistantes maternelles*, and about 17 percent attend *crèches* of one kind or another (Beyer, 2013). Starting at age two and a half, children can attend *écoles maternelles*, which are operated free of charge as part of the state school system and follow the schedule for state schools. The *écoles maternelles* are the responsibility of the Ministry of Education and financed through taxes, but the various family supports described above are financed through employer and employee contributions to the CAF, the quasi-public Family Allowance Funds that finance and administer most of the programs described here. There are 102 CAFs nationwide, administered by the National Family Allowance Fund, the CNAF.

Dynamics of the policy making process

As we have seen, family support policies in France date back to the establishment of *écoles maternelles* as part of the state school system in the 1880s, the development of employer-contribution-based funds to support families with children in the 1910s, and the passage of the Family Code in 1940. These early beginnings gave different parties a stake in perpetuating policies from which they benefitted or over which they exerted control. "Pavilions" presided over by the CAF did not turn into a state-run "palace" paid for by taxes and under the sole control of national officials. Instead, France combines centralized state control over policy with local administration of the family funds, giving interested parties a chance to participate in administrative and political decisions at both levels (Toulemon *et al.*, 2008; Martin, 2010).

What impact do early choices have on policy developments down the road? Claude Martin characterizes the French approach to family policy as a gradual accretion of new values to a fundamentally familialist perspective. In his view, family policy reflects the progressive accumulation of new priorities rather than actual policy learning: "Incrementalism and path dependency have been two main components of French family policy evolution since World War II. The 'imprint' of the first years of family policy has not disappeared, but new objectives have been piled up on previous ones, and new instruments 'layered' onto those already in existence" (Martin, 2010, 411–12).

Although change has mostly been incremental and aggregative rather than abrupt, the family policy system has made significant changes, responding to individualistic, universal claims made by the women's movement; struggling to support families in poverty using means-tested approaches; and developing a neo-liberal "free choice" rhetoric as family policies responded to increases in working mothers, soaring divorce and unemployment rates, and more diverse family types, especially single-mother-headed families. Indeed, since the mid-1980s, family policies have been increasingly subsumed under employment policies as new programs were designed to alleviate high unemployment and assist working mothers (Martin, 2010, 412–13).

The policy making process itself has also changed. It is no longer as firmly controlled by corporatist decision making carried out among employers, trade unions and familialist movements as it was during the postwar era (Martin, 2010, 415). Although academics used to have close ties to public administrators and policy makers, these have loosened with the advent of feminist scholarship in fields like sociology and political science and increased skepticism about supporting the state's policy regime. At the same time, top civil servants have become less interested in ideological confrontations and more concerned with solving technical problems. Yet the capacity of senior bureaucrats to exercise influence over policy making has declined. One marker of this was the decision to replace the central state think tank, the Commissariat générale au Plan, with the Conseil d'analyse stratégique in 2006 (Martin, 2010, 415–17).

The point is well taken: both tradition and resilience are core elements of the family policy system. There have been significant changes in emphasis and in the policy making system, but family support policies still reflect a fundamental consensus based on familialism. From here, I take up three tasks: first, I map out the mechanics of the French family support policy making system, addressing who has a privileged voice at the table and how the government prioritizes what policies it will pursue, and the influence multinational organizations like the European Union and the Organisation for Economic Cooperation and Development and exercise over France's family support policies. Second, I describe the intellectual and political contestation that characterizes the politics of insuring support for generous family policies, and point to some of the issues the work–family part of the social security system faces in the early twenty-first century. Finally, I address several puzzling issues: why has France continued to support long, low-paid parental leaves in the face of the criticism that they encourage many women to take long absences from the labor force, thereby consigning them to marginal jobs? Why has France supported private forms of childcare like AGED and AFEAMA rather than supporting the more egalitarian *crèche* system? Why has France made so little progress toward expanding paternity leaves? And why are feminist voices relatively peripheral to family policy debates in France?

France has a central state headed by a president, but it also has a parliament which elects a prime minister. The 577 members of the National Assembly are elected every five years, unless the parliament is dissolved early with a call for special elections. There is also a 348-member Senate, but the National Assembly has the sole power to pass a vote of no confidence, has final say on legislative matters, exercises primary responsibility for budgetary and social security issues, and can be dissolved and required to stand for special election.

Voters elect representatives from single-member districts in a two-stage process: in the first election, candidates from a variety of parties run, and the second is a run-off among all candidates who got at least 12.5 percent of the vote. France also elects its president every five years in a two-stage process, with multiple parties fielding candidates in the first round, and voters then choosing between the two top vote-getters in the second round. Although France does not have a PR system, the two-stage elections build strategic coalition-building considerations into the electoral system. Because the parliament is headed by a prime minister who represents the ruling political party or coalition, France occasionally has a president from one party and a prime minister from another, a situation known as "cohabitation." The ministries are responsible to the prime minister, with the majority party in the National Assembly choosing the political appointees at the top of each ministry. Many of the permanent or career bureaucrats who staff the ministries, agencies and think tanks, and many of the political appointees as well, are graduates of the elite École nationale d'administration (National School of Administration) or the Institut d'études politiques de Paris ("Sciences Po," the Institute for Policy Studies).

Political leadership changes hands fairly often, alternating among center-right Gaullist parties and the Socialist Party and its allies (the Communist Party, the Greens, etc.). There are a variety of political parties that range across the political spectrum, including the National Front on the extreme right. France has not had a Christian Democratic party since the early 1960s, probably because of a strong anti-clerical bias that has kept a social Catholic movement from taking root. Since World War II, the presidency has been held more often by the center-right; Mitterand from 1981 through 1995, and Hollande, elected in 2012, are the only socialist presidents since the Fifth Republic was established in 1958, although presidents from both left and right have had to rule in cohabitation with prime ministers from the other side of the political spectrum.

Participants in family policy making discussions and decisions represent a broad cross-section of interest groups, including pro-family groups affiliated with UNAF; representatives of the family funds, the CAF and the CNAF (the first is a network of 102 local funds, the second the national-level organization); officials from pertinent agencies and ministries; representatives of organized labor and employers' groups; and experts from research institutes that study social policy, demography, employment and labor market policy, children's well-being, and other pertinent topics. Although the Catholic-leaning UNAF has a government-mandated role in policy making, debate is conducted in secular, rationalistic, even technocratic language. The broad commitment to support families is not controversial: this is not a partisan football that leads to abrupt changes of direction every time parties alternate control of the Elysée Palace or the National Assembly.

From 1996 to 2007, the French government sponsored a yearly Family Conference, which brought together key policy stakeholders, experts and government officials to discuss and decide on the priorities the government should pursue in the coming year. Toulemon *et al.* characterize the French family policy making process during this period as

a result of a compromise between various political trends. The yearly Conférence de la famille is the place where new family policy measures are set out. Extensive dialogue with family movement associations, social protection bodies, union and management elected representatives, and experts precedes this conference. Religious institutions play a rather minor role. This intervention of the State in the private sphere has long been accepted as legitimate. The State is perceived as the main stakeholder responsible for children. The consensus on the importance of the family and State intervention goes beyond the political divide between right and left. (Toulemon *et al.*, 2008, 537, citations omitted)

Although the Conference concentrated each year on a specific issue, work–family balance issues were frequent focuses of discussion and policy proposals generated by the Family Conferences during this period, resulting in the passage of a paternity leave in 2000 and the PAJE in 2004 (Letablier, 2008, 44). With the election of Nicholas Sarkozy as president in 2007, the responsibility for setting the agenda for family policy shifted from the yearly Family Conferences to the Council on the Family (Le haut conseil de la famille). The Council on the Family has fifty-two members drawn from the family movement, its social partners, territorial representatives and relevant government agencies.[6] It is responsible for advising the government about family policy issues and demographic developments, and for proposing appropriate levels of financing for various family-related programs as well as policy innovations (Cairns.info, 2009).[7] In effect, relationships and social partnerships similar to those represented in the yearly Family Conferences persevered under the rubric put in place by the Sarkozy government, with a continued focus on coordinating groups that support working parents, family associations, family-relevant think tanks and agencies, and demographic and other research groups.

Several ministries are involved in administering work–family policies: the Ministry of Social Affairs, Health and Women's Rights (Ministère des affaires

---

[6] To encourage cooperation with the government, seven members of the Council are also members of the Ministry Designated for the Family (Cairns.info, 2009).

[7] The "useful links" part of the Council on the Family (HCF) website is a veritable Who's Who of groups interested in family support policies. For a complete list of "liens utiles," see www.hcf-famille.fr.

sociales, de la santé et des droits des femmes), the Ministry of Labor, Employment and Social Dialogue (le Ministère du travail, de l'emploi, de la formation professionnelle et du dialogue social), the Finance Ministry (Ministère des finances et des comptes publics) and the Ministry of Education (Ministère de l'éducation nationale, de l'Enseignement supérieur et de la Recherche). The Ministry of Social Affairs, Health and Women's Rights and its agencies are responsible for family assistance programs, pensions, support of young children, parenthood support, adoption, and protection for children and adolescents. The Ministry of Education supervises the *écoles maternelles*, and the Ministry of Labor attends to employment-related issues. Two units conduct research and compile statistics related to social and health matters, the DARES within the Ministry of Labor (it tracks and publishes statistics related to employment, strikes, etc.) and the DREES (Direction de la recherche, des études, de l'évaluation et des statistiques – the Research, Studies, Assessment and Statistics Directorate), an interministerial unit that conducts and disseminates research related to various social and health-related issues.

The sheer number and variety of agencies and research units involved in work–family policy issues in France is overwhelming. The big picture that I took away from discussions with various bureaucrats and researchers who worked for the government or for government-affiliated research institutes is that there is a fair degree of consensus among policy makers, and various groups and perspectives are incorporated into policy discussions and carry weight in terms of influencing policy outcomes. A little more discussion about political cleavages and what they mean may be helpful for understanding the terrain of policy debate in France.

Several government and research institute informants were kind enough to speak to me, some more than once, about the guiding values and policy processes that shape French work–family policies.[8] From these conversations, I gained a rich historical, theoretical and political context for understanding why policies have developed as they have. They emphasized the importance of redistributive issues, which are central to understanding both the aims of family policies and basic cleavages in French politics. Horizontal redistribution, which entails redistributing resources from childless families to families that are raising children, regardless of need, is a longstanding tool of family policy. Part of the reason for adopting this approach was to encourage people to have more children by providing or mandating support for childrearing, but another was to win support from across the political spectrum, as policies that

---

[8] I would especially like to note the conversations I had with Pierre Strobel, the chief of the MiRe, Mission Recherche, a research group inside the MLH; Marie-Thérèse Letablier of CEE; Laurent Toulemon of INED; and Hélène Périvier of the OFCE. I learned a lot from conversations with them, but as always any errors of interpretation or fact are my own.

support horizontal redistribution help wealthy childrearing couples as well as those with modest means. In debates since the 1980s, arguments for horizontal redistribution have often been made by political leaders on the right.

As the welfare state rediscovered the problem of poor families and turned toward targeted programs between 1975 and1985, it moved to embrace vertical redistribution by relying more on means-tested policies that are funded through progressive taxes (Martin, 2010). Politically, the Left is more likely to support policies that aid the poorest families, and the Right tends to prefer benefits and policies that benefit the wealthy (especially the 60,000 best-off families who pay the most taxes). Thus, when the Socialists took power under Jospin in 1998, they immediately decreased support for the AGED because it favored the better-off; more generally, the Left tends to support more funding for the *crèches* (Letablier, 2003).

Those who view French politics from afar are apt to notice intense controversies and protests, like the mobilization of large groups opposed to same-sex marriage in spring 2013, when Prime Minister Hollande was pushing the Bill legalizing same-sex marriage through the National Assembly. Although there are moments of intense disagreement over family policies, I think the community of discourse – the ideas that are taken seriously – is closer together than the range of approaches that are considered in the United States, for example. There is consensus that childrearing families should receive significant support, even if there is disagreement over exactly what kinds of support policies are best.

Those familiar with the French social security system worry about pressures to "throw the principal responsibility for managing all kinds of dependency, from babies to old people, back on family or local solidarities" (Strobel, 2004, 63). Pierre Strobel writes:

henceforth public action and policy will have to chart a course between several shoals: the need to respond to growing demands from individuals for autonomy, which runs the risk of subverting social cohesion and neglecting some of the responsibilities adults have toward children, and of public action which is fragmented and contradictory, liberal and modern with respect to the best off, but constrained and paternalistic toward those who are in the greatest difficulty. (Strobel, 2004, 63–4, my translation)

In the cash-starved environment since 2008, strategies that used to insure broad cross-class and cross-party support for family policies (e.g., casting policies as universalistic and aiming at horizontal redistribution) are bumping up against the need to help the neediest by designing means-tested approaches to supporting families. Policies like *crèche*-based care have lost out to leave policies that ease women out of the labor market for a time, and ones that provide private childcare and encourage women to take low-paid jobs as nannies or *assistantes maternelles*. Some think the rhetoric of choice, autonomy and individual rights is undercutting the older approach of solidarity and public responsibility for children and the needy. In his ruminations on the future of the French social security system, Strobel describes the problems facing a system torn between an older view of family policy making based on familialism and a new one based on individual claims and rights and growing financial constraints. Familialism has provided a solid mooring for French family support policies, a set of commitments to childrearing families that built on horizontal redistribution and cross-class solidarities. But policies to assist the elderly and the poor require more resources, and families and local governments are being asked to do more to take care of their own. There is more concern about helping the neediest in times of greater financial constraint, and less sense of solidarity and connection to "all of us" as potential beneficiaries.

Why are French family support policies conservative in tenor?

Given France's long-term commitment to supporting childrearing families and working mothers with varied and generously funded policies, why do many work–family policies perpetuate rather conservative patterns, such as encouraging women to take long leaves and not expanding paternity leaves? Why do so many policies benefit families without respect to income? And why are feminists relatively absent from family policy debates in France?

Aware that the parental leave law did little to encourage high-income men or women to take leaves, Hubert Brin, the president of UNAF, proposed to make leaves shorter and better-paid in the report he submitted in advance of the 2005 Conference on the Family.[9] But, so far, the government has not yet passed a short well-paid leave, and it's not clear there is much pressure to do so anytime soon.

Why has it been hard to enact better-paid, shorter leaves and longer paternity leaves that would encourage men to take more responsibility for raising children? We know that paid parental leaves have essentially been viewed as an unemployment policy: as more women took leaves and exited the labor force, the unemployment rate went down. Employment issues were also behind the AGED and AFEAMA policies that encourage families to rely on privately provided care for their babies and toddlers, since the growing demand for nannies

---

[9] Since 2006 parents with three or more children have been able to choose between three years of low-paid (€576 per month) leave and a better-paid one-year leave (€823), as we saw earlier (see p. 65 and Table 3.2 above; Toulemon et al., 2008, 539–40). But parental leaves remain more attractive to modestly paid women than to their better-paid sisters; second- and third-time mothers who stay home for three years receive €20,736 (36 months x €576), vs. €9,876 for those who opt to take twelve months off at the higher €823 monthly payment. But such financial incentives are not attractive enough to lure low-paid women into the one-year option, nor are well-paid women likely to find the payments sufficiently high to entice them into taking long breaks from working, given the high opportunity costs they would pay for lengthy interruptions.

and home care mothers increased demand for female workers in the low-paid childcare sector. The decision to reduce the working week to 35 hours in 2000 was also employment-related: if everyone worked fewer hours, more people would be hired to get the necessary work done, spreading job opportunities more broadly through French society. Measures to ease unemployment made voters across the political spectrum happy, even at the cost of providing women incentives to take long periods off from work. Many cast the issue in terms of "choice" and women's natural preference to stay home with small children (Lanquetin *et al.*, 2000, 84). Although feminists support integrating gender roles and encouraging men to do more of the childrearing, public opinion polls suggest that many accept the idea of female responsibility for childrearing and male-breadwinner norms (Morgan, 2009a, 47–50).

As we have already noted, policies that rely on horizontal redistribution that support families without respect to need are in the spirit of French familialism. Not only do they support the institution of the family, they encourage large families (Strobel interview, 2003, and 2004) and help build support for family policies among moderate right-wing parties.

But, by the mid-2000s, a central focus in discussions of work–family support policies was the difficulty of finding sufficient money to expand the *crèche* system, which is a more vertical approach to redistribution. Nicole Prud'homme, the president of the CNAF, complained in 2004 that funding for *crèches* was inadequate, noting that CNAF's budget for social action could not contribute enough money to help support construction of new *crèches* (Prud'homme, 2004). Decisions to build more *crèches* are the responsibility of local governments in conjunction with the family allowance funds (CAF) and, even though the municipalities only contribute 40 percent to the CAF's 60 percent, most cities cannot afford to undertake new construction projects because of the need to spend more on services for old people. The government's response to these financial constraints has been to provide assistance that pays for the social contributions for childcare providers rather than expanding the *crèche* infrastructure, even though poor families have to pay considerably more for such forms of care than for *crèche*-based care.[10]

Developments in family policy since the 1980s have been driven mainly by concerns with low fertility, high unemployment rates and providing childcare cheaply, with feminist concerns about insuring gender equality as a side issue. Although one certainly hears feminist arguments for redesigning paid leaves to encourage high-paid women and men to take them, and for extending "partner

---

[10] Prud'homme said that, in 2002, the average monthly cost to the family of sending a child to *crèche* ranged from €81 to €356, while the average cost of hiring a home care mother (*assistante maternelle*) was between €260 and €281 – and eight times as many children under the age of three were being cared for by *assistants maternelles* as in *crèches* (Prud'homme, 2004).

only" leaves in order to encourage fathers to take more responsibility for child-rearing and reduce discrimination against mothers in the workplace (Martin interview, 2003; Périvier interview, 2003; Brin interview, 2005; generally, see Revue de l'OFCE, 2004), they have not had as much traction in France as they have in other European countries, despite encouragement from the EU and the OECD. Politically, France seems to worry more about enlisting the support of conservative political forces and less about offending feminist voters. Since feminists are not likely to turn their backs on family support policies, even ones that are less than perfectly drawn, this probably makes sense.

Some other reasons feminists have not had more influence in shaping French family support policies might include the relatively low percentage of women elected to the national legislature in France compared to other European parliaments (Mazur, 2003).[11] Furthermore, many feminists eschew becoming involved in the family policy making process (interviews with Strobel, Villac, Toulemon and Letablier, all in 2003), choosing instead to exercise influence in other policy arenas. Feminist voices are clearly more influential in shaping policies related to parity, workplace pay equity and sexual harassment than in work–family policies. As we have seen, family support programs have been developed under the aegis of pronatalist and familialist forces, not feminist ones – under the influence of state *familialism* rather than state *feminism*. The institutional deliberative processes favor family associations, demographic concerns and mainstream corporatist interest groups like organized labor and employers' organizations. Feminists are outsiders to this process, critical of the pro-family and pronatal values underpinning many such policies.

Furthermore, French feminists are better able to exert pressure on the *work* side of work–family policies by pushing for anti-discrimination laws and pay equity in the workplace than they are to campaign for better childcare or leave policies. This is based on a strategic and historically rooted decision that reflects both the view of family policies as familialist and conservative, and the priorities of the women's movement in France, which early on advocated reproductive choice and workplace gender equality (King, 1998; Lanquetin *et al.*, 2000).[12] As we have repeatedly seen, workplace and family policy issues are often so

---

[11] In 2011, France had 19% female members in its national parliament. France lags behind most of Europe in terms of women in the National Assembly, but is ahead of the US, Korea and Japan. Recent figures for continental countries show Germany has 33% women in its parliament; the Netherlands, 39%; Spain, 37%; Italy, 21%; Switzerland, 29%; and Austria, 28%. In Scandinavia, Norway has 39%; Sweden, 45%; Finland, 43%; and Iceland, 43%. In Asia, Japan has 11%, and the Republic of Korea. 16%; finally, the United States has 17% and the United Kingdom 22% women in their national legislatures (OECD, 2013h). I discuss this issue again in Chapter 7.

[12] Such a bifurcation between arguments for gender equality and those for family policy is perhaps a bit unusual: "contrary to what has gone on in other countries, family policy and policies related to the rights of women and equality [in France] continue to be thought about and conducted separately" (Strobel, 2004, 62, my translation).

intimately intertwined that what looks like a family policy issue from one angle looks like a workplace issue from another.

Feminist engagement in labor and gender equality policies in France is echoed by European Union gender equality and work–family policy initiatives. Mazur notes that the EU calls for better reconciliation policies, and the involvement of French feminists with transnational feminist networks has helped them pursue national-level advocacy (Mazur, 2003, 517).[13] On the other hand, the EU tends toward a soft "open method of co-ordination" that has replaced hard directives as the main approach to influencing work–family reconciliation and equal opportunity policies, meaning that the EU exercises moral suasion that is often ignored (also see Martin, 2010).

In wealthy countries facing a demographic shift toward lower fertility and rapid population aging, some governments view arguments in favor of policies like job-protected paid parenting leaves, family allowances and childcare as a way to encourage women to have more children and achieve pronatalist ends, and have employed feminist arguments to support developing such policies in the face of traditional gender values and divisions of labor. In contexts like very-low-fertility Germany or Japan, developing generous work–family policies is a response to both feminist and pronatalist pressures (Mazur 2003; Henninger *et al.*, 2008). In France, where it is acceptable and normal for mothers to work full-time and leave their children in some kind of care, feminists do not have to fight for family support policies. Nor has the low-fertility–aging-society crisis hit France as hard as it has many European and Asian countries, perhaps because its family policies and a large immigrant population have been successful in supporting a near-replacement level TFR.[14]

Finally, it may be that feminist arguments are having an impact on policy change, but, because policy change in this arena is slow, it is not yet apparent. Feminist arguments in France may simply require a long incubation period (Mätzke and Ostner, 2010a, make a similar argument about the incubation

---

[13] For example, a 1992 EU directive discussed the need for "childcare services, leave for employed parents, family-friendly policies in the workplace, and measures to promote increased participation by men in the care and upbringing of children." Likewise, the EU standards for childcare arrived at during the Barcelona Council in 2002 propose that states should endeavor to provide childcare services to 90 percent of children between age 3 and school age, and 33 percent of children under three (Lewis, 2006, 430). France already meets these childcare standards, but it has not followed the recommendation for policies to encourage men to take a larger role in childrearing, as the eleven days of paternity leave have been in place several years without much movement toward extending them.

[14] Data on the TFRs of different groups within French society is difficult to obtain, as births and fertility rates are not disaggregated or identified by racial group or nationality due to the French ideal of assimilation whereby "We are all French," and differences of race, etc., should be minimized. But Toulemon (2008) has estimated that immigrant groups have somewhat higher fertility rates based on analysis of data gathered by location, which can be a proxy for immigrant status in neighborhoods that have very high percentages of immigrants.

period required for new ideas to gain familiarity, maturity and political res-
onance in the family policy area). One certainly hears arguments about the
need for policies that encourage fathers to take a larger role in childrearing and
housework, and that encourage mothers to return to work more quickly, as well
as arguments for public rather than private forms of childcare on the grounds
that more spaces in *crèches* are advantageous for poorer families. But France,
along with many other countries in Europe, also has traditional values that
support women being primary parents and secondary earners (Morgan, 2009a,
48–50). Changing such values is not easy: one might expect that feminist arguments will need to be made over and over, and that electing supportive left-wing
governments that are committed to more gender- and class-egalitarian policies
and higher levels of government spending is essential to enacting work–family
policies that reflect feminist arguments.

Conclusion

This chapter traced the trajectory of basic family policies since the mid twentieth century: the universal, pronatalist family allowances that provide funds to
families with two or more children; the *quotient familiale* that allows families
to pay taxes based on the number of dependent children in the household; the
long, low-paid parental leave established under the Mitterand government in
1985; the evolution of childcare policies from an emphasis on *crèche*-based
care to subsidies for privately provided childcare services; and the development
of eleven days of paid paternity leave. France generously supports work–family
policies, although it supports long leaves that relegate women to poorly paid
jobs, and subsidies for privately provided forms of childcare that are out of
reach for the working- and lower-middle-class members of French society.
Although one might expect France to be more egalitarian and progressive in
its policy design – more like the Nordic countries with which it is often compared – there are good reasons why it has chosen the approaches it has. These
reasons are intimately bound up with insuring widespread political backing
for family support policies, and with the policy stakeholders who play a role
in deliberating about policy innovations: the CAF, CNAF, UNAF, organized
labor, management, government ministries and demographic researchers. Many
of these groups have stakes in shaping such policies that go back to nineteenth-
and early twentieth-century concerns with pronatalism, and with treating the
bearing and rearing of children as duties deserving of public support.

4   Germany enacts change

German family policy has changed dramatically since 2007, with the introduction of a Swedish-style parental leave and significant increases in childcare for toddlers. But to understand the constellation of German family policies, and to assess and explain recent changes in such policies, we need to take a longer historical view. Germany's family support policies include its approach to direct payments and cash transfers via child allowances and tax payments, early childhood education and care (ECEC), and maternity, parental and paternity leaves. Each of these elements has developed along somewhat different tracks. After introducing the contemporary German political system, I begin by laying out how each set of policies has evolved. I then turn to the structure of contemporary family policy making processes and explanations of recent changes in Germany's approach to supporting families. Each policy area (cash supports, ECEC, leave policies) follows a rather different trajectory, making the story of family policy development a little messy to tell, but as much as possible I follow a chronological approach.

Some basic information about Germany's contemporary governmental organization is in order at the outset to help us understand the trajectory of family support policy development. Germany is a federal system, with a parliament composed of the Bundestag (lower house) and the Bundesrat (upper house). The Bundestag has 598 members who are elected every four years, with the party holding the most seats choosing the chancellor, or prime minister. The chancellor is responsible for appointing the ministers and other political leaders of the federal ministries, who play important policy making leadership roles. The Bundesrat or Federal Council is elected by the sixteen *Länder* (states). Each *Land* receives between three and six votes, depending on its population; the total number of representatives in the Bundesrat is sixty-two. While not as powerful as the Bundestag, the Bundesrat is not just a rubber stamp: the federal government has to present all legislative initiatives to the Bundesrat before they can be passed to the Bundestag; the Bundesrat has a say in any legislation related to policy areas for which the *Länder* take responsibility (e.g., education, police matters, state and local finance, land use, and transportation issues); it can veto laws passed by the Bundestag, and two-thirds of both houses must vote to approve any constitutional amendments (Conradt, 1993, 142). Further, the proportion of laws that affect *Land* interests increased from 10 percent in 1949 to 60 percent in 1993 (Bundesrat, 2012).

Germany uses a mixed single-member district – PR system to elect the members of the Bundestag: half run for single-member district seats, the other half are chosen by voting for party lists. There are several political parties: the Christian Democratic Union (CDU) and its Bavarian cousin, the Christian Social Union (CSU); the Social Democratic Party (SDP); the Free Democratic Party (FDP); the Greens; and the Left. Coalition governments are common, but there is a strong preference for two-party coalitions. The Christian Democratic parties have formed both right of center coalitions with the Free Democrats and grand coalition governments with the Social Democrats, as they did in 2005 and again beginning in late 2013. A Red–Green (SDP–Green) coalition government under Chancellor Gerhard Schroeder governed Germany from 1998 to 2005, and laid the groundwork for later changes in work–family support policies.

The German welfare state had its genesis in the 1880s under Otto von Bismarck. It is the quintessential conservative welfare state, with most people receiving benefits on the basis of employment and status rather than receiving universal or needs-based benefits. Christian Democratic parties with ties to the Catholic Church were influential in shaping the German welfare state, and subsidiarity guided the design of welfare benefits. This led to a preference for cash benefits over services, which were seen as substituting for the efforts of families and communal networks (Mätzke and Ostner, 2010a, 137).

Policies to support families generally develop later than old age pensions, and health and unemployment insurance, and this was true of Germany. From the 1950s through the early 2000s, West Germany – the Federal Republic of Germany, or FRG – was active and generous in developing policies that supported married couples and mothers and fathers who fit the model of the male breadwinner and stay-at-home housewife. However, the FRG was much less supportive of services like childcare, in part because gender complementarity was valued and seen as normal, and working mothers were excoriated as *Rabenmütter,* "raven mothers" who kicked their chicks out of the nest so they could work outside the home. The socialist state in the German Democratic Republic (GDR), East Germany, proceeded along a different trajectory, by promoting the ideal of employment for all adult men and women and providing significant supports and services to help mothers raise children and continue to work, including financial support, housing assistance, maternity leaves, and a network of full-day childcare and after-school centers. After reunification in 1989, the social infrastructure and labor market organization of the former East were subsumed to the welfare state policies developed in the FRG, although expectations about it being acceptable and normal for mothers to work and relatively plentiful childcare places continue to exist in the former eastern *Länder.*

Cash supports: tax policies and child allowances

Cash transfers are an important tool for welfare states organized according to principles of subsidiarity, and Germany first adopted family allowances for large families after World War I. The allowances were unpopular with labor unions and employers, and were soon rescinded. Compared with other continental countries, Germany's approach to family policy during the interwar period was underdeveloped (Bahle, 1998, 21).

Turning to the postwar era, Chancellor Konrad Adenauer established the Federal Ministry of Family Affairs in 1953 in a move to appease the clerical wings of the CDU and CSU, conservative parties dominated by Catholics. The early family policy model was shaped by the dominant Christian democratic parties,[1] social Catholicism and the idea of subsidiarity (Bahle, 1998; Mätzke and Ostner, 2010a). The CDU and CSU dominated national politics in the 1950s and early 1960s, and many actors with connections to Catholic and Protestant churches were given key roles in making family policy. Soon after establishing the Family Ministry, the Adenauer government introduced tax exemptions for parents (*Steuerfreibetrag*) and a cash child allowance (*Kindergeld*) for families with three or more children, based, as in France, on the idea of horizontal redistribution from small to large families (Mätzke and Ostner, 2010a, 140). Initially, the child allowance was seen as a supplement to the "family wage" earned by the father; it was employer-financed and administered by the Federal Ministry of Labor. The child allowance was revised in 1961, when the federal government introduced an income-tested tax-financed child allowance that applied to second and subsequent children, now administered by the Family Ministry (Bundesministerium für Familien, Senioren, Frauen und Jugend, BMFSFJ, which I refer to throughout either by its acronym or as the "Family Ministry"). Child allowances were broadened to include all children, beginning in 1964, and income-testing was abolished under Social Democratic leadership in 1975, so that all parents received *Kindergeld* (Mätzke and Ostner, 2010a, 142–3). The amount paid has risen substantially, especially after the federal government responded in 1996 to a Constitutional Court ruling that supported the notion that society has a duty to insure children a social minimum (Mätzke and Ostner, 2010a, 143). *Kindergeld* increased from $40 to $150 per child per month after Schroeder was elected in 1998 (Vogt and Zwingel, 2003, 468), and as of 2010, *Kindergeld* amounts to €184 per month for the first and second child, €190 for the third and €215 for the fourth and any further children. All parents receive *Kindergeld* for children up to the age of 18, and the benefit is paid up to age 25 for young adults who are in college or training. It is paid up

---

[1] CDU/CSU governments and Grand Coalition governments led by the CDU have governed the FRG, and after 1990 unified Germany, for about two-thirds of the period since the establishment of West Germany in 1949.

to age 21 for youth who are unemployed. Children who are disabled and will be unable to support themselves receive payments indefinitely (Europa, 2011).

Another key family support policy developed by the West German welfare state was income splitting, *Ehegattensplitting*, which was introduced in 1958. The policy allows a married couple, regardless of whether they have children, to add the two spouses' earned incomes together, divide by two, and pay taxes on twice that amount, so if one spouse earns €150,000 and the other nothing, the couple's taxes would be twice the tax liability for an income of €75,000, a significant benefit in a steeply progressive income tax system. Income splitting favors couples where one makes a lot and one makes little or nothing, in practice favoring a traditional male-breadwinner wage and heavily taxing a second wage within a marriage. Joint filing for married couples in the American federal tax system works in a similar way, although taxes are not as progressive, so the value of filing jointly is less, as are the incentives for the second spouse not to work.[2] There have been numerous suggestions that income splitting should be replaced by a system more like France's *quotient familiale*, whereby tax liability is reduced by the number of dependants in the family, not just the "sum and divide by two" approach (Wersig interview, 2004; Steiner and Wrohlich, 2005). But eliminating income splitting is unlikely; when the Greens and the SDP tried after the 2002 election to abolish income splitting and use the money saved to invest in childcare, they were unable to enact this measure due to political opposition from families who benefitted from income splitting, and opposition from the Right (Bothfeld interview, 2004). Furthermore, the Constitutional Court has interpreted Article 6 of the German constitution, which states that marriage and the family are under the special protection of the state, to be a barrier to eliminating income splitting (Wiesner interview, 2004).

Childcare and early childhood education

Like many early welfare states, compulsory education was one of the earliest innovations in Germany, and was first introduced in Prussia in about 1763. But from the beginning the state recognized that it would be difficult to force lower-class children to attend school, since they were expected to support their families by working for wages or helping with household chores and work. The state also recognized that it would be hard to meet the expense of providing universal education, and early on decided on a system of teaching in shifts, *Schichtunterricht*, with half the students taking morning classes and half coming in the afternoon (Hagemann, 2006, 230). But unlike most other

---

[2] American tax scholar Edward McCaffery makes the same argument in his book, *Taxing Women* (1997); in essence, the tax advantages are a significant push toward a high-earning male bread-winner, and a relationship based around gender specialization.

European nations, which eventually transformed their school systems into full-day programs, Germany stuck with this half-day schedule, which by World War I had become the norm in most urban German school districts, and is still the norm today (Hagemann, 2006, 230–1).

Looking at the origin of childcare services, Karen Hagemann traces the origins of two kinds of childcare: all-day nurseries, *Warteschulen* (child holding institutions/waiting schools), which were often free and set up to mind the children of working mothers as a kind of emergency social relief, and half-day nursery schools, which charged a fee and were conceived of as educational institutions to promote child development. Both kinds of school were typically run by private charitable or religious organizations. Around the same time, facilities for caring for elementary school children outside of school began to emerge, in the form of after-school care (*Hort*) and all-day care facilities for preschool and older children, *Tagesheim* (Hagemann, 2006, 230). In the Weimar Republic, responsibility for childcare outside the schools was viewed as a state social welfare responsibility and lodged in the Youth Welfare Offices, but parental neglect was the only legitimate reason for providing such care (Hagemann, 2006, 232).

Childcare in Germany evolved under National Socialist leadership in the Third Reich in the direction both of quasi-martial groups like the Hitler Youth, and of providing more space in childcare centers so that mothers could work in war support industries during the war. The proportion of children between ages 3 and 6 attending kindergarten increased from 13 percent in 1930 to 31 percent in 1940. Some of this increased capacity to care for preschool-age children endured for a time after the war, as Germans coped with extreme poverty, a large number of widows raised children alone, and society suffered from the destruction of infrastructure due to wartime bombing (Hagemann, 2006, 232–3).

After the division between the Federal Republic of Germany and the German Democratic Republic, two welfare states evolved with very different approaches to early childhood education and childcare. The postwar period in the FRG saw a retreat into privatism and depoliticization along with respect and protection for the family, which was regarded as a key source of stability during this period of social and economic disruption (Hagemann, 2006, 234; Mätzke and Ostner, 2010a, 136–7; Ostner, 2010, 221). The West German governments of the 1950s and early 1960s were dominated by the CDU and CSU, and Social Catholic views held sway over social policy development. West Germans took a hostile view of working mothers, and saw the necessity of women working as something which should fade away as the German economy rebounded. People began to criticize dual-career families and working mothers as "materialistic" because they were viewed as being too interested in making money and as not

Table 4.1 *Childcare institutions in East and West Germany before unification*

Country	Year	Toddlers < 3	preschool children, ages 3–6	length of school day incl. lunch	care outside school hours	female labor force partic. (ages 15–64)
FRG	1989–90	3%	79%	4–5 hrs	4%	53%
GDR	1988	80%	94%	5–6 hrs	82%	78%

Source: Hagemann, 2006, 226 (note that most children attending preschool in the FRG were only receiving care and instruction for a part-day schedule: 240).

sufficiently committed to caring for their children (Mätzke and Ostner, 2010a, 139–40).[3]

Building on the legacy of half-day schools and a split between custodial social services for neglected or abused children and pedagogically advanced part-day preschool services, the FRG developed a half-day school system that depended on mothers being present to care for their children after school. Its kindergarten system was also part-day; before 1960, it never served more than a third of three- to six-year-olds. As Hagemann puts it, during this period

the chief opponents of the expansion of childcare and all-day schools in West Germany were the Catholic Church, the Christian Democratic Party (CDU), the Christian Social Party (CSU), and conservative Christian interest groups, as well as sections of the teaching profession (mainly the conservative high school teachers associations, the *Philologenverband*) and many physicians. As in the interwar period, opponents continued to argue that such a policy would alienate children from the family and threaten the very substance of its child-rearing potential. In Catholic circles, this position was rooted in the notion . . . that the family was created by God as an end in itself, and that, by its very origin, it enjoyed priority over the state and society. The state had the obligation to care for the family, but the family was not there for the sake of the state. (Hagemann, 2006, 235, citations omitted)

In addition to subsidiarity and broadly negative attitudes toward working mothers, the FRG is a federal system that places responsibility for education with the *Länder*, with few tools at the federal level to influence education or childcare policy. This is in contrast to the GDR, where the state took responsibility for developing a network of childcare centers that accommodated upwards of 80 percent of toddlers, preschool-age children and elementary school children in after-school care (see Table 4.1).

---

[3] Von Wahl discusses the negative connotations of the word for dual-earner couples, *Doppelverdiener*, generally used to describe double-earner couples as greedy and taking jobs away from men who needed them, an attitude that has persisted until quite recently (2008, 37).

These contrasting childcare systems reflected very different gender ideologies and expectations about good mothering, with intensive mothering and limited part-day services for children under age 3 being contrasted with a system in which almost all mothers worked and entrusted their children to state-provided childcare centers from the time their maternity leaves ended. Cold War tensions exacerbated friction between the two systems, with West Germans embracing mother-care, a hands-off approach to the family's responsibilities, and animosity to the GDR's approach to early childhood education, which was broadly viewed as subjecting children to "socialist indoctrination" because of the state's role in providing full-day care to most children. Even so, the West German male-breadwinner – female-caregiver system changed gradually in the 1960s and 1970s as labor needs brought more women into paid work. A new model developed, based on male breadwinners combined with women serving both as caregivers and as supplementary earners as West German women steadily increased their participation in the workforce, albeit with most mothers working part-time. Ironically, this pattern was echoed faintly in the East as well, which developed a model of the "two full-time workers/ housewife family," based on the expectation that women would both work full-time and do most the work of raising children (Hagemann, 2006, 244).

In an interview with a former East German feminist activist in Berlin, I was struck by the huge differences in goals she described between women's movement activists before 1989 in the GDR and FRG: the East German women's movement was quite concerned with the supply and quality of childcare, while West German feminists scarcely had anything to say about such issues (Kirner interview, 1997). Hagemann helps make sense of this by observing that there were two main reasons why the West German women's movement did not argue for full-time childcare or school days:

first, the majority of the young and educated women in the students' movement and the new women's movement simply had no children; thus, childcare and school education were not important issues for them. And second, all of these movements shared a critical attitude toward the state and its institutions, a position that is not surprising, given the Nazi past. Consequently, they developed an "autonomous" political approach and sought independence from the state. (Hagemann, 2006, 243)

Instead of seeking state assistance for setting up or funding childcare centers, many new Left parents started and volunteered in childcare collectives that offered part-day schedules, in part because of their deep suspicions of the state and in part because they accepted the idea that mothers and fathers ought to be responsible for raising their own children.

After reunification in 1989, the dramatic differences in provision of full-day childcare in the former East and West continued, as the infrastructure of childcare centers and the expectation women had of working while raising

Table 4.2 *Women's working hours according to their children's ages, 1999*

Mothers' employment	% Children < 3		% Ages 3–6		% Elementary school age	
	West	East	West	East	West	East
Full-time	5	12	10	36	16	40
Part-time	18	15	43	29	48	28
On maternity leave	47	44	0	0	0	0
Jobless/Job seekers	2	6	8	23	3	23
Not employed	28	23	39	12	33	9

Source: Hagemann, 2006, 221, Table 1, drawn from Esch and Stöbe-Blossey, 2002.

Table 4.3 *Childcare infrastructure in East and West Germany in 1999 (in percentage of children covered)*

	New federal states (East)	Old federal states (West)
Availability of spaces in day nurseries (children < 3)	36	3
Proportion of all-day spaces in nursery schools	98	19
Availability of spaces in after-school care centers	19	4

Source: Hagemann, 2006, 221, Table 2, drawn from Esch and Stöbe-Blossey, 2002 (more recent figures from the BMFSFJ show improvement on the percentage of children who attend after-school care, to 40.8% in the East and 8.9% in the West, though figures for spaces in nurseries and all-day places are largely unchanged: Wiesner interview, 2004).

children did not disappear overnight. Drawing on 1999 data, Hagemann illustrates the continuing gap between the new and old *Länder* with respect to spaces in childcare centers and proportions of mothers with young children who work, especially those who work full-time vs. those who work part-time (see Tables 4.2 and 4.3).

Immediately after unification, the total fertility rate fell dramatically in the former East as the family support policies that had encouraged young people to have children were eliminated or no longer reliably guaranteed, and the job prospects of those who had been employed by the socialist state were suddenly quite grim. As a consequence, some of the childcare centers that existed in former eastern *Länder* had to close because of lack of demand for services. There was a widespread expectation that the family support policies and childrearing and work expectations of the former East would over time approximate those of the West – that is, there would be sharp cuts in the kinds of supports that the state had offered, a "leveling down" to the norms and laws of the FRG.

In 1992, Germany passed a Pregnant Women and Family Assistance Law (Schwangeren- und Familienhilfegesetz) that guaranteed every child over the age of three a place in childcare as a matter of right, starting in 1996. The law was a compromise aimed at easing the adoption of West Germany's more restrictive abortion law by improving access to childcare (Grebe, 2009, 138–9), the idea being that no mother should have to seek an abortion because of difficulty in combining work and childcare. The Act signaled several important shifts: first, the redefinition of mothers as part-time workers whose earning power was increasingly necessary; second, recognition that childcare was a means of helping working mothers reconcile work and family life; and third, the recognition that children are an endangered species whose well-being should be a dual responsibility of the state and the family (Ostner, 1998, 131–2).

After the 1998 election, the Social Democrats (SDP) and Greens formed a "Red–Green" coalition government. Although both parties had formulated gender-egalitarian and feminist goals in their party platforms, they took up fundamental family policy reforms gradually, focusing on revising the parental leave law in 2001, building new sources of support in civil society through the Alliance for the Family, an initiative launched in 2003, and expanding public childcare services in 2004. Although the Red–Green coalition discussed the possibility of enacting a Swedish-style wage replacement approach to parental leave, they never proposed this sweeping new approach to work–family reconciliation policies, perhaps because they hoped such a proposal would form the linchpin of an SDP platform for the 2005 election. Nor did they propose legislation to require a new statutory right to a place in childcare for children between the ages of one and three, part of the sweeping package of reforms that the Grand Coalition government enacted in 2007–8. But the more modest changes made under the Red-Green coalition were important for setting the stage for the leave and childcare reforms that came later.

Under the leadership of Family Minister Renate Schmidt (SDP), the Family Ministry launched the Alliance for the Family in 2003. The campaign aimed to build support among different societal actors (employers' associations, trade unions, local governments, church groups and companies) for "sustainable" family policy (Klammer and Letablier, 2007, 677; Von Wahl, 2008, 34; Blum, 2010, 101). Such policies would be *sustainable* in several senses: they would lead to higher fertility rates, better education for small children, and an increase in the number of better-skilled workers, due both to women being able to return to work more quickly and to children being better educated (Klammer and Letablier, 2007, 677).[4]

---

[4] Ulrike von Keyserlingk, the section head in the BMFSFJ in charge of local networks and engagement, spoke with me at length about this initiative, which appeared to be a pro-business, public relations-oriented approach to building support at the local and regional levels for work–family policies that would make it easier for women to return to work after giving birth (von Keyserlingk interview, 2004).

Prime Minister Hans Schroeder (SDP) set out his Agenda 2010 in 2003, a wide-ranging plan to cut taxes, unemployment benefits and pension and health payments as a way to cut high unemployment rates and boost economic productivity. One of the aims of Agenda 2010 was to provide new sources of federal funding (eked out of savings from spending cuts to other programs) to the *Länder* and cities to help fund extended-hour childcare, all-day kindergarten and other innovations (von Bassewitz interview, 2004), as well as increasing the number of places in childcare for children under the age of three (Wersig interview, 2004; Fleckenstein, 2011, 551).

Drawing on this funding, the Day Care Expansion Act, Tagesbetreuungsaus-baugesetz (TAG), was passed by the Bundestag in December 2004 and took effect on January 1, 2005. The TAG aimed both to improve the quality of child-care and to add 230,000 places for children under the age of three. Unlike the 1992 abortion compromise law, however, this law did not create a statutory right to a place in a childcare institution (Grebe, 2009, 145). Although the implementation of the program was left to the municipalities, the federal government pledged €1.5 billion in support obtained from savings realized under the Hartz IV reforms that were at the heart of the Agenda 2010 merger of unemployment benefits and social welfare. The law stipulated that childcare providers should be given better training, and proposed hiring individual "child-minders as an equal alternative to the day care institutions . . . [who would be] provided with better social security," presumably in a manner similar to France's AGED and AFEAMA laws (Child and Youth Services, 2009).

These reforms were followed in December 2008 by a major initiative from the Grand Coalition government headed by Angela Merkel to increase child-care facilities for children under age three to 750,000 spaces by 2013, at a projected cost of €12 billion. To encourage and assist the *Länder* with this major expansion of the childcare system, the federal government promised to spend €4 billion over five years to build new centers, and an additional €770 million yearly to support their operational costs. The idea behind the law was to increase coverage of this age group from 15.5 percent to 35 percent, which the government thought would meet available demand. The law also provided that, after 2013, children over the age of one would have a legal right to a place in childcare, similar to the legal entitlement to a place in kindergarten for all children over age three declared in the 1992 Pregnant Women and Family Assistance Law (Fleckenstein, 2011, 552–3). The federal government's ability to exact substantial efforts from municipal and *Länder* governments to expand the childcare infrastructure is being put to the test.

Has Germany succeeded in meeting its goals for expanding childcare for children under the age of three? Certainly the capacity of the childcare system has expanded greatly since 2002, when only 9 percent of children under three were in formal care. By 2008, this figure had doubled, and by 2013, 23 percent of children under three were in some kind of childcare. But Germany has

Table 4.4 *Summary of German work–family reconciliation policies*

Family allowances (*Kindergeld*, child payments)
Parents receive €184 per month for each of the first 2 children
Parents receive €190 for the 3rd child, and €215 for each subsequent child
Parents receive payments until children reach 18, or until 25 if in school or training

Income splitting
A form of joint taxation that benefits couples where one earns much more
A major expenditure to support married couples

Childrearing leaves
Maternity leave is 14 weeks at 100% of pay
Parental leave is 12 months at 67% pay to a cap of €1,800
Paternity leave is 2 months at 67% pay to same cap as above

Childcare and early childhood education
Home care mothers
Childcare centers: 18% of children under 3 in formal care in 2008
Kindergarten (ages 3–5): 94% of children 3–5 enrolled

This table is a summary of information presented in this chapter and Chapter 2; *Kindergeld* figures are from the BMFSFJ website, 2014; childcare and kindergarten enrollment from OECD, 2013l.

not yet achieved its goal of 35 percent of children in childcare (Blum, 2010, 95). The supply of childcare and preschool for children between three and six is much more plentiful, accommodating 94 percent of German children (see Table 2.9).

Note, however, that when data are cited by scholars they often do not distinguish between part-day and full-day care. A few observations are in order: first, the statistics on part-day vs. full-day care are not very easy to come by, but it would appear that much of the childcare that is being analyzed by scholars like Blum is part-day, for these reasons: first, the head of the section on childcare and kindergartens at the BMFSFJ in 2004, Dr. Reinhard Wiesner, told me that the Ministry defined "full-time" care as six hours a day – which is not enough to cover full-time working hours. Second, *Länder*-level data treat seven hours as the threshold for full-time care (see Figure 4.1). Third, the average child under the age of three attending childcare spent 22.89 hours a week in childcare in 2008.

One should also observe that childcare is not increasing evenly across Germany. The number of spaces available to children under the age of three more than doubled between 2002 and 2010, but spaces are much more plentiful in the new (former East German) *Länder* than in the old West German ones. Almost three times as many children in this age group attend childcare in the new *Länder* as in the West (48.1 percent vs. 17.4 percent; see Figure 4.1 for a

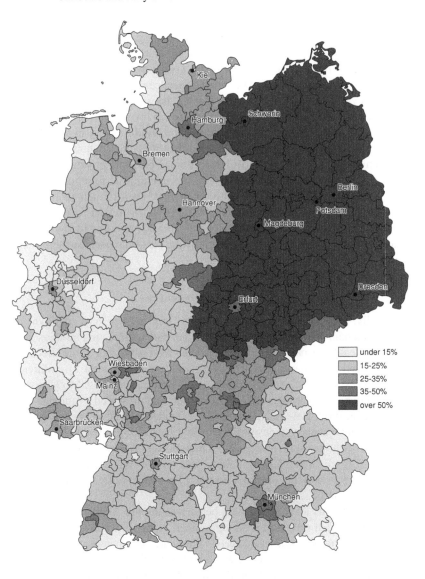

Figure 4.1 Percentage of children under age three in full-time childcare (defined as 36 hours a week), March 2013
*The legend indicates 5 categories: under 15% in childcare (lightest); 15–25%; 25–35%; 35–50%; and over 50% (darkest)
Source: Kindertagesbetreuung regional, 2013, 11.

striking map of these differences). Germany, like many other European countries, expects most children to attend half-day kindergarten.

While Germany might be close to providing spaces for 35 percent of children under the age of three in childcare facilities, it is not clear how many spaces are for full nine- or ten-hour days. There will almost certainly continue to be a lot of regional variation in childcare coverage, and between rural and urban areas. Greater reliance on *Tagesmütter,* home day care providers, was part of the 2004 TAG legislation, and it appeared to be integral a rapid increase in the number of spaces available for children under three. But it is unclear how committed German municipal and *Länder* governments are to pursuing privately provided care as a way to increase the numbers of places in childcare for children under three. The unstated assumption seems to be that, even though the German government is clearly trying to encourage mothers to return to work more quickly by increasing the availability of childcare and providing twelve months of parental leave, many mothers are still working part-time because there is not enough full-time care to meet the demand.

Maternity, parental and paternity leaves

Historically, maternity and parental leaves in Germany began as employment bans for pregnant women and mothers, aimed in part at protecting mothers' and children's health, in part at excluding women from the labor force. Because mothers' workforce participation was regarded as detrimental to children's health and development, it was widely viewed as morally wrong. Mothers who continued to work were regarded as bad mothers and pressured to quit and stay home (Grebe, 2009, 163–4). Nazi Germany extended the employment bans that had become increasingly widespread in the first decades of the twentieth century into a Mutterschutzgesetz (Maternity Protection Act or "law for the protection of mothers"), which remained in force after World War II, as consecutive conservative governments judged it immoral for mothers of young children to work for pay (Grebe, 2009, 164).

Modern maternity leave in Germany began with another Maternity Protection Act in 1968, which provided working mothers with six weeks of paid leave prior to their due date and eight weeks afterward, compensated at 100 percent of their average daily wages, with employers picking up the bulk of the tab.[5] Responding to pressure from the women's movement and a 1974 report

---

[5] In the case of multiple births, the postpartum part of the leave can be extended to twelve weeks. The text of the German 1968 Maternity Protection Act (Mutterschutzgesetz) can be found at Eurofound, a website sponsored by the EU that provides information on industrial relations and living and working conditions in Europe: www.eurofound.europa.eu/emire/GERMANY/ MATERNITYPROTECTION-DE.htm, accessed June 28, 2012.

commissioned by the Social Democratic – Liberal coalition government that recommended paid parental leave, the first parental leave law was passed in 1979. The 1979 Maternal Leave Act (Mutterschaftsurlaubsgesetz) applied only to working women, and lengthened the maternity leave from fourteen weeks to six months. The first part continued to be compensated at full pay, and the part from the third through the sixth month was paid the same as sick leave, up to €375 per month. Compensation was reduced in 1984 to €255 (Schönberg and Ludsteck, 2007, 8; Grebe, 2009, 165–6).

The 1979 law was replaced by a parental leave law developed by Christian Democratic political leaders in 1986, the Federal Child Raising Benefit (Bundeserziehungsgeldgesetz: Grebe, 2009, 168). The new law combined a job-protected leave with modest flat-rate payments which either parent could receive, though not both parents at the same time. It expanded paid leave from six to eighteen months, by stages between January 1988 and July 1990, and payments were made to all mothers, not just working mothers, at a rate of 600 DM (or about €307) per month for the first six months; after that the payment was means-tested and the amount depended on the family income. The Child Raising Benefit allowed the parent taking the leave to work up to 19 hours a week and still receive some payment (Grebe, 2009, 168; Blum, 2010, 91).[6] The law was amended in 1992 to lengthen the parental leave to three years and the paid leave to two years, allowing women to take a third unpaid year off and have their jobs protected. As with France's three-year parental leave, the flat-rate, low-paid leave appealed more strongly to lower-paid or nonworking women, since taking a long leave comes with high opportunity costs for highly paid workers. It tended to re-familialize domestic work by encouraging women to take long low-paid leaves and to depend on their husbands for support. As Timo Fleckenstein puts it, the law "constituted a normative framework of motherhood that implicitly formulated the expectation that women would leave the labor market to care for children" (Fleckenstein, 2011, 550). In addition, parents who stayed home for up to three years caring for children full time were allowed to count those years of full-time childrearing toward their pension (O'Reilly and Bothfeld, 2003, 110; Blum, 2010, 91; Fleckenstein, 2011, 549).[7]

---

[6] The 1986 law grew out of a Constitutional Court ruling that stipulated the equal value of unpaid housework and paid employment, and proposed that housework be compensated (Mätzke and Ostner, 2010a, 146). However, the maximum amount paid under *Erziehungsgeld* was not enough to live on, nor did the amount change between 1986 and 2001, which meant "that the percentage of those who qualified for the maximum amount of €307 decreased from 83.6 percent to only 48 percent during that time" as more women worked part-time (Blum, 2010, 91).

[7] Note that the law was putatively gender neutral, but more than 98 percent of those who took the leave were women.

The Red–Green coalition in power from 1998 to 2005 amended the parental leave law and renamed it *Elternzeit* ("parent time") in 2001. *Elternzeit* permitted leave takers to work up to 30 hours (instead of 19) a week while receiving pro-rated benefits, and allowed parents greater flexibility.[8] Parents were also granted a legal right to part-time work, although employers were not required to accede to their requests for part-time schedules if they only had a few employees, or if doing so would cause hardship for their business. The Family Minister under the Red–Green coalition government, Renate Schmidt (SDP), in 2004 leaked a plan to introduce a short, well-compensated parental leave, and in 2005 the Social Democrats ran on a platform of introducing an earnings-related parental leave benefit and expanding spaces in nurseries for children under the age of three. But when the SDP lost the election, the Red–Green coalition was replaced by a Grand Coalition (SDP–CDU) government under the control of CDU Chancellor Angela Merkel (Blum, 2010, 100; Fleckenstein, 2011, 551). Although the SDP was a coalition partner, the CDU/CSU claimed credit for the childcare and leave policies enacted in 2007 and 2008.

The new parental leave law granted twelve months of parental leave compensated at 67 percent of usual wages, up to a cap of €1,800 per month (that is, 67 percent of a salary of €2,700), with an additional non-transferrable two months of leave available for the non-primary parent. Low-wage and non-working parents can also take the leave, but they are paid a flat rate of €300 per month for up to fourteen months (this comes to €4,200, far less than the €7,200 they received under the previous two-year flat-rate version of *Elternzeit*). The law was a remarkable departure from the approach Germany had taken up to that time. First, it represented a clean break from the long, low-paid parental leave policy that Germany had used for twenty years, which was premised on the notion that mothers should make childrearing their first priority. Second, the law required "a considerable overall increase in spending for families (estimated costs: €3.87 billion per year)," and it shifted "resources from needy parents to working parents." Rather than aiming primarily to help poor parents, the cash benefits during parental leaves aimed to compensate working parents for a temporary loss of income and to encourage well-educated women to have children, since a growing number of them remain childless in Germany. In addition, the new benefit is financed through general taxes, marking a completely new structure in the German welfare state (Klammer and Letablier, 2007, 675).

---

[8] Both parents could take the leave at the same time; one year of the three years provided by the law could be used at any time prior to the child's twelfth birthday, and parents could opt for the "budget plan" and take twelve months paid at €450 a month rather than twenty-four months paid at €300 a month.

Passing the new law was not easy for a government led by conservatives (Fleckenstein, 2011, 548). CDU Chancellor Angela Merkel appointed Ursula von der Leyen (also from the CDU) as her Family Minister, who forthrightly pursued the employment-centered family policies that the Red–Green coalition had nurtured through the first half of the 2000s. Predictably, many within the CDU and CSU were aghast at this turn of events. One of the ways of appeasing the German religious Right (especially the Bavarian CSU and Catholic bishops, who accused von der Leyen of pursuing a feminist agenda) was to offer a concession to stay-at-home mothers: at the same time the government proposed to introduce a right to public childcare for one- and two-year-olds, it also proposed a modest care allowance for parents whose children were not enrolled in publicly funded childcare facilities, both to go into effect beginning in 2013 (Fleckenstein, 2011, 552–3).[9] Despite the heated opposition it inspired, the Bill passed in the Bundestag in late 2012 as a quid pro quo for earlier support from conservative factions in the CDU/CSU for the sweeping policies to support working mothers (Müller and Theile, 2012).

The new parental leave law encourages educated working women with relatively well-paid jobs to have a child and return to work after a brief and well-paid leave. This avoids the criticisms many level at France's long low-paid leave: that long breaks will lead women's skills to atrophy and keep them stuck in low-paid jobs. Germany aims to encourage productive workers to have more children and to get them back on the job quickly, whereas the old flat-rate paid leave was likely to encourage low-paid or non-working women to have children. Demographically, the very groups that were likely to have higher fertility rates (low-skilled immigrant women, for example) are now faced with a leave law that is not encouraging them to have babies as much as it used to. Some argue that the new law has a hard edge to it, encouraging high-earning, well-educated women to have more children and pushing less skilled women into returning to work and being responsible for supporting their families (Henninger *et al.*, 2008).

With a strong move toward Swedish-style parental leave and a pledge to expand childcare services massively, Germany's work–family reconciliation policies have undergone a fairly radical change in course since the mid-2000s.

---

[9] In June 2012, Chancellor Merkel's Cabinet approved a Bill that allocates about €400 million to create an allowance for parents who keep their one- and two-year-olds out of state-run day care. Pro-childcare groups argued that it made no sense to be spending so much to subvert the cause of state-supported childcare when the *Länder* and municipalities were struggling financially to provide new spaces for children under age three. In response, the Family Minister, Kristina Schroeder, argued that a monthly allowance of €150 would give families the choice of how they want to care for their young children: they could use it to help pay for an au pair, nanny or privately run childcare center, or to augment the family's income while the mother stayed home (Eddy, 2012).

How do we explain this change in course, and just how dramatic a change do the new leave policy and expansion of childcare constitute?

Work–family reconciliation policies: conservatism and continuity before 2000

Thomas Bahle remarks that family policy developed later in Germany[10] than elsewhere due to the early development of the German welfare state, followed by the social and political disruption in Germany during the 1920s and 1930s, which were the formative period for family policy elsewhere in Europe. Christian Democrats didn't want to intervene in family matters because of subsidiarity, so early developments focused on cash payments such as child allowances, tax benefits (including deductions for dependants and income splitting), and paid maternity and childrearing leaves that encouraged mothers to take long breaks from employment. There was a long-standing consensus that mothers caring full-time for their own young children is best, and a strong animus against working mothers. Such values were reflected in and reinforced by policies like parental leaves and the evolution of kindergarten and state schools as part-day institutions. Early family policies aimed to steer women into sequential harmonization of work and family: women were expected to take a few years off for childrearing, and then to work part-time (if at all) once their children were in school.

In Mätzke and Ostner's nice phrase, Germany is a "semi-sovereign" state, sharing power with the *Länder* in a federal system in which many of the functions related to working parents (especially childcare and education) are under the control of local governments (Mätzke and Ostner, 2010a, 141). Indeed, Bahle links the necessity of sharing power with various nongovernmental organizations to subsidiarity, writing that

federalism and subsidiarity are based on historically strong intermediary structures in German society. A major consequence is that there are no universal policies in this area. The aims, structures and organization of services vary widely between *Länder*, local communities and welfare organizations. In this subsidiary framework it is not possible to organize services around one central aim, such as compatibility between employment and family. (Bahle, 1998, 22)

Difficulty orienting work–family policies around a central aim like encouraging working women to have more babies is accentuated by the relative powerlessness of the Family Ministry. Many sources indicate that the BMFSFJ is relatively weak and lacking in competence (in the sense of limited formal

---

[10] The following discussion is based on the former FRG, or West Germany. Obviously different policy approaches and assumptions about maternal obligation were at play in the GDR, as we have already noted.

influence and jurisdiction, not lack of experience or ability), clout and money (Bahle, 1998; Kull interview, 2004; Naumann interview, 2004; von Keyser-lingk interview, 2004). But others indicated that, while not the most powerful ministry, the Family Ministry can prosper and be influential when the Minister is well organized and has clout in the Cabinet (Helmke interview, 2004; Klam-mer and Letablier, 2007; Blum, 2010; Mätzke and Ostner, 2010a; Fleckenstein, 2011).

Each legislative session since 1968, the Family Ministry has issued a family report to the Bundestag. The reports are discussed in the Bundestag and elicit extensive government commentary. Although Bahle believes that "The Fam-ily Ministry and the family reports have contributed to the institutionalization of debate on the family" (Bahle, 1998, 25), these reports are less influential than the ones prepared for the yearly family conferences in France through the mid-2000s. There is less of a self-conscious sense that there is a "wel-fare elite" that circulates among government ministry positions, think tanks, university jobs and research institutes than in France. The involvement of the permanent bureaucracy and associated scholars and experts in German family policy making seems relatively low-key.

In contrast to the powerful role bureaucrats play in France and Japan, political leaders in Germany exercise more control over policy making than do elite bureaucrats. Consultation with a variety of experts, academics and interest groups is normal, and representatives of the full spectrum of political viewpoints are invited to the table (business, labor and groups from across the social spectrum – religious, family, feminist, welfare provider and welfare client – and representatives of different political parties). The Family Ministry plays a formal, institutionalized role in debating, crafting and enforcing family policies, but it is not a powerful or dominant force in this process – that seems to be a role that falls to political leaders and occasionally to the Family Minister. There is a lot of variation in opinion about work–family policies and especially provision of childcare facilities across Germany, due in part to the historic division between the FRG and the German Democratic Republic and the very different policies they developed to support working parents. Germany is a federal state; it has to cooperate with and engage the support of the *Länder* and municipalities, as well as social actors, in a system that has traditionally dispersed welfare functions (including education and childcare) to private service providers.

New players, new arguments: the lead up to family policy change

So how do we explain the radical break with traditional, longstanding ap-proaches to family policy represented by Germany's passage of the parental leave and childcare expansion laws in 2007 and 2008? Do we need to abandon intellectual frameworks that emphasize continuity and a "stability bias" and find new ways to think about social policy making that can help us understand how dramatic change can occur (Fleckenstein, 2011)? I think both stability and change are important for understanding German family policy making. Let us consider the significance of new actors and the political leadership of Ursula von der Leyen and Angela Merkel, and the importance of new ideas and arguments related to "sustainable" family policy, the importance of early education, and feminist arguments about women, work and family.

As we saw earlier, one of the initiatives undertaken in 2003 by the Red–Green coalition and its Family Minister, Renate Schmidt, was an effort by the BMSFSJ to establish a broad set of Alliances for the Family[11] that would draw together diverse actors, including local mayors and city governments, companies, representatives of employers' associations and trade unions, churches, the media, families, volunteer-sector groups, welfare organizations, and a Service-buro within the Family Ministry whose job it was to give organizational advice to local alliances (von Keyserlingk interview, 2004; Klammer and Letablier, 2007, 678; Blum, 2010, 101). The aims of the Alliances for the Family were to make social actors conscious of the importance of the family for society, to facilitate a broad range of measures and activities aimed at improving work–life balance, and to enlist partners "in a dialogue on family-friendly business culture, sustainable family policies and . . . initiatives to reach these goals" (Klammer and Letablier, 2007, 677; Blum, 2010, 101).[12]

The Alliances for the Family changed the fundamental dynamic with respect to private sector support for family policies. Employers had long opposed the extension of social services, but this campaign mobilized them to support family-friendly policies, particularly the new parental leave law (Vogt and Zwingel, 2003; Blum, 2010, 101–2). The Alliances put "family policy on the political agenda for action," a dramatic change from the perception that work–family reconciliation policies were only of interest to women (Blum, 2010, 101). The Family Ministry's endeavors to mobilize business support for work–family policies seem to have increased consciousness of family-friendly policies markedly between 2003 and 2007 (Klammer and Letablier, 2007, 682). The 2006 Seventh Family Report indicated that 1,200 enterprises, more than half the local chapters of the chambers of industry and commerce, and many trade unions were involved in the alliances (BMFSFJ, 2006, 4). The Alliances for the Family continued to grow and flourish after the 2005 election and the

---

[11] In German, the local Alliances are called "Lokale Bündnisse für Familie," and the website for the *Bündnisse* (which is linked to the BMFSFJ site) is www.lokale-buendnisse-fuer-familie.de/lokale-buendnisse-fuer.html.

[12] Some examples of topics taken up by different local alliances include organizing public child-care and elder care, setting up flexible working-time arrangements, modifying timetables for public transport, and arranging family-friendly opening hours for city governments and services (Klammer and Letablier, 2007, 678).

change in leadership from Schroeder's Red–Green coalition government to Merkel's Grand Coalition one.

Mobilizing business support for work–family reconciliation policies hinged on explaining that increasing productivity was tied to being able to increase the participation of highly skilled women in the workforce by adopting policies that make it easier to combine work and family. Such policies would also increase the overall fertility rate and insure more workers for the future. Improving the supply of spaces in childcare and kindergarten was framed in terms of giving all children a better start in life, so that they would all be prepared to start school and learn well, a highly salient argument for a country that had been worrying about PISA scores[13] for German children that were much lower than those of children in peer European countries (Kull interview, 2004; BMSFSJ, 2006, 19).

Operating across the government–society divide, the BMFSFJ and its minister were making new and important allies who could effectively back the policy reforms that were at the core of "sustainable family policy": a big expansion of childcare for younger children, a right to a place in childcare for all one-year-olds by 2013, and a Swedish-style parental leave policy.

After the Social Democrats lost in the 2005 election and formed a Grand Coalition government with the Christian Democrats with Merkel as chancellor, the coalition agreement between the CDU/CSU and the SDP ended up importing every one of the family policy reforms that the Social Democrats had run on into the new government's agenda. By late 2008, all of these key reforms had been enacted, a set of sweeping changes in direction that indicated "a critical break with the traditional policy trajectory of the conservative welfare state in Germany" (Fleckenstein, 2011, 544–5).

The new employment-based family policies ran counter to expectations about stay-at-home mothers and male breadwinner wages that had long been core to Christian Democratic values and beliefs about the family. How did the Christian Democrats come to turn their back on the traditional male-breadwinner model and pursue "social democratic" family policies guided by the adult worker model? Three things made this possible. First, policy ideas had time to ripen and become familiar. Second, the CDU/CSU cared more about winning than ideological consistency, so they were willing (along with conservative business interests mobilized by the Alliances for the Family) to adopt a new family policy regime. Third, the leadership of Angela Merkel and her Family Minister, Ursula von der Leyen, was timely and effective.

---

[13] The PISA, Program for International Student Assessment, is an internationally recognized test of student performance that is broadly used to gauge how well a nation's children are doing in school, and the 2002 results suggested broad deficits in how well Germany's children were being prepared to engage the challenges of the adult work world.

Ideas about how best to support families have been discussed for a long time, based on awareness of other countries' approaches to supporting working mothers. Germany, like all the countries in this study, participates in epistemic communities that involve feminist academics and advocates. These communities often use international nongovernmental organizations as fora for discussing ideas about the "best practices" related to women's equality, workforce participation, and family policies like parental leaves, family allowances and ECEC (Mätzke and Ostner, 2010a, 150–1). New ways of thinking about work–family balance and gendered divisions of labor were formulated and debated under the Red–Green coalition in policy and campaign platform documents and coalition agreements. Under Renate Schmidt's leadership, they were also circulated and discussed in the ranks of the Family Ministry. These new ideas had time to gestate and become familiar to political and governmental actors, as well as ordinary citizens (Mätzke and Ostner, 2010a). But these ideas did not just become more familiar, they also became more convincing to groups that might typically be expected to oppose them, especially representatives of big business and employers. Being able to articulate the idea of sustainability in terms that linked higher fertility rates and better, universal early childhood education with increased economic productivity was essential to getting pro-business groups and the CDU/CSU on board (Seelieb-Kaiser and Toivonen, 2011).

Intraparty strategic considerations were also key to the story of how the Christian Democrats came to support employment-based family support policies. After the CDU's defeat in 1998, Merkel and other insiders in the CDU were keenly aware of the fact that their constituency was getting older and that they badly needed the electoral support of young women and urban dwellers – who were increasingly not voting for the Christian Democrats – if they wanted to continue to be politically successful (Fleckenstein, 2011, 556; Williarty, 2011). They took note of the fact that family policy was a key issue area where they needed to modernize their positions if they wanted to regain ground in the political center, and they took steps to get an intraparty commission to develop new family policy ideas and to convince the party, little by little, to take new positions in favor of expanding childcare and increasing family allowances. This group stepped up their efforts after the 2002 defeat in the general election, seeking to adopt a set of policies that would appeal to younger women (Fleckenstein, 2011, 557–8). After the 2005 election, the CDU/CSU became the surprising advocates for the new parental leave and childcare policies, garnering important support from business interests that had been cultivated for years in the Alliances for the Family under the leadership of the Family Ministry. Although these positions certainly aroused controversy and opposition among conservative elements in the CDU and CSU, the party leadership cared more about winning votes and political leadership than they did about ideological purity or content. The pragmatic desire to win and lead the country overcame the desire for policy consistency, and the decision to champion the modernization of family policy gained them crucial support among young female and urban voters (Fleckenstein, 2011, 559–61, 565). The CDU/CSU's pragmatic decision to change its long-held views on family policy lent the credibility of the major conservative political party to enacting a dramatically different approach to family support.

Other political actors were also active and important: many commentators mention Family Minister Ursula von der Leyen, who was appointed by Angela Merkel in 2005, as a policy entrepreneur who pushed forcefully and effectively for passage of the new family policies. Indeed, much of von der Leyen's task was to shepherd the proposed laws through a torrent of criticism from the right wing of her own party, as many of the proposed policy changes led to pitched battles with the conservative elements of the CDU/CSU (Fleckenstein, 2011, 559–61).

Von der Leyen's decision to keep some of the senior political staff in the Family Ministry from the previous Social Democratic administration, instead of replacing them all, also helped her engage in policy entrepreneurship. By keeping those who had introduced the policy ideas she wanted to pursue, and who were familiar with the arguments and ideas that she was advancing, she was able to enlist some of the organizational connections, expertise and credibility of those appointed by the Red–Green government to help her advance this legislation (Fleckenstein, 2011, 562). Some suggest that this decision signaled a new policy making role the BMFSFJ was taking on in the mid-2000s, a point made by Klammer and Letablier, who believe this points to the emergence of "a broader concept of social policy for the future German welfare state." They believe the Family Ministry's ability and willingness to assume new roles, moving from being a benefit provider to "regulator, motivator and moderator, integrating other social actors, in particular companies, in fields such as childcare and reconciliation policy" point to the emergence here of "a broader concept of social policy for the future German welfare state" (Klammer and Letablier, 2007, 688).

Whatever new role may be emerging for the Family Ministry, we should not underestimate the importance of von der Leyen's leadership for the emergence of a new family policy regime. Blum interviewed a CDU leader who remarked on von der Leyen's leadership:

For us as a party, this has been a paradigm change, and it would have been much more difficult to follow a different family minister . . . She has seven children and knows the balancing act between job, family, and childrearing . . . And the Chancellor supported her without reserve. Whenever anything happened, Merkel came to her defence and said: "We are going to do this!" (quoted in Blum, 2010, 102)

The changes in work–family policies were a signature accomplishment of Merkel's first term in office, and she fully supported her Family Minister (and exploited the rhetorical importance of appointing a mother of seven to this job) in order to push them through.[14]

Dramatic change, or change-and-continuity?

Germany unquestionably adopted new ideas and policy approaches to dealing with work–family issues in the late 2000s, and many argue that its approach represents genuine paradigm change (Klammer and Letablier, 2007; Blum, 2010; Mätzke and Ostner, 2010a, 2010b, 2010c; Fleckenstein, 2011). What is the best way to understand the current situation regarding German Family support policies?

In recent years, a variety of new ideas have entered public discourse and affected understandings of what Germany needs to do to support families. Central to these new ideas is the idea of demographic crisis: almost every recent commentary on German family policy mentions Germany's low fertility rate and the issue of rapid population aging, and some make this a central part of their explanation for why Germany decided to adopt a new approach to family policy (Bundesministerium für Familien, Senioren, Frauen und Jugend 2006; Klammer and Letablier, 2007; Henninger et al., 2008; Von Wahl, 2008).

Germany has of course had a very low total fertility rate for decades (see Table 2.1). Declining fertility was first discussed in the 1970s, but only among Christian Democrats; the Social Democrats dismissed such talk as "needless panicking" (*Panikmache*) (Ostner, 2010, 221). In the 1980s, Heiner Geissler and Rita Süssmuth, CDU Family Ministers under Chancellor Kohl, became the first postwar politicians to discuss openly falling birth rates and policies to help families have more children; they were attacked as 'pro-natalists' by feminists and those on the Left. Ostner notes that, even thirty years ago, worries about low fertility were nudging policy makers to engage feminist policy ideas: "Süssmuth already argued from a child's perspective and in favor of equally shared parenting. She was the first who claimed that a better balancing of work and family life may encourage women to have children – laying some of the fundaments of more child-centered and also maternal employment oriented policies" (Ostner, 2010, 223).

Now demographic urgency has been given an accessible tag line via the phrase "sustainable family policy," which appears in policy documents and discussions beginning in the early 2000s (von Bassewitz interview, 2004;

---

[14] After the 2009 election, Merkel kept von der Leyen on in her government, appointing her to be Minister of Labor and Social Affairs, and appointing Kristina Schroeder to succeed her as Family Minister.

Bundesministerium für Familien, Senioren, Frauen und Jugend, 2006; Klammer and Letablier, 2007). Klammer and Letablier describe "sustainable" policies as revolving around the assumptions that: "(a) German society needed a higher fertility rate, that (b) the economy needed qualified workers and a higher labour market participation of women, and that (c) children needed (better) education and guidance in their early years" (Klammer and Letablier, 2007, 677). In other words, "sustainability" is understood in a straightforwardly economic sense of maintaining productivity by raising fertility rates, reproducing the workers and taxpayers of tomorrow, enlisting more mothers in the workforce, and insuring that all children get a good start so that they make the most of their education. This has cachet and has clearly been consequential for justifying the view, and convincing key players, that policy change was needed, even changes that move toward gender equality in the workplace and at home (Seelieb-Kaiser and Toivonen, 2011).

In addition to recognizing that low fertility is a problem that family policy ought to address, many began to criticize the bias toward cash spending, which had long been fundamental to the design of the German welfare state. The problem was not that Germany wasn't spending enough on family support policies, but that it was prioritizing the wrong policies, ones that exacerbated class differences and did little to address the reasons why women were having fewer babies (Bundesministerium für Familien, Senioren, Frauen und Jugend, 2006). Many think Germany needs to expand childcare services and spend less on supporting marriage through income splitting. Ostner argues that expanding cash transfers to families has done little to prevent child poverty or boost birth rates. Indeed, marriage-related benefits have generally reduced women's labor market participation. Pointing out the cash bias of German family policy, she cites a 2002 study by Spieß and Bach that shows that "Germany spent 180 billion € (9 percent of GDP) on family-related matters in 2001, of which about one-third went to family-related tax policies, two-thirds as income transfers to families." But despite the fact that, according to Ostner, Germany paid for 46 percent of the cost of children, birth rates have remained low, mothers tend to work part-time, and child poverty has been increasing. On top of all that, "since 2000 the OECD Program for International Student Assessment (PISA) has repeatedly exposed Germany's failure to equalize children's educational opportunities and promote upward social (educational) mobility of children from lower class families." For these reasons, German politicians and policy makers have increasingly argued for changes in the way money for family policy is spent, "from marriage-based tax allowances to family splitting, if not individual taxation, from cash transfers for children to the funding of early on daycare and childhood education" (Ostner, 2010, 224).

The common wisdom is that if Germany wants to improve its PISA scores, it needs to invest more in early childhood education and childcare facilities, and encourage the enrollment of at-risk children. From the perspective of poor families, the 2007 parental leave law is somewhat perverse. It gives well-paid, well-educated women incentives to have children and return to work quickly, and discourages poorer women from having children by limiting to twelve months the length of time they can be paid for staying home with their children. Poor women too are urged to return quickly to work, using the prod of financial need to push them into the workforce, where they will be lucky to find low-paid jobs (Henninger *et al.*, 2008, 299).

Many are puzzling over how to explain why Germany adopted a new approach to work–family policies that was a major departure from the policies that supported married couples and reinforced a male-breadwinner, supplementary-earner/housewife division of labor (Fleckenstein, 2011, 546). Some argue that approaches that presume continuity – especially histor-ical institutionalism, but also feminist analyses, idea and discourse-based approaches (see Fleckenstein, 2011) – are inadequate for capturing the abrupt-ness and novelty of Germany's new policy departure. It is not entirely clear to me how dramatic these changes have been. I think students of policy change tend to emphasize intellectual and ideological coherence and to take claims of breakthroughs and novelty at face value, when it might be more reasonable to see how things shake out in the long run: are the promises contained in new laws met? Are the laws adequately enforced? Do all the parties chip in the money they promised? Do the intended beneficiaries of the policies change their behavior – that is, once they find the tensions between work and family have eased, will they decide to have more babies?

Part of my skepticism about the import of Germany's recent policy changes is rooted in the difficulty of getting the local governments, *Länder* and munici-palities, to live up to their promises to construct and renovate childcare facilities during a time of economic austerity. Because providing childcare is the respon-sibility of local governments, the federal government's plan to grant parents a legal entitlement to a place in kindergarten for children aged one and over involved bargaining with multiple veto players at the *Länder* and municipal levels. The federal government finally worked out a compromise: if the *Länder* and local governments expanded childcare facilities by 2013, the federal gov-ernment would spend enough to provide places "for every third child under three" (Henninger *et al.*, 2008, 294).

Although new ideas have been introduced that support mothers and fathers both taking on some of the burden of childrearing, and more gender equality in the workplace, there are enormous residual biases, customs and preferences to overcome. Germany has adopted a leave program that encourages parents to return to work quickly, but it seems likely that the childcare spaces for children aged one and two will mostly be part-day spaces that do not adequately support mothers who want to pursue full-time jobs. Germany has a long tradition of preferring part-day schooling in kindergarten and state school, as well as hands-on mothering: its childcare system does not appear to be ready to accommodate large numbers of one- and two-year-olds in full-day care, its school system is still organized around part-day schedules and offers little after-school care, and values regarding working mothers and good mothering are still in flux. It appears that the efforts of the German federal government to enact policies that would enable women to return to work after a twelve-month parental leave, and work full-time if they chose to do so, are bumping up against the rather durable message that women who work while their children are little are not good mothers (Vogt and Zwingel, 2003, 462; Bundesministerium für Familie, Senioren, Frauen und Jugend, 2006, 11; Grebe, 2009).

As we have seen, there is still enormous regional variation in the availability of spaces in childcare centers and kindergartens, and the variation has to do in part with Catholic vs. secular or Lutheran parts of Germany. Attitudes about intensive mothering and working mothers are durable, and the announcement of policies to provide more spaces in childcare cannot make those attitudes disappear.

An interview I conducted in 2004 with a young female graduate student who was working as an RA for a specialist in German family law has resonated for me in the years since we spoke. In the context of a conversation about choice, she asserted that of course German women have choices: "We can choose between having careers and having families; we are free to choose either course, we just can't choose both" (Wersig interview, 2004). I thought to myself,

but men get to choose to do both if they want to; why is the gendered character of this either-or choice she's describing so opaque to this woman? Why has she bought into the notion that women are free to make choices and decisions, with a rather strong sense that they are responsible for making the right choices and accepting the tradeoffs involved?

I think this woman was rather typical of young female academics in Germany at that time. But in recent years this precise matter of being able to choose to have a career *and* a family has been held up to scrutiny, and there is more consciousness now that this young woman's matter-of-fact acceptance of her "choices" is problematic. Germany wants smart young women to have babies, and realizes that the older approach needs to yield to a new generation of young women who expect more equality and sharing with their partners or spouses, and want concessions from employers, laws and services – including the availability of well-paid leaves and good all-day care for their children – that make the decision to have children easier for high-earning women.

It is worth remembering that Germany has two parallel traditions with respect to gender norms and expectations about working mothers: women in the eastern

Länder consider it normal to have careers and families, and to have their children attend childcare centers, while the internalized values of mother-intensive childrearing continue to be more powerful in the western *Länder*. Values change slowly, and the process of change is still on-going. Older attitudes that working mothers are *Rabenmütter* or that "*real* career women can't raise families" are still embedded in many women's psyches, as well as in the social expectations of their bosses, colleagues, friends, neighbors, husbands, family members, etc. These have not been eradicated, and they partly explain why it is an uphill fight at the local level, particularly in more conservative parts of Germany, to come up with adequate full-time care and after-school care for elementary school age children.

Similarly, Hagemann argues that the legacy of the family as the locus for teaching children and the role of women as nurturing mothers have had lasting consequences for the "time politics" of childcare. The family system is founded on the assumption of

a "mother at home," who not only prepares the lunch but also takes care of the children in the afternoon and supervises their homework. In this sense, the mother is drafted – willingly or not – as a "substitute teacher." The better educated she is, the better her children's chances in school. Thus, the German half-day school system, in combination with a nearly invisible after-school care program, is not only a major problem for working mothers, but also a reason for the great differences in the school performance of children from different social and ethnic backgrounds. In this sense, the time politics of German schools reinforces not only gender differences but also class and ethnic differences throughout German society. (Hagemann, 2006, 247)

The current school system and design of childcare have both been shaped by gender roles that dictate that women should take a major role providing unpaid care and being available for their children. Familialism has long been key to the design of education and the role women played at home and at work. When we consider the dramatic changes in work–family policies that have been afoot since the early 2000s in Germany, we need to bear in mind that familialistic policy designs and social expectations have been paramount in Germany for a long time, and still inform people's expectations of what it means to be a good mother, leading to characteristic tensions between work and mothering, even while these very norms are being forthrightly addressed and criticized by the Family Ministry and in various policy papers (Rürup and Gruescu 2003; Bertram, Rösler and Ehlert 2005; Bundesministerium für Familie, Senioren, Frauen und Jugend, 2006).

It seems evident that significant changes have occurred in German work–family policies over the last several years. But I think the changes represent what Streeck and Thelen call "layering," as new policies have come into being while old approaches and policies (like income splitting and child allowances) continue along uninterrupted, sometimes undermining or disrupting the attempt to set up a new policy regime (Streeck and Thelen, 2005, 19–29; Ostner, 2010). New ideas about gender equality and encouraging well-paid women to return to work after childbirth sit uneasily alongside well-entrenched ways of thinking about good mothering and established standard operating procedures, like the part-day school schedule that is still part of German society. Perhaps the Family Ministry is in the process of what Streeck and Thelen call "conversion," redeploying its bureaucratic apparatus to encourage social actors to cooperate in offering new services to working parents, and enlisting new forces (especially corporations and social welfare organizations) to support its policies and endeavors. But these changes are incomplete. We may not be able to judge the extent or success of the new reforms put in place in 2007–8 for a while to come.

5 Japan confronts low fertility and rapid aging

Japan's work–family policy landscape has changed dramatically over the last twenty years. Like Germany, Japan has recently undertaken to make fundamental changes in its approach to family support policies to address its low-fertility crisis, launching several initiatives in the early 1990s. An early area for policy innovation was the effort to provide more spaces in licensed childcare centers by adopting measures to encourage innovation, privatization and more user-friendly services.[1]

Japan first passed a parental leave law in 1992, and has since made it a one-year paid leave and increased the reimbursement rate several times (it is now 50 percent). The 2010 revision of the parental leave law provides for two months of partner leave, also reimbursed at 50 percent of wages, which increases the length of paid parental leave to fourteen months if the non-primary parent takes two months of the leave (MHLW, 2009). Except for the reimbursement rates (50 percent vs. 67 percent), the Japanese leave program resembles Germany's 2007 parental leave law.

Japan uses both tax deductions for dependent children and cash child allowances to help support childrearing families. It established child allowances in 1972, and has expanded them repeatedly since 1999 to increase coverage and payments. In addition to expansions in childcare services, paid parental leaves and family allowances, Japan also pursues a variety of programs that aim to educate corporate employers about family-friendly policies, as well as encouraging men to return home from work early enough to interact with their families and take more responsibility for childrearing. (For a brief summary of Japanese work–family policies, see Table 5.1).

---

[1] Japan introduced two five-year "Angel Plans" (1995–9 and 2000–4), which were inter-ministerial initiatives that aimed to increase childcare spaces, especially for infants. The Angel Plans were succeeded by a variety of programs aimed at addressing long waiting lists for places in childcare centers: the Policy on Support for Balancing Work and Childcare (the zero children on waiting lists campaign), 2001; the New Strategy for No Wait-listed Children at Day-care Centers, 2008; and the "Taking in Advance" Project for Reducing Wait-listed Children in 2010. Other measures encouraged couples to have more children (Plus One Measures to Halt the Declining Birth Rate, 2002; Act on Advancement of Measures to Support Raising Next-Generation Children, 2003; New Measures for Declining Birth Rate, 2006).

Table 5.1 *Summary of Japanese work–family reconciliation policies*

Family allowances
Parents receive ¥15,000 per month for each child under the age of 3
For 2 children, parents receive ¥10,000 for each child from ages 3 to 12
Each subsequent child aged 3–12 adds ¥15,000 per month
Parents receive ¥10,000 per month for all children 12–15; payments stop after age 15

Dependent spouse allowance
Main earner gets ¥96,000 yearly allowance if the secondary earner earns
less than ¥1.03 million a year

Childrearing leaves
Maternity leave is 14 weeks at 67% of pay
Childcare leave is 52 weeks at 50% of pay
Paternity leave is 2 months at 50% pay

Childcare and early childhood education
Childcare: 28% of children under 3 in formal care in 2008
Kindergarten/childcare: 90% of children 3–5 enrolled

Campaigns to educate the corporate public
Various icons, marks and ads aim to educate and reward good corporate citizens

Source: MHLW, 2009; OECD, 2013l.

Before turning to policy origins and historical and institutional analysis, I briefly discuss the Japanese political system, which is unusual in the sense that it functioned as a one-party system under the control of the Liberal Democratic Party (LDP) for thirty-eight years, from 1955 through 1993, when changes in the electoral system began to produce different electoral and governing strategies as one-party dominance gave way to coalition governments and the rise of opposition parties that could occasionally defeat the LDP.

Japan's political system: the 1955 system and now

Japan's Diet[2] is comprised of two bodies. The lower house, the House of Representatives, is the more powerful body, although the upper house, the House of Councilors, is not toothless. The prime minister, chosen by the majority party in the lower house or by the governing coalition, appoints the Cabinet, drawing largely on party leaders and loyalists from the Diet. The permanent bureaucracy is considered the policy making elite in Japan. Bureaucrats are recruited from excellent graduates of top universities and acknowledged for their expertise and hard work. Adding to their power in the political process is the fact that government ministries are the main source of data and analysis for Diet members,

---

[2] The Japanese parliament.

who do not have independent sources of information like the American Congress. The reputation of career bureaucrats has, however, suffered from several crises and scandals in recent years, and between 2009 and 2012 voters expressed frustration with the inability of the Democratic Party of Japan (DPJ) to exercise political control over the ministries and rein in bureaucratic indiscretion.

Japan adopted a mixed electoral system in 1994, electing members of the House of Representatives (HR, the lower and more important house of the Diet) through a combination of majoritarian single member district elections (300 seats) and proportional representative (PR) votes for party lists (180 seats). The mixed system first took effect in 1996, ushering in an era of coalition government and enabling a new opposition party, the DPJ, to win national elections and set up governments. The DPJ governed from September 2009 to December 2012, when the LDP swept back into power with a large majority in the House of Representatives.

Japan does not have a strong labor or socialist party; the Democratic Party of Japan is left of center without being the party of organized labor. Japan's version of corporatist bargaining is rooted in the postwar deal between employers and labor unions: corporations agreed to provide job security, decent fringe benefits and pay, and dependable raises in return for labor's acquiescence in refraining from labor militancy or strikes that might cause serious disruptions. Unions are company-based rather than sectoral, and rather domesticated. Although organized labor is represented on most deliberative committees (*shingikai*) that are appointed to consider policy problems or bills, business interests have more say in rules for the economy and political and policy change. By and large, unions go along to get along, and see their fates as linked to those of big business.

Before 1990, the politics of social welfare policy making revolved around the fact that Japan was a single-party system, ruled over from 1955 to 1993 by the LDP. The "1955 political system" was rooted in electoral contests in which multiple LDP candidates competed with one another for seats in the Diet, and ideological positions and party labels were not the main cues that determined voting decisions. Rather, successful candidates were ones who could establish personal campaign support networks based on generous campaign contributions. Being able to do this was predicated on a clientelistic approach to policy making that pursued welfare goals by enacting public works laws, subsidizing farmers, supporting powerful groups like the Japan Medical Association, and protecting companies from competition. Welfare support measures were packaged in such a way that legislators could claim that they had effectively championed policies with discrete, tangible rewards for well-organized supporters, oftentimes in the form of pork barrel projects like highway construction, senior centers or hospitals.

Electoral incentives had spin-off effects for Ministry of Health and Welfare[3] bureaucrats, the key ministry in Japan responsible for social welfare policy. Under the period of LDP dominance, MHW bureaucrats understood that they needed to work effectively with the LDP leadership in various policy making fora[4] and cultivate appropriate relationships with key stakeholders, including big business, labor and affected welfare providers (e.g., proprietors of private childcare centers, hospitals or nursing homes). Bureaucrats invariably appointed representatives of stakeholder groups to serve on the consultative committees that discuss and review bills. Bureaucrats were also attentive to the importance of cultivating *amakudari* ("descent from heaven") positions[5] with client industries and interest groups with an eye toward insuring that they would land in cushy post-retirement jobs (Estevez-Abe, 2008, 88–94).

With the adoption of a new approach to choosing Diet members that gives more power to unorganized groups like middle-class urban voters, these bases of electoral support and the policy making approaches they spawned have shifted. Because one-third of the lower house are now chosen in proportional representation elections, LDP candidates must now run against candidates from other parties, rather than relying on the earlier approach of personality-based campaigning and pork-barrel-focused policy making. Margarita Estevez-Abe has predicted that, as Japan's electoral contests increasingly favor candidates who court median voters rather than attentive monied interests, Japan will adopt more of the universal, modestly funded welfare measures that such voters prefer, and less of the pork barrel policies that benefit well-organized constituencies. She also thinks there will be broadening support for the MHLW and the welfare policies that fall under its jurisdiction, particularly new programs to assist senior citizens and childrearing families (Estevez-Abe, 2008, 83, 98, 224).

Estevez-Abe thinks that family support measures that passed in the early 1990s – paid parental leave, Long-Term Care Insurance for the elderly (which

---

[3] Note that in 2000 the Ministry of Health and Welfare and the Ministry of Labor combined into one ministry, the Ministry of Health, Labor and Welfare. Since I conducted interviews with MHW and MHLW bureaucrats over the time span before and after the two ministries merged, in the text I use the acronym that is accurate for the time period I am writing about.

[4] Such fora included the General Affairs Committee of the LDP (the *Sōmukai*), which reviewed bills before the Cabinet could submit them to the Diet, and the Policy Affairs Research Committee (PARC, the *Seichokai*), whose subcommittees corresponded to each ministerial jurisdiction. Generally bills were drafted by the ministries, debated in deliberative councils (*shingikai*) that were set up by the ministries or by the LDP leadership, then shepherded by the ministries through the LDP policy "tribes," intra-LDP factions (*habatsu*), and the LDP's General Affairs Committee, then brought to the floor of the Diet for debate, voting and passage into law.

[5] Most bureaucrats retire young in Japan, between the ages of 50 and 55, when the first person in their cohort or entering class of civil servants retires. This practice leaves these talented and ambitious former bureaucrats eager to find positions where they can use their previous government connections to help out regulated industries.

aimed to relieve middle-aged women of some of the unpaid care work they do for their parents-in-law), the Angel Plan (which expanded and diversified childcare services) and an increase in the consumption tax from 3 to 5 percent to pay for these new measures – reflect the power of new veto players in both houses of the Diet to promote the interests of opposition parties and less organized constituents, and to force the LDP to adopt legislation that would never have passed under the 1955 political system (Estevez-Abe, 2008, 237–44). She underlines the connection between systemic electoral change and social policy change:

> Without the veto power that the opposition parties had gained in the Upper House, the LDP government would have never introduced a child care leave policy benefiting wage earners. In the context of partial minority government, however, a new kind of legislative alliance emerged between the Ministry of Labor and the opposition parties [which resulted in passage of the parental leave law]. The general lesson here is that shifts in the political structure are necessary if new policies are to be enacted, regardless of the socioeconomic factors at work. (Estevez-Abe, 2008, 234)

In this chapter, I examine the politics of passing work–family policies and consider the claim that structural change was essential to passing parental leave laws and the Angel Plan reforms aimed at expanding childcare services. The LDP has had to engage in coalition politics to maintain leadership since 1989, and after the move to PR in 1994, it has frequently formed governing coalitions with parties that have used their leverage to push it to accept more far-reaching work–family policies than it otherwise would have supported. The period of more than three years of rule by the more progressive Democratic Party of Japan from September 2009 through December 2012 also brought about important changes in this policy arena. So the political story is a rich one, to which I shall pay due attention. I organize the rest of this chapter around four main policy areas: childcare, leaves, child allowances, and workplace-oriented policies and campaigns. Let us begin by going back in time to the origins of childcare policies.

The evolution of childcare policies

Japan developed its first day care facilities in the 1890s, located near major employers like spinning factories and coal mines and aimed at keeping children safe while their mothers worked – but not seeking any educational objective (Lambert, 2007, 5). Focusing on two sets of urban day care centers, social historian Kathleen Uno explains how these early experiments in providing childcare helped provide a basis for a national childcare system (Uno, 1999). Futaba Yōchien in Tokyo was intended to be a *hinmin yōchien*, a pauper's kindergarten. Its founders wanted to instill lessons of frugality, discipline and hard work in children from poor families and their parents at a moment when the specter of class unrest seemed to threaten Japan's burgeoning capitalist economy (Uno, 1999, 77).

These early childcare centers provided a model for centers that followed, and their practices and goals were approved by government officials and industrialists who wanted to build support for social stability and economic productivity (Uno, 1999, 141). The early day care centers aimed at providing a counterbalancing socialization to children who might otherwise have turned into unproductive ruffians. As Uno writes,

> By the end of the nineteenth century social observers noted with alarm the distressing sight of gangs of children roaming city streets. Private observers and government officials feared a rise in crime and economic dependence should large numbers of urban youth grow up without proper moral training and discipline. If idle children grew up to be useless as workers, soldiers, and citizens, economic productivity would fall, and wars would be lost. The nation would face a dismal future. This heightened concern for the character of children as future citizens established a basis for receptivity to day-care centers as institutions instilling useful values in children early in life. (Uno, 1999, 17)

Although most prewar day care centers were privately run, they received strong support from government officials in the 1910s and 1920s and sizeable subsidies from the Home Ministry as key child-welfare-related projects that helped cultivate labor efficiency (Uno, 1999, 136).

The number of day care centers expanded as need for women's labor grew: there were 2,200 such centers at the height of the Russo-Japanese war, almost all of which had shut by 1912 (Lambert, 2007, 5). But after the onset of World War I and the 1918 rice riots, day care centers expanded steadily in number, from 265 centers in 1926 to almost 1,500 centers by 1938, almost all located in the industrial centers of Osaka and Tokyo, where labor demand was highest (Lambert, 2007, 6). The Social Enterprises Law, passed by the government in 1938, provided subsidies to institutions that safeguarded children's safety, including day care centers. Although day care centers expanded during World War II, by the end of the war there were only 873 left because so many had been destroyed (Lambert, 2007, 6).

In addition to early development of day care centers, most of which were privately run but received government financial support, Japan enacted various forms of labor protection in the first quarter of the twentieth century. The Factory Act of 1911 aimed to protect women and children from exploitative working conditions and limit how many hours they could work. It also required a five-week maternity leave. The law was revised in 1923 to establish an eleven-hour day for female and child workers, bar women from working nights, extend maternity leave to ten weeks (four prenatal and six after the baby was born) and require two thirty-minute nursing breaks a day for mothers of infants.

Regulating work conditions for women and children was seen as important for insuring the fitness of future Japanese workers and soldiers (Lambert, 2007, 4–5).

In addition to labor regulations aimed at protecting women's and children's health, the prewar period also gave rise to demographic concerns. The Population Problems Research Institute (PPRI, jinkō mondai kenkyuujo) became part of the Ministry of Health and Welfare when the ministry was established in 1939. The Guidelines for Establishing the Population Policy (jinkō seisaku kakuritsu yōkō) set a target of reaching a population of 100 million by 1960, and wartime population policy unabashedly urged Japanese women to "give birth and multiply" ("umeyo, fuyaseyo") (Takeda, 2005, 79–80). The capacities of the Ministry of Health and Welfare, developed under the exigencies of total war, were useful after the war, when the Occupation relied heavily on the rehabilitated MHW to deal with serious social and financial crises. Policy historian Hiroko Takeda argues that a variety of prewar practices, personnel and institutions were utilized for economic recovery and competition in the postwar period, and ended up having an impact on policy developments related to child welfare, demographic issues and work–family policies (Takeda, 2005, 78–91).[6] The idea of population control, sometimes in the vein of encouraging pronatalist policies, sometimes in the vein of encouraging population control and contraception, still carries weight in Japan.

After the end of World War II, Japan was burdened with enormous numbers of war orphans, children and families living in poverty, and single parent households. A variety of women's groups organized to press for measures to protect maternal and child health and to help single mothers with childcare. Japan passed the Child Welfare Law in 1947, which set up the postwar childcare system, elaborating on the responsibility of local governments to provide care for children in need, and the placement system (*sochi seido*) whereby government officials were obliged to find a place in a childcare center once the parents were accepted into the system (Lambert, 2007, 9).[7] Building on the prewar notion that childcare institutions were meant to insure child welfare when parents were unable to give children proper care, the Child Welfare Law acknowledged social responsibility for childrearing and emphasized child welfare and protection (Lambert, 2007, 7–8).

---

[6] For example, the NIPSSR (the National Institute for Population and Social Security Research, kokuritsu shakai hoshō jinkō mondai kenkyuujo), an outgrowth of the earlier PPRI, is still a research institute operated under the MHLW.

[7] A variety of laws aimed at protecting mothers' and children's health and ability to control conception were passed around this time. For example, the 1949 revision of the Eugenic Protection Law, which was established for "motherhood protection," legalized abortion for economic reasons, making the decision to perform an abortion a matter of a doctor's medical judgment that did not require any oversight. The 1965 Mother and Child Health Law provided medical coverage and monitoring for expectant mothers and later for their infant children as well (Takeda, 2005, 110).

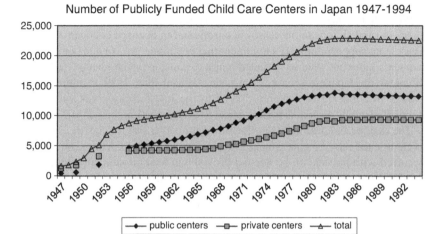

Figure 5.1 Number of publicly funded childcare centers in Japan 1947–1994
Source: Lambert, 2007, 11, Fig. 2.

The contemporary childcare or *hoikuen* system, which the MHLW oversees, is set up to care for children for about eleven hours a day, and it covers children from three months of age until they are ready to attend elementary school. Japan also has a substantial kindergarten or *yōchien* system. Kindergartens typically offer three or four hours of instruction per day, and do not offer classes during summer and other holidays. Their mission is to help small children prepare to focus and concentrate on lessons, and they are administered by the Ministry of Education, Culture, Sports, Science and Technology (MEXT).

As we have seen, when they were first established, childcare centers were regarded as *hinmin yōchien* (poor people's kindergartens), and *hoikuen* retain some association with the working class, in contrast to *yōchien* which are associated more with middle-class and well-to-do families. Many *yōchien* require three-year-olds to take entrance examinations because they are seen as gateways to admission to good elementary, middle and high schools. Though parental attitudes toward kindergarten and childcare are changing, welfare bureaucrats continue to view childcare centers as child welfare facilities that take care of children whose parents are unable to provide care because of work, illness or other reasons. Local government welfare officials admit children to childcare centers on the basis of need. Poorer families are admitted ahead of better-off ones, and fees are charged on a sliding scale, according to the family's ability to pay.

The number of childcare centers grew quickly from about 1964 until around 1978 (see Figure 5.1), responding largely to increased demand for women's labor during Japan's high-growth period. After the oil shocks of the 1970s led to economic retraction, childcare capacity declined slightly until the mid-1990s, when concern about falling fertility rates and rapid population aging again spurred significant increases in enrollment in licensed childcare centers. These data support Lambert's argument that economic growth and demand for women's labor are what have fueled major expansions of childcare – although of course the Japanese economy has been stagnant since 1989, so more recent growth in childcare is probably related to the low fertility crisis which has dominated public discourse for more than twenty years (Lambert, 2007, 11–12).

The decline in enrollments in the 1980s probably also reflects the decision to change the ratio of government funding for licensed childcare services that occurred with passage of the Second Provisional Commission on Administrative Reform in 1980 (Dainiji Rinji Gyōsei Kyōsakai, or Second Rinchō), which resulted in cutting the contribution of the national government toward paying for welfare services, including payments to support licensed childcare centers, from 80 percent to 50 percent. This left prefectural and local governments to come up with the other 50 percent of funds required to subsidize childcare services, which squeezed many cities that simply could not easily pay for this bigger slice of the support burden for such services. User fees cover some of the cost of childcare, too, but since those fees are based on a sliding scale, with poorer families paying less than better-off ones, the devolution of childcare services to the prefectures and cities was financially devastating to some localities (Peng, 2002, 433; Lambert, 2007, 23–34).

Commenting on the decision to cut the national government share of funding for childcare, Lambert remarks that "the common theme running through postwar Japanese history is that... working mothers' demands were viewed with disapproval." Economic downturns in the 1970s were accompanied by moves to repress the demand for childcare and the decision in 1980 to reduce national subsidies for childcare (Lambert, 2007, 23). Such moves make sense from the point of view of elite national bureaucrats who accepted that women workers served as economic shock absorbers, easily hired in boom times and easily laid off during economic downturns because they were likely to work in irregular positions (as temporary or contract workers, or part-timers). Further, many of the social welfare bureaucrats and experts with whom I spoke in the late 1990s voiced the opinion that mothers should stay at home with their children until they are three (Shimbo interview, 1997; Amino interview, 1999; this perspective was also voiced in an Economic Advisory Council report from 1963 – Lambert, 2007, 14).

Such long-term reluctance to support working mothers notwithstanding, the 1.57 shock in 1989[8] precipitated a sense of urgency about falling fertility rates

---

[8] The "1.57 shock" is a reference to an abnormally low-fertility year, 1966, that was based on the superstition that girls born in the year of the fiery horse, *hinoeuma*, would be especially

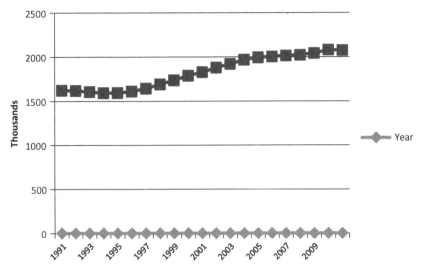

Figure 5.2 Enrollment in licensed childcare, 1991–2011
Source: MHLW, 2008, 2012a.

that got the Japanese government to begin working in earnest on policies to combat low fertility. By the early 1990s the MHW found itself dealing with a sea-change precipitated by the demographic crisis facing Japan. The public discourse on childcare for infants and good mothering began to shift as it sank in that, by 1992, there were already more dual-earner couples than male-breadwinner, stay-at-home-wife ones, a trend that has become more pronounced since then (MHLW, 2010, 176). The influx of working women into the labor force and the evident tensions between working and raising children led experts and advisory groups to recommend that Japan expand and diversify childcare services. Indeed, it appears that measures undertaken by the government to expand childcare spaces in response to the low-fertility crisis resulted in sizeable increases in the number of children enrolled in licensed childcare centers, even during the period since 1989 of prolonged recession and slow growth (see Figure 5.2, which shows rising enrollment in childcare centers from 1995 to 2010).

Enrollment of children under age three increased by more than 50 percent between 1995 and 2010, and the overall number of children enrolled increased

strong-willed, and hence unlucky. When Japan reached the same level of total fertility rate, 1.57, in 1989 due to natural decreases in fertility, it provoked a stir in the press and set up an atmosphere of crisis, initiating an on-going public discussion of the *shoshika mondai*, the "few child problem."

Table 5.2 *Developments in childcare, 1991–2010*

	1991	1995	2000	2005	2010
Total children in licensed childcare	1,622,326	1,593,873	1,788,425	1,993,796	2,080,072
# of children under 3 in childcare		470,000**	584,000**		750,000
% of children under 3 in childcare		10.1*	15.6	18.6	24
After-hours centers		2,530**	7,000**		16,245
After-school care: # of programs / children enrolled	6,708*	5,220**	10,994/ 392,893	15,184/ 654,823	810,000

* Figures from Lambert, 2007. ** Figures from Peng, 2002 for 1994, 1999. Other data are from MHLW, 2008, 2011, 2012a.

by 28 percent between 1991 and 2010 (see Table 5.2). In an era when total fertility rates have been declining, this represents substantial growth, because demand for spaces in childcare has remained robust despite the fact that fewer children are being born. In fact, despite the steady growth in spaces in *hoikuen* we see above, there have been persistent waiting lists for children seeking admission to licensed childcare centers, especially among children under the age of three.

I interviewed about three dozen academics, scholars in think tanks, activists, union members, MHW bureaucrats and political leaders between 1996 and 2011. Many of my early interviews took up details of reforms to the childcare system that were being undertaken under the Angel Plans: encouraging a variety of unique approaches or services, like centers with a focus on teaching English or music; experimenting with "eki-gata" centers close to train stations; relaxing standards for licensing in order to expand capacity and serve more children who were on waiting lists for childcare services; and allowing parents to choose which center their children will attend rather than leaving this to the official in charge at the city hall where they applied to register their children for childcare. Often policy changes were defended in neo-liberal terms as a good way to increase competition and innovation, cut costs and enhance consumer choice (a metaphor I heard a lot in these discussions was that of being able to choose from a menu rather than having to eat the *teishoku*, the meal of the day).

It struck me that the reason the themes of deregulation and privatization of services recurred in these conversations was that ministry bureaucrats were attempting to bring about policy innovation without spending a lot of money. A key strategy was to increase the proportion of private childcare centers in order to help contain costs, since both public and private centers can be licensed and receive government subsidies, and private ones generally cost less. The reason public childcare centers cost more is because they are staffed by childcare teachers who belong to the public childcare teachers' union, but the private centers are not. Unionized teachers get paid more, and are able to insist on working eight-hour shifts and other particulars of staffing, including the overall proportion of part-time teachers in a center. Further, the MHW, with its well-established connections to the LDP, LDP pro-business supporters and the powerful LDP welfare "tribe" in the Diet,[9] was no friend to the public employees' day care teachers' union, which had long-term ties to left-wing political parties (Horie interview, 1999). Both the desire to economize and hostility to the teachers' union help explain why the MHW pushed to license more privately run centers (Horie interview, 1999). At the beginning of the campaign to increase the number of spaces available in childcare centers (around 1995), the ratio of public to private licensed centers was 58 to 42. Private centers first surpassed public ones in terms of the number of children enrolled in 2005, and as of 2011 the ratio had reversed, with private centers serving 59 percent of the children enrolled in licensed childcare centers (MHLW, 2012a, 182).[10]

Privatization and deregulation have raised concerns about quality, as new regulations allowed centers to rely on more part-time workers, be less stringent about training and experience requirements, and pay teachers less. A related concern is that, with persistent long waiting-lists to get children into licensed childcare facilities (affecting around 20,000–45,000 children yearly since 1995), many families are using unlicensed forms of care so that they can continue to work. The data in Figure 5.3 on the numbers of children attending unlicensed forms of care suggest that a significant amount of "overflow" from the licensed centers are children being cared for in such facilities, which include private centers (both nonprofit centers and for-profit chains), on-site day care facilities in the workplace, and baby hotels. The MHLW did not, however, include figures for children cared for by *hoiku mama*, nannies or baby sitters in the "other" category.[11]

In 2011, there were 2.075 million children enrolled in licensed childcare centers (from data for Figure 5.1) while 246,000 children were attending some

---

[9] "Tribe" or *zoku* is the word used for groups of legislators in the House of Representatives with substantive expertise in and close connections to particular policy areas. The welfare tribe (*Kōsei zoku*) used to be quite powerful.

[10] From a chart titled "Detailed Data #1: Changes in Number of Day-Care Centers, etc." based on author's calculation (MHLW, 2012a, 182).

[11] It is tempting to translate "hoiku mama" as home care mothers (like French *assistantes maternelles*), but in fact they are usually described as trained nurses who watch children in a private apartment (Kato, 2009; Nishizawa interview, 2008). Unlike in France, such services are neither regulated nor subsidized. The number of children being cared for by *hoiku mama* in 2009 was approximately 2,600 (Kukimoto, 2013a).

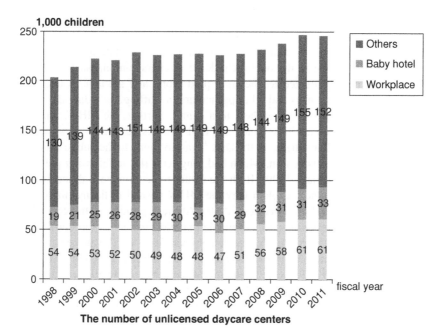

Figure 5.3 Number of children attending unlicensed forms of care, 1998–2011

Source: MHLW, 2013. "Baby hotels" are facilities that provide care past 8.00 p.m. (sometimes even all-night care), or in which more than half the children use part-time care (Kukimoto, 2013a).

form of unlicensed care.[12] Many of the latter are infants, because it is harder to find spaces in licensed centers due to expense and care standards (the required ratio is three children to each adult for infants under age one, six for each adult for babies between one and two). High demand for childcare has pushed people to turn to private forms of care that are not regulated, sometimes not high-quality, and expensive.[13]

[12] I think these figures underestimate how many people use unlicensed forms of care because the national government relies on local and prefectural governments to report these data. Numbers are also underreported because unlicensed facilities are looked down upon.

[13] Kukimoto reports that families she interviewed paid between ¥60,000 and ¥140,000 per month for unlicensed childcare, which is equivalent to $632-$1,475 a month. (Kukimoto, 2013b). Some cities subsidize unlicensed forms of care, but this varies from place to place. Additionally, some families that are desperate to enroll their children in licensed care game the system by sending their children to unlicensed care providers because they know they will receive extra "points" toward pushing their children to the top of the waiting list for licensed care if they pay out of pocket for unlicensed care services. Clearly this is a game that only relatively well-off families can afford to play, and Kukimoto criticizes this policy on the grounds that it favors the well-to-do (Kukimoto, 2013b).

The DPJ-headed governments from 2009 to 2012 attempted to address long waiting lists for childcare by setting up a "Zero Waiting List Team"[14] and combining day care centers and kindergartens into "kodomoen," an idea originally introduced by the LDP.[15] Although, for decades, enrollment in kindergartens exceeded enrollment in childcare, the proportion enrolled in the two systems has shifted in recent years, until now there are more children attending childcare than preschool. With falling fertility rates leading to lower demand for preschool services and closure of hundreds of kindergartens, at the same time as childcare centers continue to have persistent waiting lists, the Kan administration in 2010 proposed a new hybrid *kodomoen* ("children's centers") system that would fuse educational and caregiving functions for children over age three, providing care for eleven hours a day. The idea was to use existing infrastructure to provide more spaces in full-day childcare by converting underused kindergarten facilities into childcare centers, perhaps creating a new ministry to supervise the centers and other work–family policies (Takahara, 2010; MHLW, 2012a, 177ff.).

Tomoko Okazaki, a DPJ member of the House of Councilors familiar with the party's work–family policy proposals, discussed the *kodomoen* proposal with me. Although the two systems have competing perspectives, she believed streamlining *hoikuen* and *yōchien* into one integrated system would save the government money by eliminating bureaucratic redundancy. Councilor Okazaki argued that the MHLW and MEXT, the two ministries administering the *hoikuen* and *yōchien* systems, are parallel structures responsible for doing the same thing, caring for and teaching small children, and that the government could save money if it eliminated this redundancy (Okazaki interview, 2011).

But the proposal foundered on intense political opposition. Supporters of the kindergarten system worried that the educational credentials of *yōchien* would be eroded by such a merger, and day care supporters worried that the training and experience required of childcare teachers would be lost. But the battle is about more than credentialing, as two separate ministries and their bureaus, two vocal and competing unions, and two different cultural and class perspectives are at stake.[16] Although a few *kodomoen* have been launched on an

---

[14] The aim of the team was to devise a solution for children waiting for places in day care by increasing the number of childcare centers and personnel. It does not sound new to MHW/MHLW watchers; the zero children on waiting lists initiative from 2001 and the "New Strategy for No Wait-listed Children at Day-care Centers" from 2008 are precursors (MHLW, 2012, 177).

[15] "Kodomoen" literally means "child garden," from the word for "child" + "en," which is part of the words *hoikuen* and *yôchien* and evokes a mixture of both.

[16] Recall that kindergartens appeal to middle-class and affluent families who are keen to insure that their children get a head start in the battle for educational advantage that will culminate in their graduating from a good university, while childcare centers are associated with working-class parents and child welfare.

experimental basis, the DPJ recognized that the plan to get rid of *hoikuen* and *yōchien* and produce a whole new system of integrated centers was arousing tremendous opposition, and in early 2011 backed off its initial ambitious goals, instead adopting a plan to offer generous subsidies to centers that agreed to try the integrated approach (MHLW 2011; Takahara 2011b).[17]

Since the LDP won the December 2012 election and Shinzo Abe took over as prime minister, he has developed "Abenomics," which aims to stimulate the economy, end the atmosphere of gloom and doom, and encourage more women to be active in the labor market. He too has announced plans to attack the problem of children on the waiting list by adding 400,000 spaces in licensed childcare centers by 2017, though how he means to accomplish this has not been specified (Mie, 2013).

The approaches Japan has taken to increasing the number of spaces in licensed childcare centers since the first Angel Plan went into effect in 1995 have produced some important changes: spaces for children and infants expanded from 1.6 to 2.1 million; the percentage of children under the age of three in childcare expanded by half; centers offered more varied services, including more centers that offer extended hours; spaces in after-school programs expanded substantially; and the ratio of private and public licensed centers flipflopped, from 60–40 public–private, to the reverse. But as the difficult economy has pushed more wives to work to support their families, the number of dual-income households has increased from 6 million to 10 million since 1980.[18] Despite the government's best efforts, the capacity in licensed childcare centers has remained flat at around 2 million since 2004. Consequently, there is a lot of unmet demand for childcare, especially in big cities.[19] Because infant care is expensive and relatively scarce, most of the children are waiting for spots in infant rooms. Many parents who want or need to return to work rely on private, unlicensed forms of childcare to care for their children while

---

[17] When I last went to Tokyo to complete research for this book, I stumbled across a small street demonstration outside of the MHLW offices in Kasumigaseki that was protesting against the new *hoiku seido*, daycare system. It seemed to consist of childcare teachers, parents and some children. Evidently there have been many such protests; they are not large-scale, and do not receive much media coverage, but there is plenty of evidence of opposition to the *kodomoen* idea among those who are supporters of both the *hoikuen* and *yōchien*.

[18] The *Japan Times* reports that, by 2012, some 54 percent of mothers in Tokyo had taken jobs to bolster family income, compared with 48.3 percent in 2007 (Mie, 2013).

[19] Earlier we noted that there have been waiting lists of between 20,000 and 45,000 every year since 1995. In fact, many believe these figures severely underestimate the number of children who are waiting for spaces in licensed daycare centers. For example, the MHLW reported that there were 24,800 wait-listed children in 2012, but the advocacy group Hoikuen wo kangaeru oya no kai (Parents Thinking About Day Care) reported that there were more than 55,000 children waiting for spaces that year, explaining that the government figure does not count children whose parents declined admission to day care centers that were not of their choosing, or children who were accepted by unlicensed day care facilities that receive government subsidies (Mie, 2013).

they wait for spaces in licensed centers, often spending more for lower-quality childcare.

With the exception of brief spells in the early 1990s and the period of DPJ rule from 2009 to 2012, the LDP has led the national government through most of the "too few children" crisis period which began in 1990, although it has often done so by leading coalition governments. Despite predictions to the contrary by Estevez-Abe and others, through most of this period policies were still being shaped by ministries working with LDP leadership groups. Despite the electoral incentives that have undercut particularistic and clientelistic policies, such behaviors are still evident in the area of work–family policy making. For example, in the mid-1990s the MHW helped establish a public interest foundation, the Kodomo Mirai Zaidan (KMZ, The Foundation for Children's Future).[20] The MHW had, and still has, close ties to KMZ, which initially worked closely with the Ministry to decide which childcare businesses would receive subsidies to set up experimental centers, such as *eki-gata hoikujo*, childcare centers across from train stations used by commuters in central Tokyo. The KMZ also worked with for-profit childcare and baby care companies like Pigeon and Pasona Foster, Inc.,[21] and a number of former MHW bureaucrats occupied leadership roles at KMZ.[22] From the major "subcontractor" role played by the KMZ in designing and implementing new childcare measures, I surmised that the "business as usual" approach to bureaucratic decision making was still flourishing. Yes, the Ministry was responding to the exigencies of the "few child" crisis, but it was doing so by relying on a loosely supervised public interest foundation that was an *amakudari* haven specializing in cozy ties with for-profit childcare businesses. Reliance on the KMZ fit tongue-and-groove with the overall move in the 1990s and 2000s toward privatization and

---

[20] The KMZ initially had *fukushi hōjin* status, literally, "social welfare legal person," meaning it was a private company run in the public interest, with some funding and direction from the government.

[21] The Kodomo Mirai Zaidan had a special fund of ¥3,000 oku ($2.454 billion in 1998–9 dollars) in the late 1990s to disburse to different groups to foster a variety of experimental programs. In addition to its role in implementing innovative childcare programs, until 2011 the KMZ produced glossy English-language brochures titled "Child Welfare: Information from Japan" that provided a digestible summary of current policy initiatives to promote childcare, government and corporate efforts to promote work–life balance, and the like, drawing on data from the MHLW. They still produce such brochures in Japanese (see their website, www.kodomomiraizaidan.or .jp). When I expressed some surprise about this relationship, I was told that KMZ's role was to administer programs and implement policies once they had been decided, not to provide data or attempt to influence policies (Amino interview, 1999).

[22] Estevez-Abe also mentions Kodomo Mirai Zaidan as an *amakudari* haven (2008, 238). Beyond the KMZ, many of the people I interviewed in think tanks and research positions in universities or research foundations (e.g., Saimura Jun of the Japan Child and Family Research Institute, 日本子ども家庭総合研究所, and Amino Takehiro of Sophia University) were former MHW bureaucrats, which is why they were able and willing to provide me with information and insight on how policies are made.

deregulation, especially the MHW's decision to relax the rules for licensing private centers, which benefitted groups like the Japanese Federation of Private Childcare Centers (zenkoku shiritsu hoikuen renmei, 全国私立保育園連盟) and for-profit childcare operations.[23]

Despite the 1994 electoral reforms which created incentives to represent median voters rather than special interests, it appears that ministry officials still cultivate warm relations with powerful groups, devolving some of the research and informational work related to setting up innovative day care programs to private foundations like KMZ. Cutting cozy deals with the government's money when there might be some political or financial gain to be had can co-exist with a more electorally responsive approach to policy making that takes the median voter and his or her interests to heart (Estevez-Abe, 2008; Noble, 2010). Quiet, behind-the-scenes deal-making is deeply rooted in the way politics-as-usual has proceeded, and I think political–bureaucratic backscratching (including a few new players and groups) is still commonplace.[24]

This is a rather different explanation of childcare reform than that offered by scholars who emphasize the importance of women's groups taking advantage of a new opportunity to demand more and better childcare policies, even though these groups were not as vocal or demanding as the Hahaoya no Kai (the Mothers' Association), and its demands for "posuto no kazu hodo hoikusho o" ("as many childcare centers as postboxes") from the early 1960s (Lambert, 2007, 14). Peng argues that the demographic crisis gave women's groups an opening to apply pressure for change, although her discussion of their tactics mostly refers to young women's tacit refusal to go along with traditional gender and family values by having fewer babies (2002, 424). This is more a response to circumstances that make having and raising children difficult than it is a political movement aimed at making a specific critique or arguing for specific policy changes. The more assertive tactics used by women's groups that lobbied in the late 1980s for long-term care insurance (LTCI) for the elderly, especially the Women's Committee for the Betterment of the Ageing Society (Korei shakai wo Yokusuru Josei no Kai), paid off in giving women access to deliberative bodies,

---

[23] Another example of a think tank with close ties to the MHW is the Japan Child and Family Research Institute, which is also a beneficiary of MHLW funding and a source of post-retirement jobs for former MHLW bureaucrats.

[24] Interestingly, the KMZ moved from its offices in the Ginza to a new location in 2004 or 2005 in Nishi-Shinbashi, which is close to ministry offices located in Kasumigaseki. The last time it produced glossy pamphlets in English was for "Child Welfare 13," published in 2010. It has not operated an English-language version of its website for about two years, and has no information archived in English. The website now announces that, as of April 1, 2013, "一般財団法人に変わりました" (it changed into a general foundation, rather than a public interest one). It appears that the KMZ is no longer trying to address international audiences but is focusing instead on a narrower domestic mission of providing information about baby sitters and care-provider businesses.

where (in addition to their actions and arguments in other public fora) they helped shape the LTCI debate. Some credit women's groups with effectively lobbying for more woman-friendly work–family laws as well (Peng, 2002; Eto, 2000, 2001). But, in the family policy context, I think feminist arguments are not as broad-based as they were when women's groups mobilized to support the LTCI, and are taking place mostly among elites, including public intellectuals like Mari Osawa, members of the Diet like Tomoko Okazaki, and some feminist bureaucrats.[25]

Maternity and childcare leaves

Maternity leaves have been part of Japan's social policy since the early twentieth century, and when the Japanese state got back on its feet after World War II, the Labor Standards Law of 1947 guaranteed mothers twelve weeks of paid maternity leave reimbursed at 60 percent of usual wages. This was later extended to fourteen weeks. The law also provided penalties for employers who did not grant maternity leaves (Lambert, 2007, 7). Maternity leave now is paid at 67 percent of usual pay (Tokyo Pregnancy Group, 2011).

Unionized women workers in the 1960s began to demand a longer childcare leave,[26] because lack of infant care forced women to quit their jobs to take care of their babies. Companies that relied on highly skilled female employees, like NTT, the national telephone company, were the first to enact such leaves. In response to the demands of the telecommunications union, Zendentsu, in 1968 NTT granted its female workers a three-year unpaid leave, which was reimbursed by an allowance paid by the mutual aid society (Lambert, 2007, 19). What ensued after this was a decades-long effort centered around the mobilization of women-dominated, powerful unions to extend childcare leave from private agreements with employers to a public law with universal application. Particularly important were the efforts of women in the powerful Japan Teachers' Union, Nikkyōso, to obtain a leave policy. The union spent three years in the early 1960s fighting hard to arrive at a position on the issue, then began to lobby for changes to the national law. The Japan Socialist Party in 1967 introduced a law that would grant to female school teachers a one-year leave

---

[25] Lambert's explanation of family policy change focuses on women's sections of unions, and unions that represent large numbers of skilled women workers, like the NTT (Nippon Telephone and Telegraph) union and one representing textile and garment workers (Lambert, 2007, 14–15, n. 26). She argues that the two crucial forces responsible for the expansion in childcare coverage in the 1970s were the need for women's labor and recurrent electoral pressures on the LDP, rather than the women's movement.

[26] *Ikuji kyuugyō* is the Japanese name for the policy I analyze here, which translates into English as "childcare leave." I will refer to it as "childcare leave," since that is the normal usage in Japanese. But readers should know that it is equivalent to what I call "parental leave" in other countries: a paid job-protected leave for a parent, gender neutral.

paid at 80 percent of wages, which was defeated three years in a row, with the LDP and the Finance Ministry both opposed to passing it. Finally, with backing from the Ministry of Labor, a watered-down leave law, the Women Workers Welfare Law, passed in 1972, which admonished employers to "make efforts" to provide women workers with childcare leaves (Lambert, 2007, 19–20). Shortly after this, the Diet passed a one-year unpaid leave that applied to women workers in schools, hospitals and childcare centers (Lambert, 2007, 20–1).

Advocates for leaves argued that highly skilled women workers – teachers, nurses, telephone operators – should be encouraged to stay in the workforce after giving birth, but business opposed them. Labor unions and parties on the left pushed for paid childcare leaves in the 1970s and 1980s, and when it seemed important for the LDP to support such measures because they were losing electoral support and did not want to be regarded as unreasonable or oblivious to the value of women workers, bills made progress. But just when, in 1981, it looked as though a paid leave bill might pass,

the four largest business groups – the Japan Federation of Employer Associations (*Nikkeiren*), the Japan Chamber of Commerce (*Nisshō*), the Japan Committee for Economic Development (*Keizai Dōyuukai*), and the Federation of Economic Organizations (*Keidanren*) – submitted a joint statement opposing legislation of childcare leave on the grounds that it would place too heavy a burden on firms and that a single standard should not be applied to all firms. (Lambert, 2007, 22)

At that point, the LDP abandoned all attempts to pass a childcare leave measure, and voted down all subsequent attempts to pass a bill until 1991, when Japan finally did pass such legislation (Lambert, 2007, 22).

In the run up to passage of the childcare leave law in 1991, the opposition pressed for a paid twelve-month leave reimbursed at 60 percent of usual wages, reinstatement to the same job when a worker returned from leave, and penalties for employers who violated the law.[27] But the LDP, concerned that this would impose too heavy a burden on small and medium-sized businesses, took the side of the employers' association, Nikkeiren, in opposing these requirements. Although the childcare leave law eventually passed under the tutelage of the Ministry of Labor, initially it was an unpaid leave that provided no sanctions for employers who were not in compliance (Estevez-Abe, 2008, 232–3). (Indeed, the MHLW still prefers to avoid writing sanctions for non-compliance into its laws, opting to "encourage" the desired behavior and to conduct educational and public relations campaigns and find ways to reward exemplary companies (Seelieb-Kaiser and Toivonen, 2011, 353–4; Tsukasaki interview, 2011).)

---

[27] Opposition parties included the Japan Socialist Party, Kōmeitō, the Democratic Socialist Party, and the Social Democratic Alliance, and they were able to push the parental leave bill forward in the upper house, where the LDP did not have an absolute majority.

The job-protected childcare leave has been modified several times since 1991: it was made a paid leave reimbursed at 25% of usual salary in 1995, upped to 40% in 2001, and to 50% in 2010. One half of salaries up to ¥430,200 per month are reimbursed, i.e. ¥215,100 which is equivalent to $2,213 per month. The most recent version of the law provides for two months of "daddy leave," that is, paid childcare leave (at the 50% rate) that the non-primary parent must either use or lose. This law allows families to take up to fourteen months of paid childcare leave, with the option of being able to take another four months of leave if the family is unable to find a space in childcare for their child (MHLW, 2009).[28] What I find particularly interesting about the childcare leave law is the government's explanations for and responses to male and female uptake rates. In official documents, the percentage of women who take the parental leaves is shown as a proportion of working women who continued to work after having a baby. So, for example, a table based on the Fourteenth Japanese National Fertility Survey (NIPSSR, 2011) shows the percentages of working mothers and fathers who have taken childcare leave from 2004 through 2011; the percentage for women varies from 70.6% to 90.6% over that period, and for men from 0.50% to 2.63% (MHLW, 2012a, 173). A typical government response to such data is to decry the low percentage of men taking the leave and to devise plans and set goals for increasing the percentage of men taking the leave five or ten years later.

But the percentages of women who take the leave are figured on the basis of women who continue to be employed after they give birth, not on the basis of all women who became pregnant while they were working. Therefore, women who quit or "retire" from their jobs when they get pregnant or give birth are excluded from the figures.[29] If one calculates women's uptake rate for childcare leave on the basis of the total number of women who were working when they became pregnant, it is far lower, ranging between 9.3% and 24.2% over the period from 1985 to 2009 (see Table 5.3). Figured this way, although the percentages of women taking childcare leave have gone up over this 24-year

---

[28] In addition, fathers are urged to take up to eight weeks off right after their baby is born, without it counting toward the two months of paid parental leave – so, in essence, fathers get four months of paid parental leave, if they take two months right after birth, and two months after their wives go back to work (MHLW, 2009).

[29] The MHLW can calculate uptake rates for parental leave any way it wants to. But this way of figuring uptake rates would make statisticians and social scientists in countries like France, Germany and the United States scratch their heads. They would probably puzzle over the high percentage of women who quit outright when they give birth to their first child, and try to explain why so many young women quit working upon giving birth in their twenties or thirties. Linguistically as well, the reference in Japanese to young women "retiring" from their jobs seems to normalize this pattern of workforce participation; in English, we refer to people "retiring" after working for thirty-five years or more; when a young worker leaves a job after working five or ten years, we would say she quit, or maybe she was fired, depending on the circumstances.

Table 5.3 *Percentages of all previously working women who take childcare leave*

	% of women working when they became pregnant	% of all women who became pregnant who "retired"	% of all women who became pregnant who kept on working w/o taking a leave	% of all women who became pregnant who took childcare leave	% of all previously working women who took childcare leave
1985–9	61.4	37.4	18.3	5.7	9.3
1990–4	62.1	37.7	16.3	8.1	13.0
1995–9	63.5	39.3	13.0	11.2	17.6
2000–4	67.3	40.6	11.9	14.8	22.0
2005–9	70.7	43.9	9.7	17.1	24.2

Source: NIPSSR, 2011, 19.

period, they are still quite anemic. A couple of other changes are noticeable from the data in the table: first, more women are working before their first baby is born than used to be the case; and, second, the percentage of women who "retire" from the workforce because of pregnancy increased somewhat between 1985 and 2009. The fact that more women are working for pay is not surprising; it confirms the rise in dual-income couples, and makes sense in light of the tough economic times Japan has faced in recent years. But the data above piqued me to wonder: why is a larger percentage of women than before quitting when their first baby is born, and why do so few Japanese women take parental leaves to which they are legally entitled?

Women might quit rather than taking a leave because they want to spend time with their infants. This makes sense of the fact that the percentage of women who "retire" when they get pregnant is increasing: in an era when women are having fewer babies – maybe just one, or maybe none at all – those women who do get pregnant may have looked forward to the opportunity to take some time off to be at home for a few years. Other explanations also make sense: perhaps women quit because they know it will be difficult to find a space in a licensed childcare center for a one-year-old, so they might as well just take two or three years off to stay home with their child. Or perhaps they have been warned that their job is likely to be filled by someone else when they come back from leave (bosses quietly communicate such expectations with a smile, a "congratulations," and an envelope with severance pay, and most employees know that it puts their employers out to find replacements to do their work if they are gone for a year, given the cost and difficulty of training someone in the firm-specific skills that are expected of a Japanese employee). Or the woman considering a leave may anticipate hostility and tension upon returning to work after taking a year of childcare leave, as her colleagues most likely were expected to pick up the slack while the new mother was absent, and are apt to feel resentful about the extra burden she caused (Muraki interview, 2001). Indeed, these are not either-or explanations; women may be taking several of them into account as they decide whether to take parental leaves, and survey data suggest as much.

Whatever the reasons, the fact that relatively few working women continue to work after their first child is born or use the paid leave policy is important for understanding Japan in comparative context. The tendency to drop out of the labor market rather than taking a one-year leave is especially significant in Japan, where the decision to interrupt one's work tenure for a year or more usually means that women who take time off to raise children never get back on track with full-time regular jobs, but are pushed into part-time or other kinds of irregular work, at a substantial cost in terms of pay and advancement.

The reasons why uptake rates are low for men are familiar: men tend to make more money than their wives. From the point of view of the family's income, a husband taking a leave at half of his usual pay is usually more financially burdensome than doing without the wife's pay. Men who take time off for childcare leave are also regarded as not being very "otokorashii," or manly, despite various campaigns to make caregiving dads seem appealing and sexy (e.g., the "Sam" campaign recounted in Roberts, 2002, or the Ikumen campaign, which I discuss below). More to the point, in a labor market in which good regular jobs are relatively scarce, men are not likely to take a childcare leave that will make their bosses regard them as slackers.

The peculiar gap between the letter of the law and its actual operation is a reminder of an important tradition in Japan of bureaucratic and legal informality. Recall that when the Diet passed the childcare leave law in 1991, the LDP sided with big business interests and refused to include penalties for employers who disobeyed the law. Indeed, the law still depends on efforts to inform, educate and persuade companies to go along with its requirements (see Upham, 1987, for an excellent discussion of this aspect of Japanese law). If a woman takes a one-year leave from her job after she gives birth, and her boss replaces her with someone else, leaving her jobless at the end of the year, she cannot bring a lawsuit to demand that her employer rehire her for the same or a similar job. As long as there is no legal remedy for women whose bosses fire them, women are faced with some tough choices: they can continue to work (and have no babies); they can continue to work (and take no childcare leave); they can have babies and spend a year at home, and deal with the possibility that their job will not be held for them or their colleagues will be nasty when they return to work after their year's leave – or they can simply quit their jobs and spend a reasonable amount of time at home with their babies, in the knowledge they will probably never hold a full-time regular position again. Bureaucrats attempt to persuade employers to obey the letter of the law via campaigns and promotions (more on this in the "Workplace benefits and regulations, and campaigns to publicize WLB" section below). Meanwhile, the MHLW scurries around trying to convince employers to obey the law, to convince young women that the childcare leave will be there for them if they decide to have a baby, and reminding everyone that it is in the best interest of the country if couples continue to marry and have two babies each. But everyone knows that employers can flout this law with impunity, and efforts at moral suasion are often ineffective.

Child allowances

Childcare allowances (*jidōteate*) were introduced in 1972 at the height of the high-growth era, and initially covered preschool children between birth and six years old. From the early 1980s until 1999, it was cut back and only covered children through age three (Peng, 2002, 439, n. 29). Payments were modest and pronatalist in design: families received ¥5,000 (roughly $51) a month for the first two children, and ¥10,000 ($102) a month for third and subsequent children, until the child's third birthday. I repeatedly heard that child allowances were too small to make a difference in a family's decision about whether to have children: bureaucrats liked to say that it only amounted to enough to pay for cigarettes. When asked about the efficacy of different approaches, most told me they thought providing childcare was a more effective way to encourage people to have more children than the modest child allowance program.

Despite this skepticism, the child allowance law was reformed in late 1999 to double its coverage (children would receive the same monetary benefits as before, but they would get them until their sixth birthday) and to ease the eligibility ceiling so that instead of only 60 percent of families qualifying for child allowances, 80 percent would receive them (Peng, 2002, 439, n 29). Because the economy was in bad shape, coming up with extra revenue to pay for this expansion in the child allowance program was not feasible. So it was financed by cutting dependent-child tax deductions for children under the age of sixteen from ¥480,000 to ¥380,000 (from $5,823 to $4,602). The net impact on the government's books was revenue neutral, but the redistributive effect was to give extra cash to lower-middle-class families by cutting tax deductions that were particularly helpful to middle- and upper-middle-class families – a constituency that had traditionally been solid LDP supporters (Kobayashi interview, 1999; Honda interview, 2001).

The policy change reflects the changed political circumstances of the political parties, and of the bureaucrats as well. In 1999 the LDP headed a coalition government that relied on the support of Kōmeitō, the political party associated with Sōka Gakkai, which promoted Nichiren Buddhism. Kōmeitō viewed lower-middle-class families as its primary constituency, and it made its support for the coalition contingent on passing a big revision in the child allowance program. In order to hold the political coalition together and retain power, the LDP supported the changes in the child allowance law. Even though few LDP or MHW policy experts thought the expanded payments would have much impact on people's decisions to have more babies, party leaders and ministry officials had to go along with Kōmeitō's ultimatum.[30]

The child allowance program was revised again in 2007, this time giving ¥10,000 ($102) a month for each child under age three, then reverting to the above pattern of ¥5,000 ($51) a month for the first two children and ¥10,000 a month for third and subsequent children, until the child turns twelve (MHLW, 2007). The most recent revisions, in 2010 and 2012, expanded coverage yet again. Now all children receive ¥15,000 ($153) per month until their third birthday; the first two children age 3 through 12 receive ¥10,000, and third and subsequent ones receive ¥15,000, and all middle school children (ages 12–15) receive ¥10,000 (MHLW, 2012b).[31]

The 2007 increases again reflect the presence of Kōmeitō in the ruling coalition led by the LDP: the increases built on the deal to extend child payments in late 1999, expanding amounts and doubling the age to which children receive these payments from six to twelve. By 2009 and the campaign leading up to the elections that swept the DPJ into office in September, it was clear that the DPJ was also campaigning on a promise of an even more generous expansion in child allowances: it promised a monthly child allowance of ¥26,000 for every child through the end of junior high school (age 15), regardless of parental income (Kato, 2009). The DPJ took this approach in order to attract support from voters worried that Japan does not adequately support childrearing families. But other reasons have been suggested as well: it was a cash amount that represented a quantitative goal, something that could be measured and achieved. It would immediately address the criticisms of those who compare Japan with European countries, and rank it near the bottom of the OECD in terms of the percentage of GDP it spends on family support (Okazaki interview, 2011). It

---

[30] A bureaucrat familiar with the child allowance reform gave me this brief explanation in 2001 of the change in family allowance policy: "There are three kinds of cash support for childrearing: payments for dependent wives and children that come from employers (*haigusha* and *fuyōteate*), supports from tax deductions, and child allowances (*jidōteate*). Decreasing the tax deductions and increasing the *jidōteate* effects an income transfer from wealthier to poorer families; it's strongly supported by Kōmeitō (whose base of support is lower income families) but not by Jimintō, whose base is upper-middle class and wealthy families who find the tax deductions more advantageous." These changes resulted in 3 million people getting more from increased child allowances, and some 19 million people losing some of the tax deductions they had been receiving (Honda interview, 2001).

[31] The intention had been to expand the amounts for child allowances even more, so that children would be receiving ¥26,000 each per month. But the earthquake and tsunami in March 2011 derailed plans for these big increases, and the government scaled back the amounts paid to the figures indicated in the text (Takahara, 2011a).

was not as difficult and intractable as solving the problem of all the children waiting for spaces in childcare centers (Kato, 2009).[32] A huge natural disaster, however, disrupted the ambitious program for expanding the child allowance plans. When the March 11, 2011 earthquake hit northeast Japan, causing a tidal wave that destroyed much of the Fukushima nuclear power plant, Japan's spending priorities were transformed overnight into disaster relief, and the Kan administration was forced to scale back its plans to double the child allowance payments, which is why the amounts presented above are more modest than those that were discussed on the campaign trail.

The amounts being paid to childrearing families through child allowances have increased significantly; under the latest revisions, families with one child under the age of three receive about $1,800 a year, and about $1,225 per year for one child from age three to age fifteen. For families raising two children, the amounts double, and more than triple if there are three children in the home. Neither the cost of providing increased child allowances nor the gain to the families is trivial. But by comparative standards, Japan's child allowances are not as generous as Germany's or France's. German families receive €184 per month for each of the first two children, €190 for the third child, and €215 for subsequent children up until age 21, or until 25 if the child is in school, training or military service. For a one-child family, this amounts to €2,208 per year, and it is paid six to twelve years longer than in Japan. The basic family allowance in France is €129 a month for two children and €295 for three children, paid until the child turns 20.[33] In addition to this basic allowance, France has several other cash supports to help pay for childcare, buy school clothes and the like (CLEISS, 2014). (The United States, on the other hand, provides no family allowance, and its dependent Child Tax Credits and deductions are rather modest.) Because Japan's cost of living is higher than France's and Germany's, even its expanded child allowance program probably only has a modest impact on decisions to have a(nother) child.

Workplace benefits and regulations, and campaigns to publicize work–life balance

In this section, I discuss several other work–family policies that are crucial for understanding Japan: dependent spouse allowances and regulations governing contributions to health and pension coverage; laws regulating jobs and work

---

[32] Kato's article in the *Japan Times* quotes the director of the Japan Research Institute, Yuri Okina: "I think they are resorting to distributing cash, because it is complicated to fundamentally change the system and regulations on child care" (Kato, 2009).

[33] Notice that French family allowances only cover families with two or more children; the first child receives nothing, a pronatal aspect of French policy design.

hours (required overtime work, permitting parents to opt for reduced hours while their children are young, allowing workers to have family leave to take care of sick children or elderly relatives); plus an array of policies that loosely fall under the rubric "work–life balance" (WLB).

Feminist scholars often criticize spousal tax deductions and grants from private employers for dependent spouses (*haigusha teate*). The spousal tax deduction cuts the taxable annual income of the household's main earner by ¥380,000 if the dependent spouse earns less than ¥1.03 million a year (Shiota, 2000). Although there was talk of cutting the deduction by half starting in 2004 because of the disincentive it provided for women to work full-time, the deduction has not changed in decades (this system was introduced in 1961). In addition, many private employers offer dependent-spouse allowances that work in the same way: if the dependent spouse earns less than ¥1.03 million, the main earning spouse receives ¥96,000 (about $980) as an allowance, a benefit the family loses when the lower-earning spouse earns above this level. Furthermore, once the lower-earning spouse earns more than ¥1.03 million, she is responsible for paying into the pension and medical insurance funds (rather than being covered as a dependent), and the amount required is significant (about $1,235 a year). Taken together, the financial incentives encourage most married women to keep their earnings below the ¥1.03 million figure, which usually means that they only work part-time and at rather low-paid jobs (¥1.03 million is only about 24 percent of an average production worker's earnings: OECD, 2003, 184–5). This common form of fringe benefit supplied by employers has a big impact on women's earning patterns in Japan.

Regulation of working hours has been a focus of work–life balance initiatives and policies to counter low fertility in Japan. Jiyeoun Song discusses some of the efforts the government has made to discourage employers from requiring long hours of overtime. She explains them in light of the government's growing awareness of long work hours as a problem, and the new political possibilities in an electoral system that reflects the preferences of median voters (Song, 2010, 1025–31). As part of the new work–life balance approach, the Council on Economic and Fiscal Policy in 2006 proposed "to enhance diversity and flexibility in employment and working conditions" by increasing premiums for overtime pay and thereby encouraging firms to reduce working hours and allow workers to spend more time with their family (Song, 2010, 1030). The LDP-led coalition government proposed excluding overtime pay for most white-collar workers in order to help firms keep their labor costs low, but the LDP's coalition partner, New Kōmeitō, opposed this because it would undermine the party's focus on family-friendly policy. As originally written, the bill would have increased overtime pay from 25 percent to 50 percent when overtime exceeded 80 hours a month. But MHLW bureaucrats rewrote the bill under pressure from Kōmeitō and the opposition DPJ to require that employees receive a 50 percent premium when overtime exceeds 60 hours a month, a concession to the labor union base of the opposition DPJ (Song, 2010, 1030).

In addition to increasing the bonus workers receive for working overtime once they exceed more than 60 hours in one month, other "family-friendly" regulations of work hours include: the right of workers with children under the age of three to work six hours instead of eight; the right of workers responsible for caring for a child under three to be exempt from overtime; a cap of 24 hours of overtime per month for workers with preschool-age children; the right of workers with preschool-age children to be exempt from late night hours and to have five days a year to care for a sick child or family member (MHLW, 2012c, 4).[34] The point of these measures, part of the revised Childcare and Family Care Leave Law (CCFCLL) which took effect in 2010, is to allow parents the time and flexibility they need to deal with sick children and elderly relatives, and to work shorter hours while their children are young. However, the enforcement mechanisms for this law are based on encouragement, education and publicizing the names of employers who violate the law (Okazaki interview, 2011; Tsukasaki interview, 2011; MHLW, 2012c, 5). There is no right to bring a lawsuit seeking specific performance or damages in cases where employers do not obey the recommendations contained in the law, and the provisions for monitoring the law's effectiveness sound like they are based completely on voluntary compliance in response to very mild carrots and sticks. If companies are found to comply with nine different standards (which are in essence the measures in the CCFCLL discussed above), then they qualify for the "Kurumin Mark" (see Figure 5.4) which signifies that "ko sodate sapouto shiteimasu," "we support childrearing." If they are not in compliance, then their names can be published on a website as not in compliance with the CCFCLL. Furthermore, the requirements of the law only apply to companies that have 100 or more employees (MHLW, 2009, 2012d, 5–8; Tsukasaki interview, 2011).

Japan's Basic Law for a Gender Equal Society took effect in 1999, and resulted in the establishment of the Gender Equality Bureau and Council within the Cabinet Office, which moved some basic policy thinking and coordination away from the MHLW and into the prime minister's hands, in an effort to exert more political control. The consolidation of resources in the Cabinet Office makes it easier for a skillful and powerful prime minister to exert control over the policy process, but when weak leaders are in power (which has often been the case in Japan), the policy making initiative is likely to revert to the ministries.

I spoke with four bureaucrats who were working for the Cabinet Office Gender Equality Promotion Section, "on loan" from the MHLW, in 2008. The

---

[34] It is a little difficult to see how a 60-hour work week, no matter how well paid, can be seen as "family-friendly."

Figure 5.4 Kurumin Mark for childrearing-friendly businesses
Source: this mark is found in numerous MHLW publications related to work–family policy, beginning in 2009.

group was headed by a woman, Yūko Tsukasaki, the head of the Section. We focused on issues related to expanding after-school care for elementary school children and relying more on *hoiku mama* to care for children, an approach that they viewed as a feasible, inexpensive way to provide care and afford parents greater choice.[35] The gender bureau group was hopeful that the government would be able to increase consumption taxes by 1 percent in order to generate sufficient funds to be able to increase spending on childcare and other family-friendly policies by about ¥2.4 trillion, or $29.14 billion.[36]

---

[35] This struck me as an interesting shift from earlier discussions of *hoiku mama* and *bebi hoteru* (or "baby hotels," unlicensed facilities that offer drop-in and long hours infant care services) as suspect or not quite safe ways to care for children. The Cabinet Office bureaucrats seemed to think these were acceptable alternatives for providing care that could be brought "on line" quickly and easily.

[36] In fact the timing was not good for a tax hike, given that the ruling LDP coalition government was feeling vulnerable with the DPJ newly in control of the upper house of the Diet, and fearing a big shift in favor of the DPJ, which indeed occurred when voters swept the first DPJ

In contrast to my earlier interviews with welfare bureaucrats from the MHLW, this group focused on the job market, especially the move toward young people not being able to get good "regular" jobs when they graduate and having to work as temps, contract workers or part-timers. They saw the paucity of good jobs as a fundamental reason why people were postponing getting married, as most young couples want to have a good job that will permit them to move into a reasonable apartment or house before starting a family. These four relatively young officials understood that long work hours are family-unfriendly: they talked at length about Japan's long-work-hours culture, particularly the problem of workers being expected to put in a lot of "social overtime" (*tsukiai zangyō*) and "service overtime" (*saabisu zangyō*). The first means you can't go home until your boss does, the second is unpaid overtime, and both are ubiquitous in Japanese workplaces. These practices are costly to family life, because when workers have to put in long hours of overtime, they can't get home in time to pick up their children from childcare, make dinner, read to their kids, give them baths, or talk to their wives, and they spend very little time taking care of children and doing daily chores (see GEB, 2006, 17; and Figure 2.5). The group discussed the idea of "part-time regular" work, that is, secure jobs which would entitle workers to good pay and benefits while working shorter hours, as in the Netherlands.

This "cross-disciplinary" group of policy bureaucrats, led by a woman who herself has children, were discussing work–family issues in a more complicated, richer way than the more circumscribed discussions I had previously had with MHW and MHLW officials. This was reflected in their awareness that long hours of overtime and young people being locked out of regular jobs are key work–family issues.[37] I was also struck by the weariness they expressed about their own bosses' expectations for overtime work: despite their clear understanding that long hours of overtime are difficult for couples raising a family, they couldn't discuss the issue in their own offices (Tsukasaki interview, 2008).

A humorous interlude during this rather sober discussion about work conditions and low marriage and birth rates occurred when two of the men in the group dug up copies of a campaign they were familiar with, which urges men to return home early from work so they can spend time with their kids, and urges families to be more understanding of the dads' diligent commitment to work hard. They showed me a picture book featuring a cute little green frog hopping

government into office fifteen months later. In any case, the LDP did not risk trying to pass a tax increase under these circumstances. The tax hike eventually passed in October 2013 under the Abe (LDP) government, and took effect April 1, 2014.

[37] On the other hand, it was not clear how much influence they had over agenda setting or drafting and promoting particular bills, especially as the consensus-building done by deliberative councils still occurs largely within the ministries (Weathers, 2005; Song, 2010).

「やさしさ」と「思いやり」が
響きあう社会へ。

「ライフ」のハーモニーがとれてくると、
ココロに余裕がうまれてくる。そうすると
新しい何かをはじめたくなったり、仕事や毎日を楽しくしちゃう
アイデアが浮かんできたり、なんだかいいこと、いっぱいありそう！
それに、きっと周りの状況がよく見えてきて、周りの人にも、
もっとやさしくなれそうじゃない？ たとえば、駅でベビーカーを運ぶ女性に
手をさしのべたり、仕事場で「明日が家族の誕生日」なんて聞いたら
「何か手伝おうか？」って声をかけたり…そんな「やさしさ」と「思いやり」が
響きあう社会になると、うれしいね。

Figure 5.5 はたら区カエル野の仲間たち: A community/field full of working frogs

his way home from work, playing on the pun in the word "kaeru," which means
both "frog" (カエル) and "to return home" (帰る) (this booklet appears to have
been the collaborative effort of the MHLW, Cabinet Office work–life balance
program, and the Kodomo Mirai Zaidan – KMZ, 2009).

The book is illustrated in a genuinely cute way, featuring a working dad frog
who reflects on his life and all the commitments he's made. It's a fun, easy read
aimed at getting adults to think about the balance between their children and
work. The booklet was the icing on the cake, coming at the end of a far-ranging,
thoughtful interview that suggested the possibilities for more integrative, cross-
disciplinary thinking about work–family balance issues (Tsukasaki interview,
2008).

By the time I spoke with Ms Tsukasaki again in 2011, she was back to
working for the MHLW, this time working on corporate compliance with the
Child Care and Family Care Leave Law, including reporting requirements and
standards for receiving the Kurumin Mark. She was also spearheading the
"Ikumen" campaign to promote nurturing fathers who take time off to care
for their children (Tsukasaki interview, 2011). "Ikumen" was coined by the
Hakuhodo advertising agency, and combines the "iku" from the word "ikuji"
(育児, "childrearing") with the English word "men" to create the sexy, macho-
sounding "Ikumen" (which means "nurturing men" – see Figure 5.6 below). The
ministry launched the Ikumen Project in June 2010 with the aim of increasing

育てる男が、家族を変える。社会が動く。

Figure 5.6 Ikumen logo

the number of fathers who take childcare leave and participate in childrearing – and, along the way, "Ikumen" became the most popular new Japanese word of 2010 (Fukue, 2010).

It is evident to any scholar of Japanese work–family policies that the art and graphics departments at the MHLW devote significant amounts of time and attention to designing campaigns, very much in the spirit of advertising campaigns. This was evident even in the covers of Ministry White Papers, reports on the Angel Plan, reports on data about work–family initiatives, and particular slogans and images that were used in educational or advertising-type posters one might see in the workplace or on a train – cherubic little babies floating around in the air, young couples sitting down for an idyllic picnic (MHW White Paper 1998), chipper little frogs returning home from work, display ads run on the trains and in newspapers featuring the fey machismo of an actress's husband ("Sam") holding their infant to his chest and looking into the camera under a caption suggesting that, if you're really manly, you aren't afraid to hug your baby (Roberts, 2002, 76–82). A great deal of effort has been put into these campaigns; but who are they for, and what good do they do? Raising public awareness of the obstacles facing young people who would like to marry and have a couple of children; idealizing a particular notion of fulfillment or happiness; presenting that notion to public audiences in an appealing, attractive way so as to shape their dreams and hopes; and educating powerful members of Japanese society (the bosses and corporate managers worried about productivity and bottom-line issues) about the public good at stake in having young people continue to procreate – these seem to have been the aims for these images (Coleman interview, 2011).

Analysis

We have examined policy developments related to childcare, parental leaves, child allowances, company-level policies granting dependent-spouse allowances and regulating hours, and a variety of campaigns aimed at publicizing policy aims and encouraging individual men to be more present as nurturing fathers, and corporations to go along with allowing parents to take childrearing and family leaves and work shorter hours. The policy changes I have recounted already suggest that political forces and processes were changing during this period; here, I offer an explicitly political analysis of changing work–family policies.

It might be helpful to introduce some organizing themes at the outset. One theme is the resilience of established ways of doing business in the MHW, revolving around doing the necessary groundwork with potential stakeholders and veto players in deliberative councils and the Diet. Another is the interaction between elite career bureaucrats and political leaders. The complexion of electoral contests has changed significantly over precisely the time period that I studied, and that is part of what makes examining the political back story so interesting and important. A third is the organizing question: why have changes in work–family policies been so slow, compromised and vestigial?

A more complicated approach to consultation

The moment in late 1999 when the LDP and the MHW recognized that they had to give in to the demands of the Kōmeitō for a more generous child allowance program represents a political turning point in Japan's work–family policy development. The political environment in which social welfare policies were shaped had fundamentally changed. Systems for moving legislative ideas from agenda setting through passage into law that revolved around close collaboration with the LDP policy coordination institutions and comfortable working relations between the MHW and key LDP supporters had been disrupted. New, unpredictable political competition required the LDP to form coalitions if it was to govern. Wakō Kobayashi, the section head for the Child and Family Planning Section at the MHW at the time of the *jidōteate* battle in late 1999, described the changing political situation poetically: "kazeatari dete-kuru" ("strong winds are blowing"). The political forces unleashed by coalition governments were unsettling the well-established procedures for bringing new policies into being, and making the policy making process more cumbersome, irrational and difficult. Because the views of the MHLW bureaucrats and powerful politicians were increasingly discordant, it was becoming harder to iron out differences between bureaucrats and political leaders. Since coalition governments were likely to be the wave of the future, Kobayashi thought it probable that policy making would require dealing with coalition members flexing their political muscle, with policy initiatives, ideas and agendas coming from more places, and requiring more work to reconcile differing viewpoints and priorities (Kobayashi interview, 1999).

He was of course describing exactly the situation that political reformers were aiming for, a bureaucracy that is more accountable to the political will of elected officials, and, indirectly, to the people. But his affect in describing the changes from the 1955 system – in which wielding political influence meant mastering the channels of power within the LDP – to the much more volatile situation in place by 1999 was one of girding himself for a challenging policy making environment, with a lot more wild cards and unpredictable actors. In his opinion, this was exacerbated by the fact that the increased reliance on privatization, deregulation and administrative reform gave the bureaucracy fewer levers of power to wield than in the past (Kobayashi interview, 1999).

The child allowance policy reforms of 1999, 2007 and 2010 all involved multi-sided negotiations with multiple coalition members and veto players: Kōmeitō was the LDP's coalition partner in 1999 and in 2007, and in 2010 the DPJ was the ruling party, trying to pass decisive spending increases that would put an end to Japan's reputation for being a family policy laggard. This policy area helped me see that multi-sided political negotiations and greater uncertainty were transforming the national-level policy making process in ways that extended beyond the child allowance issue. In another late 1999 interview, a professor of social welfare at Sophia University in Tokyo, who had worked for the MHW for eleven years, expressed profound respect for the intelligence and efficiency of bureaucrats. He contrasted it with the "debased" political debate carried on by party politicians and the public. But he also acknowledged that there had been a shift away from the inflexible, unresponsive approach to leadership used by bureaucrats before the LDP lost its vise-like grip over Diet politics. They could no longer act as though they didn't need to listen to anyone else's views and could simply use *shingikai* (deliberative councils) as rubber stamps for the policies they had already decided upon. In the new climate, the bureaucrats had to be more open and responsive, cultivating different kinds of political support and responding to a variety of political pressures (Amino interview, 1999).

My impressions of a nascent move away from an approach to policy making based on quiet consultations and deal-making, toward a more unpredictable, multi-sided approach that ministry officials were less able to control, were confirmed in a later conversation I had with Tomomi Hihara. Hihara worked for the MHLW for twenty-two years before retiring to take a job as a researcher at a health policy research institute. She told me in a 2011 interview that her senior colleagues at the ministry had talked about how it was easier for MHW to accomplish policy goals when the LDP was the sole governing party.[38] Under the 1955 system, the policy making process involved working closely with the LDP policy leaders and organizations, including the "welfare tribe" and the General Affairs Committee. One could talk with this relatively limited, manageable group of political leaders, gauge their responses, and make sure any reservations or objections were discussed and resolved before submitting a bill to the Diet. This careful vetting of bills with key interest groups, legislators and leadership groups more or less insured positive consideration of the bill or report in question.[39] But now, Hihara explained, the policy process is more complicated. There are more steps to go through, and more parties and points of view to listen to and try to accommodate. It takes more time and trouble to do a competent job of bringing along the different political actors to support particular bills (Hihara interview, 2011).

In addition to the fact that coalition governments have become the norm, the DPJ led the government from 2009 until 2012. Both these developments have made the process of consultation more complicated. On top of that, Hihara believes the situation was exacerbated by the fact that the MHLW bureaucrats had lost the public's trust due to issues related to waste and corruption. In a universe of limited financial support, the MHLW does not have many choices left with respect to how to accomplish its policy goals. Although the surfeit of old people insures plenty of support for national health and pension programs, Hihara thinks support for childcare is relatively weak (Hihara interview, 2011).

[38] I interviewed Hihara twice, once in 1999 when she was working for the Childcare Section of the Child and Family Bureau at MHW; and again in 2011, after she had retired from the MHLW and was working for the Institute for Health Economics and Policy.

[39] Similarly, a conversation with a senior researcher, Saimura Jun, at the Japan Child–Family Interdisciplinary Research Institute (日本子ども家庭総合研究所) who had also worked for the MHW for several years confirmed my sense that established ways of doing business were slowly fading away at the end of the 1990s. When I asked how MHW bureaucrats convinced legislators to pass bills they favored, he told me that the standard way they did business was through "nemawashi" (doing groundwork), by engaging in appropriate interactions with political leaders whose support would be needed to push proposals through the Diet. Presumably these interactions consisted of friendly conversations intended to express respect and keep Diet members informed of a bill's progress, although Saimura's description evoked an old boys' network, while Hihara's sounded more like careful, nuanced explanation and sharing of reservations. Saimura's imagery reflects the settled ways of doing business that grew up around the era of LDP dominance (Saimura interview, 1999).

Hihara repeatedly expressed frustration with a tendency to blame bureaucrats for not being able to address persistent problems effectively, like long waiting lists for childcare. Bureaucrats are not insensitive to, or out to subvert, the will of the people: they *should* listen to the people's voice. The problem is, it is not always easy to figure out exactly what the people's express will is. Thus the people voted overwhelmingly for the DPJ in 2009, but the election did not provide an unambiguous mandate that the public would support raising the consumption tax from 5 to 10 percent or other ways to raise money to pay for policy expansions. Hihara repeatedly expressed frustration with scenarios in which political leaders come up with new ideas and goals, and ask bureaucrats to bring these goals into effect without providing the necessary resources. She stated that "Sometimes the best response a bureaucrat in this situation can make is to say 'this is the best we can do right now, and if you want more than that, come up with the necessary resources to pay for the goals you want us to pursue'" (Hihara interview, 2011, my translation). Her frustration seemed to derive from feeling she and her fellow bureaucrats were being blamed for not being able to accomplish what had been asked when the means for doing so were simply not available (Hihara interview, 2011).

The policy process is more fractious than it used to be, with career bureaucrats less able to explain bills and garner support from a Diet that is more divided and harder to control. But Hihara reminded me that the divisions and disagreements that are part of the current process are not necessarily a bad thing. For example, she mentioned that the bureaucrats from the welfare side of the MHLW support mothers taking parental leaves, while those from the labor side support building up the supply of childcare so that mothers can return to work quickly after giving birth. She thinks this kind of difference of opinion can be constructive, and lead to more synthetic, creative ways of thinking about policies, and perhaps to better solutions (Hihara interview, 2011).

Tomiko Okazaki, the member of the House of Councilors from Miyagi appointed by DPJ Prime Minister Hatoyama to be the minister in charge of low fertility countermeasures in September 2009, provided a fascinating counterpoint to Hihara's irritation at being asked to accomplish policy goals with inadequate resources.[40] Councilor Okazaki offered insightful analyses of childcare and child allowances, and discussed relationships between politicians and permanent bureaucrats at length. She began our interview by reminding me of the importance of gender equality and work–family harmonization issues for the DPJ. These were the issues the DPJ campaigned on, and their credibility hinged on being able to make substantial progress on them. She and other DPJ leaders saw the permanent bureaucracy as an obstacle to bringing about the political agenda that the DPJ favored for dealing with low-fertility issues.

---

[40] She served in this post for four months, stepping down in January 2010.

In Councilor Okazaki's view, the voters expressed their desire for change by strongly backing the DPJ in the 2009 election. Political leaders have to be responsive to the people's will if they want to be (re)elected, and they are judged by their ability to enact the policies and positions they ran on. But bureaucrats are not elected or subject to changing political moods, and not likely to be as concerned as the political leaders with responding to the people's will. The gap between the political leadership and the MHLW widened after 2009. As Councilor Okazaki put it, "After fifty years of LDP rule, the voters were fed up and voted for the DPJ in 2009. But because of the long dominance of the LDP, it is difficult to change the entrenched interests and the power of bureaucrats who have long worked with the LDP and its leadership" (Okazaki interview, 2011, my translation).

In other words, the DPJ had staked its political fortunes on addressing low-fertility issues, and promised to introduce more effective and innovative work–family policies. But they faced pushback from the MHLW, whose bureaucrats had developed a reputation for frequently prevailing in policy debates. This influence was rooted in the fact that senior MHLW bureaucrats had long cultivated close, mutually beneficial relationships with LDP leaders. Given that the DPJ was trying to make its reputation around innovative work–family policies, DPJ leaders were keen to clip the wings of the MHLW by increasing the power of the political leadership over career bureaucrats, and the ministry was resisting the DPJ's efforts to exercise greater control.

More general observations

Moving beyond discussions of how specific policy issues were debated and decided, I conclude this chapter with some more general considerations. Scholars of Japanese work–family policies note that worry about Japan turning into an old people's country was crucial for pushing work–family policies onto the policy agenda and building support for the Angel Plan and other measures (Peng, 2000, 2002; Lambert, 2007). Yet, despite the growing sense of crisis and electoral changes that favor median voters over special interests, reforms in work–family policies have been halting. This is not what one would expect from a competent and resilient state policy machinery. So what explains why change has been so slow and hesitant?

Some of the reasons for halting responses despite an acute sense of crisis are apparent. From the late 1990s to the present, bureaucrats have been coping with a situation in which they have less leverage and cannot exert the same influence over policy making that they did in the 1980s and early 1990s. There have been a number of tricky political cleavages with which they had to reckon: Kōmeitō's concern with increasing child allowances, *jidōteate*, in order to benefit its lower-middle-class base vs. the LDP's concern for its upper-middle-class constituency; left-wing public day care teachers' unions pitted against influential groups representing private childcare centers and demands for cost cutting; urban areas where childcare shortages were extreme vs. rural ones where centers were undersubscribed; resistance from employers to laws that would force them to keep positions open for women taking a year of childcare leave, and so on. Japan's demographic and financial situation (its declining population; a shrinking proportion of working-age, contributing members of society having to pay taxes to support a ballooning cohort of elderly people; the collapse of the bubble economy in 1989 and the stuttering economy since then) has also presented serious challenges. In addition to political cleavages and economic crisis, I think there are four other reasons for ineffective policy responses in this area, related to cultural values, conflict between political leaders and bureaucrats, difficulty raising taxes to fund expansive new programs, and the inherent tensions involved in relying on the corporate welfare state. I address each in turn.

First, there is still a strong consensus behind two conservative cultural norms: not having children out of wedlock, and mothers staying home to take care of their children until they are three years old. Single mothers and single parent headed households are frowned upon and uncommon, and almost all babies are born to married couples. It is worth noting that high-fertility countries like France, Sweden and the United States also have high out-of-wedlock birth rates, and the decision to have children is often made before the parents decide to marry, or without them ever marrying. Culturally, this is unlikely to change in Japan. Marriage is a precursor to childbirth; very few 35-year-old Japanese women are deciding to have babies on their own. But as more young people delay and forgo marriage, these decisions (often driven by poor job prospects and the tendency to live at home with one's parents longer) have an impact on fertility rates. Expectations of mother-care lead women to want to take a few years off while their babies are small. They may also feel that there are pleasures and milestones they can only experience if they are hands-on mothers, and that their role in childrearing is crucial to getting their children off to a good start.

Such cultural values are not an explanation for underdeveloped or compromised family policies so much as an explanation for young people making decisions that delay and reduce their fertility. They marry later or not at all; they start having babies later; they work a few more years before getting pregnant; and women who feel that it is important to spend the crucial years of infancy at home with their children decide not to take a one-year leave so that they can stay home longer, even though this obviously imperils their ability to hold full-time regular jobs in the future. This is not just an imposed cultural "thou shalt," but a deeply internalized hope and desire for many women. Not only do they want to be full-time mothers for a stretch, but many feel like balancing baby care and a full-time job is daunting.

This kind of expectation of intensive mother-care is fine for families that can afford to live on one salary, but, as the job market has become harsher, more women and men have been forced to take non-regular (part-time, contract or temporary) employment. Such jobs pay badly and do not include various job-related benefits or guaranteed raises and promotions, increasing the financial pressures on young people and leading many to postpone marriage and having children. The difficult job market has led more women to want to work for a few years longer before marriage, or to devote themselves to their careers instead of marrying. Japanese women continue to pay an extremely high cost for having children and staying home with them for a year or more, as labor market practices punish workers who do not continuously devote themselves to their jobs.

Second, in recent years the political leadership and the bureaucratic machinery have not worked smoothly with each other, as the foregoing discussion of children's allowances and the paired Hihara–Okazaki interviews illustrate. Although changes in electoral incentives have enhanced the power of political parties like Kōmeitō and the DPJ and made it easier for them to push for work–family policy changes, some of the institutional power holders that shape policy in this area (career bureaucrats, powerful business interests) have not been eager to respond to these new policy agendas.

Again, this is a little odd: given the prominence of low-fertility issues in Japan in the 1990s and 2000s, one might have expected the MHLW to see the low fertility crisis as an opportunity for expanding its policy responsibilities and budget, and to take a more entrepreneurial approach to expanding the childcare system and pushing for more vigorous enforcement of the paid leave policy for working mothers.[41] But that is not what I observed: my impression was that bureaucrats viewed the move away from LDP dominance toward a more open electoral system in which leaders were more responsive to unorganized voters as complicating the standard avenues for communication and influence that they had developed, not as an opportunity for expanding the purview of the MHLW. Around the turn of the twenty-first century, officials were trying to deal with greater uncertainties and more confusing avenues for policy influence than those that prevailed under the 1955 system, when ministry bureaucrats knew how to communicate with the LDP leadership in the Diet, and understood that their job was to convince the LDP to go along with their views about proper policy (Kobayashi interview, 1999). Rather than embracing new possibilities and a weightier profile in the overall government, MHLW bureaucrats seemed to be cautiously feeling their way with respect to learning how to work the system.

---

[41] Indeed, Peng claims that the Child and Family Bureau within the MHW saw its objectives as coinciding in a timely way with the demographic interests of the Population Problems Bureau, which would pave "the way to interbureau policy consensus" around support for expanded child welfare issues (2002, 425–6).

In addition to the more fractious relationship between the career bureaucrats and the political leadership, a third challenge to developing effective family support policies in Japan has been difficulty finding the money to pay for expanded policies. Japan needs to spend more if it wants to get rid of the long waiting lists of children who are queued up in large cities for spaces in high-quality, affordable licensed childcare centers. For a long time, the inability to raise taxes for fear of arousing the ire of the voters has limited the adaptability of the Japanese welfare state. An increase in the consumption tax from 5 to 8 percent was finally approved in October 2013, and took effect in April 2014.

But a key question remains: *which* median voters are making their voices heard? There is much more support for pensions, long-term care and health care – old and middle-aged people's issues – than there is for spending more to pay for childcare centers – a young people's issue. When I think about Hihara's comments about democratic accountability and the lack of a clear mandate to raise taxes in order to pay for expanded childcare services, it strikes me that this may be a vicious cycle related to population aging. Of course old people support funding old people's services, but as the cohort of younger voters shrinks, their piece of the fiscal pie (as determined by voter mandates) is likely to shrink too.

As much as Japan talks about modernizing its family policies, and as essential as this is to overcoming women's reluctance to have children, it is not clear the state has the financial or political wherewithal to fund major expansions in childcare facilities. Bureaucrats often engage in trying to accomplish policy goals without much budgetary expansion – for example, by moving toward more private childcare centers and a less expensive teaching workforce as a way to expand childcare spaces, or by taking money from dependent-child tax deductions to fund increased child allowances. But Hihara's comments illustrate how frustrating it is to try to accomplish ambitious goals at the political leadership's request with inadequate financial support. Another example of trying to accomplish its mission with limited resources is the bureaucracy's orchestration of clever campaigns to educate and persuade corporations and individuals to go along with childcare leave and overtime laws (e.g., Kurumin, Ikumen), in lieu of being able to compel compliance.

Fourth, Japan faces a contradiction between the well-established pattern of relying on private employer-provided benefits and developing functional work–family policies. Several scholars of the Japanese welfare state note the importance of recognizing a broad "range of policies that cushion workers and citizens from market forces, including job protections, regulations that limit competition, financial system interventions, and public works spending." For example, policies that encourage employers not to lay off workers, and ones that help marginal companies eke their way through tough economic times, protect workers' jobs, and their access to corporate welfare, and thus offer them the same income security as unemployment policies whereby the government writes them checks when they are laid off (Schoppa, 2010b, 97; see also Estevez-Abe, 2008, 30–7; and Steinmo, 2010). Recognizing that employment-based benefits provide for workers' welfare, the government provides incentives to encourage private employers to provide for their workers' well-being through measures like company housing, job security, lifetime employment, and dependent child and spouse subsidies to the primary wage earner. Yet some of these policies, especially ones that support the male-breadwinner system, undercut governmental work–family policies. Many employees provide a dependent-spouse benefit as long as the secondary earner, usually the wife, does not earn more than ¥1.03 million (or roughly $10,000) a year, reinforcing a pattern of women working for low wages in marginal part-time jobs. Women who need or want to earn more than this face a huge disincentive from the private welfare state. Similarly, the legally mandated one-year paid childcare leave, aimed at getting women to return to work full-time after having a child, is also subverted by corporate employment practices, which discriminate against workers who interrupt their workforce participation – for example, women who take time off to raise children.

Japan's lean welfare state relies on employment-based welfare measures to take the place of more conventional public welfare programs, and, in such a regime, protective measures to keep companies from going under and laying off workers are a key strategy for insuring the welfare of workers and families. As Sven Steinmo puts it, "The simple truth is that employers *are* the social safety net in Japan: When unemployment rises social welfare declines" (Steinmo, 2010, 134). But the labor market in Japan places a premium on firm-specific skills that require significant upfront investment in workers. This makes employers reluctant to hire women for permanent career-track jobs because they are likely to quit upon marriage or childbirth (Estevez-Abe, 2007). Part of the thinking is that women are less committed to the workforce, likely to quit and spend a significant stretch at home raising children, and therefore not worth a heavy investment in training, or expensive and inconvenient accommodations like paid parenting leaves.

Note the self-fulfilling, systemic quality of employment practices here: most women are pressured to quit when their first child is born, and workplace expectations are not compatible with being the primary parent of a young child. Women who decide to have children and stay home for a few years generally return to work after their children start school, typically working at low-paid part-time jobs in order not to exceed the threshold for their husbands to receive dependent-spouse benefits. While German policy makers successfully argued that policies to help women return to work quickly after having babies would spur economic growth, private corporate welfare and labor practices in Japan send the opposite message, relegating women, especially mothers, to low-paid jobs. In effect, Japan has decided it does not need to use the productive capability of women to help it compete in the global economy, a move Steinmo thinks is very costly, both because women's talents are too valuable to waste and because barring them from good jobs keeps Japan's demographic time bomb ticking (Steinmo, 2010, 140–2). Prime Minister Shinzo Abe, elected in December 2012, has been touting the importance of encouraging more women to work, hoping to increase the female labor force participation and boost Japan's economic productivity, but his speeches say nothing about the long-established practice of shunting women into marginal jobs, and little about how he will bring about the work–family policies needed to enable more women to work. Until these issues are addressed forthrightly, there is good reason to be skeptical about Japan's ability to back strong work–family policies.

This chapter charts key developments in American family support policies, explaining how certain assumptions and approaches came to be taken for granted. In contrast to the other three countries we have examined, US policies are premised on the notion that childrearing and work–family conflicts are the responsibility of families and individuals, best left to the private realm of familial choice and responsibility and market-provided services that families pay for. American family support policies draw on deep-rooted traditions and policy repertoires, including poor relief, maternalism, a strong presumption of personal responsibility and notions of deservingness that are tied to class, race and gender, modest government spending, and reliance on purchasing care services in the marketplace. I take up these topics in greater detail below.

The development of approaches to protecting children and mothers

The idea that state support for families is tinctured with blame goes back to the founding of the United States and the tradition of poor relief that threw jobless adults into poor houses and compelled them to work. If indigent parents were not deemed to be raising their offspring according to prevailing norms of morality and respectability, children could be removed from their parents' care and put up for adoption, fostering or apprenticeship. Almshouses, orphanages and the Child Saving Movement of the nineteenth century, which resulted in 100,000 poor and working-class children from the east coast being placed with "suitable" rural families, are part of this early history of outdoor relief whereby the poor were expected to work (Davidson, 1994).

Despite this dismal start, political arguments about child and maternal welfare and family support were gaining traction by the early twentieth century. Virtually all the states adopted mothers' pensions between 1911 and 1931. The women's groups and social reformers who fought for passage of such laws wanted to help widowed mothers maintain custody of their children by providing public aid that was "intended to be honorable and adequate, a

147

predictable salary of sorts for public service," similar in kind to the public services performed by army officers or school teachers (Skocpol, 1992, 465). Prior to the passage of mothers' pensions laws, fatherless poor families had few good options: children could be placed in orphanages or foster homes, or the children and mother could work at low wages to support the family, or they could seek handouts or charity (Skocpol, 1992, 166).

Although some states considered extending support to unmarried mothers, over 80 percent of those receiving mothers' pensions in 1931 were widows, and almost none were unmarried mothers (Skocpol, 1992, 469). Even at that, the pensions were often administered and funded begrudgingly: recipients were regulated closely by social workers who visited them to assess the adequacy of their homes and childrearing and to give them advice about hygiene, parenting and the kind of work they could do that was compatible with receiving a stipend. Even widows who were deemed "worthy" were often given such small amounts that they or their children had to work to support their families. Because funds were limited, eligible women were often asked to wait for long periods of time before being enrolled for a pension, or were held up to judgment about how deserving their families were (Skocpol, 1992, 468–79). Organized women's groups played a crucial role in the first third of the twentieth century in arguing that well-brought-up children were a public good deserving of support, and pushing states to pass mothers' pensions laws. This is noteworthy even though the mothers' pensions were poorly funded and receipt of such support often required the beneficiaries to undergo minute inspection of their homes and mothering styles.

The maternalist leanings of the early American welfare state can be seen at the federal level with the establishment of the Children's Bureau in 1912. Julia Lathrop, the first chief of the Children's Bureau, worked tirelessly to build support among women's and consumers' groups for the projects the Bureau undertook.[1] Lathrop proposed a maternal and infant health education program that would be administered at the state and local levels and paid for through matching federal and state funds. The legislation, co-sponsored by Senator Morris Sheppard (D-TX) and Representative Horace Mann Towner (R-IA), aimed to promote maternal and infant health through universal preventive-care education. The Sheppard–Towner Act (STA), officially titled the Federal Act for the Promotion of the Welfare and Hygiene of Maternity and Infancy, passed

---

[1] These included compiling statistics on births and infant and maternal mortality; publicizing links between mortality rates and husbands' salaries and women's early return to work; encouraging women's groups to write letters to members of Congress to protest a threatened refusal to increase the Bureau's funding in 1914 (the resulting flood of mail kept the funding level where Lathrop wanted it); sponsoring a "Baby Week" in 1916 and 1917 to educate communities about infant care; sponsoring the "Year of the Child" in 1918; and a White House Conference on Standards of Child Welfare in 1919 (Skocpol, 1992, 490–6).

in 1921. The law was administered by the Children's Bureau, greatly augmenting its budget, visibility and mission as a federal agency devoted to women's and children's welfare (Skocpol, 1992, 480–1).

But in 1927, six years after passing the STA, Congress decided to rescind the Act, partly in response to the rise of groups opposed to it, especially organized medicine. The American Medical Association launched a campaign attacking government's role in educating women across the nation about maternal and infant health, arguing that private doctors could provide pediatric care without a mandate from the federal government. The termination of the STA marked a turning point toward making maternal and child health the private responsibility of prudent families (and their doctors) and away from the notion that well children are a collective good.

The United States enacted Old Age and Survivors' and Dependents' Insurance and the Aid to Dependent Children (ADC) program as part of the Social Security Act (SSA) of 1935. The SSA extended protections to women by giving working women a pension upon retirement,[2] providing health services to eligible pregnant women and mothers of eligible children, paying a lump-sum death benefit to survivors of insured workers, and offering public assistance to children under age sixteen who did not have "breadwinning parental support and who continued to live with a relative engaged in their full-time care" (Mink, 1995, 130). But the social security provisions treated women differently according to whether they were widows or were single mothers for some other reason: widows received pension support as an entitlement, without having to show need to be paid, whereas the ADC program benefitted poor children whose mothers were staying home to raise them only if they could prove need and demonstrate that they were providing their children a wholesome home environment (Mink, 1995, 137). ADC was left to the states to administer (if they chose to participate in the program at all), and many states used illegitimacy as a way of deciding that mothers – especially African American mothers – were not providing an adequate moral environment for their children and should not receive assistance (Mink, 1995, 144–5; Gilens, 1999, 105). State discretion over funding and eligibility rules allowed many southern states to spend far less than the national average of $13 per eligible child per month in 1940; Martin Gilens reports payments to black children in Arkansas of only $3.52, and in South Carolina of just over $4 per child (Gilens, 1999, 105). African American families were poorly integrated into this New Deal family security policy: even though large numbers of black families were unemployed and in need of assistance, in 1939 over 89 percent of the families receiving assistance from ADC were white (Mink, 1995, 140–1).

---

[2] However, many jobs done primarily by women were excluded from this provision, e.g. clerical and sales work, teaching and nursing, and domestic and personal service.

In addition to ADC allowing the states to set up racial distinctions between deserving white and undeserving black mothers and children, many New Deal welfare programs recognized and institutionalized distinctions between male earners and female dependents. Thus, unemployment insurance and pensions were funded through payroll taxes and paid out as a matter of established right with no requirement to demonstrate need, whereas programs like survivors' benefits and ADC assisted women in their capacity as wives of deceased workers or mothers of children living in poverty without the support of a wage-earning father. Their claim to aid as dependents was written into the way the benefits were administered, just as men's independence and deserv-ingness were written into the way pensions and unemployment benefits were structured (Fraser and Gordon, 1997). Claims brought under the second, means-tested tier of welfare benefits were more likely to be scrutinized minutely, and claimants to be viewed as less deserving than those who "earned" their pensions by paying into the system, despite the fact that Social Security pensions were also redistributive welfare payments judged to be important for avoiding poverty and preserving dignity in old age. As a result, funds to pay for pensions have been largely immune from political attack and budget-cutting axes, while funds for ADC and its policy heirs, Aid to Families with Dependent Children (AFDC) and Temporary Aid to Needy Families (TANF), and, more distantly, Medicaid and Food Stamps / SNAP,[3] have often been attacked by political opponents and subjected to budget cuts.

Racialized opposition to welfare policies

In terms of overall welfare efforts, by the mid-1990s the United States had three main areas of welfare provision: education (about 25 percent of all govern-ment social spending); social insurance programs like Social Security pensions, Medicare, retirement programs for public employees, workmen's compensa-tion and unemployment insurance (47 percent), and means-tested programs for the poor, like ADC, Food Stamps, Medicaid, Supplemental Security Income (SSI) and housing assistance (17 percent) (data are from Gilens, 1999, 15–16). Given the relatively small amount that goes for means-tested antipoverty mea-sures, it is striking that these programs attract so much opposition and antipathy in the United States. Why is this, and what does it tell us about the attitudes toward welfare state measures there?

---

[3] Medicaid provides medical care to those who do not have medical insurance through their employment and who meet income thresholds. SNAP, Supplemental Nutrition Assistance Pro-gram, is the new acronym for the Food Stamps program, which provides money to families that need help with paying for adequate amounts and kinds of food. They are family support policies that share the general public dislike and reluctance to fund that ADC/AFDC and TANF programs have experienced.

One of the most prominent lightning rods for public disapproval has been the Aid to Dependent Children / Aid to Families with Dependent Children program (renamed in 1962). The program grew slowly from the late 1930s through the mid-1960s,[4] then nearly tripled in size between 1965 and 1975, from a program that benefitted 2.2 percent to one that served 6.4 percent of all American families. Its budget also mushroomed, growing from $10 billion in 1965 to $27 billion in 1975, although average payments declined significantly over this period, with assistance spread more thinly to cover more poor people (Gilens, 1999, 19). As AFDC increased in size, the program began to serve a larger percentage of African Americans.[5] The recognition of poverty as a first-order social problem in the 1960s (including the publication of Michael Harrington's book *The Other America* in 1962, and President Johnson's declaration of an unconditional "war on poverty" in his State of the Union speech in 1964) led to the commitment of more federal resources to programs like AFDC, job-training, housing assistance and early childhood education (Head Start, a means-tested preschool program for at-risk children, was launched in 1965). The Civil Rights Movement and urban riots of the mid-1960s made the poverty and discrimination faced by blacks apparent, and also increased the racialization of poverty in news media depictions.

Gilens argues that the striking degree of opposition to welfare (understood as cash payments to able-bodied adults) among Americans is related to media coverage in the mid-1960s that depicted undeserving poor people as mostly black and unwilling to work to support themselves and their children. African Americans have never been a majority of AFDC recipients, but the media began to publish and broadcast a large number of stories that portrayed poverty and problems with anti-poverty programs as issues particularly affecting blacks in America's inner cities.

Largely because of the construction of blacks as lazy and undeserving in media portrayals and public discourse, many whites came to reject the story that welfare payments are temporary assistance that allows people who have hit a rough patch to get back on their feet, instead seeing welfare as a trap that keeps people down by undercutting their desire to work hard (Gilens, 1999, 172). Depictions of welfare recipients as black, lazy, not working and partaking of a "culture of welfare" related to sexual promiscuity, drug use, teenage and out-of-wedlock births and welfare scamming were underscored by a number of influential books that argued that welfare sets up perverse

---

[4] Gilens notes that average monthly payments grew from $360 in 1940 to $581 (in constant dollars) in 1960, and the number of families on the ADC rolls went from 370,000 in 1940 to 800,000 in 1960 (1999, 18).

[5] In the 1930s, about 12% of recipients of ADC assistance were black. The largest proportion of black families receiving AFDC was 42% in 1973, falling to about 35% in 1995 (Gilens, 1999, 106).

incentives for recipients to have children out of wedlock, avoid marriage, refrain from identifying the fathers of babies born out of wedlock, and keep having children in order to increase welfare payments (Murray, 1984; Mead, 1986; also see Fraser and Gordon, 1997, who describe and critique this literature).

In sum, maternalism and racism are both important legacies of family support policies in the United States. As we saw with widows' pensions in the 1910s, the Sheppard–Townsend Act of 1923, and the Aid to Dependent Children program in 1935 and its heirs, states frequently agreed to go along with national legislation as long as they could exercise discretion in implementing the policies, often in ways that discriminated against or excluded African Americans.[6] The pattern of national legislation premised on partial funding and implementation at the state level reflects the decentralized federal system in the United States. It also reflects the fact that race was an issue for southern legislators who exerted leverage to make sure that policies like ADC could be administered at the state level in ways that pressured black mothers to work for low pay as domestics or agricultural workers to support themselves and their children.

The notion that the state should support mothers to stay home and raise their own children was never whole-heartedly accepted in the United States: white mothers and children were seen in a more sympathetic light than black ones. When TANF superseded AFDC in 1996, the notion that children deserve to be cared for by their mothers was abandoned altogether, as the law requires all mothers to work to support their children. There is now a lifetime limit of five years of cash assistance, and after that mothers are expected to earn enough to support their families.

Core work–family support policies – childcare, tax payments and parental leaves – have been shaped by some of the same class, gender and race assumptions and biases of these early policies to support mothers and children. The rest of this chapter focuses on the development of childcare measures, tax expenditures and parental leaves.

Childcare

Childcare practices in nineteenth-century America included indenturing children with other families, boarding out children, baby farms, day nurseries and homes for infants – all practices associated with poverty, family crisis and the need for uplift (Michel, 1999, 47). The early twentieth-century women's groups that pushed for widows' pensions and the Sheppard–Townsend Act were not

---

[6] Many African Americans and women were de facto excluded from coverage under the Social Security Act because jobs disproportionately held by blacks or women were exempted from social insurance protections like unemployment insurance or pensions (e.g., personal service, domestic, casual, clerical and sales work, teaching, nursing and agricultural work) (Mink, 1995, 130, 137; Glenn, 2012).

eager to support childcare; indeed, they supported policies that would enable women to stay home and care for their own children, not ones that would help them work outside the home. Childcare was understood from early on as a form of social welfare rather than being seen as a public responsibility like universal public education, crucial for enhancing the human capital of the next generation (Michel, 1999, 48–9).

The first national-level childcare policies developed in the crucible of the Great Depression in the 1930s; they aimed at promoting child welfare and creating jobs. In response to widespread poverty and unemployment, the Federal Emergency Relief Administration (FERA, which later became the Works Progress Administration, WPA) set up Emergency Nursery Schools (ENS) as a job creation program. Although the Schools emphasized their educational mission, and the ENS program was advised by the National Advisory Committee on Emergency Nursery Schools, ENS were inextricably connected to the emergency relief agencies (FERA and the WPA) and the need to create jobs and serve low-income parents (Michel, 1999, 120–5). Because the Women's Bureau was not anxious to push for childcare services so that women could work, the program was adopted by the Children's Bureau, and the Schools were oriented toward child welfare rather than pursuing educational or labor policy goals.

Some 1,900 Emergency Nursery Schools were set up between 1933 and 1935, serving about 75,000 children in forty-three states (Michel, 1999, 119). By 1942, their number had shrunk to 944 schools just as the need to develop childcare services for the children of defense workers was becoming urgent with the onset of American involvement in World War II. The 1940 Lanham Act provided federal funds for community needs in war-boom areas, including child day care centers (Tuttle, 1995, 96). The Federal Works Agency (FWA), which was charged with supervising Lanham Act funds, urged expansion of group childcare facilities, but the Children's Bureau, the US Office of Education and the Federal Security Agency lobbied against group childcare outside the home on the grounds that it would undermine parental authority. Even in the throes of the national mobilization for World War II, legislation was proposed to curtail federal involvement in funding childcare facilities. The Bill was defeated in mid-1943 and Congress appropriated extra funds to build childcare centers, since without childcare it would be difficult to recruit and retain women for industrial jobs (Tuttle, 1995, 97–8). A coalition of labor unions, community leaders, women members of Congress and FWA officials joined together to appeal for funding to expand the wartime child day care program and by spring of 1944, day care center enrollments were rising rapidly, reaching a peak in July 1944 with 129,357 children enrolled in 3,102 centers (Tuttle, 1995, 98–9). The Lanham Act day care centers eventually received federal funds totaling $52 million, with states and localities contributing matching funds. One of the important lessons of the Lanham Act was that in a national emergency the federal government could see childcare as a public responsibility and commit to supporting subsidized care for children (Tuttle, 1995, 99).

The need for childcare to enable women to work in war-time industries was also met by several private corporations that set up nursery facilities near factories (for example, Douglas Aircraft in Santa Monica, California; Curtiss-Wright in Buffalo, New York; and two Kaiser shipyards in Portland, Oregon). The Kaiser centers each served about 1,000 children at their peak in September 1944, and demonstrated the ability of private employers to provide quality center-based childcare services when faced with the need to accommodate large numbers of essential workers. These centers were often described as innovative in design and well staffed and run (Tuttle, 1995, 101; also see Michel, 1999).

In addition to public and privately run day care centers, in 1942 the federal government offered $400,000 to the US Office of Education and the Children's Bureau as seed money to promote and establish Extended School Services (ESS) for school-age children of working mothers.[7] ESS programs operated from 6.30 or 7.00 a.m. until 6.30 or so in the evening, covering summer vacations and in some cases Saturdays. Large numbers of children were cared for through these programs: in mid-1943 the Office of Education estimated that 320,000 children were being served, and more than that by the war's end (Tuttle, 1995, 104). The ESS programs were well publicized, conducted in an innovative, do-it-yourself spirit, and fairly comprehensive in terms of offering extended-hour care and other services (meals, health care) for children from ages six to twelve.

The federal government's mobilizations to address the emergencies of the Great Depression and World War II demonstrate that, when a crisis leads citizens to view women's work as essential, state and private actors can be mobilized to meet childcare needs. Note, however, that, as the national emergency ended and the need for mothers to work abated, funding was abruptly terminated for Lanham Act-funded childcare centers. Concerted lobbying efforts to push for subsidized childcare and government action to provide it have been surprisingly rare since the end of World War II.

Even though women constituted 31 percent of the non-agricultural workforce in 1951–2, childcare was not a front-burner issue in the postwar period, despite the fact that "child care facilities were on the whole overcrowded, discriminatory, costly, and uneven in quality" (Michel, citing a study by the Women's Bureau: 1999, 177). Childcare facilities nationwide received little funding, either through the states and cities, or through charitable sources. Some

---

[7] The ESS program was financed from parents' fees, contributions from community foundations, school districts, state school boards, Lanham Act money and the initial seed money from the federal government, which expired in 1943.

43 percent of childcare was offered through private, commercial nursery schools or centers, which tended to charge more than centers operated through churches, philanthropies or institutions of higher education (Michel, 1999, 177–8).

Even though much of the existing childcare was expensive and of poor quality, few rationales emerged for making the case that childcare deserved national support. Out of the disorganized stew of actors in the postwar era who might have taken an interest in pushing for better childcare policies, middle-class women were notably absent, making it seem as though childcare was primarily an issue for working-class and low-income women. Not even advocates for early childhood education articulated childcare as an enriching experience for "normal" children from "functional" families (Michel, 1999, 190). When the Children's and Women's Bureaus cast around for rationales for pursuing childcare policies, the one that kept resurfacing was the notion of childcare

as a support for working-class and low-income mothers. Although this approach tapped into Americans' traditional eagerness to prevent pauperism by helping the poor help themselves, it created another kind of problem. By ruling out a definition of child care as a universal provision linked to women's right to work, it reinforced the class-based and racial divisions among wage-earning mothers – between those who could, apparently, resolve their child care needs privately, and those who had to turn to the state for help. (Michel, 1999, 191)

Defining childcare as an issue for working-class and poor families attracted support from those who saw childcare as a solution for juvenile delinquency, child neglect and inadequate mothering. But embracing childcare as an approach to remediating children in poverty was a dangerous move, because it undercut the argument that childcare and early childhood education should be services that everyone needs and uses, like state schools. This move hobbled political support for childcare from its inception in the United States.

Another formative development in postwar childcare policy was the change in the US tax code in 1954 to allow working adults, single or married, to deduct up to $600 for childcare as long as its purpose was to permit the taxpayer to be employed (Michel, 1999, 205–6). Michel believes this was the most significant breakthrough in childcare policy in the 1950s, and it represented the single largest federal expenditure for childcare. Of course, tax measures cannot address issues of supply, distribution or quality, which were ignored by members of Congress who assumed that childcare problems would be resolved privately in the market or the family. Indeed, congressional hearings on the childcare tax deduction did not even consider such issues because no childcare advocates were invited to testify at hearings which were controlled by the Republican Party, the majority party in the 1950s. Being excluded from the hearings brought home to advocacy groups like the Child Welfare League of America that they would have to take the initiative in pushing for generously supported high-quality childcare, a point the Women's and Children's Bureaus had long argued (Michel, 1999, 209–10).

Two White House conferences in 1960 helped focus attention on working mothers, childcare and other child welfare and education issues: one a White House Conference on Children and Youth, the other a conference on day care. Building backing for childcare policy, however, was not a matter of orchestrating events or building a broad grassroots movement, as was done for the Civil Rights, women's and anti-Vietnam war movements. Rather, as the number of women working outside the home steadily increased, it required slowly involving groups that recognized the need for more and better childcare. The advocacy coalition that formed around childcare included a variety of women's religious, childcare, early childhood education and labor groups, the same groups that the Women's and Children's Bureaus pulled in to help plan the 1960 White House conference on day care.[8]

Labor Department statistics presented at the 1960 day care conference predicted that increased demand for women's labor by 1970 would fuel increased need for day care, and, indeed, the proportion of mothers with children under age six in the paid labor force rose from 30 percent in 1960 to nearly 60 percent in 1991. Although the number of childcare slots also grew, they did not keep up with demand: in 1990, of the children under age five whose mothers worked for pay, only 38 percent attended childcare centers. Another 20 percent were cared for by home day care providers, and a third were cared for by relatives or unrelated caregivers at home. Furthermore, the quality of care in centers and family day care homes was erratic, with regulation and credentialing weak or nonexistent. Poor quality was also related to the lack of state financial support or regulation of care providers: the United States, unlike France, did not subsidize the social costs (contributions for pensions and health care) of hiring care providers, leaving families scrabbling to find care that they could afford on their salaries. As a result, many childcare providers were paid low wages, and many who provided care from their own homes or worked as nannies received no benefits (Michel, 1999, 229, 236–7).

---

[8] These included the Intercity Council for Day Care (ICC); Christine Heinig, who had been involved in running WPA nursery schools and now worked for the American Association for University Women; representatives of the American Federation of Labor – Congress of Industrial Organizations; the National Association for Nursery Education; the General Federation of Women's Clubs; United Church Women; and the Parent–Teacher Association. Note, however, that organized labor did not uniformly back childcare: a few labor representatives argued in the early 1960s that more childcare was needed as mothers' contributions to household incomes were growing, but this was a departure from the traditional labor union insistence on family wages. Despite the efforts of several mainstream organizations to gain broader acceptance for maternal employment, the federal and most state and local governments ranked day care low on their lists of priorities (Michel, 1999, 220, 223–4).

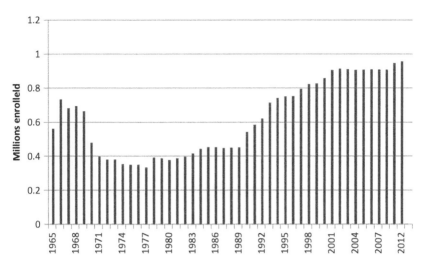

Figure 6.1 Enrollments in Head Start, 1965–2012
Source: Office of Head Start, 2013, 2014.

At the same time as the United States was beginning to recognize that it was facing a childcare crisis, the federal government initiated the Head Start program, a means-tested preschool program that targeted children from poor families. Undertaken in response to President Lyndon Johnson's declaration of a "war on poverty," Head Start started in 1965 as an eight-week summertime pilot program to help children develop skills that would prepare them for kindergarten and elementary school (Office of Head Start 2013). After its first two years of operation, Head Start (HS) developed into a year-round program to provide childcare and a pre-kindergarten educational program for children ages three through five. Early Head Start (EHS), which provides care for children from birth to age three, was initiated under the Clinton administration in 1995. In contrast to the part-day schedule and educational mission of Head Start in its early years, both Head Start and Early Head Start now provide longer hours of care that enable mothers to work. As many as 92 percent of EHS children attend more than six hours a day for a four- or five-day week, while about half of the HS children attend for this long. Head Start is the larger program, serving a cumulative enrollment of 946,000 in 2011–12, while Early Head Start had a cumulative enrollment of 167,500 for that year (Office of Head Start, 2012).

As Figures 6.1 and 6.2 show, variations in Head Start enrollments roughly correspond to Republican or Democrat control of the White House, with the periods of growth in enrollment corresponding to the presidencies of

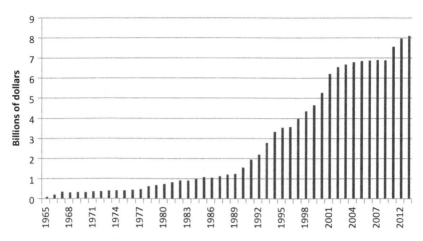

Figure 6.2 Appropriations for Head Start, 1965–2013
Source: Office of Head Start, 2013, 2014.

three Democrats, Johnson (1965–9), Clinton (1993–2001) and Obama (2009–present). Growth in funding increased steeply from 1992 to 2002, flattening out during Republican George W. Bush's term (2001–9).[9]

Head Start is an example of one of two typical patterns one sees in American work–family policy development: a targeted policy aimed at providing remedial care for children from needy families. The other is tax expenditures aimed at helping middle-class families pay for care choices that suit their tastes, budgets and needs, which I discuss later in this chapter. That said, the United States has occasionally managed to mobilize organized interests and congressional sponsors to pass comprehensive childcare legislation that transcended both of these modes. The most notable instance of this since World War II was the Comprehensive Child Development Act (CCDA) of 1971, a Bill that would have provided childcare services to a broad range of families. Under the CCDA, low-income families would have received free childcare, and others would have been charged on a sliding scale. A broad group of supporters, including feminists, labor leaders, civil rights and welfare activists, and early childhood educators argued that it would have a positive effect on racism and child development, and the Bill passed both houses of Congress. Debate over the measure reflected enormous polarization. At one extreme, feminists and progressives demanded 24-hour day care centers, connected childcare to women's right to economic independence, and argued that childcare facilities

---

[9] Despite modest growth in the Head Start and Early Head Start programs in recent years, the first only serves 40 percent of income-eligible children, and the latter only reaches about 4 percent of eligible infants (National Women's Law Center, 2011).

should be seen as fundamental public services like libraries and state schools. At the other extreme, conservatives argued that universal childcare would bring about Orwellian social engineering reminiscent of the Nazis or communists and produce a "classless" society that would "Sovietize" American youth. In the context of bitter struggles over the use of busing to bring about racial integration in the state schools, anxiety about creating a public service that would mix young children of different races was an important subtext in the debate about the CCDA. President Nixon did not openly discuss race when he vetoed the Act; his veto message relied on more acceptable rhetoric about preserving the American family and opposing increased government services, even likening the CCDA to proto-communist regulation (Michel, 1999, 248, 250–1).

Despite its vociferous opposition to universal childcare, the Nixon administration had no qualms about expanding childcare for the poor in order to push welfare mothers into employment. After blocking the CCDA in 1971, federal childcare assistance moved back to the pattern of providing early childhood education and care to poor families through means-tested programs. Two such laws, Title XX of the Social Security Act, which connected childcare to workfare[10] recipients and "at-risk" populations, and the Aid to Day Care Centers Act (ADCC), which increased funding in order to raise standards in public day care centers, passed in 1974 and 1976 (Michel, 1999, 251–2).

Non-poor parents were increasingly left to rely on private alternatives, leading to the proliferation of various types of private sector childcare and a widening gap between publicly supported childcare services for the poor, and private, market-based care for the middle class and the wealthy. Michel notes the role tax credits played in fostering the privatization of childcare: "From the mid-1970s through the mid-1980s, a broadening of tax relief to individual parents through the child care credit, along with failed attempts to enforce federal child care regulations, fostered the growth of these alternatives but at the same time widened the gap between public and private provisions and their constituencies" (Michel, 1999, 237).

Childcare legislation again reached the federal agenda in 1987 amid a public dismay about the "childcare crisis" stemming from the burgeoning number of working mothers and lack of high-quality childcare. The Act for Better Child Care was introduced that year. It aimed to address three critical issues – availability, affordability and quality of services – by setting up a federally funded infrastructure for childcare delivery across the nation, and requiring states to comply with minimum standards set by a National Advisory Committee on Child Care Standards (Klein, 1992, 41).

---

[10] Workfare programs required mothers receiving welfare payments to receive job-training and find paying work.

The law that eventually passed in 1991, the Child Care and Development Block Grant Act (which is now commonly known as the Child Care and Development Fund, CCDF) accomplished much less than this. It allocated a modest $732 million for fiscal year 1991 (and somewhat more for following years), one quarter of which was reserved for quality improvement and early childhood services, with the rest available for use at states' discretion. Funding levels were lower than initially called for, and "choice" with respect to childcare providers soon became a mantra: childcare providers of all kinds – religious, voluntary, for-profit and home care – could receive CCDBG money to subsidize childcare services (Klein, 1992, 53–5). National standards for quality were abandoned, and states were given the discretion to set their own standards as long as they covered particular health and safety issues. Congress did in fact pass a childcare law that the president signed, which made the CCDBG more successful than the 1971 Comprehensive Child Development Act. But the Alliance for Better Child Care – a broad coalition consisting of child welfare groups, labor unions, early childhood professionals and the Children's Defense Fund – that lobbied for this law found themselves having to make deep compromises over principles and financial support in order to pass it, a tradeoff common in American work–family policy making and referred to by Anya Bernstein as the "moderation dilemma" (Bernstein, 2001).[11]

Since its passage in 1991, CCDF has supported care for large numbers of children, on the order of almost twice as many children as are enrolled in Head Start (see Figure 6.3). Most CCDF users must pay part of their children's childcare fees; on average, their co-payments come to 6 percent of their monthly income. They receive vouchers from the government to pay for the rest, which must be redeemed at licensed centers (attended by 66 percent of recipient children) or home day cares (24 percent of children), or are used to pay for care in the child's home or group homes (CLASP, 2011).

The gendered and racialized character of American social welfare programs has long been apparent. We saw how many states were reluctant to use widows' pensions in the 1920s to support women who had babies out of wedlock, and particularly black women. We noted that various New Deal programs made assistance to men a matter of entitlement, but designed policies for women that were needs-based and emphasized women's dependency, and excluded several female and black-dominated occupations from key benefits like pensions and unemployment insurance. We described the increasing hostility to AFDC as

---

[11] Michel and Klein both discuss the decision by Marian Wright Edelman, head of the Children's Defense Fund (a key lobbying group for childcare legislation), to accede to Republican demands that church-run facilities be allowed to receive federal funding, noting that this compromise demolished support among those who wanted a strict separation between church and state, but was deemed to be a concession worth making to gain support for childcare (Michel, 1999, 277; Klein, 1992).

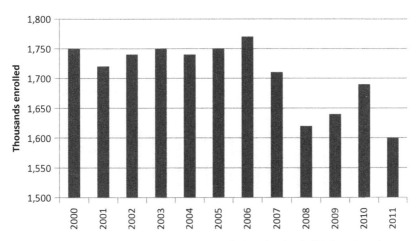

Figure 6.3 Number of children enrolled under the Child Care Development Fund, 2000–2011
Source: CLASP (2011).

the program's size and the proportion of non-white recipients grew, and noted the racial tensions behind President Nixon's decision to veto the CCDA. Here I scrutinize the impact of race, class and gender on American childcare policies over the last generation.

As we noted earlier, public support for AFDC eroded through the 1960s as the racial composition of the recipients shifted quickly from being 86 percent white in 1960 to 54 percent by 1967, and the numbers served by the program mushroomed. Job-training and workfare programs were increasingly favored by members of Congress seeking new ways to bar blacks and unmarried mothers from receiving AFDC benefits (Michel, 1999, 244). But workfare and job-training programs were dependent on the availability of childcare. Gradually, federal support for childcare came to be discussed as a crucial anti-welfare policy, rather than as a universal program aimed at providing high-quality childcare for all working parents. The decision to replace the AFDC program with Temporary Aid to Needy Families in 1996 was the culmination of a long campaign to characterize welfare recipients as lazy and undeserving. TANF eliminated entitlements for poor mothers and their children, established a lifetime cap of five years for payments, and invited the states to develop approaches to encourage single mothers to enter the labor force. Central to the welfare-to-work orientation of the TANF program was the expectation that mothers would work to support themselves and their children. As women transitioned away from welfare into the workforce, savings in monthly TANF assistance payments were available for states to use to provide subsidies to

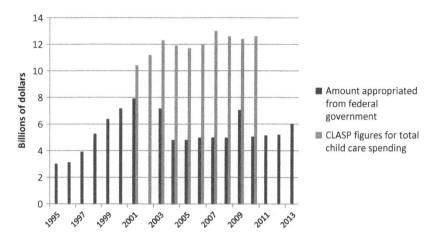

Figure 6.4 Federal appropriations to Child Care Development Fund, 1995–2013; total appropriations, 2001–2012
Sources: US Congress (2004); Child Care and Development Fund (2013); CLASP (2011; these figures include TANF rebates and state and federal contributions).

help pay for childcare services. Because states were (and still are) able to move federal TANF funding into Title XX Social Services Block Grant and CCDF, since the late 1990s funding for TANF has moved fluidly between cash assistance and support for childcare and other family services (Administration for Children & Families, 2011). The total combined childcare funding from state and federal monies redirected from TANF was on average more than the direct federal childcare subsidies (see Figure 6.4) between 2001 and 2010, with amounts that ranged from $10.4 billion in 2001 to $13.0 billion in 2007 (CLASP, 2011). Outlays for CCDF grew under President Clinton (1993–2000) but have been modest and flat under presidents George W. Bush and Barack Obama. The Center for Law and Social Policy reports that only about 14 percent of income-qualified children are served by CCDF, indicating that the federal program to subsidize childcare services for low-income families is severely underfunded (CLASP, 2011).

As the 1971 CCDA and 1987 Act for Better Child Care (ABC) efforts illustrate, the United States has repeatedly failed to adopt comprehensive laws that would mandate national enforceable standards for childcare services and universal availability of affordable services.[12] What has worked are approaches that target support for childcare to the neediest families. One can see this in the

---

[12] What I have in mind here are standards setting minimum requirements for teacher education and training, teacher–child ratios, and pay, as well as health and safety.

passage of the Head Start program in 1965, the 1991 CCDF program, and in a variety of provisions that support childcare in order to encourage low-income mothers to work in order to prevent welfare dependency, including the Work Incentive Program from the 1960s, the Comprehensive Employment Training Act of 1973 and Title XX of the Social Security Act (Michel, 1999, 243–4, 251).

Tax expenditures for the middle class

In addition to targeted spending to support early childhood education and childcare for poor families, tax expenditures have been a popular way to support childcare in the United States. In addition to the 1954 law which permitted parents to deduct $600 of childcare expenses from their taxable income, the Reagan administration enacted several tax measures aimed at supporting childcare in the 1980s. Under the 1981 Dependent Care Assistance Plan, individuals were allowed to exclude the value of employer-provided childcare services from their gross income, and employers were given tax benefits to encourage them to provide childcare facilities on-site or nearby. The Child and Dependent Care tax credit was increased in the early 1980s, and taxpayers were allowed to shelter some pretax dollars in Flexible Spending Accounts for dependent care services. Although tax credits and deductions are often not viewed as government spending, Michel points out that "the total value of these foregone taxes more than tripled between 1980 and 1986, constituting by far the greatest single expenditure for child care in both of those years" (Michel, 1999, 256).[13]

Using tax expenditures to reduce the cost of out-of-pocket expenses incurred in purchasing childcare services in the private market is appealing for a number of reasons. First, reducing tax liability does not seem like an expenditure in the same way a tax-funded program like AFDC or TANF does. When a tax credit or deduction allows someone to reduce taxes owed, money a taxpayer would otherwise pay the government is not collected, but stays in that taxpayer's bank account, increasing her or his spending power. Thus tax reductions are easier to defend politically than increased government expenditures under CCDF to help pay for the costs of childcare services, even though the net impact on the budget of reducing tax revenue or spending more through a government program is identical. In particular, tax cuts are more politically palatable to the right than direct spending, and therefore easier to pass and maintain. Republicans often

---

[13] However, the overall spending is not particularly generous. Thus, the amount of subsidy received per family compared with the total costs of paying for childcare is modest indeed. Families earning between $30,000 and $40,000 in practice get somewhere between $1,000 and $1,500 in tax credit to help pay for the annual cost of childcare under the Child and Dependent Care tax credit. See Maag, 2013.

bristle at the idea of "tax and spend" big government, but are more likely to favor ways of accomplishing social policy outcomes through manipulating the tax code. Not coincidentally, most tax deductions and credits have a middle- or upper-class skew, because they assist taxpayers who actually owe taxes. Generally, the more the taxpayer owes, the more tax expenditures are likely to benefit her or him. For example, dependent care tax credits are not refundable, so if filers do not owe the government very much tax, they may not benefit from the deduction or credit that is intended to help subsidize their childcare expenses (Hacker, 2002; Abramovitz and Morgen, 2006).

The development and expansion of tax breaks in the 1980s was intended to foster a vibrant private market in childcare options to meet every taste and pocketbook, and succeeded famously in doing so.[14] As childcare chains prolif- erated, so did the National Association of Child Care Management (NACCM), whose members were owners and managers of proprietary centers. NACCM members were opposed to federal standards that would require them to increase staffing levels or salaries, so they were pleased when the 1981 Omnibus Budget Reconciliation Act (a measure passed soon after Ronald Reagan took over as president that drastically cut domestic spending) converted Title XX childcare funding into block grants controlled by the states, and effectively deprived Washington of its power to regulate childcare (Michel, 1999, 261). The path- dependent effect of private modes of provision is evident in US childcare policy: the inability to build broad support for public services that would be pitched toward the tastes and needs of middle-class families, "coupled with strategic tax incentives to both individuals and corporations, has had the effect of building up the supply of child care in the private sector, creating a constituency for this type of provision and deflecting demands upon the state for universal services" (Michel, 1999, 279).

In order to understand how important tax expenditures are as an approach to funding work–family policies, notice that tax expenditures rival or exceed direct, tax-funded spending to pay for the Head Start, CCDF and TANF pro- grams. Taking fiscal and direct spending figures for 2003, the direct expendi- tures for Head Start were $6.67 billion, and $12.3 billion in total expenditures for CCDF (see Figures 6.2 and 6.4). The dependent care tax credit was $2.3 billion (see Table 6.1 below), but other tax expenditures to support families with children were more sizeable. Tax outlays included $19.13 billion for the Child Tax Credit (which provides families with a refundable tax credit of $1,000 for

---

[14] Private for-profit childcare chains mushroomed in numbers and in terms of the number of children served between the late 1970s and the mid-1980s, leading to a situation where "child care became big business, as the chains and franchisers took over the industry." Nonprofit centers simultaneously proliferated at YWCAs, churches, synagogues, etc. These rapid increases in centers led to a fourfold increase in the number of families using new center-based services between 1958 and 1982 (Michel, 1999, 256–7).

Table 6.1 *Family support related tax expenditures (in millions of dollars)*

Function and provision	Total revenue loss/expenditure						
	2000	2001	2002	2003	2004	2005	2006
Child Tax Credit (effect on receipts)*	19,330	19,310	18,980	18,410	18,000	17,430	16,790
Child Tax Credit (effect on outlays)**	809	790	760	720	660	630	590
Total child credit expenditures	20,139	20,100	19,740	19,130	18,660	18,060	17,380
Dependent care tax credit	2,390	2,360	2,330	2,300	2,280	2,250	2,220
EITC (effect on receipts)	4,644	4,692	4,963	5,225	5,456	5,688	5,965
EITC (effect on outlays)	26,099	25,923	26,983	27,875	28,545	29,373	30,165
Total EITC expenditures	30,743	30,615	31,946	33,100	34,001	35,061	36,130
Mortgage interest deduction	60,270	63,190	65,750	68,050	70,470	73,100	76,150
State and local property tax deduction	22,140	23,920	25,570	27,220	29,080	30,980	33,220

* Money the government does not take in once the credit offsets tax liability
** Money refunded to taxpayers because the credit exceeds their tax liability
Source: US White House, OMB, 2002.

every child under the age of seventeen in the household); $2.30 billion for the Dependent Care Tax Credit; $33.10 billion for the Earned Income Tax Credit (which is an anti-poverty policy that supplements the incomes of working poor taxpayers); and $68.05 billion for mortgage interest deductions (taxpayers can deduct the amount spent on interest on their home mortgages from their taxable income, a policy aimed at promoting home ownership, but also one that disproportionately benefits those who can afford to buy expensive and multiple homes). Taking the figures for direct welfare state spending from above, in 2003 the US and state governments combined spent $12.3 billion for the Child Care and Development Fund, $6.67 billion for Head Start, and $22.86 billion for Temporary Aid to Needy Families. Comparing these two strands of family support policies, overall tax expenditures (money that the federal government never collects due to tax breaks of various kinds) totaled $122.58 billion, and direct spending programs totaled $41.83 billion. Direct welfare spending is only a third as much as the amount of the total tax expenditures. I should also point out that family support measures are not necessarily intended as work–family policies; the Child Tax Credit (CTC) was increased in 2001 to a maximum of $1,000 per child as a politically expedient response to Democratic proposals to increase funding for childcare. The CTC supports parents raising children without tying the support to childcare: families with a stay-at-home mom get the payment along with those where all parents are working. Far from redistributing income toward relatively poor families raising children, the

CTC provides tax reductions to middle- and upper-income taxpayers with dependent children under the age of seventeen, whereas "poverty-level families with incomes below the refundability threshold receive no tax benefits from the child tax credit" because it is not a fully refundable credit (Esenwein, 2006). In terms of attracting Republican support, the CTC was a smart tool, cast as a "put money back in the pockets of hard-working taxpayers" measure that would not give working parents anything that stay-at-home parents didn't also receive, and was more likely to benefit better-off families. As we noted above, tax expenditures are a convenient way to enact family support policies, as they are more politically acceptable, easier to pass, and less likely to be exposed to public scrutiny and debate than direct spending measures. Just how much the United States spends in forgone tax collections, and who precisely benefits from these expenditures, is harder to unearth and less likely to be discussed, analyzed and criticized than spending of a similar magnitude that is funded through direct spending provisions (Hacker, 2002).

To put the point in comparative perspective, American social policy typically relies on tax expenditures to reward or subsidize certain behaviors rather than directly funding childcare programs, subsidizing users or providing services, as the French, German and Japanese governments commonly do (Japan also uses its tax code substantially to encourage private provision of benefits, just not ones related to childcare). The preference for tax spending over direct spending is consonant with neo-liberal preferences for private provision, markets and the rhetoric of choice which have long characterized the American approach to providing social welfare benefits. Relying on tax forgiveness rather than direct expenditures is emblematic of Americans' deeply engrained opposition to the intervention of the state into "private" life, and of their evident reluctance or inability to make powerful public claims for state intervention to address work–family tensions.

Parental leaves: the Family and Medical Leave Act

The last branch of work–family policy I address is the Family and Medical Leave Act (FMLA), passed in 1993. The United States had no national-level leave laws until the FMLA was adopted. The FMLA requires employers to give employees an unpaid twelve-week job-protected leave, and only applies to relatively large businesses (those with fifty or more employees working within a 75-mile radius). The FMLA stands out for its late adoption, limited applicability and being short and unpaid (see Table 2.8 for a comparison of leave policies). I explain why passing a leave law was so difficult in the United States, and why there have been no changes to make the law more broadly applicable, to lengthen the leave, or to make it a paid one, in the twenty-plus years since it was adopted.

Twelve states and the District of Columbia had passed family and medical leave laws by 1993, and the campaign to pass the FMLA built upon the experiences at the state level. Since the FMLA became law, three states have extended coverage beyond the federal requirements by providing paid leaves (California, Washington and New Jersey), and three more provide paid maternity leaves under their temporary disability insurance (TDI) programs (Hawaii, New York and Rhode Island, in addition to New Jersey and California, which have both paid family leaves and TDI funding for medical leaves – see Fass 2009).[15] Several states – Connecticut, the District of Columbia, Hawaii, Maine, Minnesota, Oregon, Vermont, and Wisconsin – have extended the reach of the employees covered under the FMLA (Ray, 2008, 32–3).

In the United States, it is difficult to pass labor laws that require employers to pay workers while they are unable to work or insure their jobs for them while on leave, because business is a well-organized, attentive interest group with plenty of money to contribute to campaigns, and lobbies strongly to oppose regulations it deems too costly or intrusive. Generally, arguments about the impact of such regulations on the bottom line (and therefore employment and productivity) carry weight, especially during tough economic times when political leaders are loath to pass laws that could affect hiring, productivity, profit and decisions about relocation. The view is that everyone benefits, including workers and ordinary citizens, when the economy flourishes, and since burdening business with costly regulations threatens economic growth, such burdens must be minimized. On the other side, the groups that one might expect to argue vigorously for paid family leaves – organized labor, women's groups, parents of young children, and children's rights groups – have not been able to create a powerful social movement to demand generous paid leaves.

Even so, nineteen states and the federal government did eventually pass family leave laws. In her book examining successful and failing efforts to pass family leave laws in several states and at the federal level, Anya Bernstein argues that successful efforts made good use of institutional resources (e.g., powerful leaders who had a stake in promoting childcare leave laws), framed family leave in terms of supporting families rather than casting it in more polarizing terms as a feminist or labor rights issue, and engaged in "insider" politics based on bargaining and compromise rather than taking the moral high ground and making nonnegotiable demands for change or adopting confrontational political strategies, as activists drawn to a cause by principled arguments sometimes do. Bernstein found that states were more likely to pass laws when advocates for family leave built alliances with conservative politicians and

---

[15] Note that the Pregnancy Disability Act of 1978 requires that state disability plans must treat pregnancy-related disabilities the same as any other work-related disability, so all states that have TDI plans cover pregnancy.

groups and found exemplary corporate citizens who would testify at legislative hearings that adopting corporate-level family leave policies, far from hurting their companies' bottom lines, helped them attract and retain talented workers. Astute political work that reflected familiarity with political and policy processes and norms of reciprocity and compromise was also crucial to the success of state leave laws. Being able to attract influential Bill sponsors and supporters from both political parties, and making common cause with conservative and religious groups like the American Association of Retired People and the US Catholic Conference helped advocacy groups succeed. But building this kind of broad-based support required a high degree of willingness to compromise and bargain in order to craft a diverse coalition of groups to support family leave laws. The result was what Bernstein calls the "moderation dilemma": the incremental strategies aimed at finding common ground with business and conservative groups meant settling for much less than advocates of leave policies wanted. The laws were generally weak, only covering about half of the workforce for a short period of time, and none of the laws passed by 1993 provided for paid leaves. This meant that, for many workers, the FMLA and state counterpart laws were unusable, because they couldn't afford to take twelve weeks off from work without pay. But it was clear to all that an unpaid leave was the price of passing any law at all: had advocates insisted that the FMLA or state leave be paid, they would fail to gain crucial support from the business community (Bernstein, 2001).[16]

Many believed that accepting half a loaf in order to pass any law at all (in this case, accepting leave provisions that were much weaker than advocates wanted in order to pass any kind of leave law) was justified because getting a law on the books at the national level was an important first step toward legitimizing family leaves, and that future fights would aim to extend the leave to more workers and to make sure that it was paid. To a degree, this has occurred: three states passed paid leave policies in the 2000s: California in 2002, Washington in 2007, and New Jersey in 2008. But the lengths of these paid leaves are generally short (six weeks each in California and New Jersey, five weeks in Washington), and the amounts are low (55 percent of weekly pay up to a cap in California, 66 percent in NJ, and a flat rate of $250 a week in Washington: Fass, 2009). However, implementation of these laws has been slowed by the economic downturn in the United States that began in 2008, and Washington has delayed enforcement of its law until 2015 because of budget shortfalls (Guerin, 2013).[17]

---

[16] Bernstein recounts the story of what happened in Massachusetts, where activist feminists insisted on a paid leave, and the Bill did not pass (2002, Ch. 3).

[17] Nor has Congress yet passed the Federal Employees Paid Parental Leave Act, a Bill introduced in every Congress since 2000 that would give all federal employees four weeks of paid leave (govtrack.com, 2013).

Table 6.2 *Summary of US work–family reconciliation policies*

Family allowances
The United Statesdoes not offer universal cash family allowances; TANF benefits are means-tested and have a lifetime cap of 5 years; levels vary by state

Tax code provisions
Joint filing produces some tax benefits for married couples where one earns much more than the other
Numerous tax credits & deductions: common tool for work–family goals

Family leaves
12 weeks of unpaid leave for birth or family medical emergency
Some states offer brief paid parental leaves, as do some employers

Childcare and early childhood education
Childcare: 31% of children under 3 in formal market-based care in 2008
Kindergarten/childcare: 67% of children 3–5 enrolled
Most ECEC is private, market-based care that parents purchase on their own

Source: OECD, 2013l; summary of content in chapter.

The fact that the United States took so long to develop a family leave policy, and adopted one that is so meager that many people are unable to use it, can be explained by the power of business interests in a dispersed federal system where capital is mobile, and the existence of many veto points can enable business to block reforms (Pierson, 1995, paraphrased in Bernstein, 2002, 7–8). Many Americans accept the idea that parents should plan for childbirth, and be financially prepared to support their newborns and themselves, should they desire to spend time out of the workforce with a new baby. The notion that the state should support families through this eventful transition is hardly discussed. (For a summary of American work–family policies, see Table 6.2).

Policy making processes and actors

There are two houses in the US Congress: the 100-member upper house, the Senate, has two senators from each state, regardless of population; and the 435-member lower house, the House of Representatives, is elected from districts that are based on population, although each state gets at least one representative. The Senate is not a majoritarian system, but over-represents scantly populated (generally more conservative) states. Elections are winner-take-all contests, which means electoral contests are largely between the two major parties struggling for majorities – the United States has neither PR nor coalition governments, and tends to produce centrist-conservative governments that can attract broad majorities. Presidents are elected independently of the Congress, and it is common for one or both houses of the US Congress to be under the control of the opposition party, especially since personality-based campaigning and split-ticket voting are common. Divided governments often result in deadlock and inability to pass controversial legislation, as passing legislation requires that both houses of Congress pass language cast in identical terms, then signed by the president and enforced by necessary guidelines and interpretations from the federal departments, their agencies and the federal courts.

Because the United States is a federal system, a variety of policy matters are left to the states, including those related to public education, childcare and kindergarten, and family formation and dissolution. The federal government rarely takes the initiative to pass major policies to support working parents on the grounds that this is properly the states' prerogative.

At the national level, American government is less institutionally competent than the other three countries we have examined, in the sense that it does not have a powerful central state that can readily push through an active social welfare agenda. Overlapping areas of jurisdiction with the states adds to the institutional complexity of work–family policy making, with federal laws often building in discretion and authority for the states to fund and enforce laws.[18] The permanent bureaucracy, which is under the control of the sitting president who chooses the top layer of political appointees, is not as active or respected a policy making body as in France, Japan or Germany. Departments and agencies rarely play an active role in introducing legislation. Instead, they work with members of relevant House and Senate committees, who draw on bureaucratic expertise in drafting bills that they will introduce in Congress.[19]

In the course of researching this chapter, I spoke with about a dozen members of the national work–family policy making community, including both political appointees and career bureaucrats from the US Department of Health and Human Services (HHS) and representatives from a number of research institutes and activist groups. In speaking with government officials at the Administration for Children and Families and the Child Care Bureau within the ACF (both housed in HHS) in 2003, I was struck by their defensive tone during conversations we had about US childcare policies like CCDF and Head Start. This might be related to the fact that the leadership of the HHS and its sub-agencies were political appointees who represented the political perspective of Republican President George W. Bush. In any case, these officials were skeptical of the utility of comparing the United States to Japan, telling me that the values of Japanese society were more group-oriented and conformist than would ever be acceptable in an American day care setting (Tvedt et al.

---

[18] We have seen several examples of this split authority in this chapter, including AFDC, TANF and CCDF.

[19] There are often cozy relationships between regulatory agencies, regulated industries and congressional committees, although this is not as pronounced as in Japan.

interview, 2003).[20] They explained the utility of adopting a means-tested, targeted approach to providing support for childcare, and were frankly dismissive of the idea of the United States adopting universal pre-kindergarten or childcare programs, despite the success of such policies elsewhere (Rolston interview, 2003). Like bureaucrats in the other three countries, they were familiar with the programmatic details of the policies they administered, as well as a variety of research on child development and well-being (Tvedt et al., 2003; Rolston interview, 2003).

When I asked about possible tensions between career bureaucrats and political appointees, responses were guarded; no one was willing to directly address this issue in a mixed group of career bureaucrats and political appointees. My impression was that both the political and career bureaucrats at HHS were more involved in program evaluation and administration than in preparing legislative language or proposals, or in testifying at congressional hearings regarding the pros and cons of particular approaches to childcare or parental leave.[21]

The policy terrain at the national level includes a variety of interest groups that are vitally concerned with promoting (or defeating) active work–family policies, including advocates of work–family policies like the Children's Defense Fund, the National Partnership for Women and Families, the Center for Law and Social Policy and Legal Momentum. Lobbyists on the other side include pro-business groups like the National Association of Manufacturers, the Business Roundtable and the US Chamber of Commerce, which lobby hard against flexible scheduling, paid leaves and the like on the ground that they will hurt the corporate bottom line and economic productivity. Because money-based politics is crucial to electoral contests, the latter set of groups tends to carry more clout than the first. In addition, groups that represent providers, such as for-profit childcare providers, are well-mobilized and relatively effective in shaping policy.

Conclusion

This chapter has reviewed the record of efforts to pass work–family policies in the United States over the last hundred years. As we have seen, such laws have had sporadic success and often been deeply flawed. Early measures to support mothers and children took a maternalist approach, reaffirming women's role as mothers who should be supported to stay home and care for children. These early policies were also framed and implemented in such a way that "deserving"

---

[20] They were also skeptical of comparing the United States to France and Germany. All in all, I was struck by how parochial and smug the career leaders of the Child Care Bureau were, especially given the apparent shortcomings in quality and supply of the US market-based approach.

[21] This is episodic, of course, and there is no doubt action at present in response to President Obama's repeated calls for a federal program to encourage universal pre-kindergarten education.

mothers were usually white, and African American women were excluded from coverage. The crises of the Great Depression and World War II briefly resulted in broad-scale support for childcare. But by 1947, support for such approaches had evaporated, and never materialized again, even when large numbers of women entered the workforce between 1970 and 1990. Without strong unified support from across the spectrum of users, childcare policies evolved into two tracks, public programs that targeted the poor through underfunded programs like Head Start and the Child Care Development Fund, and modest tax benefits that help middle- and higher-income families pay for childcare in the private market. Associating public support for childcare with anti-poverty programs meant that middle-class women, who might otherwise have exerted substantial influence in favor of universal childcare policies, instead embraced the minimal tax supports that helped them pay for childcare options they chose in the private market. One of the consequences of the bifurcated American approach to childcare policy is that quality has suffered: regulations are rudimentary and poorly enforced, even in centers that receive CCDF funds.[22] Regulation has largely been left to the states, and many of them lack the personnel and funding to enforce what standards they have. Parental leave laws have been slow to pass and minimal in their coverage, premised on deep compromises to assuage conservative (especially business) opposition. The United States is unique among the wealthy industrialized countries of the world in not having a national law guaranteeing paid maternity or parental leaves. Its spending levels for family-related policies put it at or near the bottom of the range for OECD countries, and these low levels of funding for work–family policies matter. For example, CCDF funds only cover about 14 percent of income-qualified families – that is, families who earn 85 percent or less of the state median income. Curiously, the American women's movement has not been very successful in pushing for generous work–family policies. I think the reasons for this are three-fold. First, American feminists have largely taken a rights-based orientation reflecting a commitment to "sameness": women should be treated the same as men, with the same chances for admission to good schools and elite careers, and men should be viewed as potential fathers and nurturers, rather than assuming that either paid or domestic work (and childrearing) are necessarily gendered realms. Second, the women's movement has had a hard time reckoning with issues of class and race that divide women, and has not

---

[22] The language of the Child Care and Development Block Grant Act of 1990 requires that a small percentage ("not less than 4 percent") of the funds a state receives to carry out subchapter SEC. 658G of the law be set aside "for activities that are designed to provide comprehensive consumer education to parents and the public, activities that increase parental choice, and activities designed to improve the quality and availability of child care (such as resource and referral services)" (CCDBG Act, 42 USC 9858).

always seen the importance of a united front pushing for universal, generous benefits with respect to childcare and parental leaves. Policy strategies that gave poor women publicly supported childcare and gave middle-class and wealthy women a bit of tax support to purchase private, market-based childcare didn't provoke a "we're all in this together, we have to fight for high-quality subsidized public care for all children" strategy from women's groups. Without the attention, organization and mobilization of middle-class women, the fight for universal high-quality childcare is bound to fail. Third, feminists have not developed arguments about social citizenship, and the need for policies that would permit women to enter the workplace on a similar footing to men, that are commonplace in Europe. The American women's movement seems to have accepted the idea that it is not the state's responsibility to help pay for adequate family leaves or good childcare options. Sonya Michel links these arguments, writing

Without focused feminist leadership and propelled by a policy that persistently linked public provisions to welfare-related goals, wage-earning mothers divided along class and racial lines instead of joining together . . . it is precisely because the discourses surrounding child care have become so fractured by race and class that this deeply flawed policy has been allowed to develop in the first place. By unifying the constituency for child care, it may be possible to change the terms of provision and insist on universally available services that are high in quality. (Michel, 1999, 279–80)

Is change possible in such a context? Like many others, I study work–family policies because I think and hope that the United States can do better with respect to supporting working families. But if one wants a realistic approach to changing work–family policies in the direction of greater inclusivity and generosity, higher-quality care for babies and preschoolers, and paid parental leaves, one must understand why the United States has pursued particular policy approaches and grapple with the forces that have brought us to where we are now. The way forward depends on political processes of change, not on the family-policy tooth fairy coming down to grant us three wishes.

Work–family policy scholar Jennifer Glass offers a tough-minded assessment of what will be necessary for the United States to enact more generous policies, focusing on two tracks: regulations aimed at requiring employers to provide benefits, and direct provision of services by the state (Glass, 2009, 233). Glass explains why neither approach has so far been successful.

Fleshing out the first track, Glass thinks that as jobs in the manufacturing sector were gradually cut or moved elsewhere, workers began to worry that their jobs might be "outsourced to lower-waged workers in developing countries or automated out of existence," and "demands for paid parental leave, elimination of mandatory overtime, or schedule flexibility" came to seem utopian

(Glass, 2009, 235). Furthermore, working mothers were too small and weak a constituency, both politically and in terms of their presence in the workplace, to negotiate work–family concessions. In fact, most women worked in

low-wage jobs in which they were readily replaceable, and so had little bargaining power with which to gain work modifications to accommodate family care . . . In this changed economic environment, conservative fears that regulation would lower productivity, hurt job growth, and reduce capital investment in the United States took precedence over the very real difficulties of working families caught between the 24/7 economy and their families' needs for care. Clearly, any analysis of the state of work–family policy in the United States must grapple with the strong antipathy toward employer regulation that exists in both the business community and major political parties. (Glass, 2009, 235)

Turning to the second track, Glass notes that government regulation and provision of services have fared badly since neo-liberal concerns with protecting business's bottom line and minimizing government regulation became paramount in the 1980s: "The ideology that lowering taxes and government spending would help families more than government-sponsored provision of education, child care, family leave and health care prevailed throughout the Republican administrations of the 1980s to the present" (Glass, 2009, 236). In this atmosphere, neither party has pushed for generous work–family policies, in part because of other priorities that have taken precedence, and in part because political candidates are careful to consider bottom-line arguments and policies that create jobs, as most depend on pro-business constituencies to finance their campaigns. Clearly, many legislators buy into neo-liberal thinking that makes the expansion of the economy the highest priority: "federal mandates for paid leaves, scheduling flexibility, part-time benefit parity, and other policies might shrink profits, depress wage growth, and hamper new job creation. Surely that is not in the public interest" (Glass, 2009, 244). Indeed, such concerns that government regulation could depress job and wage growth are even more pronounced during a prolonged recession like that which began in 2008.

Lack of action on the work–family policy front is also related to the ebbs and flows of workers' needs for policies to help them with care responsibilities over the life cycle. This means that, at any given time, "the primary constituency for any particular family policy" is somewhat thin, which allows politicians to refuse to take action "without paying a huge penalty with voters in the next election" (Glass, 2009, 238). Glass's advice to those who would like to enact such laws is that they should provide empirical evidence that work–family policies will enhance, not hurt, bottom lines: if one can prove that they are cost-effective, then they are more likely to be adopted. Arguments about cost-effectiveness must take into account the impact of family supports on workers' mental and physical health, and on their children's acquisition of human capital (Glass, 2009, 247).[23]

President Obama used his bully pulpit to make cost-efficiency and justice arguments for investing in universal early childhood education in his 2013 State of the Union address. Here is what he said in pertinent part:

Study after study shows that the sooner a child begins learning, the better he or she does down the road. But today, fewer than 3 in 10 four year-olds are enrolled in a high-quality preschool program. Most middle-class parents can't afford a few hundred bucks a week for private preschool. And for poor kids who need help the most, this lack of access to preschool education can shadow them for the rest of their lives. Tonight, I propose working with states to make high-quality preschool available to every child in America. Every dollar we invest in high-quality early education can save more than seven dollars later on – by boosting graduation rates, reducing teen pregnancy, even reducing violent crime. In states that make it a priority to educate our youngest children, like Georgia or Oklahoma, studies show students grow up more likely to read and do math at grade level, graduate high school, hold a job, and form more stable families of their own. So let's do what works, and make sure none of our children start the race of life already behind. Let's give our kids that chance. (Obama, 2013)

Of course, State of the Union speeches are wish lists of policies and priorities the president would like to undertake, and Obama's mention of this issue was brief and met with little serious discussion and no effort to introduce legislation. But he made important arguments in a forum where a large audience was paying attention, and put the authority of his office and leadership behind a federal–state partnership to provide universal preschool education, potentially a way to help working parents find excellent care for their children, and certainly a way to insure that all children get a good start in life, which is crucial in the United States where class inequalities in access to good education are marked.

Obama's arguments are important and might in the long run influence early childhood education policies. But we need to be tough-minded and realistic about the political obstacles to passing more generous work–family policies. These include the developments and debates over work–family policies since the economic reorganization of the 1960s and 1970s, the turn toward neoliberalism in the 1980s, as well as the kinds of family policy repertoires and discourses that have become dominant in the United States. It is of course unlikely that the United States will adopt work–family policies as generous as those in France or the social democratic Nordic countries (see Gornick and Meyers, 2009). Change will require opening policy windows that have been

---

[23] Nancy Folbre also argues that excellent care for children is a collective good, suggesting that care work be included in calculations of the GDP, and that taxpayers be called upon to consider how they have benefitted from government supports and payments of differing kinds, so as to defuse conservative objections to socializing care (2009).

painted over and stuck firmly in place for many decades. Effective lobbying and action will require groups to work together who have long viewed one another with enmity and suspicion, including organized labor, welfare recipients, poor people, women, child welfare advocates and young adults, many of whom are worried about finding good jobs and being asked to pay more into the pension system than they will ever draw out. The United States needs to mobilize to create an effective political movement that cannot be ignored, that can make strong and persuasive arguments about the public stake in making sure all children get a good start in life, no matter what families or neighborhoods they are born into. Such a movement will need to show that early childhood education and high-quality childcare are cost-effective in the long run, by producing citizens who work at necessary jobs, pay their taxes and contribute to the economy. Perhaps some external jolt which cannot be foreseen – a sense of public crisis due to military or environmental threat, or public anxiety about declining populations of working-age people and mushrooming numbers of elderly people – will spark broad support for universal and high-quality childcare and early childhood education policies, as the sense of crisis over low fertility and population aging has done in Germany and Japan. I return to the question of feasible suggestions for policy change in Chapter 8.

This chapter asks how well the various policies we have examined work along several dimensions. Are work–family policies increasing fertility rates? How well do they support working mothers? Are they promoting gender equality? Do they help all children get a good start in life? Do work–family policies contribute to overall social equality? How expensive are they? My aim is to establish what the best practices are in this area, so that policy entrepreneurs and legislative leaders have a good idea which policies to emulate and adopt. The next chapter takes up the question of what is politically feasible.

First I compare standard work–family reconciliation policies – childcare and early childhood education, leave policies, direct cash transfers, tax expenditures, and policies and practices related to work hours – in terms of policy design, generosity and how well they work, then I move into evaluative mode, assessing different countries' approaches along the above dimensions. I include data for Sweden in here in order to provide a benchmark for a high-spending social democratic welfare state in order to be able to compare family policies across four groups of countries: high-spending, universalistic social democratic welfare states; conservative continental ones (France and Germany); the Asian variant on conservative welfare states, Japan; and liberal welfare states, as epitomized by the United States.[1]

Spending figures for two dozen OECD countries dramatically illustrate the differences among them with respect to supporting childcare and early childhood education (see Figure 2.8). The biggest spenders are four social democratic Scandinavian countries, followed by a mixed group (the UK, France, Finland and New Zealand), a group of conservative welfare states (the Netherlands through Germany) in the 0.5 to 0.9 percent range, and the lowest spenders (0.4 percent and below), Ireland through Greece, a group that includes Japan and the United States. Except for the four highest-spending countries, early childhood education and care (ECEC) spending levels are not categorizable by welfare regime types.

---

[1] These comparisons also allow me to consider important intra-group differences between France and Germany, which have long supported families in quite different ways.

Table 7.1 *Percentage of children in formal childcare or preschool, 2010*

Country	Ages <3	Ages 3–5
Sweden	46.7	92.9
France	48.0	100.0
Germany	23.1	93.9
Japan	25.9	90.3
US	43.2	66.5

Figures include privately and publicly funded care. *Source*: OECD, 2012a

Turning to the share of children served by public and private financed childcare and kindergarten, Table 7.1 shows that just below 50 percent of children under the age of three attend childcare in Sweden and France, 43 percent in the United States, and roughly a quarter in Germany and Japan. Except the United States, all these countries have large majorities of children aged three to five attending childcare or kindergarten. The figures for public spending to support ECEC and percentages of three- to five-year-olds attending childcare are low for the United States because childcare and preschool are supported through means-tested programs that serve a small minority of preschool-age children (less than 50 percent of children from income-qualified families – see Chapter 6 for details). One year of kindergarten for children who are five years old is included in the state school system.[2] Most preschool and childcare in the United Statesis privately provided, as is most preschool in Japan, which is a significant burden on young families.

Figure 2.9, which compares childcare fees, benefits and tax reductions, illuminates this financial burden. About two-thirds of the thirty countries in the figure have kept fees for childcare in check, either by providing childcare or subsidizing care providers. Seven others – Belgium, Portugal, Spain, Luxembourg, the Netherlands, Slovenia and Australia – offer generous benefits to families to offset high fees. Looking to the five countries we are comparing, we can see that 5 percent of net family income goes to paying for childcare in Sweden, double that in France and Germany (10 and 11 percent, respectively), with the figure jumping to 17 percent in Japan and 23 in the United States. As we noted in Chapter 6, the key approach to supporting childcare for middle-class citizens in the United States, the dependent care tax credit, does

---

[2] Many American school districts have adopted full-day kindergarten, which follows the same hours as elementary schools (roughly 8.30 until 3.00). Except in countries like Sweden and France that design care to accommodate working mothers, kindergarten care is still mostly part-day.

Table 7.2 *Maternity, parental and paternity leaves, 2011–2012 (duration is in weeks)*

Country	Maternity leave	% pay for maternity leave	Paternity leave, and % pay reimbursed*	Parental leave	% pay for parental leave	Total leave time	Equivalent in FT paid leave weeks, incl. pat. & mat. leaves	type of system
Sweden	14	80%	10 @ 80%	60	64.3	84	57.8	dual earner
France	16	100%	2 @ 100%	26–156	18.9	174	50.8	general
Germany	14	100%	8 @ 67%	52	67	74	54.2	dual earner
Japan	14	67%	8 @ 50%	52	50	74	45.4	general
US	0	0	0	12	0	12	0	market-oriented

Source: OECD, 2013c. Note that in France leave time varies between first and subsequent children. Parents of first children get 6 months of leave, everyone else gets 3 years off. Parental leave is reimbursed at a flat rate of €548 a month, expressed here as 18.9% of pay. The equivalent weeks of leave is for the maximum 3-year leave.

little to reduce the overall cost of childcare. Six of the eight countries with the highest net costs for childcare are English-speaking; the others are Japan and Switzerland, a residual stand-out among continental welfare regimes.

Turning to leave policies, official policy design is very similar in Germany, Japan and Sweden. France is an outlier from these three in that it offers up to three years of flat-rate reimbursed parental leave and eleven days of paternity leave instead of two months. In contrast to the Swedish-style leave structure that encourages women to return to work quickly and provides two months or more of use-it-or-lose-it paternity leaves to encourage fathers to spend more time engaged in childrearing, the French approach reinforces traditional gender roles. But the bigger outlier is United States, which offers twelve weeks of unpaid leave to a little over half of its workers, a policy that compels many women to return to work with little or no recovery time after giving birth.[3] A silver lining may be that women who must hurry back to their jobs lose little in the way of seniority or skills because they are not away from work for several months or years, thus minimizing their opportunity costs of giving birth.

As we saw in the country chapters, France, Germany and Japan pay universal family allowances (see Table 7.3 below). France and Japan pay about 2 or 3 percent of an average worker's (AW) salary per year per child, up to age twenty in France and fifteen in Japan. France's family allowance is, again, pronatalist in design, as families receive it only if they have two or more children. (Note that Sweden is roughly in line with Japan on this benefit.) Germany is more generous, as *Kindergeld* amounts to about 5 percent of AW salary, and these payments are also supplemented by a means-tested child allowance (*Kinderzuschlag*) that is meant to protect childrearing families from having to apply for unemployment or welfare benefits. The United States also falls short on this dimension of family support; indeed, the only cash benefits for families are means-tested and set up in such a fashion that a baby born while the family is receiving TANF benefits will not trigger higher payments, in order to discourage women on welfare from having more babies in order to qualify for higher benefits. There is a lifetime cap of five years for receiving TANF benefits, which is intended to encourage poor single mothers to find paying work to support themselves and their children.

Considering income tax regulations and benefits in comparative perspective, France's national income tax (structured around the *quotient familiale*) gives taxpayers with multiple dependents a tax break, effecting horizontal redistribution toward large families. The German and American joint taxation systems both reward male-breadwinner-style earning patterns; the tax payments to

---

[3] The issue of finding high-quality affordable care for newborns in the United States is not trivial, especially for the families that need the mother's income so badly that she returns to work in less than twelve weeks.

Table 7.3 *Family cash benefits*[1] (2011)

	Maximum benefit for one child aged 3–12		Benefit amount per additional child varies with[2]		Upper age limit for children (student)	Means tested?	Observations
	National currency [1]	% of AW [2]	age of child [3]	# of children [4]	[5]	[6]	[7]
Sweden	12,600	3	0	+	15 (19)	No	–
France	747	2	+	+	19	No	Family allowance: zero benefit for first child. For 2 children (under age 11) the amount per child would be €747 (2% of AW).
Germany	2,208	5	0	+ from 3rd	18 (25)	No	*Kindergeld* is a refundable tax credit in the form of a monthly tax refund (reduces SA if there is no tax liability).
	1,680	5	–	–	–	Yes	Supplementary child allowance (*Kinderzuschlag*) is paid to parents to prevent them from having to apply for unemployment benefits or social welfare benefits in order to take care of their children.
Japan	156,000	3	0	0	15	No	Supplementary child allowance available as part of SA.
United States (Michigan)	1,068	2	0	+/–	–	Yes	Temporary Assistance for Needy Families (TANF): benefit is based on family size at the time of application rather than number of children. The benefit amounts and durations vary by state.

[1] Family benefits including refundable tax credits. Benefit amounts are shown on an annualized basis. "–" indicates that no information is available or not applicable. Family benefits are not taxable unless otherwise indicated. [2] "+": increases, "–": decreases, "0": remains the same, "+/–": increases or decreases (some countries give higher rates to the youngest and oldest age groups).

SA = Social Assistance

Source: OECD, 2013i.

Table 7.4 *Average annual hours actually worked per worker*

	2000	2005	2010	2012
Sweden	1642	1605	1635	1621
France	1523	1495	1480	1479
Germany	1471	1431	1407	1397
Japan	1821	1775	1733	1745
United States	1836	1799	1778	1790

Source: OECD, 2013a.

married couples are one of the most costly policies in Germany's family support repertoire. Although the impact is less dramatic in the United States, where the tax schedule is less progressive than in Germany, both countries' tax codes are advantageous to couples where one earner earns all or most of the income, and both penalize couples who earn close to parity (for US marriage penalty and bonus figures, see Kahng, 2010, 658, Table 1).

As we saw in Chapter 6, tax payments to support specific purposes are a common strategy in the United States for packaging social welfare spending as simply putting money back in taxpayers' pockets. The United States is more likely to use the tax code to support families than to adopt programs that require direct government outlays to support big, universal schemes, such as state-provided early childhood education or childcare. But such payments are not very redistributive, as they are more advantageous to higher-earning taxpayers who owe more in taxes to the government. Tax expenditures that benefit the well-to-do, and controversial and underfunded means-tested direct spending programs, are the two basic approaches the United States uses to support working families.

Japan is the only country of the four studied here that eschews joint taxation and taxes spouses separately using individual taxation. But it provides a dependent-spouse tax deduction to the main earner in the family, as well as a dependent-spouse payment provided as a fringe benefit by many employers, both of which require that the dependent spouse not earn more than ¥1.03 million (roughly $10,000) a year. These policies, which encourage many women to limit their earnings and accept part-time work which is not well paid, also provide tax incentives that support a male-breadwinner–female secondary-earner pattern (Shiota, 2000; OECD, 2003; Morinobu and Nakamoto, 2013).

Although work hours are not specifically work–family policies, the amount of time men and women spend on paid and unpaid work is of interest in evaluating how well countries support working families. Table 7.4 provides recent data on average number of hours worked per year per worker, a figure which includes all workers, those who work part-time as well as full-time. Given that many more workers (especially women) have part-time jobs in Japan than in the United States, the figures for these two countries mask how long the typical hours are for full-time (usually male) employees there. These data are a useful addition to the information contained in Table 2.7 (a comparison of standard working hours and vacation days), giving a glimpse into the relative amount of free time that workers have to spend on childrearing and family-related activities and chores. In France and Germany, which have 35 and 37 hour working weeks respectively, workers have two or three more hours a week at their disposal than their American and Japanese counterparts. Sweden, France and Germany have more paid vacation days per year (34, 36 and 29) than Japan (25) and particularly the United States (10). Nor are workers in these countries reluctant to take paid vacation days, while many Japanese workers feel they should not take all the time off available to them. Recall also the graph from Chapter 2 showing unpaid work by mothers and fathers of at least one preschool-age child (Figure 2.5): Swedish dads are the champions with respect to time spent on unpaid care work at 189 minutes a day, while Japanese dads average only 60 minutes a day, with the rest falling in between these extremes. The Japanese mothers clock a massive 447 minutes a day on unpaid care work, while mothers in the other countries log between 314 (in Sweden) and 371 minutes a day (in the United States). In addition to the raw number of hours that workers put in on the job (and for some the work day could include a long commute and quasi-mandatory after-hours socializing), norms about parent care and gender expectations about mothers' and fathers' roles in housework and childrearing also bear on who spends how much time on childrearing and housework. Interestingly, the sum of mothers' plus fathers' contributions to unpaid care work is highest for Americans, despite the long average hours workers put in on the job in the United States.

How do the different work–family reconciliation policies stack up? Table 7.5 summarizes the policy approaches described above along a continuum from most to least generous social welfare / work–family policy regime, based on the preceding review of policy design and generosity. I include Japan in the "conservative" category and suggest some nuances related to how different policies work in practice. The rest of this chapter evaluates these countries attending to six criteria: total fertility rates, support for working mothers, gender equality, insuring that all children get a good start in life, overall economic and social equality, and cost (see Thévenon, 2011, for a similar evaluative schema).

Demographic health

In some countries, total fertility rates have been so low for so long that policy makers have responded by passing family-friendly policies in the hope they

Table 7.5 *Types of welfare/work–family policy regime*

Country	Welfare regime type	ECEC system	Equivalent fully paid weeks of leave	Family allowances	Taxation	Avg. hours worked per year
Sweden	social democratic, dual earner	public	58	generous		1621
France	pronatalist and pro-family conservative, female secondary earner	mostly public	51; only 2 weeks paternity lv.	generous	*Quotient familiale*: horizontal redistribution	1479
Germany	conservative, male breadwinner	mostly public; CC not widely available	54	generous	Income splitting: favors male BW	1397
Japan	conservative/pro-business, male breadwinner	public/mixed; demand exceeds supply	45	modest	Dependent-spouse tax deduction: favors male BW	1745
United States	liberal, female secondary earner	private/market-based, scant regulation, expensive	0; no paternity lv.	none	Joint taxation: favors female secondary earner	1790

CC = childcare; BW = breadwinner
(Author's table, based on material discussed above)

will induce more young women to have babies. How well have these policies worked in reversing demographic decline?

Recalling the data in Table 2.1 for the five countries we are comparing here, in 2010 the total fertility rates for Sweden and France were virtually tied at 1.98 and 1.99; the United Stateswas at 1.93; and Germany and Japan both had TFRs of 1.39. On that basis, one might judge Swedish and French work–family policies, which were consciously crafted to make it easier for women to work and raise children, successful at encouraging young people to have babies at close to replacement levels. Fertility rates in the United States have been fairly steady since 1970, and there has been little public discussion or angst about the need to adopt work–family policies to encourage people to have more babies. Indeed, the United States has a sizable immigrant population and has been able to rely on the robust fertility rates of immigrants, especially Hispanics, to bolster its overall TFR. The steady forty-year decline in total fertility rates in Japan and Germany, on the other hand, reflects a situation in which young women apparently see pursuing satisfying careers and raising children as largely incommensurable. Work–family policies adopted in response to these countries' very low fertility rates do not as yet appear to have had much impact in reversing this trend, perhaps because they are not speaking to the most important issues facing young women and couples, or not addressing them vigorously enough.[4]

Support for working mothers

We surely ought to judge work–family policies on the basis of how well they support working mothers, and to ask *which* working mothers they support. Work–family policies in Sweden, France, Germany and Japan aim to support families in broadly similar ways: they use a mixture of subsidized childcare and early childhood education, paid maternity, parental and paternity leaves, family allowances, and tax payments to support specific family types (dual-earner couples in Sweden, families raising children in France, and dependent-spouse–male-breadwinner couples in Germany and Japan). American work–family policies, in contrast, revolve around market provision of care services with modest financial assistance, brief unpaid leaves and extensive use of the tax code.

---

[4] Although some commentators see lowest-low fertility rates as an indictment of societies that do not adequately support working mothers – see Esping-Andersen, 2009, ch. 3 – the United States and liberal welfare states in general fly in the face of this argument, since most of them have near-replacement TFRs alongside rather meager work–family policies. This might lead reasonable people to disagree about using fertility as a basis for judging the efficacy of work–family policies, since it suggests that decisions about having children are not necessarily a reflection of how easy or difficult it is to manage childrearing and work.

Taking a more fine-grained look, Sweden supports all working mothers with universal and generous paid leaves, easy access to high-quality childcare, laws that allow parents to scale back working hours to three-quarters time until their children start elementary school, and generous family allowances. Work–family policies in the three conservative welfare regimes, as we have seen, vary in policy design. France combines universal policies (e.g., *école maternelle*) with ones that target different groups. Its long flat-rate-reimbursed parental leaves are attractive to women in low-paid jobs, who are likely to use them fully, especially if they cannot find a space for their child in the *crèche* system. High-earning women with skills that will atrophy are more likely to return to work quickly and to utilize policies that subsidize hiring a nanny or an *assistante maternelle*. As we noted in Chapter 3, France's policy reorientation in the 1980s toward privatizing childcare and away from the *crèche* system encouraged many women to take long low-paid leaves. At the end of the day, modestly paid women may feel like their best option is to identify themselves as "family-primary," take a succession of long low-paid leaves, and make their peace with being marginal workers.

Germany's recent decision to restructure paid leaves to limit them to twelve months and link reimbursement to wages marked an important shift from policies that encouraged low-earning women to have babies and take long leaves, to ones that encourage high-earning women to have babies. The new one-year leave provides less financial incentive for poor and low-income women to have children, and pushes them to work to support themselves, sending the message that "it's OK if *you* have fewer babies, and when you do, the state will try to make sure that there are spaces for them in childcare or kindergarten so you can return to work and we can insure that your children receive good early childhood education to make up for the upbringing they get at home." In recent years, immigrant women have given birth to one-third of the babies born in Germany, and highly educated women have had very low fertility rates, which appears to be one of the reasons it adopted a policy that encourages high-earning women to give birth (Elger *et al.*, 2009, Kreyenfeld *et al.*, 2011).[5]

On paper, Japan's work–family policies resemble Germany's: both countries reinforce a male-breadwinner system; both have twelve months of paid parental leave plus two months of partner leave, and both provide child allowances. Japan's childcare system is better developed than Germany's, covering more

---

[5] I think it unlikely the new approach will boost Germany's overall total fertility rate. For that, long, flat-rate-paid leaves and plentiful high-quality affordable childcare would work better – though more immigrant and poor women would be having babies than highly educated "native" ones. It is obviously tricky to design parental leave laws that are perceived as fair and woman-friendly, and that work in demographic terms. France's long, flat-rate-paid parental leave is attacked for encouraging women to take several years off from working and hurting their long-term prospects for good work, Germany's for disfavoring poor immigrant women. See Henninger *et al.*, 2008.

children under the age of three whose parents work. However, Japan's family support policies are not always as available in practice as they appear to be. As we saw in Chapter 5, leave policies are a bit of a chimera in Japan, where a majority of women "retire" from their jobs when they give birth to their first children rather than taking the one year of paid leave to which they are entitled. Another example of the "less than meets the eye" problem is the long waiting lists for spaces for infants in licensed childcare centers: the centers are good, but there aren't enough of them. Japan's employment system also differs markedly from Germany's, especially its long-hours work culture and the sharp cleavage between regular and part-time, temporary and contract jobs.[6] And Japanese men are under intense pressure to work long hours of overtime and have less time to spend with their families than German fathers do.

Work–family policies in the United States are very modest compared with those in Sweden, France, Germany and Japan. There is no national paid parental leave, and few employers offer such benefits. Because FMLA leaves are not paid, many people cannot afford to take the full twelve weeks off. If they can arrange to do so, American families plan and save in order to take time off when a baby is born or adopted. Obviously better-off families manage to take time off around a birth more readily than poorer ones, a pattern one sees in the American market approach to care services too: those who can afford to hire a nanny or pay for a space in a well-staffed childcare center do fine, and those who cannot afford high-end care might rely on an untrained home care mother or a mediocre childcare center (often a commercial franchise), or find a family member who can care for their children without pay. Furthermore, the two means-tested programs (Head Start and CCDF) that support childcare and early childhood education are minimal, in the senses both that they are not funded generously enough to cover all needy children and that recipients are often demeaned in public debates.

Gender equality

I use several rough measures to get at gender equality here: gender and maternal pay gaps, the percentage of women elected to national legislatures, the percentage of women in senior management and professional positions, the share of women on boards of publicly listed companies, and the percentage of unpaid care work done by fathers. As we can see from Table 7.6, Sweden appears to be the most gender egalitarian overall, although France has the lowest gender and motherhood wage gaps, and the United States has more women in professional and senior management positions.

---

[6] Full-time jobs in Japan are better paid and come with valuable fringe benefits, including generous twice-yearly bonuses and job security.

Table 7.6 *Gender equality comparisons across eight countries*

Country	Gender pay gap			Mommy pay gap	% women in parliament			% women in senior mgnt.	Share of women on boards of listed companies	% women in professional positions	% unpaid care work done by fathers
	2000	2005	2010	2008–10	2000	2005	2010	2008	2009	2004	varies
OECD avg.	25.7	24.4	25.3	22.0	19.4	22.6	24.9	6.1	10.3	17	n/a
Sweden	15.5	14.4	**14.3**	21.0	**43.0**	**45.3**	**45.0**	3.5	**19.3**	19	**38**
France	**9.5**	**12.1**	**14.3**	**12.0**	11.0	12.2	18.9	6.8	18.1	12	29
Germany	21.0	22.0	20.8	25.0	31.0	31.8	32.8	3.6	3.5	11	32
Japan	33.9	32.8	28.7	60.9	5.0	9.0	11.3	n/a	3.9	n/a	12
United States	23.1	19.0	18.8	23.0	13.0	15.2	16.8	**13.9**	12.0	**22**	31

Sources: OECD, 2012d, 2013h. Data on unpaid care work are from Figure 2.5. (Bolded data indicate the country with the most woman-friendly policy for a given dimension and year.)

Sweden's generous work–family policies would seem to explain (or be explained by) the high percentage of women in the Swedish parliament, small gender pay gaps, and greater involvement of fathers in unpaid care work. But even without such policies, more American women are able to break through the glass ceiling than in other OECD countries: in addition to the 14 percent of women in upper management, 35 percent of all of management-level employees are female. Further, the costs of interrupting their work lives to have children is relatively small for American women: in lifetime earnings, mothers earn 80 percent of the income of women who do not have children (OECD, 2011b).

Ann Orloff believes American women do relatively well in competing for good jobs because the flexible, lightly regulated, general skills-based US labor market makes it easier for women to leave and re-enter the labor market, exacting less of an opportunity cost for interruptions and affording more possibilities for talented women to advance (Orloff, 2006; also recall from Chapter 1 the discussion of Estevez-Abe's argument that liberal states outrank Scandinavian social democratic ones in terms of gender equality). Access to higher education and well-developed legal protections against gender-based discrimination also make it easier for women to enter and succeed in male-dominated occupations. Even though Sweden does admirably on some measures of gender equality, its strategy of hiring women disproportionately for jobs in the public sector where their jobs are secure and tolerant of interruptions has created a female job ghetto. Although Swedish women do well with respect to the pay gap, few of them compete for high-paid jobs in the private sector.

Clearly, different national women's movements have pursued different gender equality strategies. In the United States, the women's movement has focused on marketplace equality, pursuing equal pay and nondiscrimination policies in preference to paid leaves and public childcare.[7] This has borne fruit, with women gaining greater access to well-paid elite occupations than in other countries, and structuring their lives around the demands of their jobs or professions, not their childrearing responsibilities.

Although many French feminists have criticized long low-paid parental leaves on the grounds that they hurt women's chances to advance in the labor market, they also tend to focus on pursuing non-discrimination and equal treatment and pay in the workplace rather than trying to change family policy (Lanquetin et al., 2000). Partly in response to such pressure, France passed a law in 2011 that requires employers to narrow the gender pay gap or pay a fine,

---

[7] This strategy was due in part to sharp philosophical differences between difference and equality feminists. Exponents of difference feminism are more likely to argue for maternity leaves and childcare, equality feminists to express anxiety about policies that provide benefits based on maternity and gendered childrearing responsibilities, treating women differently and better than men. Among mainstream feminists in the United States, the equality paradigm has been dominant.

which appears to have shrunk the gender gap. Gender pay gaps are narrower in France than in Germany, Japan and the United States, and historically better than Sweden as well.

There are divergent opinions about whether Sweden, France or the United States has the most gender equality, but no one would argue that Germany excels on this dimension, despite the fact that there are more women in the Bundestag than in the national legislatures of the US, France or Japan, and German fathers spend more time on care work than fathers in the other three countries. Women are paid less and more likely to work part-time than in France, Sweden or the United States, reflected in the fact that there are fewer women in senior management and professional positions as well as higher maternal and gender wage gaps. But German women are far ahead of their Japanese sisters. The gender and mommy pay gaps in Japan are huge, very few women serve on corporate boards or hold senior management or professional positions, the percentage of women in the Diet is low, and men do very little unpaid care work. Japan lags on every dimension of gender equality.

Japan's labor market practices and the private welfare system are costly to women, especially mothers. Tax deductions and the company-provided dependent-spouse allowances reinforce the male-breadwinner, stay-at-home mother pattern, and hiring practices that discriminate against women are commonplace. Most mothers quit working and stay home for a few years after giving birth, returning to work at low-paid part-time jobs once their children start school in order not to exceed the threshold for their husbands to receive dependent-spouse benefits. While German policy makers successfully linked policies to help women return to work quickly after having babies to economic growth, corporations in Japan have not supported such policies.

Demographers have shown for a generation now that there is a positive correlation between fertility rates and women's workforce participation – that is, countries where more women work have higher total fertility rates. Based on my comparative studies of work–family issues, there appears to be a similar correlation between gender equality and fertility rates. The fact that German and Japanese women are still faced with either-or choices between having children or having careers pushes many of them into the "no to kids, yes to career" camp, or perhaps postponing childrearing so long that they end up only having one child. If labor market policies were less discriminatory, attitudes toward working mothers less harsh, expectations of full-time workers in Japan less draconian, and spaces in childcare more available, these women might be more willing to commit to being working mothers. The statistics on maternal pay gaps in Japan in particular suggest a strong connection between gender discrimination, high opportunity costs and low fertility. The median full-time working mother earns 61 percent *less* than the median full-time male worker, an enormous "mommy penalty" compared to the OECD average mommy pay

Table 7.7 *Percentage children in poverty, 2008, breakdown by single parent and couple headed households*

| Country | Poverty among children | | Poverty in households with children and a working age household head | | | | |
| | | | Single | | Couple | | |
	2008	Point changes since mid-1990s	Not working	Working	No workers	One worker	Two or more workers
Sweden	7.0	4.4	54.5	11.0	46.0	18.5	1.4
France	9.3	0.3	45.7	16.5	21.8	10.5	2.3
Germany	8.3	0.2	46.2	11.6	23.2	3.7	0.6
Japan	14.2	2.1	52.5	54.6	37.8	11.0	9.5
United States	21.6	−0.6	91.5	35.8	84.1	30.6	6.6

Source: OECD, 2012e.

gap, which is 22 percent. If becoming a mother forever after relegates a woman to low-paid work, small wonder that many Japanese women are postponing or deciding against motherhood.[8]

Children's start in life

What kind of start do children get in life in the countries we have been comparing? Let us begin by looking at the percentages of children who are living in poverty in each country (see Table 7.7). About one in seven Japanese children and one in five American children were living in poverty in 2008, while less than one in ten children were in poverty in Sweden, Germany and France. Children are of course affected by the economic situation of their parents, and clearly families where no parent or other adult is working are more likely to be poor. But some countries are more likely to bail out such families with cash transfers or anti-poverty programs, others to expect the parents to find jobs to support themselves and their children. The poverty rate for single parent headed households where the household head is not working is much higher in the United States than in the other four. The message of the American Temporary Aid to Needy Families law is: "go to work or live in poverty."

What impact do work–family support policies have on children's start in life? Thinking back to Table 7.5 and the summary of basic work–family policies at the beginning of this chapter, we know the United States leaves it up to families

---

[8] Notice also that in large part gender pay gaps reflect the opportunity costs associated with mothers' decisions to take time off from work to raise children. In many countries, including France and Germany, women who do not have children make about the same amount men do (see Figure 2.4). Maternal wage gaps are the biggest reason for overall gender gaps in pay.

to support childrearing with fairly minimal tax expenditures and means-tested programs like CCDF, Head Start and TANF, while the other four countries all employ paid leaves, cash family allowances and state-supported early childhood care. They do not all support childcare and early childhood education at the same level, of course. Sweden and France have childcare attendance rates hovering around 50% for children under age three, while Germany has 23% and Japan 26%, and the United States is at 43%. But all except the United States have over 90% enrollment in kindergarten plus childcare combined. Out-of-pocket expenses for ECEC are heavier in Japan and the United States than in the other three countries, in part because of the reliance on privately purchased care and preschool.[9]

Less obvious from attendance and cost figures are the tradeoffs that low-paid American parents make as they search for affordable childcare on the private market. In 2012 about half the states had children on waiting lists to receive CCDF assistance (Schulman and Blank, 2012). In many states, high-quality childcare costs more than in-state college tuition at a public university – and these costs come at a point in the lifecycle when most parents do not yet earn hefty salaries.[10] Unlike the French *assistante maternelle* and nanny programs, which pay for the social contributions of childcare providers, many American parents pay their childcare providers under the table in order to *avoid* paying federal social security contributions, so they can keep their costs low and make sure that the full amount they pay goes into their provider's pocket. Paying workers under the table also avoids potential problems with employing illegal immigrants.[11]

In short, the American solution to providing childcare services without much public support is to rely on a large workforce of low-paid female care providers who are willing to work for low pay and without receiving benefits. The fact that the United States has a huge cohort of workers who are willing to take low-paid jobs and to work without benefits reflects a market system in which many workers are coerced to take such jobs, because they must support themselves and may not have skills that would give them many choices regarding work.

---

[9] This is particularly true in the United States, as Japan's licensed daycare centers are subsidized, but its *yōchien* system – preschool for children ages three to five – is mostly private and paid for by parents.

[10] The mean cost of full-time childcare in the United States is about $7,500 a year per child, or $625 a month. But the annual cost of full-time childcare for an infant in a childcare center varies enormously, from $4,600 in Mississippi to $15,000 in Massachusetts (ChildCare Aware, *Parents and the High Cost of Child Care: 2012 Update*).

[11] Susan Cheever points out that there are 400,000 children under age 13 in New York City whose parents both work, and fewer than 100,000 places for them in after-school and day care programs. The demand for childcare is met by an unregulated patchwork of agencies, experienced nannies, and thousands of immigrant women looking for jobs that require no training, no degrees and often no papers (Cheever, 2002, 32).

For example, TANF strictly limits how long families can receive cash benefits, and requires single mothers to work to support their children, and there are few active labor market policies to provide workers with the vocational training or education that might enable them to find jobs that pay a living wage. Coercion of a different kind may lead immigrants to come to the United States. Even if they are paid badly by US standards, they may be able earn more there than they would at home, and perhaps even send remittances back to their families. If such immigrants do not have a valid visa or green card, they can also be forced by their employers to work long hours for low pay and to put up with other kinds of abuse, on pain of being reported to the authorities and deported (see Glenn, 2012, who develops the idea of being "forced to care").

Scholars interested in interactions between care regimes and immigration policies point out that countries that spend little on ECEC are more likely to have laws that make it easier to rely on immigrant care workers (Gastineau-Grimes, 2012; Glenn, 2012; Michel and Peng, 2012, 410–11). The Catch-22 is that having large numbers of low-paid workers on hand undercuts demand for the government subsidies that might transform care work into a good job: Michel and Peng write that "the more or less continuous availability of low-paid private care workers has . . . meant that neither [the United States nor Canada] has developed much in the way of public services offering the kind of well-paid professional employment that would attract native-born workers. Instead, care-work remains largely informal, with few or no regulations, low salaries, long hours, and often exploitative conditions" (Michel and Peng, 2012, 414).

In a market-based, low-spending family policy regime, access to good care for children is controlled by the resources available to the family. The pertinent social cleavage is class, which is often interwoven with race, national origin, gender and access to education. Parents find the best childcare providers they can afford, but children from middle-class and wealthy families are more likely to receive good care than those whose parents can't afford to pay much. Building childcare around low-paid care providers means that

The average quality of child care in the United States is not high. An evaluation of the "process" quality of care (based on direct observation of the interactions between caregivers and children) in nine states revealed that just 9 percent of children aged fifteen months to three years (observed between 1996 and 1999) generally received positive caregiving, while 61 percent rarely or never did. A 1993–94 study of 749 classrooms in 401 child-care centers indicated that the quality of care was so low in 12 percent of the centers that basic health and safety needs were unmet. Quality was rated mediocre in nearly three-fourths of the centers, with only 14 percent supplying high-quality care; just 8 percent of infants and toddlers were in classrooms where the care was rated as high quality. This low process quality is accompanied by, and almost certainly related to, the deficiencies found when "structural" indicators of care such as group size, child–staff ratios, and caregiver training and pay are examined. (Ruhm, 2011, 49–50)

The problem is exacerbated for the children of poor families. In addition to limited finances, differences in access to information constrain ability to learn of high-quality care, as the contacts and networking that help parents identify good childcare centers in their communities and get their names on waiting lists well in advance of when they want to send their child to a center depend on information and cultural capital to which well-educated and well-informed parents have greater access. The lack of national standards and regulations and the patchwork of state regulations which are often laxly enforced also contribute to the extraordinarily low quality of childcare services in the United States. And as we saw in Chapter 6, for-profit childcare companies have lobbied effectively to defeat such regulations, in the belief that meeting higher standards for pay, qualifications and staffing ratios will cut into their bottom line.

Although better comparative data would bear out the significant differences in quality of early care in our countries, the statistics we have reviewed on state support for ECEC, the percentages of preschoolers and infants in ECEC,[12] the amount parents have to pay out of pocket to purchase care and preschool services, and the percentage of children living in poverty suggest that children get the best start in life in Sweden, followed by France, Germany and Japan, with the United States in last place. The start in life that children receive is extremely consequential for reproducing larger patterns of social inequality, the criterion we turn to next.

Social equality

As we have seen, in market-based systems the quality of ECEC a child receives is related to her family's resources, while in systems that are need-based or universal and that cover or subsidize the costs of care, children start out on a much more even playing field. Whether children get an equal start in life matters tremendously in terms of setting up the conditions that reinforce social equality (Esping-Andersen, 2009). Consider, for example, Torben Iversen and John Stephens's work that demonstrates how patterns of spending to support human capital acquisition (education, broadly speaking, from childcare through tertiary and vocational education) reinforce patterns of educational and

---

[12] What data would give us a sound basis for evaluating the tradeoffs in quality of care that children are receiving in the countries under comparison? It would be useful to know more about how well trained teachers are, the required ratio of teachers to children for various ages, and how high median national salaries are for childcare and preschool teachers. The OECD Family Database and the OECD Directorate of Employment, Labour and Social Affairs contain data from early 2010 on educational qualifications for teachers, and staff and teacher-to-child ratios for childcare centers and kindergartens (see the charts and discussion at "PF4.2: Quality of childcare and early education services"). But I think they are too cursory, unreliable and context-specific to be very helpful in making cross-national comparisons (OECD Family Database, accessed January 3, 2014 at www.oecd.org/els/social/family/database).

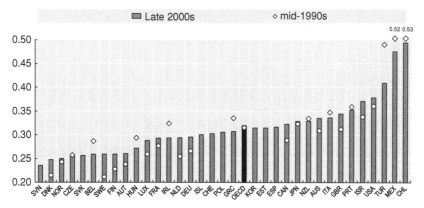

Figure 7.1 Gini index of income inequalities
Note: Data refer to mid-2000s instead of late 2000s for Greece and
Switzerland.
Source: OECD, 2011a.

employment (in)equality. They argue that different kinds of welfare states –
varying according to whether elections are structured as PR or majoritarian,
which political parties prevail, and the rules that govern the labor and capital
markets – produce distinctive patterns of investment in education (Iversen and
Stephens, 2008). Looking at Table 7.8 below, the scores for adult literacy are
much more unequal in countries that do little to support childcare, as well as
for those that spend more frugally and unevenly on public education. Moving
from the social democratic regimes to the conservative and liberal ones, the
level of support for childcare gets smaller and the gaps between the scores at
the fifth and the ninety-fifth percentiles get larger.

The point of the chart is to highlight the connection between social equality
and the generosity and universality of investments in education. Countries that
support childcare generously are able to minimize the differences in educational
outcomes among children. Countries like the United States that spend very little
on childcare, leaving most of the burden of paying for childcare to families,
compound inequalities in educational preparation for children that affect how
well they do in verbal and cognitive skills, their success in public education,
and eventually the skills they acquire that allow them to get well-paid jobs,
bad jobs, or no jobs at all (Iversen and Stephens, 2008, 616). Iversen and
Stephens convincingly demonstrate that high levels of wage dispersion and
income inequality are related to the unequal starts that children get, and show
that these are quite marked in the United States and the other liberal family
policy regimes. One can see this graphically in Figure 7.1, which shows the
Gini index of income inequalities (a standard measure of income inequality,

Table 7.8 *Measures of human capital and OECD Literacy Scores*

	Public education spending (% GDP)	Public higher education spending (% GDP)	Childcare spending (% GDP)	Vocational education (% of age cohort)	Adult scores on the OECD Literacy Test (1994–1998)			
					5th percentile	25th percentile	75th percentile	95th percentile
Social democratic welfare states								
Sweden	7.5	1.9	1.6	36	216	274	340	386
Norway	7.5	1.9	1.5	37	207	267	326	362
Denmark	8.1	2.1	2.0	31	213	264	319	353
Finland	6.6	2.0	1.2	32	195	258	322	363
Mean	7.4	2.0	1.6	34	207.9	265.9	326.7	366
Continental conservative welfare states								
Austria	5.7	1.3	0.5	22	N/A	N/A	N/A	N/A
Belgium	5.1	1.2	0.5	53	163	247	315	359
Netherlands	5.1	1.5	0.4	43	202	260	317	354
Germany	4.6	1.1	0.4	34	208	255	317	359
Switzerland	5.5	1.2	0.1	23	150	244	310	349
France	5.7	10	0.8	28	N/A	N/A	N/A	N/A
Italy	4.5	0.8	0.1	35	N/A	N/A	N/A	N/A
Mean	5.2	1.1	0.4	34	181	251.5	314.7	355.3
Liberal welfare states								
Australia	5.0	1.4	0.2	9	146	246	315	369
Canada	6.2	2.1	0.3	5	145	244	324	372
Ireland	4.8	1.2	0.1	6	151	227	306	352
NZ	6.7	1.7	0	7	158	237	313	361
UK	5.1	1.1	0.1	11	145	231	313	359
US	5.3	1.3	0.2	3	133	235	319	371
Mean	5.5	1.4	0.2	6.8	146.3	236.7	315.1	364
Asian conservative welfare states								
Japan	3.6	0.5	0.2	16	N/A	N/A	N/A	N/A

Based on Iversen and Stephens, 2008, 616, Table 3.

Table 7.9 *Gini index scores for five countries (detail)*

Country	mid-1980s	mid-1990s	2000	Late 2000s
Sweden	0.198	0.219	0.243	0.26
France	0.275	0.278	0.273	0.29
Germany	0.263	0.277	0.275	0.30
Japan	0.278	0.295	0.314	0.33
United States	0.338	0.362	0.357	0.38

where higher scores correspond to greater levels of inequality) for thirty-four countries, showing changes between the mid-1990s and late 2000s (for finer grained Gini score data covering a longer period, see Table 7.9).

In terms of income inequality, Sweden is the most egalitarian of the five countries we are examining here, although its Gini index increased significantly between the mid-1990s and the late 2000s. France did not change much over that period, while Gini coefficients increased modestly in Germany, Japan and the United States. Focusing on country-level differences, Sweden's educational policies resulted in the smallest gap between those at the 5 percent and 95 percent level for adult literacy scores and a relatively egalitarian income structure in which workers at the bottom of the pyramid earn enough to support themselves without help from the state. Politically, Sweden's policies have been possible because its PR electoral system has been dominated by Social Democrats and farmers for decades. It has a coordinated market economy (CME) in which organized labor and employers cooperate in providing rules and benefits that mitigate unbridled market competition.[13] This constellation of power is associated with more redistributive approaches to education and social policy, and helps explain policies that insure even the lowest-paid workers acquire relatively high-level skills and can work in information age industries like cell phone production (Iversen and Stephens, 2008).

France also has a CME and tries to cushion the impact of neo-liberal reforms like privatizing companies and letting uncompetitive firms go bankrupt by protecting the most vulnerable members of French society, especially the long-term unemployed.[14] France's Gini coefficient has been steady for the last generation, a period when inequality has increased substantially in many post-industrial

---

[13] CMEs are based on corporatist decision making institutions that include business and organized labor, and regulate the economy and labor market to make it more predictable and soften the impact on workers of retraction and unemployment.

[14] Although France's union density is only 9 percent, the lowest of the four countries examined here, labor discipline and strikes are more common there than in Japan or the United States (Iversen and Stephens, 2008).

countries. Although it does not fit the strong labor, social democratic profile of the Scandinavian countries and is not as redistributive as those countries, France's commitment to ideals of solidarity and support for children leads it to support childcare and early childhood education policies. Insofar as it supports high-quality public childcare, free universal preschool, primary and secondary education, and active labor market programs, France fits with countries that have coordinated market economies, PR-based electoral institutions and weak Christian Democratic parties (Iversen and Stephens, 2008, 608–9).

Germany's package of support for human capital acquisition fits Iversen and Stephens's profile of countries with PR and strong Christian Democratic parties in offering "high levels of vocational education and employment protection; medium levels of public spending on primary, secondary, and tertiary education; and low levels of spending on day care, preschool, and active labor market policy" (Iversen and Stephens, 2008, 631). Germany's lack of spending on childcare and limited spaces in full-day care and kindergarten have discouraged mothers from working, and channeled those who do work into part-time jobs (Iversen and Stephens, 2008, 616). On average German mothers earn 25 percent less than men, making its mommy gap twice as large as France's and slightly higher than that of the United States (see Figure 2.4). Although two influential studies in the early 2000s made the case for adopting a generous Swedish-style parental leave policy, feminists have not been as successful at challenging discrimination in the workplace as their counterparts in France and the United States.

Turning to Japan's record with respect to human capital acquisition, its spending on childcare, public education and public higher education are quite low: the figure for support of public education, 3.6% of GDP, is the lowest of all the rest of the countries in Table 7.8, and less than half the mean spending on public education in the social democratic countries. At 0.5% of GDP, Japan's spending on public higher education is also puny, between a half and a quarter as much as the average of the other groups of countries in this table. Its spending level for childcare is also comparatively modest: 0.2% according to Iversen and Stephens's figures, 0.3% according to 2009 OECD figures in Figure 7.1, putting it in the same league as the liberal welfare states. In part to remedy the low level of spending on public education, many Japanese families devote considerable private resources to pay for after-school cram schools (*juku*) and in some cases for private childcare.

Japan's Gini index for disposable income is 0.33, more than Sweden and the continental conservative countries but less than the United States. Income inequality has increased more steeply in Japan than in the other four countries since the mid-1980s, in part because Japanese society is rapidly aging and many elderly people have low incomes, and in part because of the way it has addressed economic downturns since the bubble economy burst in 1989.

(Japan's political economy is a focus of the next chapter, in which I address economic and job-related policies in more detail.) Not only is social stratification increasing rapidly, but there is a generational component to the winners and losers in Japanese society, with men in their thirties and forties being guaranteed they will not be laid off, at the cost of mortgaging the future because companies are hiring fewer new regular workers. Because job recruitment in Japan hinges on hiring new employees as soon as they graduate from high school or college, the decision to protect core workers has consigned many men and women who have just finished their schooling to badly paid jobs with no future. Due to Japan's longstanding, very formal approach to hiring, those who are unable to find permanent full-time positions at the appropriate moment are unlikely *ever* to be hired for a regular job. If they are not hired straight out of school, they do not get the crucial on-the-job training that new permanent employees receive and that secures their position with the company. There is no flexibility or opportunity to switch career paths later in one's career trajectory (Brinton, 2010). A consequence of this is that many young people are so financially constrained they are finding it harder to get married and have children, contributing to low fertility (Newman, 2008).

In addition to generational inequality, Japan's labor market is very tough on women. Because of statistical discrimination, women find it difficult to be hired for regular jobs, especially in a contracting economy.[15] Women are responding in divergent ways. Sven Steinmo believes it makes sense for women facing persistent discrimination to leave the labor force as soon as they can (Steinmo, 2010, 141–2). While some well-educated young Japanese women choose professional careers over having children, many still use their four years at university to find a smart, diligent young man with good prospects to marry, and settle down to the traditional *ryosai kenbo* (good wife and wise mother) ideal of Japanese womanhood, becoming attentive full-time mothers and housewives who make sure their children get every educational opportunity (Vogel, 2013). Such women are pulled into intensive mothering by the cultural ideal of raising children who do well academically and get into elite colleges, which requires mothers to push their children to excel. But the situation is harder for women who graduate from high school or two-year junior colleges and who do not have such good marriage prospects. Like their counterparts in other very-low-fertility countries facing high unemployment (such as Spain, Greece and Italy), they stay on the job longer and are more likely to see their contribution to the family income as essential to maintaining a middle-class standard of living. This group is more likely to delay marriage and childbearing,

---

[15] "Statistical discrimination" refers to making employment decisions on the basis of the statistical probability that women will take time off to have children, and that a high proportion will decide to drop out of the labor force for a period of years.

and to require infant childcare (or an available grandmother) so they can return to work soon after giving birth.

The United States stands out among the countries studied here for investing little in early childhood education and care, funding state schools unequally,[16] relying on high levels of private spending to pay for childcare, preschool and tertiary education, and having high and increasing levels of income inequality. Indeed, the Gini index figures for income inequality in the United States put it among the most unequal societies measured in Figure 7.1. High levels of inequality in the United States are rooted in its lack of policies to support high-quality care services, as we noted earlier. Because there is little government support for affordable care services, many Americans rely on being able to purchase such services for rock-bottom prices, relying on the fact there are lots of low-paid workers who may lack other marketable skills and who feel compelled to take jobs caring for children and old people. As in Japan, inequality patterns are gendered: low-paid care workers are more likely to be women, and many are also members of racial minorities or immigrants (Glenn, 2012). The issue of who takes care of the caregivers' dependents – how *they* can afford to pay for childcare or elder care – is scarcely addressed.

Iversen and Stephens explain this inequality by pointing to the fact that the United States has a majoritarian electoral system which produces center-right governments that favor employers and business, resulting in support for wide open market competition with little regulation, and education policies that exacerbate social disparities rather than minimizing them. The United States spends little on public education, public childcare, vocational education or public higher education, while using the tax code to subsidize middle-class families' expenses for higher education. This approach has generated huge educational disparities between the best and least well-educated: the United States has the lowest 5th percentile literacy scores of the seventeen countries in Table 7.8, but its scores at the 95 percent level are among the highest in the world (Iversen and Stephens, 2008, 616).[17] In countries where literacy gaps are less marked, wage differences between the least- and the best-educated are less dramatic, and there is greater social equality. The fact that the bottom 5 percent in the United States have such low skill levels means that they trail far behind middle-class wages, leading to huge wage disparities.

---

[16] The basis for such funding is mainly property taxes, so school districts in relatively poor cities or neighborhoods raise less money than those in well-off ones, a disparity in funding that, despite the fundamental importance of education, the US Supreme Court has upheld as constitutional: San Antonio Independent School District vs. Rodriguez, 411 US 1 (1973).

[17] Iversen and Stephens (2008) think that the high scores at the 95th percentile are due to the fact that North American universities are excellent, and Americans who can afford to do so devote considerable private resources, especially on their children's childcare and college education.

These wage disparities are due in part to the unregulated version of market capitalism practiced in the United States, in which personal responsibility and effort are much esteemed, and policies that interfere with market estimations of talent and value are widely derided. But the wide disparities in human capital and wages are also rooted in the history of organized labor in the United States. Due in part to reliance on semi-skilled, replaceable workers who were not inclined to insist on collective bargaining, labor unions did not develop strongly in liberal market economies, a trend that was reinforced by powerful union-busting tactics in the 1980s from leaders like Ronald Reagan and Margaret Thatcher. When assembly line-based manufacturing began to disappear, the unions were eviscerated and unable to hold onto an organizational toe-hold as service sector jobs were taken over by semi-skilled workers. This history of weak union movements is politically significant: since middle-class voters did not strongly identify with organized labor, they had no incentive to fight for a PR system over a majoritarian one. PR systems did, however, prevail in continental and northern Europe, because strong unions for skilled and semi-skilled workers were rooted in a history of guilds, artisan organizing and cooperation with farmers that dated back to the late eighteenth century. So when assembly line production declined there, the corporatist policy making systems distinctive of CMEs did not change dramatically, and labor kept its established role in economic decision making (Iversen and Stephens, 2008, 628–9).

Cost of work–family policies

Anyone who teaches courses in social policy or women's issues in an American university has probably encountered students who, whenever Sweden or France is praised for its generous support of social welfare policies, point out that taxes are much higher in those countries than in the United States. My students never fail to remind me that the low cost of work–family policies in the United States means that we don't have to pay as much in taxes. So I make the burden on taxes and government spending the last criterion for evaluating work–family policies.

Looking at Figure 2.6, which separates public spending into cash, direct services and tax measures, the countries spending in excess of 3.7% of GDP on things like child allowances, parental leave benefits and childcare support include France and three of the Nordic countries, along with Luxembourg, Ireland and the United Kingdom. Another nine countries (a mixed group of Nordic and conservative continental countries, plus Australia, New Zealand, Estonia and Hungary) are above the OECD average of 2.6%. The lowest-spending countries (below 1.5%) include Japan, Chile, Switzerland, Greece, the United States, Mexico and Korea. The five countries we are comparing here vary widely, with France spending 4% of GDP on families; Sweden, 3.75%; Germany, 3.06%; Japan, 1.49%; and the United States, 1.22%. All of them except Sweden rely partly on tax expenditures, although the highest proportions of tax spending are in the United States and Japan, where tax breaks amount to 43 percent and 36 percent of overall family spending, respectively.

Japan and the United States are among the lowest-spending welfare states within the OECD; if price tag is one's criterion, they do an excellent job of curbing high spending and keeping the tax burden low. But less public spending means that families are burdened with higher out-of-pocket expenses to care for children, or to pay for after-school supplementary lessons, cram schools or universities. Because tax deductions tend to favor relatively high-earning, high-tax-paying families, spending through the tax code is a less redistributive (or more regressive) way to support families than cash payments or providing services. Low spending is part of the reason that Japan and the United States have higher percentages of children living in poverty and higher Gini index figures than the other three countries.

Comparing cost with our other measures – demographic health, support for working mothers, gender equality, children's start in life, income equality – clearly there is a tradeoff between efficacy and cost. The countries with the policies that work best with respect to supporting children and working mothers and fostering gender and overall equality also spend the most. As we have seen, Sweden is the most egalitarian of the five countries examined in this chapter. It does well with respect to demographic health, supporting working mothers, gender equality, guaranteeing children a good start in life, and overall social equality. France is in second place: it does well on dimensions of fertility, support for working mothers and children, gender equality and social equality. Germany comes in third, combining generous support for married couples and child allowances, a low child poverty rate, and a Gini coefficient just a hair higher than France's with a low TFR, large gender and mommy pay gaps, and scant provision of full-time care for infants and preschool-age children.

More difficult than sorting out the top three is figuring out which is worse on our various dimensions for judging work–family policies, the United States or Japan. Both face serious problems that suggest the need to change how they support working families. Although its record with respect to work–family support is fairly dismal, I put the United States in fourth place. On the positive side, its population is reproducing itself, and it embraces some aspects of gender equality (mothers' opportunity costs are relatively low, and antidiscrimination laws support women's ability to compete for management and professional jobs). But on the negative side, it does little to support working mothers, fails to insure all children a good start in life, and fosters enormous economic inequality. I put Japan in last place using the criteria established here. Japan is the quintessential lowest-low-fertility country, so much so that, after Monaco,

Japan has the world's oldest median age in the world. Its work–family policies do not support working mothers effectively: it has high-quality, affordable childcare services which are not adequately funded to meet existing demand. And its leave policies, even though they sound good on paper, are not being used by a large proportion of the women and men whom they are designed to benefit. Women still face persistent discrimination in the labor market, and Japan has enormous gender and mommy pay gaps. Social inequality is relatively high: over 14 percent of Japanese children live in poverty, and many young people are being shunted into low-paid jobs, causing many to postpone marriage and have fewer children.

After factoring in how much countries spend on their policies, one might re-evaluate these rankings a bit. Yes, Sweden is the most egalitarian and supports working mothers the best, but its taxes are high and it spends a lot on those policies. Second-place France isn't quite as egalitarian or supportive, and it spends even more. Tax burdens and spending are not as high in Germany (where total support for families is 3 percent of GDP, in contrast to France and Sweden's 4 and 3.75 percent levels), and this might shift assessment of its performance a little. One might even assess the US approach positively, given how little it spends: the market does after all provide a lot of services, and government policies mitigate inequalities. Japan likewise spends very frugally, and has accomplished quite a bit in terms of policy reform to improve family support policies. I recognize that cost matters, and that, for many, keeping government spending low trumps offering the best possible work–family policies. But recognizing that children who are well cared for, nurtured and educated are a public good is at the crux of debates about family support policies, and the values we have explored here – the ability to reproduce the population, the capacity to support working mothers, gender equality, making sure children get a good start in life, and overall social equality – ought to be our touchstones for evaluating how well policies work, and not simply how cheap they are.

So why aren't countries flocking to be more like Sweden and France? And when they *do* adopt policies based on "best practices," why don't they work out so well in reality? The final chapter considers the political reasons why states are not always able to do what would be best for working parents and their children.

8   Why the United States can't be Sweden

Identifying best practices and recommending policy reforms that will help all countries to better support working mothers and children is an optimistic enterprise. It assumes countries aspire to be more just and generous by supporting young people as they raise their babies and insuring that all children get a good start in life. This book springs from this hopeful impulse; we have studied policies and policy design in detail, and Chapter 7 used comparative data to demonstrate that more generous work–family policies help cultivate demographically stable, egalitarian societies.[1]

But states are not blank slates. They come with their own policy histories and political institutions that make it more or less difficult to adopt particular policy approaches. No matter how much we might admire the approach taken by Sweden or France to supporting working parents, we need to grapple with the political, historical and institutional inheritances that shape how particular countries approach policy making in this area. We live in a less than ideal world where inefficient and biased policies are adopted because powerful interests stand to gain from them (a good example is the US health care system), and where there are deep and abiding disagreements about which values ought to be pursued. Countries have well-established constellations of political power, political rules and institutions, policy repertoires, ways of governing their markets and value systems. These shape the policy approaches they adopt to deal with particular problems, and, indeed, what they recognize as problems in need of solution in the first place. They rely on a variety of strategies to help parents manage work–life issues, strategies they develop due to deeply engrained political constraints and opportunities. Every country has a *political logic* that guides its approach to work–family policy making. While it is important to think about which policies work best, there are also crucial lessons to draw from a comparative study of the political and historical constraints on policy change.

---

[1] For other examples, see Gornick and Meyers, 2003, 2009; Jaumotte, 2003; Sleebos, 2003; Adsera, 2004; Bettio and Plantenga, 2004; D'Addio and Mira Ercole, 2005 and 2006; Immervoll and Barber, 2006, and the "Babies and Bosses" series from the OECD (OECD, 2003, 2007a).

We know that some countries do a much better job of supporting working parents than others; I want to understand *why* this is so. What constrains different countries' approaches to crafting work–family policies? Sometimes such policies may lack popular support, or fail to garner the support of powerful stakeholders. Sometimes well-designed laws don't work very well in practice because of inadequate funding and enforcement, or deep-seated values and practices that keep people from fully utilizing the services or claiming the rights to which they are entitled. Occasionally laws send contradictory messages, with some encouraging egalitarian dual-earner arrangements and others pulling people back toward male-breadwinner ones. Some countries confront ideological barriers to considering and adopting work–family supports. Or there may be institutional, structural reasons why governments do not act decisively to support work–family reconciliation policies, such as the difficulty of overcoming multiple veto points, or the division between the national and subnational governments in federal systems.

Because the organization of the labor market is important to women's and men's decisions about work, we also need to think about how states and markets interact. Are there formal rules governing flexible and part-time work? Does the state provide job-training programs for workers who are laid off? Are employers required to give their workers paid parental or maternity leaves? What kind of skills regime does the labor market embrace? What rules, norms and practices shape expectations of what constitutes a good worker, and how do these affect women and men differently?[2]

My study of work–family policies suggests that we need more than ideal types or templates for good policy: we also need to understand what impedes and facilitates adopting such policies. This chapter identifies different kinds of constraints on change by discussing how the following themes play out in our four countries:

1. the political economy of family policy: the connections among power resources, political institutions, the organization of markets, and work–family reconciliation policies;
2. institutional competence;
3. policy repertoires;

---

[2] I am beholden here to approaches to the political economy of family policy that combine power resource analysis with an appreciation for market regulation and skills regimes in order to provide insight into the development of policies that support working mothers (Thelen, 2004; Estevez-Abe, 2007, 2008; Rosenbluth, 2007; Iversen and Stephens, 2008). Iversen and Stephens in particular argue that we need to attend both to the organization of capitalism and to explanations rooted in political power and structure in order to understand the variation in support for policies that promote skills acquisition, ranging from childcare and early childhood education, to state schools, vocational training, tertiary education and active labor market policies.

4. the relationship between historical institutionalism and policy change and continuity;
5. cultural and ideological factors.

Though I focus here on barriers to change, I am not arguing that policy approaches are forever set in stone, or that change is impossible. Although I think it unlikely that countries like Japan and the United States will fully adopt "gold standard" approaches to dealing with work–family issues, they have changed and adopted better policies, and can continue to do so. I argue that their chances of bringing about meaningful reforms will be better if policy makers understand the political logic of policy change, are aware of and attend to deep-seated values, build on familiar policy repertoires, and bring along powerful interests. With this in mind, I suggest some feasible change strategies for each of my four countries. Even if the United States will never be Sweden, it can certainly aspire to be more like Australia or the United Kingdom.

I conclude with some general considerations about the value of an inductive approach that starts with consideration of policy histories and the logic of the policy making process.

The political economy of work–family policies: states, politics and labor markets

In political economic terms, France's coordinated market economy (CME) tries to cushion the impact of neo-liberal reforms, such as the privatization of companies and letting uncompetitive firms go bankrupt, by protecting the most vulnerable members of French society, especially the long-term unemployed. In the context of political debate about unemployment, work–family policies that ease mothers out of the workforce for a period of time are seen as reducing high unemployment rates and helping long-term unemployed people find jobs.

In France, most women work, and most of them work full-time (which is thirty-five hours a week, another CME accommodation to ease high unemployment). Children commonly are cared for at home until they start childcare (at a *crèche*, with a nanny or in the home of an *assistante familiale*) or preschool at age two and a half.[3] Little blame is levelled at working mothers in public discourse; in fact, some commentators praise the acceptance of working mothers in France and contrast it to the negative attitudes toward working mothers in Germany (Fagnani, 2002).

In 2007, German family policies shifted profoundly from an approach that favored stay-at-home mothers and male breadwinners to a "modern" family

---

[3] There are a variety of childcare options aimed at parents from different classes, and high-quality universal preschool.

policy approach that facilitates women's workforce participation, relies on state childcare centers, and encourages fathers to be more involved in childrearing. The adoption of a Swedish-style paid parental leave law in 2007 was an enormous change, hailed as a "sustainable" family policy that would revitalize the German economy and boost its total fertility rate. Implicit in the new leave law is the recognition that talented women should be encouraged to give birth, but also to return to their full-time responsible jobs reasonably quickly, keeping their interruptions for childrearing short. Business leaders, the Christian Democratic Union and the Christian Socialist Union have long backed the traditional male-breadwinner family, supporting long leaves and interruptions from the workforce for mothers, and opposing expanded childcare and kindergarten spaces. But they adopted a new course in the mid-2000s as they recognized that they would need to court young urban female voters, who wanted more progressive work–family policies, if their parties were to remain electorally competitive. This bit of political expediency, combined with a receptive audience for feminist arguments and a coalition of local notables and business leaders mobilized by the Family Ministry's campaign for the "Alliance for the Family," was decisive in garnering political support for ECEC and short well-paid parental leaves.

Similar policy changes in Japan appear to be less successful, in part because of business and political opposition to genuine reform of the labor market. Comparing family policy reforms in Germany and Japan, Martin Seelieb-Kaiser and Tuuka Toivonen argue that two key differences explain why reforms have been less successful in Japan than in Germany. First, German parental leave laws had always been mandatory; they never relied on voluntary compliance or permitted loopholes or exceptions. Against this baseline, employers were receptive to shorter leaves and to getting women back into the workforce quickly (Seelieb-Kaiser and Toivonen, 2011, 352). Japan, on the other hand, initially allowed only regular employees to take parental leaves, excluding part-time and temporary workers from coverage, and it provided no sanctions to force employers to comply with requests for paid parental leave (Seelieb-Kaiser and Toivonen, 2011, 344, 352–3).

Second, Germany courted business support for its breakthrough family-friendly legislation in the early 2000s, first under the leadership of an SDP–Green coalition government, then under the Grand Coalition government led by Angela Merkel. That campaign convinced business that it would be in Germany's best interest to make good use of the talents of women workers by facilitating their ability to give birth and return quickly to work.

But whereas German policy makers succeeded in convincing business leaders to support policies to help women return to work quickly after having babies, the Japanese Ministry of Health, Labor and Welfare has not convinced Japanese business leaders or political conservatives that progressive work–family policies will revitalize Japan's economy or reverse its long steady plunge in fertility.

Not having buy-in from big business in Japan is telling, because deliberative councils considering labor policy reforms always include representatives of big business and organized labor. For example, the initial work–life harmonization committee that formulated the Work–Life Balance Charter of 2007 was anchored by representatives from business (Keidanren) and organized labor (Sōren). The Charter embraced such goals as cutting the share of workers who work more than sixty hours a week, increasing productivity, encouraging workers to take all their paid holidays, and increasing the percentage of women who return to work within a year of giving birth. But Keidanren insisted on treating the Charter as a vision statement that exhorted companies and workers to do better without establishing any enforceable rights, because it "was adamant that the promotion of work–life harmonization should be based on self-directed, voluntary initiatives of companies and their workers – no uniform regulations or laws should be imposed by the state since suitable measures would vary according to company scale, type, and employment system" (Seelieb-Kaiser and Toivonen, 2011, 351). Indeed, most of Japan's workplace-related laws are voluntary, essentially setting goals and admonishing companies to behave well. The MHLW has been reluctant to take a confrontational approach to dealing with employers: it rewards exemplary companies, and tries to shame those that are not in compliance, but it will not sanction those who fail to comply with the law (Seelieb-Kaiser and Toivonen, 2011, 353–4; Tsukasaki interview, 2011).

In contrast to Germany's cultivation of conservative and business support for "sustainable" family policies, neither Keidanren nor the Liberal Democratic Party backs enforceable leaves in Japan. In part this is related to the structure of Japan's labor market, which relies on well-compensated and hardworking full-time workers who put in a lot of overtime, and underwrites this expense by relegating large numbers of women and young men to "irregular" (that is, part-time, contract or temporary) jobs that do not come with benefits, are badly paid, and do not lead to promotion.

Because Japan's CME prizes firm-specific skills, long absences for childrearing make a worker less valuable since she will be expensive to train and hard to replace during temporary absences for childrearing leaves. As I noted in Chapter 1, discrimination against women as potential mothers is both economically rational and difficult to eradicate: it doesn't make sense to invest in training a woman who will probably leave in five or six years (Estevez-Abe, 2007; Rosenbluth, 2007). This pattern of discrimination explains why Japan's maternal and gender pay gaps are so much higher than in Sweden, France, the United States or Germany (see Table 7.6, and Steinmo, 2010, 141).

The job system has been a focus of debate during Japan's long economic downturn since 1990. Because Japan did not want to increase the size and activity of its welfare state and create European-style policies to cushion high unemployment rates, it supported full employment by bailing out unproductive businesses. Instead of letting struggling companies fail and adopting active labor market policies that redeploy labor in response to market signals, the national government cushioned uncompetitive companies from the impact of market forces that threatened to push them out of business and *blocked* labor market adjustments. Having gone down that road, it became progressively more difficult to adopt liberalizing reforms because there were no welfare policies to compensate the laid-off workers who would have to bear the costs of adjustment (Levy, Miura and Park, 2006, 95–6, 132).

Protecting uncompetitive firms has come at a high cost: the percentage of employees in regular positions declined from 80 percent to 67 percent between 1990 and 2005, with the bulk shifting into irregular jobs (Steinmo, 2010, Table 3.11, 133). Even though this shift is creating wide-scale poverty and inequality, especially among younger workers, the government has done little to take up the slack (Steinmo, 2010, 133). As Sven Steinmo puts it, "The simple truth is that employers *are* the social safety net in Japan: When unemployment rises social welfare declines." Indeed, to the extent the government increased social spending in the 1990s, the increases mostly went to programs to support the aged, not to improving unemployment insurance or anti-poverty programs (Steinmo, 2010, 134; also see Levy, Miura and Park, 2006, 132).

The state's willingness to acquiesce to corporate decisions to protect the jobs of mid-career men, and consequently to hire fewer entry-level employees into regular jobs, has forced more young Japanese men and women to take jobs that do not provide benefits. In a country with a tiny welfare state like Japan, access to corporate-provided social security is essential to having the financial wherewithal and confidence to marry and establish a family. Perversely, barring large numbers of young people from such jobs and relegating them to part-time and other non-regular jobs greatly undermines the pronatalist work–family policies Japan has enacted over the last twenty-five years.

Thus, the organization of the labor market subverts Japan's well-intended work–family reconciliation policies. Bosses assume that women all quit work for several years when they have their first baby, limiting women's job prospects. Most women are relegated to bad jobs, except for a few ambitious, talented and well-trained women who compete for good jobs and accept that they must, like their male peers, minimize career interruptions. The state relies on company-provided dependent-spouse allowances that reinforce the male-breadwinner, stay-at-home mother pattern, and tolerates hiring practices that discriminate against women. Such labor market practices are hugely costly to women, especially mothers.

Like Japan, the United States also relies on employment-based benefits as a source of social welfare, including health insurance, pensions and paid parental leaves. According to a recent survey, 10 percent of private sector workers have access to paid family leave, a fringe benefit which is provided to attract and retain highly educated and trained workers and rarely covers low-paid workers with replaceable skills (Sundbye and Hegewisch, 2011).[4] But at least the United States has unemployment insurance financed through federal Social Security payroll taxes, and cushions the impact of companies downsizing and laying off workers.

Some American corporations have adopted voluntary human relations policies like flexible scheduling and part-time hours, anticipating the demand, from mothers particularly, for the opportunity to work shorter and more flexible hours when their children are small. But studies by labor sociologists have shown that in practice such policies are often not very accessible. Women who ask to cut back on their hours are sometimes subject to retaliation, and apt to find that they are excluded from working with important clients and on projects that require working under deadline pressure (Crittenden, 2001; Stone, 2007; Hochschild and Machung, 2012). Relying on corporate munificence is not a reliable approach to work–family reconciliation.

The absence of strong unions and a labor party in the United States, and the existence there of a majoritarian electoral system that favors two centrist parties have contributed to low social welfare spending and light labor market regulation.[5] Business has a favored position in politics and the policy making process, in large part because of its crucial role in campaign finance. Even after the 2008 financial meltdown, American labor and capital markets continue to be largely unregulated. Most employers do little to welcome or accommodate parents who have infants or small children, and business groups have been vocal and effective opponents of parental and family leave laws (Bernstein, 2001).

The United States is a general skills regime, which values degrees and credentials that workers acquire from training programs and educational institutions. Such skills are readily transferrable, allowing workers to take their skills from one position to another (in contrast to firm-specific skills, which are not transferrable and require the company to make a big investment in the worker). As a result, the American labor market is relatively mobile and flexible. It neither does much to protect workers from layoffs, nor acts to block them from re-entering the job market after taking time off. Thus American mothers find it relatively easy to obtain work after taking time off to raise children, and are

---

[4] Of workers in the highest earning quartile, 16 percent had access to paid family leave, while only 4 percent of those in the lowest earning quartile did (Sundbye and Hegewisch, 2011, 3, and table 3).

[5] This is in contrast to PR-based electoral systems, which facilitate multiple political parties representing several distinct ideological positions, and are associated with coalition governments and more generous social welfare provisions.

less likely to be shunted into part-time jobs than their German and Japanese counterparts (although this depends somewhat on their education and training). This keeps the opportunity costs of taking time off from work to raise children relatively low, as do strong federal laws that require equal pay for the same job[6] and prohibit gender- and pregnancy-based discrimination in the workforce[7] (O'Connor, Orloff and Shaver, 1999; Orloff, 2006).

France and Germany are sectoral skills regimes (which means workers acquire skills that are useful for the sector they work within, e.g., banking or auto assembly; they are more transferrable and easier to acquire than firm-specific skills). They are CMEs, based on corporatist governance of markets, jobs protection, and active labor market policies that help retrain workers who have been laid off so they can get new jobs (Iversen and Stephens, 2008, 616, Table 3). Japan is also a CME, organized around firm-specific skills and key workers who have secure jobs, plus a growing proportion of workers in irregular jobs. The United States is a liberal market economy which puts a premium on general skills. Market governance is light, and controlled more by employers than workers; there is lots of labor mobility and big variations in the level of income. With respect to political economy, Japan and the United States are both pro-business, market-oriented regimes, but organized labor has more voice in Japan than in the United States, and Japan does more to support companies that wouldn't be competitive in a truly free market. France and Germany are both responsive to workers and business interests, and protective of families – but France looks after children while Germany supports couples and spends less on childcare and kindergarten.

Institutional competence

There is a growing sense of crisis in countries faced with declining fertility rates and economic productivity, and the conundrum of having to finance benefits for a growing elderly population with a shrinking cohort of employed adults. At the same time many countries find it difficult to respond with well-judged, generous policies to ease work–family tensions and encourage working women to have families. The degree of control that national governments are able to assert over policy making is crucial for their ability to respond to new needs or crises as they arise. When states can exercise power and authority with alacrity, with few political or structural impediments to action, they are more likely to respond to the needs of working mothers, who are now an important segment of the workforce in most wealthy countries.

---

[6] For examples, the Equal Pay Act of 1963 and the Lily Ledbetter Act of 2009.
[7] Two such measures are Title VII of the Civil Rights Act of 1964 and the Pregnancy Discrimination Act of 1978.

Power can be mobilized more easily when the executive and legislative branches of the government are controlled by the same party. Power sharing, which is fairly common in the United States and France because presidents are elected independently of the national legislature, can make this kind of singular exercise of power difficult. So can federal systems in which governments at national and state (or prefectural or *Länder*) levels share governing responsibility, especially since many of the issues that are central to work–family reconciliation (especially childcare and early childhood education) are decided at the sub-national level. Dispersion of responsibility to geographically distant, politically, socially and culturally diverse local governments introduces the likelihood of regional variation, and increases the difficulty of overcoming differing values and political biases to arrive at standardized national regulations or approaches.

To take a case in point, Germany's federal system and longstanding preference for subsidiarity have made it difficult for the national government to mandate that the cities and *Länder* build and operate more state-regulated, subsidized childcare centers. As we saw in Chapter 4, the percentage of children attending full-time care varies enormously by region (see Figure 4.1). Furthermore, what constitutes "full-time" care is informed by Germany's longstanding preference for short school days, which end around 1.00 p.m., when children return home to eat lunch (Hagemann, 2006). Many German sources consider "full-time" childcare to be as little as six hours per day, which is not enough to cover a full-time work schedule.

Although Germany has undertaken real and dramatic change in its approach to work–family policies, whether it will be able to increase its total fertility rate will depend on the availability of childcare to permit women interested in well-paid careers to manage childrearing and work at the same time. The impetus for fundamental change came from the federal government, but the *Länder* must actually build, staff and administer the new childcare centers. It remains to be seen what the real magnitude of these changes will be. Although Germany set a target for itself of providing space for one third of children aged one and over to attend full-day childcare by 2014, so far it is laboring to attain that target.[8]

In addition to the difficulties presented by federalism, procedures that require multiple institutions to pass or fund a law, which are central to national-level policy making in the United States, constitute a series of consecutive veto points that make it easy to derail legislation, particularly when there are deep divisions

---

[8] In March 2012, 23.4% of all children younger than three had a place in a public childcare institution. In addition, 4.3% were cared for by publicly financed childminders. Of this 27.7% total, 51% are in full-time care (defined as 36 hours and above per week), 27% have part-time places (26–35 hours) and 22% attend childcare less than 25 hours a week (data are from Statistisches Bundesamt, 2012).

of opinion, as is often the case with issues related to family responsibilities. Because laws must be passed by majorities or supermajorities in both houses of Congress and signed into law by the president, there are many points where a single institution can refuse to pass a law and stop it in its tracks.

Veto points can be built into a country's formal political institutions, as in the United States, or in more informal policy making processes, as one can see with Japan's reliance on deliberative councils where business is always represented. Big business exercises veto power over tough, enforceable work–family laws in Japan, insisting on "soft" measures like suasion and education as the only appropriate tools for encouraging employers to cooperate with laws about hiring and firing parents. States with multiple or strong veto points built into their formal or informal policy making processes are less able to respond quickly and affirmatively to work–family issues than ones that are more centralized, where policies can be enacted by a simple parliamentary majority and implemented by a ministerial apparatus under the prime minister's control.

In addition to federalism and veto points, countries vary considerably with respect to how readily executive branch actors can exert control over the social policy making process. Both France and Japan have strong national bureaucracies that are composed of well-trained, competent graduates of elite universities. Bureaucrats in both countries are responsible for introducing policy measures and shepherding them through the legislative process. Government ministries and their allied think tanks and research institutes constitute an elite policy making body, respected as expert and understood as having continuing projects, missions and goals regardless of the government in power. Even though the career bureaucrats in Germany's Family Ministry, the BMFSFJ, were constrained by the fact that the federal government is not responsible for childcare or early childhood education, by the early 2000s they recognized that policy windows were opening, in the sense that the political leadership of the SDP was pushing for briefer and more generous parental leaves and expanded childcare for young children (Helmke interview, 2004), initiatives which the CDU-led Grand Coalition government continued to champion after it took power in 2005. The BMFSFJ became an integral player in terms of bringing business leaders and local mayors and members of civil society into an "Alliance for the Family" which backed a profound change in work–family policy orientation, including a deal between the federal government and the *Länder* to expand spaces in childcare for children aged one and over.

Japan's national ministries – the Ministry of Health, Labor and Welfare, the Ministry of Education, and the Cabinet Office Gender Equality Bureau under the Prime Minister's office – have been the architects of policy deliberation and change, albeit with weaker party and prime ministerial political leadership and less support from key business constituencies than in France or Germany. Various changes (electoral reforms, widely publicized stories of ministerial malfeasance and corruption, and efforts to streamline and more closely regulate government ministries) have affected the role that bureaucrats play in the Japanese policy process. They are still respected and competent, but they operate in a political climate that is more uncertain and skeptical, where the levers of power are harder to control.

In contrast to in France, Germany and Japan, the national-level bureaucracy has not played a key role in fostering work–family policy innovation in the United States. A career working as a federal bureaucrat is not the preferred destination of most top graduates of the US's most prestigious social science university programs (business and law are). Policy innovation is much more likely to originate from the president or one of the two houses of Congress than from the executive branch departments. Congress has its own sources of information and policy analysis, and does not rely on the executive branch for data or expertise, which shifts policy making initiative and power toward the legislative branch. Within Congress, the upper house (the Senate) often invokes rules for ending debate that require a sixty-vote supermajority, which has the effect of making it quite difficult to muster consecutive majorities to pass generously supported social spending bills, and, since each state has two senators, the Senate over-represents sparsely populated, relatively conservative states.

Policy repertoires

Turning next to the importance of policy repertoires for understanding why some approaches are more congenial to policy makers than others, I want to begin by considering the familiar historical institutionalist argument that starting points matter. Paul Pierson uses the example of the QWERTY keyboard to explain how an early technological innovation foreclosed development of more logical or easier-to-use keyboard layouts: once typewriters started being made with this layout and secretarial schools began to teach people how to type on them, too many powerful interests had a stake in preserving this approach for it to be able to change (Pierson, 2004, 23). Likewise, early and ubiquitous policy approaches have had path-dependent effects in the work–family policy making process in each of our countries, which continue to shape their approaches. For example, France set up the Family Allowance Funds (the CAF) 100 years ago as employers set up voluntary funds to help working fathers support their families. The CAF have grown into a well-articulated infrastructure that still collects the contributions that pay for many of France's family support policies, and they have spawned myriad groups who have an interest in continuing to administer family policies this way (the CAF and the CNAF employ administrators, clerical staff and researchers; union and business leaders sit on their governing boards; care providers and teachers are paid out of funds they collect; and millions of citizens count on funds and services paid for by the CAF). There is a kind of institutional inertia to the CAF: they are rooted in localities and particular enterprises, they are represented in governmental bodies and decision making, and their continued existence and role in policy making is taken for granted. Though its roots are more recent, another good example of path dependency is the law passed in the postwar period granting the UNAF (National Union of Family Associations) a formally recognized role in deliberations about family policy. This guaranteed that concerns about large families and pronatalism would be voiced in family policy circles.

In Germany, the ideal of families or local charitable and other organizations taking responsibility for meeting welfare needs (subsidiarity) is a policy legacy that continues to shape policy making. The Alliances for the Family aim to build support for new work–family policies through a network of local mayors, businesses and employers, church groups and others interested in welfare, children and education. Working on support for work–family policy in this grassroots fashion reflects a deep-rooted pattern of wanting local actors to take responsibility for social welfare. Another example of path-dependent policy development is Germany's system of having students attend school until early afternoon, then returning home for a late lunch. Such part-day school schedules made sense when children were needed to come home to do farm chores or work at home or in the family business; arguably they do not make much sense today, when it might be a help to working parents to have their children in school until 3.30 in the afternoon, and after-school care available later than that. But teachers and school administrators, the clerks in shops and grocery stores (whose schedules allow them to be home by 7.30 or 8.00 in the evening and on Sundays because stores have limited hours in Germany) and the unions that represent them are not eager to change the school schedule.

Japan has long used an approach to regulation called administrative guidance, which sets forth goals and expectations for desired results but does not punish those who fall short of such goals. As we saw earlier, this regulatory approach reflects the veto power that business interests exercise over more stringent approaches that would require compliance with policies or laws. It is also a good illustration of a well-ensconced standard approach to policy making that continues to shape policy design. Relying on suasion and education as tools to convince employers to go along with family-friendly laws clearly builds on this approach, which reflects a cultural preference for harmony and cooperation over confrontation and discord.

Another example of path-dependent policy development is the strategy of relying on private corporate welfare, particularly the practice of protecting workers from layoffs. In Japan, protecting companies from harsh competition and market forces that would otherwise force them to declare bankruptcy has become a functional equivalent to providing unemployment insurance and active labor market policies like retraining programs. But this policy repertoire has undermined Japan's commitment to functional work–family policies in three ways: first, bailing companies out takes a lot of money that might be used to build more childcare centers and provide more spaces for children needing care. Second, protecting the jobs of mid-level male employees has pushed more women and young men into irregular employment because companies cannot afford to hire as many people as in the past. This in turn has had a negative impact on family formation and fertility rates, as regular jobs are the key source of company-provided welfare benefits, and young people who work as part-timers do not have access to them. Third, employers reinforce traditional male- breadwinner arrangements by providing dependent-spouse benefits and by pushing women to leave the workforce once their first child is born, creating a massive mommy penalty as mothers are relegated to badly paid irregular jobs.

Several historians of the American welfare state analyze the distinctive politics of relying on tax expenditures to subsidize privately provided welfare services (Howard, 1997, 2007; Hacker, 2002, 2005; Abramovitz and Morgen, 2006). Tax credits and deductions give money back to taxpayers to help them pay for such things as dependent care providers, but they do not appear as budget outlays: the government simply forgoes revenue it would ordinarily receive from taxpayers because of reductions in the amount the individual or family has to pay. Tax breaks are easier to pass and maintain than direct spending laws because they are not very visible, and do not arouse as much opposition as conventional welfare measures. Typical budgeting practices make tax expenditures easy to maintain once they have passed,[9] and they can be enacted with greater ease and more frequently than public programs (Abramovitz and Morgen, 2006, 48–9; Howard, 2007, 123). As a result, measures like the Dependent Care Tax Credit and deductions and credits for dependent children are commonly used to help families pay for childcare and other services. Notice, however, that tax payments are biased in favor of relatively well-off citizens who make enough money to owe the federal government taxes; families who are poor or struggling often receive no benefit from tax credits or deductions, which generally only count against taxes owed (the exceptions here are refundable tax credits like the dependent Child Tax Credit and the Earned Income Tax Credit).

In addition, a range of other family support laws have been designed as means-tested benefits, such as Aid to Families with Dependent Children (until 1996), Temporary Aid to Needy Families (since then), the Head Start program for babies and preschoolers, and the Child Care Development Fund. Advocates of this approach argue that means-tested benefits cost less than universal ones, and insure that those who need assistance the most will get help. However,

---

[9] Generally tax expenditure items are carried over from one year to the next with little discussion or change (Howard, 1997, 180, 183).

universal programs are higher in quality and less vulnerable to attack and de-funding, and, when used for early childhood education and childcare, they insure that all children will get a good start in life (French preschool is a good example). Because the United States has largely relied on means-tested approaches to childcare and early childhood education, it is difficult to enlist middle-class support for universal high-quality affordable childcare services, as many middle-class parents either do not use childcare or have been able to find reasonably good and affordable care for their children, so they have little reason beyond altruism or enlightened self-interest to push for a generous universal program. But such laws are impossible to pass without middle-class support when there are provider groups – especially the for-profit childcare sector – who have a vested interest in insuring that most childcare continues to be market-provided and lightly regulated (Michel, 1999; Morgan, 2006, 141–2).

Historical institutionalism and policy change vs. policy continuity

When I first tried to write about the theoretical underpinnings of this book, a colleague suggested that I needed to figure out whether the central dynamic in the work–family policy area was stasis or change. I construed this advice as a warning: committing myself to a historical institutionalist approach would amount to buying into a story of continuity that might not be very useful for understanding dynamic processes of change that are transforming work–family policies in many countries.[10] But, as I reflected on the matter, I came to think that the antinomy my colleague proposed between continuity and change was too stark. Paying attention to historical starting points and institutional evolution does not blind one to change and innovation. Indeed, whether work–family reconciliation policies are fundamentally continuous and incremental or are new departures that stake out fundamental policy changes, any sensible interpretation of social policy making has to pay attention to starting points in order to understand the political forces and dynamics that reinforce patterned approaches to policy making.

Taking the United States as an example, Jacob Hacker argues that the American failure to respond over the last few decades to expanded needs as more mothers are working outside the home has opened up a widening gap between the needs that families face and the services and payments that the federal government provides (Hacker, 2005, 44, 50–51). Although less visible than the changes that have resulted in the adoption of new policies to help working

---

[10] For example, a number of work–family policy scholars argue that ideas and framing play a crucial role in bringing about policy innovation, an approach which is somewhat at odds with attending to path-dependent policy developments (Beland, 2005, 2009; Fleckenstein, 2011).

mothers in Germany and Japan, inaction in the face of broad social changes that have brought most mothers into the workforce is a form of policy change, too. Hacker describes this policy dynamic as one of *drift*, whereby approaches that have long been dominant continue in place, perhaps with efforts from opponents striving to curtail the expansions needed to keep up with expanded needs. The point is that the refusal to keep up with growing needs, although it looks like stasis rather than motion, amounts to retrenchment or backsliding insofar as it results in more unmet need. As Hacker writes,

In a context where social risks are changing and policy drift is ubiquitous and consequential, conservatives have not had to enact major policy reforms to move toward many of their favored ends. Merely by delegitimizing and blocking compensatory interventions designed to correct policy drift or ameliorate intensified risks, opponents of the welfare state in the United States have gradually transformed the orientation of social policy. (Hacker, 2005, 71)

Hacker makes the point that policy change in the United States is occurring in patterned, predictable, path-dependent ways. Because so much of American social policy relies on tax payments and private provision of services, policy and institutional design already favor conservative outcomes, as tax payments and purchasing services in the market favor the wealthy. He argues that the political process in the United States makes it easy for conservatives and stakeholders who benefit from current policies to block efforts to expand tax payments and to oppose approaches that would define problems and solutions in more encompassing, interventionist and expensive ways. As a scholar of the American welfare state who argues that much of the welfare effort is provided privately, through employment-based benefits, Hacker reminds us that private programs also develop in path-dependent ways. He argues that privately provided benefits have thrived in the United States *because* of their low visibility, and because their supporters include both direct beneficiaries and highly organized and resourceful sponsors and providers of benefits.[11]

Setting up institutions and policy making processes creates a bias in favor of vested interests that gain from continuing to rely on these approaches, and insures that they will be consulted and heeded when new approaches are being considered. Even when change is afoot, this kind of deep institutional conservatism is a force to reckon with. As Hacker puts it, "Path dependency does not preclude change but instead systematically conditions it. This argument has begun to correct the strong tendency in previous historical institutional research to privilege stability in description and explanation and therefore treat

---

[11] Advocates for private provision of family support services include private for-profit childcare chains and big business groups like Business Roundtable and the US Chamber of Commerce, the same groups that oppose expanding the state's role in supporting childcare or requiring employers to grant longer job-protected paid leaves to parents of young children.

institutional change as exogenous. What is emerging is a more variable and dynamic conception of path dependency" that sees path-dependent institutional changes as internally generated, and exhibiting strong continuities over time (Hacker, 2005, 72).

In short, I think the change vs. continuity dichotomy is a bit of a red herring. Whether we observe continuity or change, path-dependent effects are inevitable, and important focuses for scholars of the policy process. We need to understand how starting points and institutional arrangements condition change and affect the ability of groups and interests to be active and effective in shaping policy development on down the road. This is true not just in the United States but in France, with its commitments to familialist groups and arguments; in Germany, with its legacies of intensive mothering, part-time school days and subsidiarity; and in Japan, with its reliance on corporate-provided welfare and administrative guidance.

Cultural and ideological factors that undermine support for work–family policies

Both Germany and Japan subscribe to norms of male responsibility for earning a living and intensive mothering that undercut some of their progressive policy reforms. Men who dare not seem uncommitted to their jobs are unlikely to embrace paternity leaves, and mothers who work full-time often feel that they are not providing their children with proper nurture. German and Japanese mothers are well aware of the social norm that babies need to be cared for full-time before the age of three, and in Germany the term *Rabenmütter* ("raven mothers") is still used to disparage mothers who work outside the home.

Conflicting policies also send mixed messages about gendered divisions of labor. On the one hand, the provision of two months of paternity leave encourages greater sharing of childrearing work between parents. On the other hand, Germany has held fast to its income-splitting approach to joint taxation, despite feminist arguments that this policy pushes women to work part-time, accept low wages or stay home (Wersig interview, 2004; Wersig, 2006).[12] Similarly, Japan continues to offer dependent-spouse tax deductions and special payments, reinforcing gendered divisions of labor, even as it has adopted two months of use-it-or-lose-it paternity leave.

An important reason why Japan's work–family policy reforms do not work very well in practice has to do with the greater weight given to one's identity as an employee who is committed to the workplace, as opposed to the merely

---

[12] The Federal Constitutional Court for decided in the early 1980s that income splitting, one of the most expensive of Germany's family policies, could not be altered and remain consistent with constitutional protections for married couples (Wersig, 2006, 6–7).

private concern with one's own family. I begin by situating this argument about the conflict between family and work priorities in the context of an argument that Leonard Schoppa makes about young women struggling with whether to have babies or careers. Schoppa relies on Albert Hirschman's notions of "exit" and "voice" to explain why women do not speak up to ask for work–family reconciliation policies that would help them pursue careers while raising children. If there were lots of young women struggling to "do it all" in Japan, trying to raise children and return promptly to work in order to keep their careers alive, then one would hear more about the challenges they face, the policies they would find most helpful, and their demands for government action. But Schoppa believes the group of women opting for kids and careers is small, because most Japanese women exit the kids-or-career dilemma, either by remaining childless and pursuing a career, or by having children and giving up on a career. Because there are few young Japanese women struggling to do both at the same time, there has not been a sizeable constituency with a stake in pushing for working-mother-friendly policies, hence no exercise of voice via protest votes, manifestos, or organized groups pushing for policy change or insisting on representation in deliberative councils (Schoppa, 2006, 2010).

But this insight sidesteps a fundamental question, which is *why is it* women have been so prone to adopt one or the other of the "exit" strategies and not to exercise "voice" and struggle for policies that would help them manage the messy but satisfying life of the mother with a lifelong career? The answer is rooted in the deep tension between what in Japan are regarded as the "public" needs of the workplace or corporate employer and the "private" need to be a nurturing, present mother to a small child.

As we noted earlier in discussing the political economy of Japan's work–family policies, there is a certain economic rationality to discriminating against women as potential mothers which has led some women to internalize the norm that their first loyalty should be to the workplace if they value their job and want to prosper and be promoted: they adopt the life course of a typical male by acquiring few familial responsibilities. Conversely, women who decide to have children are made to feel that they are making special demands if they ask for a year of leave, even though this is guaranteed under the law and their employers are in theory supposed to honor that. Only about a quarter of women who become pregnant plan on continuing to work after they give birth; the other 75 percent exit the dilemma of how to manage as a working mother with a full-time, lifelong career. Most of them spend a stretch as full-time stay-at-home mothers, then return to work once their children are in school (recall the discussion of this in Chapter 5). A surprisingly large number of women opt out of the committed, lifelong labor market trajectory, even though the opportunity costs – what they will lose in forgone earnings because they decided to have children – are extremely high. Why aren't more of them struggling to stay on the job and demanding policies that will help them raise children *and* work?

They quit because they know that they will be given the cold shoulder by their colleagues and supervisors if they ask for a leave. They will perforce put their colleagues to a lot of trouble, since employers are not keen to hire and train temporary workers to take their place, given the firm-specific skills required in Japanese workplaces. Co-workers will be asked to take up their responsibilities while they are absent, and this is likely to evoke resentment and chilliness once women return to the workplace from their parental leave (on this point, recall the discussion in Chapter 1 of Estevez-Abe's arguments about parental leaves causing resentment in firm-specific skills regimes). If they ask for their leave, they are insisting, in essence, on the importance of their merely private desire to be devoted mothers for a year, and those are held to be trivial and selfish next to the concerns of workplace harmony and corporate productivity and profitability.

Seelieb-Kaiser and Toivonen get at this tension when they argue that the structural dynamic that makes it difficult to hire replacement workers when someone takes a leave, "combined with a strong cultural aversion to 'causing trouble to others' (*meiwaku wo kakeru*) that tends to dampen individual assertions of entitlements, has . . . limited the propensity of many Japanese employers to support robust parental leave schemes for even professionally well-trained women" (2011, 353). Private claims don't carry much weight when juxtaposed to the public importance of the company and the collective good of one's colleagues.[13]

Being a good mother and a good worker conflict sharply in Japan, where responsibility for having and raising children is associated with the private sphere. As we can see from the chilly reception of women whose needs for time off impinge on their colleagues, women as mothers do not belong in the Japanese workplace.[14] It has also been difficult to recognize childrearing as a focus for public support in the United States. Americans still largely view childrearing and unpaid domestic work as private matters that families should arrange with minimal official scrutiny or interference. Since the Reagan

---

[13] Many people still believe that the source of a working man's identity and well-being is his employer, and the good of the company is the source of the collective good of the economy and state. On the other hand, many women are horrified by this view and take pride and pleasure in being good mothers and nurturers, in touch with a range of meanings and values that are coded as feminine in Japan.

[14] Steinmo recounts a memorable story in this vein, of the dean of the faculty of a university publicly shaming a female professor who had asked to take parental leave (2010, 141). See Boling (1990) for a fuller discussion of the valences of public and private in Japan.

Revolution of the 1980s changed the political discourse in the United States toward suspicion of expensive tax-financed public programs administered by bloated, intrusive state machineries, many Americans uncritically accept the argument that it is good to keep taxes low and shrink the size of the federal government. Respect for the privacy of family arrangements and "choice" are treated as talismanic. The lobby for affordable, high-quality childcare and preschool argues often and ably against this position, but without much traction.[15]

What policy changes are possible?

Policy change is a matter of intelligent strategy, not just aspiration and exhortation. So what should advocates and policy makers who would like to advance generous work–family policies *do*? I briefly sum up where each country is at, and suggest directions for change that make sense for each of them.

Of the four countries we have studied, France's work–family support policies are the most generous, varied, deep-rooted and stable. France has managed innovation and change alongside deep currents of continuity; it uses income-targeted policies alongside universal and pronatalist ones. Varied and encompassing approaches have been possible because family support policies have been relatively uncontroversial in France. Work–family policies favor inclusion of all families, garner solid and continuing support, and rarely become partisan political issues.

France has already achieved the generosity and flexibility many countries aspire to, but it might consider making parental leaves shorter and better paid, increasing the number of spaces available in *crèches* so that women who cannot afford to hire a nanny or *assistante maternelle* could return to work after a one-year leave, and adopting a use-it-or-lose-it paternity leave that pays at least two-thirds of usual wages for two or more months. Although all of these suggestions have been discussed, the persistent problems of high unemployment and a stagnant economy make it likely that France will continue to rely on long low-paid leaves as a device for getting women to exit the labor market for a period of years.

I think there is support for extending the eleven-day "daddy leave" to encourage men to be responsible, nurturing parents who spend a significant stretch out of the workforce when their babies are born or adopted, and to keep up with the approaches adopted in Germany and Scandinavia (Martin interview, 2003).[16]

---

[15] For example, groups like the Children's Defense Fund, the National Partnership for Women and Families, the Center for Law and Social Policy, and MomsRising.

[16] Although France's eleven-day "daddy leave" allows fathers to be supportive around the time of a new baby's birth, it supports the notion that childrearing is women's responsibility and makes it easier to marginalize caregivers.

But changing the parental leave from a flat-rate three-year leave to a one-year leave reimbursed at two-thirds of usual pay in order to introduce two months of well-paid paternity leave would be financially and politically difficult – and without generous reimbursement, few fathers are likely to take such a leave. An increase in spaces in *crèches* would underscore France's commitment to helping women of modest means return to their jobs promptly, a good move if funding could be found.

Germany stands as an example of the possibility for convincing conservative groups – big business, Christian Democratic parties – of the need to adopt policies to support working mothers if the country and the economy are to flourish. But there are contradictory forces at play in Germany. Countering the feminist and economic growth arguments for modernizing German family policies are cultural and institutional forces that pull in the opposite direction: deep-seated expectations about intensive mothering, male responsibility for wage earning and subsidiarity; longstanding policies like income splitting and short school days; and local and *Länder*-level authority over schooling and social welfare. All of these suggest that Germany's family policies will continue to revolve around a part-time track for mothers with young children, rather than moving vigorously to accommodate full-time working mothers.

What could change this? The German federal government could push the *Länder* with regulations and monetary incentives to extend full-day care to more preschool and school-age children via childcare and more after-school care programs. This would entail adopting longer hours not just for childcare centers and schools, but also for retail businesses, since grocery stores that shut in the early evening and on Sundays are not very convenient for mothers who work full-time. Such changes will not be easy, both because of the longstanding short-hours school day and deeply engrained expectations about good mothering.

Another possibility might be to provide federally funded subsidies for licensed, well-regulated private care providers, along the lines of France's subsidies for home care mothers and nannies. This might enable the federal government to exercise leadership in an area that has traditionally been governed by the *Länder*. Relying on private care providers would also transform the issue of part-time vs. full-time schedules into a matter of individual choice and negotiation, and perhaps be less politically fraught than fighting for public childcare facilities that stay open ten or more hours a day.

A third possibility would be for Germany to adopt the Dutch approach and insure that workers who work part-time receive wages and benefits commensurate with those received by full-time workers. The Netherlands suggests another model for intervening in the definition of good work and good workers so that part-time workers are not deprived of access to benefits and good wages, and can if they wish return to full-time careers when their family responsibilities abate.

Like Germany, Japan has undertaken expansions in family support policies to address its low-fertility crisis, launching the Angel Plans to increase spaces in childcare, paid parental leaves, increases in family allowances, and measures to make workplace hours more family-friendly. Yet its work–family policies have sputtered. The reasons for ineffectual policy responses are varied: inadequate funding for childcare, which has led to long waiting lists; parental leave laws that are not enforceable; a cultural preference for intensive mothering; the animosity that colleagues and co-workers direct at women who take leaves; and the move to protect mid-level workers' jobs, which has led to increased inequality and marriage delay as more young people are forced to work in part-time, contract and temporary jobs.

With a substantial infusion of cash from the national government, Japan might aggressively increase the supply and affordability of childcare while maintaining high standards. One idea would be for the national government to increase spaces for babies and toddlers by renovating out-of-use kinder-gartens and also building new childcare centers. Japan might also establish a free universal high-quality preschool system for all children starting at age two and a half, like France's *écoles maternelles*. Such schools could provide universal education and care to all children aged two and a half to six. If they were designed with affordable and readily available add-on care, they would make it easier for mothers to combine work and childrearing.[17] By guaranteeing that all children get a good start in life, universal kindergarten would help arrest the move toward greater income inequality in Japan in recent years.

Some of the suggestions I made for Germany are relevant for Japan as well. Adopting French-style subsidies to help families pay for licensed, well-regulated private care providers might help Japan address shortfalls in childcare quickly without costing as much as expansions in childcare or preschool. Or Japan could borrow the Dutch approach of requiring employers to treat and pay part-time workers generously as a way to accommodate the cultural value of intensive mothering while keeping the opportunity costs of taking time off to raise children relatively low.

Indeed, addressing the structure of the labor market in Japan would be the most effective way for Japan to address its low-fertility crisis. Limiting the standard work week to thirty-nine or forty hours, capping overtime at 5 hours a week, and eliminating unpaid overtime could be transformative. Such changes would necessitate hiring more workers, which would make it easier for new graduates to find entry-level positions, and hence to consider marriage and having babies. It would also necessitate employers relaxing their expectations

---

[17] Perhaps it could be called *kodomoen*, like the idea floated in policy circles in Japan since 2011, which combines elements of childcare and kindergarten (MHLW, 2012a, 180–1).

of full-time workers, which would enable men to spend more time with their families and make it easier for women to hold down career-track jobs.

Further, if workers were not expected to be so devoted to their jobs that they worked long hours and declined to take all their paid leave time, more women might take their year of parental leave and return to work without fear of being given the cold shoulder. The state might pass antidiscrimination laws to penalize employers who discriminate against women and mothers. Reducing the high opportunity costs of having children so that women no longer feel that having children disqualifies them for challenging and well-rewarded work would go a long way toward addressing Japan's low-fertility crisis. But such changes seem unlikely, given the enormous power of business in Japan.[18]

The possibility of permitting more immigration has been much discussed, and, indeed, Japan increasingly relies on immigrants from the Philippines and Indonesia to be caregivers for the elderly. But I think a measure that would encourage permanent immigration in order to counter Japan's population decline and provide more workers has little chance of being adopted, given the deep political opposition to such measures and the concern with preserving "Japanese-ness."

If women and young people were to become more vocal about the policies they need and want, to pressure political leaders for change, and to vote for parties that supported work–family policies and were willing to stand up to powerful business interests, changes that presently seem impossible might be more plausible. But such grassroots movements will have to work uphill against established interests and the numeric weight of old people, who are an ever-expanding chunk of the Japanese population. Japan needs to develop a discourse about enlightened self-interest that would help corporate interests and the elderly both to embrace fair treatment of young people, women and mothers in the labor market, and to spend more on services to support childrearing.

Conservatives in the United States worry that regulation that requires employers to bear the costs of workers' caregiving needs would lower productivity, hurt job growth and reduce capital investment. They advocate reducing

---

[18] Kathryn Ibata-Arens optimistically writes that, if Prime Minister Shinzo Abe could push through decent work–family policies, he would have "an opportunity to forge a triple win: a larger pool of professional women can provide his Liberal Democratic Party with much needed new constituents to replace its dying (literally) base, these women will become more likely to have children, and best of all, boost growth in the Japanese economy in the long-term" (Ibata-Arens, 2013). Ibata-Arens seems to envision Japan's political leader mounting a successful campaign to get business to back work–family policies, as Germany did in the early 2000s. Despite the buzz this argument has elicited, I remain skeptical of both the political leadership's will and its ability to push business to do this. The government has tried to enlist business support in the past for a variety of work–life balance policies, but its efforts to educate and pressure companies into voluntary compliance have not been very effective. See the discussion in this chapter of the voluntary nature of the parental leave law, and in Chapter 5 of campaigns urging companies to embrace family-friendly policies.

government spending and lowering taxes based on the theory that putting money back into the pockets of childrearing families, to spend as they see fit, is preferable to regimented, one-size-fits-all government-supported ECEC. In addition to the ideological commitment to a small welfare state and low taxes, the United States faces a variety of institutional barriers to change, including substantial veto points, a federal system that places the responsibility for ECEC with the states, a two-party majoritarian political system that tends to elect center-right governments, weak organized labor and a liberal market economy that abhors workplace regulations.

Given all of these obstacles, what kinds of political strategies and changes make sense? One approach would be to build on accepted policy repertoires and ask for refundable tax credits for dependent-care expenses, so that taxpayers would receive them whether or not they owe federal taxes. The credits would need to be redesigned to give families financial assistance with paying for childcare services, say up to $5,000 or $6,000 for each preschool-age child who is in childcare.

A second recommendation would be to expand kindergarten programs funded through the state schools to cover children as young as three. Lest this seem too ambitious, resolutely conservative and comparatively poor Oklahoma has made preschool universally available to children from the age of four since 1998 (Kristoff, 2013). Early childhood education delivered and paid for by the states through their state school systems with encouragement and financial support from the federal government[19] would be a form of universal education that most parents would welcome, and that would insure that all children get a good start in life. Given the very low scores for Americans in the 5 percent literacy bracket and the high level of inequality in the United States (see Tables 7.7 and 7.8, and Figure 7.1), there are strong arguments for measures that would equalize educational outcomes and lift the skills and literacy of the least well-educated and lowest-paid members of society. In the long run, it is cheaper to insure that even the least-educated have adequate skills to be hired for jobs that pay decently than it is to pay for means-tested benefits like SNAP, TANF and the EITC or a burgeoning prison system. Cost–benefit analyses are a good way to appeal to the self-interest of most Americans, including business interests and advocates for keeping government small and frugal (Glass, 2009, makes excellent business-oriented arguments for policy change, see Chapter 6).

Final thoughts

This chapter has addressed the cultural, institutional, economic and political barriers to adopting generous work–family policies, and tried to identify the

---

[19] President Obama included this idea in his 2013 State of the Union message (and again in 2014 and 2015), although it has not as yet produced much legislative action.

political logics and policy repertoires that France, Germany, Japan and the United States have developed. It is meant to be an antidote to the optimistic "let's learn from the rest of the world and copy the countries that are doing it right" approaches that assume that policy learning is not problematic, and solutions can be copied and borrowed, regardless of the political and policy environment at home. I have argued instead that what we need is a tough-minded political assessment of policy change that takes into account political power and institutional constraints as a critical part of the story. Policy makers who understand how political choices and institutional repertoires shape and constrain policy are in a better position to bring about meaningful change that pushes their countries closer to the "best practices" of northern Europe.

Work–family policy development occurs at the intersection of deeply held and hotly contested values about gender roles, pre-existing policy approaches, labor markets that seek particular kinds of workers and resist or accept various kinds of state regulation, and debate about the appropriateness of state interventions in the private sphere of the family. The fact that the policies are contested and contentious is part of what makes studying policy development in this area so interesting.

My aim here has been to show that taking seriously historical context and institutional–political organization and power is crucial to getting the story right. I hope that this approach will lead researchers to ask new and better questions about the politics of how policies are made in different countries. Paying attention to fine-grained, contextual research on problem identification, policy framing and implementation makes us more aware of national particularity, which is valuable in its own right. It can help us to notice and understand variation within welfare regime types, to identify new regime types (I think of Japan as an "Asian conservative" welfare state) – and perhaps even to be skeptical of the idea of regime types altogether.

A whole generation of work on family support policies has been inspired by Gøsta Esping-Andersen's influential typology of welfare states, which has often been used to predict or explain policy outcomes on the basis of the rather general and formal models of politics in the three different "worlds" of welfare capitalism: social democratic, conservative and liberal. Although the "three worlds" typology has guided my decision to stick to advanced post-industrial countries (the wealthy, older OECD countries) and motivated me to include data on Sweden in Chapter 7 so that I could evaluate work–family policies from countries that represent all three regime types, for the most part I have started from the other end of the elephant. My thinking has been nurtured by the particularity and detail of policy histories, oodles of comparative data, and qualitative research on the role of different policy actors and institutions in shaping and implementing policies. I think attending to values, power dynamics, institutions and policy histories can help us understand the particular policies countries pursue, and why they chose those policies and not others. Given my background as a political theorist, this is a very different book than I expected to write, as I have eschewed grand theory for empirical analysis of how governments approach crafting work–family policies. Someone else may take the accumulated work of this and other similar studies and put them together into an elegant typology or theory, maybe one that both refines existing categories and moves beyond the world's wealthy countries to include many more types of work–family regimes. I shall be content if my investigations point future researchers toward more grounded and insightful ways to think about how states insure social welfare in this area.

Bibliography

Abramovitz, Mimi, and Sandra Morgen with the National Council for Research on Women (2006). *Taxes Are a Woman's Issue: Reframing the Debate*. New York: The Feminist Press at CUNY.

Administration for Children and Families, US Department of Health and Human Services (2011). "Fiscal Year 2011 Child Care Development Fund (CCDF), Summary of Expenditures by Categorical Items." Retrieved December 7, 2014 from www.acf.hhs.gov/programs/occ/resource/fy-2011-ccdf-state-expenditure-data.

(2013). "FY 2013 Budget Overview – Executive Summary." Retrieved July 13, 2013, from www.acf.hhs.gov/sites/default/files/assets/ExecutiveSummary.pdf.

Adsera, Alicia (2004). "Changing Fertility Rates in Developed Countries: The Impact of Labor Market Institutions," *Population Economics* 17(1): 17–43.

Afsa, Cedric (1998). "L'allocation parentale d'éducation: entre politique familiale et politique pour l'emploi," *INSEE première* 569: 1–4.

Akabayashi, Hideo (2006). "The Labor Supply of Married Women and Spousal Tax Deductions in Japan – A Structural Estimation," *Review of Economics of the Household* 4: 349–78.

Ambler, John S. (1991). *The French Welfare State: Surviving Social and Ideological Change*. New York University Press.

Ashford, Douglas E. (1991). "Advantages of Complexity: Social Insurance in France," in John S. Ambler (ed.), *The French Welfare State: Surviving Social and Ideological Change*. New York University Press, 32–57.

Badinter, Elisabeth (2003). *Fausse route: réflexions sur 30 années de feminisme*. Paris: Odile Jacob.

(2004). "La place des femmes dans la société française," *Lettre de l'OFCE [Observatoire français des conjunctures économiques]* 245: 1–4.

(2010). *Le conflit, la femme et la mère*. Paris: Flammarion.

Bahle, Thomas (1998). "Family Policy in Germany: Towards a Macrosociological Frame for Analysis." *Eurodata Newsletter*. Retrieved June 23, 2012, from www.mzes.uni-mannheim.de/eurodata/newsletter/no7/familypolicy.html.

Béland, Daniel (2005). "Ideas and Social Policy: An Institutionalist Perspective," *Social Policy & Administration* 39(1): 1–18.

(2009). "Gender, Ideational Analysis, and Social Policy," *Social Politics* 19(2): 558–81.

Béland, Daniel, and Randall Hansen (2000). "Reforming the French Welfare State: Solidarity, Social Exclusion and the Three Crises of Citizenship," *West European Politics* 23(1): 47–64.

Bernstein, Anya (2001). *The Moderation Dilemma: Legislative Coalitions and the Politics of Family and Medical Leave.* University of Pittsburgh Press.

Bertram, Hans, Wiebke Rösler and Nancy Ehlert (2005). Nachhaltige Familienpolitik. Zukunftssicherung durch einen Dreiklang von Zeitpolitik, finanzieller Transferpolitik und Infrastrukturpolitik. Gutachten im Auftrag des Bundesministeriums für Familie, Senioren, Frauen und Jugend. Retrieved December 6, 2014, from www.bmfsfj.de/RedaktionBMFSFJ/Broschuerenstelle/Pdf-Anlagen/Bertram-Gutachten-Nachhaltige-Familienpolitik,property=pdf.

Bettio, Francesca, and Janneke Plantenga (2004). "Comparing Care Regimes in Europe," *Feminist Economics* 10(1): 85–113.

Beyer, Caroline (2013). "Le gouvernement annonce 275.000 'solutions d'accueil' pour les moins de trois ans" (June 3, 2013). *Le Figaro.* Retrieved February 17, 2014, from www.lefigaro.fr/actualite-france/2013/06/03/01016-20130603ARTFIG00449-le-gouvernement-annonce-275000-solutions-d-accueil-pour-les-moins-de-trois-ans.php.

Blum, Sonya (2010). "Between Instrument Tinkering and Policy Renewal: Reforms of Parental Leave in Germany and Austria," *German Policy Studies* 6(3): 83–118.

Boling, Patricia (1990). "Private Interest and the Public Good in Japan," *Pacific Review* 3(2): 138–50.

Bongaarts, J., and T. Sobotka (2012). "A Demographic Explanation for the Recent Rise in European Fertility," *Population and Development Review* 38(1): 83–120.

Brewster, Karin L., and Ronald R. Rindfuss (2000). "Fertility and Women's Employment in Industrialized Nations," *Annual Review of Sociology* 26(1): 271–96.

Brin, Hubert, Patrick Midy and Philippe Steck (2005). *Enjeux démographiques et accompagnement du désir d'enfants des familles: conférence de la famille 2005.* Paris: French Ministry of Solidarity, Health and Family.

Brinton, Mary (2010). *Lost in Translation: Youth, Work, and Instability in Postindustrial Japan.* Cambridge University Press.

Budlender, Debbie (2010). *Time Use Studies and Unpaid Care Work.* New York: Routledge.

Bundesministerium für Familien, Senioren, Frauen und Jugend (BMFSFJ) (2004, June 30). *Overview of the Standard Benefits and Tax Concessions Relevant to Family Policy and the Amounts Involved in the Federal Republic of Germany.* Berlin: BMFSFJ.

——— (2006). Seventh Family Report (Summary): "Families Between Flexibility and Dependability – Perspectives for a Life Cycle-related Family Policy." Statement by the Federal Government – Results and scenarios of the report drafted by the committee of experts. April. Retrieved December 6, 2014, from www.bmfsfj.de/RedaktionBMFSFJ/Abteilung2/Pdf-Anlagen/familienbericht-englisch,property=pdf,bereich=bmfsfj,sprache=de,rwb=true.pdf.

——— (2011). "Familie: das Kindergeld." Retrieved July 21, 2011, from www.bmfsfj.de/BMFSFJ/familie,did=31470.html.

——— (2012). "Lokale Bündnisse fur Familie." Retrieved June 27, 2012, from www.lokale-buendnisse-fuer-familie.de/lokale-buendnisse-fuer.html.

Bundesrat Official Homepage. Retrieved December 31, 2012, from www.bundesrat.de.

Cairns.info (2009). "La politique familiale en 2009." Retrieved June 7, 2012, from www.cairn.info/revue-spirale-2009-1-page-219.htm.

Caisse national d'allocations familiales (CAF) (2011). "Allocations familiales, particuliers," in *Cahiers des données sociales 2011*. Paris: Caisse national d'allocations familiales. Retrieved December 7, 2014, from www.caf.fr/sites/default/files/cnaf/Documents/Dser/cahier_donnees_sociales/CDS_2011.pdf.

Caldwell, John C., and Thomas Schindlmayr (2003). "Explanations of Fertility Crisis in Modern Societies: A Search for Commonalities," *Population Studies* 57(3): 241–63.

Campbell, Andrea Louise (2003). *How Policies Make Citizens: Senior Citizen Activism and the American Welfare State*. Princeton University Press.

Campbell, John Creighton (1992). *How Policies Change: The Japanese Government and the Aging Society*. Princeton University Press.

(2002). "Japanese Social Policy in Comparative Perspective," World Bank Institute Working Paper. Washington, DC: World Bank Institute.

Castles, Francis (2003). "The World Turned Upside Down: Below Replacement Fertility, Changing Preferences and Family-Friendly Public Policy in 21 OECD Countries," *Journal of European Social Policy* 13(3): 209–27.

Chan-Tiberghien, Jennifer (2004). *Gender and Human Rights Politics in Japan: Global Norms and Domestic Networks*. Stanford University Press.

Cheever, Susan (2002). "The Nanny Dilemma," in Barbara Ehrenreich and Arlie Russell Hochschild (eds.), *Global Woman: Nannies, Maids, and Sex Workers in the New Economy*. New York: Henry Holt and Company, chapter 2.

Child and Youth Services [Kinder Jugendhilfe] (2009). "Day Care Expansion Act." Retrieved June 26, 2012, from http://kinder-jugendhilfe.org/en_kjhg/cgi-bin/showcontent.asp?ThemaID=4879&preview=print.

Child Care and Development Fund, Administration for Children and Families, US Department of Health and Human Services (2013). "Child Care and Development Fund FY 2013 Budget." Retrieved July 13, 2013, from www.acf.hhs.gov/sites/default/files/assets/CCDF%20final.pdf.

CLASP (Center for Law and Social Policy) (2011) "Child Care Assistance Profile." Retrieved June 13, 2013, from www.clasp.org/admin/site/publications/files/2010-Child-Care-Assistance-Profile-US.pdf.

Clearinghouse on International Developments in Child, Youth and Family Policies at Columbia University (2011). "France: Family Allowances." Retrieved March 27, 2011, from www.childpolicyintl.org/countries/france.html#top.

CLEISS (Centre des Liaisons Européennes et Internationales de Sécurité Sociale) (2014). "Le régime français de protection sociale, Annexe 1: Tableau récapitulatif des prestations familiales." Retrieved February 17, 2014, from www.cleiss.fr/docs/regimes/regime_francea1.html.

Clemens, Elisabeth S., and James M. Cook (1999). "Politics and Institutionalism: Explaining Durability and Change," *Annual Review of Sociology* 25(1): 441–66.

COE (Council of Europe) (2010). Country Sheet on Youth Policy in Germany. Retrieved June 28, 2013, from http://youth-partnership-eu.coe.int/youth-partnership/documents/Questionnaires/Country/2010/Country_sheet_Germany_2010.pdf.

Commaille, Jacques, Pierre Strobel and Michel Villac (2002). *La politique de la famille*. Paris: Editions La Decouverte.

Conradt, David P. (1993). *The German Polity, Fifth Edition*. New York: Longman.

Coontz, Stephanie (1992). *The Way We Never Were: American Families and the Nostalgia Trap*. New York: Basic Books.

Crittenden, Ann (2001). *The Price of Motherhood: Why the Most Important Job in the World is Still the Least Valued*. New York: Metropolitan Books.

D'Addio, Anna Cristina, and Marco Mira d'Ercole (2005). "Trends and Determinants of Fertility Rates in OECD Countries: The Role of Policies," OECD Social Employment and Migration Working Papers. Paris: OECD.

(2006). "Policies, Institutions and Fertility Rates: A Panel Data Analysis for OECD Countries," *OECD Economic Studies* 41: 7–43. Retrieved December 7, 2014, from www.oecd.org/eco/growth/40505223.pdf.

Davidson, Cherilyn. (1994). "Dependent Children and Their Families: A Historical Survey of United States Policies," in Francine Helene Jacobs and Margery W. Davies (eds.), *More Than Kissing Babies? Current Child and Family Policy in the United States*. Westport, Conn.: Auburn House, chapter 3.

Deutsch, Francine (1999). *Halving it All: How Equally Shared Parenting Works*. Cambridge, Mass.: Harvard University Press.

Deutsche Welle (2003, October 17). "A Quick Guide to 'Agenda 2010.'" Retrieved May 21, 2013, from www.dw.de/dw/article/0,,988374,00.html.

Drew, Eileen (2005). "Parental Leave in Council of Europe Member States," Directorate General of Human Rights, Council of Europe, Strasbourg, France. Retrieved May 21, 2013, from www.coe.int/t/dghl/standardsetting/equality/03themes/women-decisionmaking/CDEG(2004)14final_en.pdf.

Drobnic, Sonia, Hans-Peter Blossfeld and Gotz Rohwer (1999). "Dynamics of Women's Employment Patterns over the Family Life Course: A Comparison of the United States and Germany," *Journal of Marriage and the Family* 61(1): 133–46.

Economist (2007, June 14). "Suddenly the Old World Looks Younger." Retrieved May 22, 2013, from www.economist.com/node/9334869.

Eddy, Melissa (2012, June 6). "German Lawmakers Spar over Childcare Subsidy." *New York Times*. Retrieved May 21, 2013, from www.nytimes.com/2012/06/07/world/europe/german-lawmakers-spar-over-child-care-subsidy.html?_r=0.

Ehrenreich, Barbara, and Arlie R. Hochschild, eds. (2003). *Global Woman: Nannies, Maids, and Sex Workers in the New Economy*. New York: Metropolitan.

EIRO (European Industrial Relations Observatory on line) (2012). "Sanctions for Not Closing the Gender Pay Gap." Retrieved October 29, 2012, from www.eurofound.europa.eu/eiro/2011/12/articles/fr1112011i.htm.

Elger, Katrin, Ansbert Kneip and Merlind Theile (2009, January 26). "Immigration: Survey Shows Alarming Lack of Integration in Germany." *Der Spiegel online*. Retrieved October 7, 2012, from www.spiegel.de/international/germany/immigration-survey-shows-alarming-lack-of-integration-in-germany-a-603588-druck.html.

Engster, Daniel, and Helene Olofsdotter Stensota (2011). "Do Family Policy Regimes Matter for Children's Well-Being?" *Social Politics* 18(1): 82–124.

Esenwein, Gregg A. (2006). "Child Tax Credit," in *Tax Policy Center: Tax Topics*. Washington, DC: Urban Institute and Brookings Institution. Retrieved February 23, 2011, from www.taxpolicycenter.org/taxtopics/encyclopedia/Child-Tax-Credit.cfm.

Esping-Andersen, Gøsta (1990). *The Three Worlds of Welfare Capitalism*. Princeton University Press.

   (1997). "Hybrid or Unique? The Japanese Welfare State Between Europe and America," *Journal of European Social Policy* 7(3): 179–89.

   (1999). *Social Foundations of Postindustrial Economies*. New York: Oxford University Press.

   (2009). *Incomplete Revolution: Adapting Welfare States to Women's New Roles*. Cambridge: Polity.

Estevez-Abe, Margarita (2002). "Negotiating Welfare Reform: Actors and Institutions in the Japanese Welfare State," in Bo Rothstein and Sven Steinmo (eds.), *Restructuring the Welfare State: Political Institutions and Policy Change*. New York: Palgrave MacMillan, 157–83.

   (2005). "Gender Bias in Skills and Social Policies: The Varieties of Capitalism Perspectives on Sex Segregation," *Social Politics* 12(2): 180–215.

   (2007). "Gendering the Varieties of Capitalism: Gender Bias in Skills and Social Policies," in Frances McCall Rosenbluth (ed.), *The Political Economy of Japan's Low Fertility*. Stanford University Press, 63–86.

   (2008). *Welfare and Capitalism in Postwar Japan*. Cambridge University Press.

Eto, Murase Mikiko (2000). "The Establishment of Long-Term Care Insurance," in Hideo (ed.), *Power Shuffles and Policy Processes: Coalition Government in Japan in the 1990s*. Tokyo: Center for International Exchange, 21–50.

   (2001). "Public Involvement in Social Policy Reform: Seen from the Perspective of Japan's Elderly-Care Insurance Scheme," *Journal of Social Policy* 30(1): 17–36.

Eurofound (2012). "Germany: Mutterschutz (Maternity Protection)." Accessed June 28, 2012, from www.eurofound.europa.eu/emire/GERMANY/MATERNITY PROTECTION-DE.htm.

Europa: European Alliance for Families (2011). "Germany: Developing a Sustainable Family Policy." Retrieved June 30, 2012, from http://ec.europa.eu/employment_social/emplweb/families/index.cfm?id=4&policyId=13&countryId=6&langId=en.

European Employment Services (EURES) (2007). "Living and Working in Iceland." Retrieved May 30, 2013, from http://eures.is/files/L&W%20-%20English_21012915.pdf.

Fagnani, Jeanne (1998). "Helping Mothers to Combine Paid and Unpaid Work – or Fighting Unemployment? The Ambiguities of French Family Policy," *Community, Work & Family* 1(3): 297–312.

   (2002). "Why do French Women Have More Children than German Women? Family Policies and Attitudes towards Child Care outside the Home," *Community, Work & Family* 5(1): 103–20.

   (2006). "Family Policy in France," *International Encyclopedia of Social Policy* 3: 501–6.

Fagnani, Jeanne, and Danielle Boyer (2012). "Current Leave and Other Employment-related Policies to Support Parents." *International Network on Leave Policies & Research*. Retrieved May 23, 2013, from www.leavenetwork.org/fileadmin/Leavenetwork/Country_notes/2012/France.FINAL.9may.pdf.

Fagnani, Jeanne, and Marie-Thérèse Letablier (2003). "La réduction du temps de travail a-t-elle amélioré la vie quotidienne des parents de jeunes enfants?" *Premières*

Informations et Premières Synthèses, Direction de l'animation de la recherche, des études et des statistiques (DARES) 1(2): 1–10.

(2004). "Work and Family Life Balance: The Impact of the 35 Hour Laws in France," *Work, Employment and Society* 18(3): 551–72.

(2005). "Social Rights and Care Responsibility in the French Welfare State," in Birgit Pfau-Effinger and Birgit Geissler (eds.), *Care and Social Integration in European Societies*. Bristol: Policy Press, 135–52.

Fagnani, Jeanne, and Antoine Math (2010). "Recent Reforms in French and German Family Policies," *Sociología, Problemas e Práticas* 64: 11–25.

Fass, Sarah. (2009). "Paid Leave in the States: A Critical Support for Low-wage Workers and Their Families." New York: National Center for Children in Poverty, Mailman School of Public Health, Columbia University.

Ferrarini, Tommy (2003). *Parental Leave Institutions in Eighteen Post-war Welfare States*. Stockholm: Swedish Institute for Social Research.

(2006). *Families, States and Labour Markets: Institutions, Causes and Consequences of Family Policy in Post-War Welfare States*. Cheltenham: Edward Elgar Publishing.

Ferree, Myra Marx (2009). "An American Road Map? Framing Feminist Goals in a Liberal Landscape," in Janet C. Gornick and Marcia K. Meyers (eds.), *Gender Equality: Transforming Family Divisions of Labor*. London: Verso, 283–315.

Fleckenstein, Timo (2011). "The Politics of Ideas in Welfare State Transformation: Christian Democracy and the Reform of Family Policy in Germany," *Social Policy* 18(4): 543–71.

Folbre, Nancy (2001). *The Invisible Heart*. Cambridge, Mass.: MIT Press.

(2009). *Greed, Lust and Gender: A History of Economic Ideas*. New York: Oxford University Press.

Fraser, Nancy, and Linda Gordon. (1997). "A Genealogy of Dependency: Tracing A Keyword of the U.S. Welfare State," in Barbara Laslett, Ruth-Ellen Boetcher Joeres, Mary Jo Maynes and Evelyn Brooks Higginbotham (eds.), *History and Theory: Feminist Research, Debates, Contestations*. University of Chicago Press, 276–303.

Fukuda, Nobutaka (2003). "Comparing Family-Friendly Policies in Japan and Europe: Are We in the Same or in a Different League?" *Journal of Population and Social Security* supplement to volume 1: 31–45. Retrieved June 23, 2012, from www.ipss .go.jp/webj-ad/WebJournal.files/population/2003_6/2.Fukuda.pdf.

Fukue, Natsuko. 2010. "Four Fathers Picked as Role Models for Child-rearing Leave," *Japan Times*. September 1.

Gal, John, and Mimi Ajzenstadt (2010). *Children, Gender, and Families in Mediterranean Welfare States*. New York: Springer.

Gastineau-Grimes, Holly (2012). *Making an Exception for Care: Balancing Welfare States and Immigration Policies* (doctoral dissertation). Purdue University.

Gauthier, Anne Hélène (1996). *The State and the Family: A Comparative Analysis of Family Policies in Industrialized Countries*. Oxford: Clarendon Press.

(2004). "Choices, Opportunities and Constraints on Partnership, Childbearing and Parenting: The Policy Responses," *European Population Forum 2004: Population Challenges and Policy Responses*. Retrieved September 6, 2007, from www.unece .org/pau/epf/gauthier.pdf.

GEB (Gender Equality Bureau, Cabinet Office, Japan) (2006). "FY2005 Annual Report on the State of Formation of a Gender-Equal Society" and "Policies to be

Implemented in FY 2006 to Promote the Formation of a Gender-Equal Society."
Retrieved June 24, 2013, from www.gender.go.jp/english_contents/about_danjo/
whitepaper/pdf/ewp2006.pdf#page=3.

Gelb, Joyce (2003). *Gender Policies in Japan and the United States: Comparing Women's Movements, Rights, and Politics*. New York: Palgrave MacMillan.

Genda, Yūji (2007). "Jobless Youths and the NEET Problem in Japan," *Social Science Japan Journal* 10(1): 23–40.

Genda, Yūji, and Masako Jurosawa (2001). "Transition from School to Work in Japan," *Journal of the Japanese and International Economies* 15(4): 465–88.

Gerring, John (2004). "What Is a Case Study and What Is It Good For?" *American Political Science Review* 98(2): 341–54.

Gerson, Kathleen (2010). *The Unfinished Revolution: Coming of Age in a New Era of Gender, Work, and Family*. New York: Oxford University Press.

Gilens, Martin (1999). *Why Americans Hate Welfare: Race, Media, and the Politics of Antipoverty Policy*. University of Chicago Press.

Glass, Jennifer (2009). "Work–Life Policies: Future Directions for Research," in Ann C. Crouter and Alan Booth (eds.), *Work–Life Policies*. Washington, DC: The Urban Institute Press, chapter 13.

Glenn, Evelyn Nakano (2012). *Forced to Care: Coercion and Caregiving in America*. Cambridge, Mass.: Harvard University Press.

Godot, Michel, and Evelyn Sullerot (2005). "La famille, une affaire publique." Conseil d'analyse économique. Retrieved April 29, 2014, from www.laprospective.fr/dyn/francais/ouvrages/057.pdf.

Goldin, Claudia (2006). "The Quiet Revolution that Transformed Women's Employment, Education, and Family," *American Economic Review, Papers and Proceedings* 96: 1–21.

Gornick, Janet C., and Marcia K. Meyers (2003). *Families that Work: Policies for Reconciling Parenthood and Employment*. New York: Russell Sage Foundation.

(2009). "Institutions that Support Gender Equality in Parenthood and Employment Transforming Family Divisions of Labor," in Janet C. Gornick and Marcia K. Meyers (eds.), *Gender Equality: Transforming Family Divisions of Labor*. London: Verso, 3–64.

Gottfried, Heidi, and Jacqueline O'Reilly (2002). "Reregulating Breadwinner Models in Socially Conservative Welfare Systems: Comparing Germany and Japan," *Social Politics* 9(1): 29–59.

Govtrack (2013). S. 1697: Strong Start for America's Children Act. Retrieved January 29, 2014, from http://www.govtrack.us/congress/bills/113/s1697.

Govtrack.com (2013). H.R. 517: Federal Employees Paid Parental Leave Act of 2013. Retrieved July 13, 2013, from www.govtrack.us/congress/bills/113/hr517.

Graziano, Paolo, Sophie Jacquot and Bruno Palier (2011). *The EU and the Domestic Politics of Welfare State Reforms: Europa, Europae*. Houndmills: Palgrave Macmillan.

Grebe, Cornelius (2009). *Reconciliation Policy in Germany 1998–2008: Construing the "Problem" of the Incompatibility of Paid Employment and Care Work*. Wiesbaden: VS Verlag für Sozialwissenschaften.

Guerin, Lisa (2013). "Paid Family Leave in California, New Jersey, Washington, and the District of Columbia." Nolo Legal Encyclopedia. Retrieved July 13, 2013, from www.nolo.com/legal-encyclopedia/paid-family-leave-states-29854.html.

Haas, Peter M. (1992). "Introduction: Epistemic Communities and International Policy Coordination," *International Organization* 46(1): 1–35.

Hacker, Jacob S. (2002). *The Divided Welfare State: The Battle over Public and Private Social Benefits in the United States.* New York: Cambridge University Press.

(2005). "Policy Drift: The Hidden Politics of the US Welfare State Retrenchment," in Wolfgang Streeck and Kathleen Ann Thelen (eds.), *Beyond Continuity: Institutional Change in Advanced Political Economies.* New York: Oxford University Press, 40–82.

Hagemann, Karin (2006). "Between Ideology and Economy: The 'Time Politics' of Child Care and Public Education in the Two Germanys," *Social Politics* 13(2): 217–60.

Hall, Peter A., and David Soskice (2001). *Varieties of Capitalism: The Institutional Foundations of Comparative Advantage.* New York: Oxford University Press.

Harrington, Michael (1962). *The Other America: Poverty in the United States.* New York: Macmillan.

Harris, Fred R. (2006). *The Baby Bust: Who Will Do the Work? Who Will Pay the Taxes?* Lanham: Rowman and Littlefield.

Harris, Marvin (1981). *Why Nothing Works: The Anthropology of Daily Life.* New York: Simon and Schuster.

Hegewisch, Ariane (2005). "Individual Working Time Rights in Germany and the UK: How a Little Law Can Go a Long Way," in *Working Time for Working Families: Europe and the United States.* Washington, DC: Friedrich Ebert Stiftung, Chapter 6.

Heinen, Jacqueline, and Heini Martiskainen de Koenigswarter (2001). "Framing Citizenship in France and Finland in the 1990s: Restructuring Motherhood, Work, and Care," *Social Politics* 8(2): 170–81.

Henninger, Annette, Christine Wimbauer and Rosine Dombrowski (2008). "Demography as a Push toward Gender Equality? Current Reforms of German Family Policy," *Social Politics* 15(3): 287–314.

Hirsch, Martin (2005, April). *"Au possible nous sommes tenus": rapport de la Ministère des solidarités, de la santé et de la famille. Commission familles, vulnérabilité, pauvreté.* Paris: Ministry of Solidarity, Health and Family.

Hirschman, Albert O. 1970. *Exit, Voice, and Loyalty: Responses to Decline in Firms, Organizations, and States.* Cambridge, Mass.: Harvard University Press.

Hochschild, Arlie, and Anne Machung. 2012. *The Second Shift: Working Families and the Revolution at Home.* New York: Penguin Books.

Hook, Jennifer L. (2006). "Care in Context: Men's Unpaid Work in 20 Countries, 1965–2003," *American Sociological Review* 71(4): 639–60.

Houser, Linda, and Thomas P. Vartanian (2012). "Policy Matters: Public Policy, Paid Leave for New Parents, and Economic Security for US Workers." Rutgers Center for Women and Work. Retrieved February 17, 2013, from www.cww.rutgers.edu.

Howard, Christopher (1997). *The Hidden Welfare State: Tax Expenditures and Social Policy in the United States.* Princeton University Press.

(2007). *The Welfare State Nobody Knows.* Princeton University Press.

Huber, Evelyn, and John D. Stephens (2001). *Development and Crisis of the Welfare State: Parties and Policies in Global Markets.* University of Chicago Press.

Hugh, Edward (2007). "Fertility in Europe." *Fistful of Euros.* Retrieved October 4, 2008, from http://fistfulofeuros.net/afoe/fertility-in-europe.

Ibata-Arens, Kathryn (2013, January 22). "How Promoting Women Could Get Japan out of this Crisis." *Quartz.com*. Retrieved January 27, 2013, from http://qz.com/46052/how-promoting-women-could-get-japan-out-of-this-crisis.

Immergut, Ellen M. (1992). *Health Politics: Interests and Institutions in Western Europe*. New York: Cambridge University Press.

(2000). "The Theoretical Core of the New Institutionalism," *Politics and Society* 26(1): 5–34.

Immervoll, Herwig, and David Barber (2006, January 16). "Can Parents Afford to Work?" DELSA/ELSA, OECD Social, Employment, and Migration Working Papers. Retrieved May 21, 2013, from http://ftp.iza.org/dp1932.pdf.

Index Mundi. Retrieved May 29, 2013, from www.indexmundi.com/facts/switzerland/labor-participation-rate.

INED (Institut national d'études demographiques) (2008). "Total Fertility Rates from 1970–2006 for EU and OECD countries." Retrieved October 18, 2008, from www.ined.fr/en/pop_figures/developed_countries/total_fertility.

Ingraham, Patricia W. (1987). "Building Bridges or Burning Them? The President, the Appointees, and the Bureaucracy," *Public Administration Review* 47(5): 425–35.

Inter-Parliamentary Union (2012). "Women in National Parliaments – Situations as of March 31, 2012." Retrieved May 31, 2012, from www.ipu.org/wmn-e/classif.htm.

Iversen, Torben, and Frances McCall Rosenbluth (2010). *Women, Work, and Politics: The Political Economy of Gender Inequality*. New Haven: Yale University Press.

Iversen, Torben, and John D. Stephens (2008). "Partisan Politics, the Welfare State, and Three Worlds of Human Capital Formation," *Comparative Political Studies* 41(4): 600–37.

Japan Times (2011, May 10). "Children's Day and Japan's Future." Retrieved March 11, 2013, from www.japantimes.co.jp/opinion/2011/05/10/editorials/childrens-day-and-japans-future/#.UT3q8hyG3zg.

Jaumotte, Florence (2003). "Labour Force Participation of Women: Empirical Evidence on the Role of Policy and Other Determinants in OECD Countries," *OECD Economic Studies* 37: 52–108. Retrieved March 2, 2013, from www.oecd.org/economy/growth/34562935.pdf.

Jenson, Jane, and Mariette Sineau (2001). *Who Cares? Women's Work, Childcare, and Welfare State Redesign*. University of Toronto Press.

JMC (Japan Management Consulting) (2014). "Japan Maternity and Child Care Leave." Retrieved February 22, 2014, from www.japan-payroll.com/japan-maternity-leave.

Johnson, Chalmers (1982). *MITI and the Japanese Miracle: The Growth of Industrial Policy, 1925–1975*. Stanford University Press.

Kabashima, Ikuo, and Gill Steel (2010). *Changing Politics in Japan*. Ithaca, NY: Cornell University Press.

Kahng, Lily (2010). "One Is the Loneliest Number: The Single Taxpayer in a Joint Return World," *Hastings Law Journal* 61: 651–86.

Kasza, Gregory J. (2002). "The Illusion of Welfare 'Regimes,'" *Journal of Social Policy* 31(2): 271–87.

(2006). *One World of Welfare: Japan in Comparative Perspective*. Ithaca, NY: Cornell University Press.

Kato, Mariko. 2009. "Parties Wave Flag for Child-rearing: But Policies Intended to Woo Young Voters Don't Address Failings in Caring for Kids: Critics." *Japan Times*, August 29.

Kaufmann, Franz-Xaver (2002). "Politics and Policies toward the Family in Europe: A Framework and an Inquiry into Differences and Convergences," in Franz-Xaver Kaufmann, Anton Kuijsten, Hans-Joachim Schulze and Klaus Peter Strohmeier (eds.), *Family Life and Family Policies in Europe: Problems and Issues in Comparative Perspective*, Volume II. New York: Oxford University Press, 419–89.

Kawabata, Eiji (2008). "Reforming the Bureaucracy," in Sherry L. Martin and Gill Steel (eds.), *Democratic Reform in Japan: Assessing the Impact*. Boulder, Colo.: Lynne Reiner, 101–22.

Khor, Diana (2002). "The Construction of Gender through Public Opinion Polls in Japan: The 'Problem' of Women's Employment," *US–Japan Women's Journal*, English Language Supplement 22: 107–37.

Kindertagesbetreuung Regional (2013). "Statistische Ämter des Bundes und der Länder." Wiesbaden: Statistisches Bundesamt. Retrieved February 19, 2014, from http://www.destatis.de/DE/Publikationen/Thematisch/Soziales/KinderJugend hilfe/KindertagesbetreuungRegional5225405137004.pdf?__blob=publicationFile.

King, Leslie (1998). "France Needs Children: Pronatalism, Nationalism and Women's Equity," *The Sociological Quarterly* 39(1): 33–52.

Kittay, Eva Feder (1999). *Love's Labor: Essays on Women, Equality, and Dependency*. New York: Routledge.

Klammer, Ute, and Marie-Thérèse Letablier (2007). "Family Policies in Germany and France: The Role of Enterprises and Social Partners," *Social Policy Administration* 41(6): 672–92.

Klein, Abbie Gordon (1992). *The Debate over Child Care: 1969–1990, a Sociohistorical Analysis*. Albany: State University of New York Press.

KMZ (Kodomo Mirai Zaidan) (2009). "はたら区カエル野の仲間たち." (A community/field full of working frogs). Retrieved June 24, 2013, from http://fukuoka-roudoukyoku.jsite.mhlw.go.jp/library/fukuoka-roudoukyoku/5kanto/wlb/wlb02_04.pdf.

Knijn, Trudie, and Monique Kremer (1997). "Gender and the Caring Dimension of Welfare States: Toward Inclusive Citizenship," *Social Politics* 4(3): 328–61.

Kobayashi, Yoshi (2004). *A Path toward Gender Equality: State Feminism in Japan*. New York: Routledge.

Kondo, Ayako (2007). "Does the First Job Really Matter? State Dependency in Employment Status in Japan," *Journal of the Japanese and International Economies* 21(3): 379–402.

Korpi, Walter (2000). "Faces of Inequality: Gender, Class, and Patterns of Inequality in Different Types of Welfare States," *Social Politics* 7(2): 127–91.

Krauss, Ellis S., and Robert J. Pekkanen (2011). *The Rise and Fall of Japan's LDP: Political Party Organizations as Historical Institutions*. Ithaca, NY: Cornell University Press.

Kreyenfeld, Michaela, Krystof Zeman, Marion Berkimsher and Ina Jaschinski (2011). "Fertility Data for German-speaking Countries: What is the Potential? Where are the Pitfalls?" Max Planck Institute for Demographic Research, MPIDR Working Paper. Retrieved October 7, 2012, from www.demogr.mpg.de/papers/working/wp-2011–003.pdf.

Kristoff, Nicholas D. 2013. "Oklahoma! Where the Kids Learn Early." *New York Times*, November 9.

Kukimoto, Mikoto. 2013a. Personal communication on June 20, 2013, conveying the data and graph included in Figure 5.3, "Number of Children Attending Unlicensed Forms of Care, 1998–2011."

2013b. "Working Mothers and Childcare Services: Changes and Challenges." Paper presented at the Association for Asian Studies conference, San Diego, Calif., March 21–24.

Lambert, Priscilla A. (2007). "The Political Economy of Postwar Family Policy in Japan: Economic Imperatives and Electoral Incentives," *Journal of Japanese Studies* 33(1): 1–28.

(2008). "The Comparative Political Economy of Parental Leave and Child Care: Evidence from Twenty OECD Countries," *Social Politics* 15(3): 315–44.

Lanquetin, Marie-Thérèse, Jacqueline Laufer and Marie-Thérèse Letablier (2000). "From Equality to Reconciliation in France?" in Linda Hantrais (ed.), *Gendered Polities in Europe: Reconciling Employment and Family Life*. Basingstoke: Macmillan, 68–88.

Laufer, Jacqueline (2003). "Equal Employment Policy in France: Symbolic Support and a Mixed Record," *Review of Policy Research* 20(3): 423–44.

LeBlanc, Robin (1999). *Bicycle Citizens: The Political World of the Japanese Housewife*. Berkeley: University of California Press.

Lee, Ronald (2003). "The Demographic Transition: Three Centuries of Fundamental Change," *Journal of Economic Perspectives* 17(4): 167–90.

Leitner, Sigrid (2010). "Germany Outpaces Austria in Childcare Policy: The Historical Contingencies of 'Conservative' Childcare Policy," *Journal of European Social Policy* 20(5) 456–67.

Lenoir, Remi. 1991. "Family Policy in France Since 1938," in John S. Ambler (ed.), *The French Welfare State: Surviving Social and Ideological Change*. New York University Press, chapter 5.

Letablier, Marie-Thérèse (2003). "Fertility and Family Policies in France," *Journal of Population and Social Security*, supplement to Volume 1: 245–61.

(2008). "Work–Family Policies in France: Principles, Contents and Outcomes." Paper presented at the International Symposium on Work–Family Balance Policy across Countries (Korean Women's Development Institute – KWDI) in Seoul, South Korea, August 25–26.

Levy, Jonah, Mari Miura and Gene Park (2006). "Exiting Etatisme? New Directions in State Policy in France and Japan," in Jonah Levy (ed.), *The State after Statism: New State Activities in the Age of Liberalization*. Cambridge, Mass.: Harvard University Press, 93–136.

Lewis, Jane (1992). "Gender and the Development of Welfare Regimes," *Journal of European Social Policy* 2(3): 159–73.

(1998). *Gender, Social Care and Welfare State Restructuring in Europe*. Aldershot, Hants.: Ashgate.

(2006). "Work/Family Reconciliation, Equal Opportunities and Social Policies: The Interpretation of Policy Trajectories at the EU Level and the Meaning of Gender Equality," *Journal of European Public Policy* 13(3): 420–37.

Lewis, Jane, Trudi Knijn, Claude Martin and Ilona Ostner (2008). "Patterns of Development in Work/Family Reconciliation Policies for Parents in France,

Germany, the Netherlands, and the UK in the 2000s," *Social Politics* 15(3): 261–81.

Lister, Ruth (1997). *Citizenship: Feminist Perspectives*. Basingstoke: Macmillan.

Lovell, Vicky, Elizabeth O'Neill and Skylar Olsen (2007). "Maternity Leave in the United States: Paid Parental Leave is Still Not Standard, Even Among the Best US Employers," *IWPR Fact Sheet #A131*. Washington, DC: Institute for Women's Policy Research.

Maag, Elaine (2013). "Taxation and the Family: How Does the Tax System Subsidize Child Care Expenses?" in *Tax Policy Center: Tax Topics*. Washington, DC: Urban Institute and Brookings Institution. Retrieved February 17, 2011, from www.taxpolicycenter.org/briefing-book/key-elements/family/child-care-subsidies.cfm.

Mahon, Rianne (2002). "Child Care: Toward What Kind of 'Social Europe'?" *Social Politics* 9(3): 343–79.

(2006). "The OECD and the Work/Family Reconciliation Agenda: Competing Frames," in Jane Lewis (ed.), *Children, Changing Families and Welfare States*. Cheltenham: Edward Elgar, 173–97.

Maier, Friederike, and Zorica Rapp with Catherine Johnson (1995). "Women and the Employment Rate: The Causes and Consequences of Variations in Female Activity and Employment Patterns in Germany," in *German Report for the EC-Network, Women and Employment*. University of Manchester, Institute of Science and Technology.

Mandel, Hadas, and Moshe Semyonov (2005). "Family Policies, Wage Structures, and Gender Gaps: Sources of Earning Inequality in 20 Countries," *American Sociological Review* 70(6): 949–67.

Marshall, T. H. (1964). *Class, Citizenship and Social Development: Essays by T. H. Marshall*. Garden City: Anchor Books.

Martin, Claude (2010). "The Reframing of Family Policies in France: Processes and Actors," *Journal of European Social Policy* 19(5): 410–21.

Martin, Claude, Antoine Math and Evelyne Renaudat (1998). "Caring for Very Young Children and Dependent Elderly People in France: Towards a Commodification of Social Care?" in Jane Lewis (ed.), *Gender, Social Care and Welfare State Restructuring in Europe*. Aldershot, Hants.: Ashgate, 139–74.

Martin, Sherry L., and Gill Steel (2008). *Democratic Reform in Japan: Assessing the Impact*. Boulder: Lynne Rienner.

Mätzke, Margitta, and Ilona Ostner (2010a). "The Role of Old Ideas in the New German Family Policy Agenda." *German Policy Studies* 6(3): 119–62.

(2010b). "Introduction: Change and Continuity in Recent Family Policies." *Journal of European Social Policy* 20(5): 387–98.

(2010c). "Postscript: Ideas and Agents of Change in Time." *Journal of European Social Policy* 20(5): 468–76.

Mazur, Amy G. (2002). *Theorizing Feminist Policy*. New York: Oxford University Press.

(2003). "Drawing Comparative Lessons from France and Germany," *Review of Policy Research* 20(3): 493–524.

(2007). "Introduction: Feminists Engage the Republic: Comparative Lessons from France," *French Politics* 5(3): 187–90.

Mazur, Amy G., and Susanne Zwingel (2003). "Comparing Feminist Policy in Politics and at Work in France and Germany," *Review of Policy Research* 20(3): 365–84.

McCaffery, Edward J. (1997). *Taxing Women*. University of Chicago Press.

McDonald, Peter (2000). "Gender Equity in Theories of Fertility Transition," *Population and Development Review* 26(3): 427–43.

McIntosh, Alison C. (1983). *Population Policy in Western Europe: Responses to Low Fertility in France, Sweden, and West Germany*. Armonk, NY: M. E. Sharpe.

Mead, Lawrence (1986). *Beyond Entitlement: The Social Obligations of Citizenship*. New York: Free Press.

Mendolicchio, Concetta (2005). "Gender and Private Returns to Education: A Cross-European Analysis," Département des sciences économiques de l'Université catholique de Louvain, Discussion Paper 2005–56.

Mettler, Suzanne (1998). *Dividing Citizens: Gender and Federalism in New Deal Public Policy*. Ithaca: Cornell University Press.

(2005). *Soldiers to Citizens: The G.I. Bill and the Making of the Greatest Generation*. New York: Oxford University Press.

MHLW (Ministry of Health, Labor and Welfare, Japan, n.d.). "Introduction to the Revised Child Care and Family Care Leave Law." Retrieved April 16, 2011, from www.mhlw.go.jp/english/index.html.

(2007). "Effective April 1, 2007: Scope of Coverage for the Child Allowance System Will Expand." Retrieved March 27, 2011, from www.mhlw.go.jp/english/topics/child-support/index.html.

(2008). 2007–2008 Health, Labor and Welfare White Paper 7, Section 3: "Promotion of Various Improvements in Day Care Services and Comprehensive Measures for After-School Children." Retrieved February 23, 2014, from www.mhlw.go.jp/english/wp/wp-hw2/part2/p2c6s3.pdf.

(2009). Introduction to the Revised Child Care and Family Care Leave Law. Prepared August 2009. Retrieved June 13, 2013, from www.mhlw.go.jp/english/policy/affairs/dl/05.pdf.

(2010). Child Allowance. Retrieved June 13, 2013, from www.mhlw.go.jp/english/policy/affairs/dl/09.pdf.

(2011). "Establishment of a Unified System in which the Entire Society Supports Child and Childcare: Realization of Unifying Systems, Resources and Benefits" (English translation of the language of the *kodomoen* Bill presented to the Diet in 2011). Retrieved June 12, 2013, from www.mhlw.go.jp/english/wp/wp-hw4/dl/equal_employment_and_child_welfare/2011071914.pdf.

(2012a). Equal Employment and Child Welfare, section 7 of the 2011–2012 MHLW White Paper, English Summary. Retrieved June 12, 2013, from www.mhlw.go.jp/english/wp/wp-hw6/index.html.

(2012b). "The Outline of the Act for Amending Part of the Child Allowance Act." Retrieved June 20, 2013, from www.mhlw.go.jp/bunya/kodomo/osirase/dl/100402-1u_e.pdf.

(2012c). "Promotion to Support the Balance Between Work and Family Life." Retrieved June 24, 2013, from www.mhlw.go.jp/english/policy/children/work–family/dl/psbbwfl.pdf.

(2012d). "くるみんマーク認定を目指しましょう!!!" ("Let's Aim for Getting the Kurumin Certification!"). Retrieved June 24, 2013, from www.mhlw.go.jp/bunya/koyoukintou/pamphlet/dl/26a.pdf.

(2013). Press release, "Report of Current State on Unlicensed Daycare Centers in 2011" (厚生労働省2013年報道発表資料『平成23年度 認可外保育施設の現況取りまとめ』).

Michel, Sonya (1999). *Children's Interests / Mothers' Rights: The Shaping of America's Child Care Policy*. New Haven: Yale University Press.

Michel, Sonya, and Rianne Mahon (2002). *Child Care Policy at the Crossroads: Gender and Welfare State Restructuring*. New York: Routledge.

Michel, Sonya, and Ito Peng (2012). "All in the Family? Migrants, Nationhood, and Care Regimes in Asia and North America," *Journal of European Social Policy* 38(10): 406–18.

Mie, Ayako (2013). "Maternity Leave, Day Care Still Elude Many Working Mothers: Working Moms Face High Hurdles in Efforts to Return to Workplace." *Japan Times*, June 18.

Mink, Gwendolyn (1995). *The Wages of Motherhood: Inequality in the Welfare State, 1917–1942*. Ithaca: Cornell University Press.

Mishima, Ko (1998). "The Changing Relationship between Japan's LDP and the Bureaucracy: Hashimoto's Administrative Reform Effort and Its Politics," *Asian Survey* 47(5): 968–85.

　(2007). "Grading Japanese Prime Minister Koizumi's Revolution: How Far Has the LDP's Policymaking Changed?" *Asian Survey* 47(5): 727–48.

MOF (Ministry of Finance, Japan) (2003). FY 2003 Tax Reform (Main Points). Retrieved June 24, 2013, from www.mof.go.jp/english/tax_policy/tax_reform/fy2003/index.htm.

Morel, Nathalie (2007). "From Subsidiarity to 'Free Choice': Child- and Elder-care Policy Reforms in France, Belgium, Germany, and the Netherlands," *Social Policy & Administration* 41(6): 618–37.

Morgan, Kimberley J. (2002). "Does Anyone Have a 'Libre Choix?' Subversive Liberalism and the Politics of French Child Policy," in Sonya Michel and Rianne Mahon (eds.), *Child Care Policy at the Crossroads*. New York: Routledge, 143–70.

　(2003). "The Politics of Mothers' Employment: France in Comparative Perspective," *World Politics* 55(2): 259–89.

　(2005). "The 'Production' of Child Care: How Labor Markets Shape Social Policy and Vice Versa," *Social Politics* 12(2): 243–63.

　(2006). *Working Mothers and the Welfare State: Religion and the Politics of Work–Family Policies in Western Europe and the United States*. Stanford University Press.

　(2009a). "Caring Time Policies in Western Europe: Trends and Implications," *Comparative European Politics* 7: 37–55.

　(2009b). "The Political Path to a Dual-Earner/Dual-Caregiver Society: Pitfalls and Possibilities," in Janet C. Gornick and Marcia K. Meyers (eds.), *Gender Equality: Transforming Family Divisions of Labor*. London: Verso, 317–37.

Morinobu, Shigeki, and Atsushi Nakamoto (2013). "A Revised Estimation of Japan's Income Tax Base," *Public Policy Review* 9(2): 433–55 (March). Policy Research Institute, Ministry of Finance, Japan. Retrieved January 3, 2014, from www.mof.go.jp/english/pri/publication/pp_review/ppr021/ppr021f.pdf.

Mosesdottir, Lilja (2001). "Pathways toward the Dual Breadwinner Model: The Role of the Swedish, German and the American States," *International Review of Sociology* 10(2): 189–205.

Müller, Peter, and Merlind Theile (2012). "Let Down By the Chancellor: Merkel's Passive Gender Equality Policy Could Backfire" (November 21). *Der Spiegel*.

Retrieved February 19, 2014, from www.spiegel.de/international/germany/passive-gender-equality-policy-could-backfire-for-angela-merkel-a-868343.html.

Murase, Miriam (2006). *Cooperation Over Conflict: The Women's Movement and the State in Postwar Japan*. New York and London: Routledge.

Murray, Charles (1984). *Losing Ground: American Social Policy 1950–1980*. New York: Basic Books.

National Women's Law Center (2011). "Head Start: Supporting Success for Children and Families" (November). Retrieved December 30, 2013, from www.nwlc.org/sites/default/files/pdfs/head_start_fact_sheet_2011.pdf.

New Zealand Ministry of Business, Innovation & Employment: Labor Information (2013). Retrieved May 30, 2013, from www.dol.govt.nz/index.asp.

Newman, Katherine S. (2008). "Ties that Bind: Cultural Interpretations of Delayed Adulthood in Western Europe and Japan," *Sociological Forum* 23(4): 645–69.

Nicaise, Ides, and K. U. Leuven (2011). "Building the Tools to Fight In-Work Poverty." European Commission Employment, Social Affairs and Inclusion. Retrieved May 21, 2013, from http://ec.europa.eu/social/main.jsp?catId=1024&langId=en&newsId=1390&furtherNews=yes.

NIPSSR (National Institute for Population and Social Security Research of Japan) (2011). *The Fourteenth Japanese National Fertility Survey in 2010: Marriage Process and Fertility of Japanese Married Couples* (Highlights of the Survey Results on Married Couples). Retrieved December 6, 2014, from www.ipss.go.jp/site-ad/index_english/nfs14/Nfs14_Couples_Eng.pdf.

(2012). "Fourteenth Japanese National Fertility Survey, 2010." Retrieved June 20, 2013, from www.ipss.go.jp/site-ad/index_english/nfs14/Nfs14_Couples_Eng.pdf.

(2014). "Population Pyramid for Japan: 1920–2060." Retrieved February 5, 2014, from www.ipss.go.jp/site-ad/TopPageData/pyrea.html.

Noble, Gregory W. (2010). "The Decline of Particularism in Japanese Politics," *Journal of East Asian Studies* 10(2): 239–73.

Obama, Barack (2013). State of the Union Address, February 12, 2013. Retrieved July 16, 2013, from www.politico.com/story/2013/02/state-of-the-union-2013-president-barack-obamas-speech-transcript-text-87550_Page2.html.

O'Connor, Julia (1996). "Labour Market Participation, Gender and Citizenship," *Current Sociology* 44(2): 78–108.

O'Connor, Julia S., Anna Shola Orloff and Sheila Shaver (1999). *States, Markets, Families: Gender, Liberalism and Social Policy in Australia, Canada, Great Britain and the United States*. New York: Cambridge University Press.

OECD (1999). *A Caring World: The New Social Policy Agenda*. Paris: OECD.

(2003). *Babies and Bosses: Reconciling Work and Family Life, Volume II: Austria, Ireland and Japan*. Paris: OECD Publication Service.

(2005a). OECD Employment Outlook Statistical Annex. Retrieved June 28, 2013, from www.oecd.org/employment/emp/35024561.pdf.

(2005b). Table 4–1, "Employment and Part-time Work by Presence and Age of Children, 2003," in *Extending Opportunities: How Active Social Policy Can Benefit Us All*. Paris: OECD Publication Service.

(2007a). *Babies and Bosses – Reconciling Work and Family Life: A Synthesis of Findings for OECD Countries*. Paris: OECD Publication Service.

(2007b). Table H: Earning Dispersion, Gender Wage Gap and Incidence of Low Pay, in *OECD Employment Outlook 2007*. Paris: OECD Publication Service.

(2008a). *Education at a Glance 2008: OECD Indicators*. Paris: OECD Publishing. Retrieved June 28, 2013, from www.oecd-ilibrary.org/education/education-at-a-glance-2008_eag-2008-en.

(2008b). *Labour Force Statistics 2008*. Paris: OECD Publishing.

(2011a). Graph 2.10, "Gini Index of Income Inequalities," in *How's Life?* Paris: OECD Publishing.

(2011b). *OECD Better Life Initiative*. Paris: OECD Publishing. Retrieved December 8, 2012, from www.oecdbetterlifeindex.org/topics/work-life-balance.

(2012a). Chart PF 3.2, "Participation Rate in Childcare and Pre-school Services among Children Aged 0–5 Years," in OECD Social Policy Division – Directorate of Employment, Labour and Social Affairs, Family Database (Dec. 2013 version). Retrieved January 7, 2014, from www.oecd.org/social/family/database.

(2012b). Chart SF2.3.A, "Mean Age of Women at the Birth of the First Child, 2009," and Chart SF2.3.B, "The Postponement of the First Birth in 2009, since 1970." Both drawn from OECD Social Policy Division – Directorate of Employment, Labour and Social Affairs, Family Database (2012 version). Retrieved from www.oecd.org/social/family/database.

(2012c). Figure 13.3 "The Price of Motherhood is High across OECD Countries," in *Closing the Gender Gap: Act Now*. Paris: OECD Publication Service.

(2012d). Indicators of Gender Equality in Employment. Retrieved January 6, 2014, from www.oecd.org/gender/data/indicatorsofgenderequalityinemployment.htm.

(2012e). Table CO2.2.A, "Poverty Rates for Children and Households with Children by Household Characteristics, OECD Countries, 2008." Drawn from the OECD Social Policy Division – Directorate of Employment, Labour and Social Affairs, Family Database (2012 version). Retrieved from www.oecd.org/social/family/database.

(2012f). Chart SF2.4.A, "Proportion of Births Out of Wedlock, 2010." Drawn from OECD Social Policy Division – Directorate of Employment, Labour and Social Affairs, Family Database (2012 version). Retrieved from www.oecd.org/social/family/database.

(2013a). "Average Annual Hours Actually Worked per Worker." OECD Stat-Extracts. Retrieved January 4, 2014 from http://stats.oecd.org/Index.aspx?DataSetCode=ANHRS.

(2013b). Chart PF1.1.A, "Family Spending on Cash, Services and Tax Measures." OECD Social Expenditure Database, from OECD Social Policy Division – Directorate of Employment, Labour and Social Affairs, Family Database (Dec. 2013 version). Retrieved January 16, 2014, from www.oecd.org/social/family/database.

(2013c). Chart PF2.1.A, "Child-related Leave Periods by Duration of Unpaid Leave and the Duration of the Full-Rate Equivalent of the Leave Period if Paid at 100% of Last Earnings, 2011/2012"; Chart PF2.1.B, "Spending on Maternity and Parental Leave Payments per Child Born, 2009." OECD Social Expenditure database (preliminary data for 2008 and 2009). Retrieved from www.oecd.org/els/social/expenditure.

(2013d). Chart PF3.2.A, "Enrolment Rates of Children under Six in Childcare and Early Education Services." OECD Social Policy Division – Directorate of

Employment, Labour and Social Affairs, Family Database. Retrieved February 9, 2014 from www.oecd.org/els/social/family/database.

(2013e). Chart PF3.4.B, "Net Childcare Costs for a Dual-earner Family with Full-time Arrangements of 167% of the Average Wage, 2008." OECD Social Policy Division – Directorate of Employment, Labour and Social Affairs, Family Database (Dec. 2013 version). Retrieved February 22, 2014, from www.oecd.org/social/family/database.

(2013f). Incidence and Composition of Part-time Employment: Persons Aged 15 and Over, Percentages. *OECD Employment Outlook 2013*. Paris: OECD Publication Service.

(2013g). "Percentage of Employed in Involuntary Part-time Employment, by Sex and Age Group." Retrieved January 6, 2014, from www.oecd.org/gender/data/indicatorsofgenderequalityinemployment.htm.

(2013h). "Share of Women in Parliament: Percentage, 1995 and 2011," in *OECD Factbook 2013*. Paris: OECD Publishing. Retrieved June 28, 2013, from www.oecd-ilibrary.org/economics/oecd-factbook-2013/share-of-women-in-parliament_factbook-2013-graph272-en.

(2013i). Table PF1.3, "Family Cash Benefits." OECD Social Policy Division – Directorate of Employment, Labour and Social Affairs, Family Database (Dec. 2013 version). Retrieved January 5, 2014, from www.oecd.org/social/family/database.

(2013j). Table PF2.1, "Key Characteristics of Parental Leave Systems." OECD Social Policy Division – Directorate of Employment, Labour and Social Affairs, Family Database (Dec. 2013 version). Retrieved February 22, 2014, from www.oecd.org/social/family/database.

(2013k). Table PF3.1, "Public Spending on Childcare and Early Education, 2009." OECD Social Policy Division – Directorate of Employment, Labour and Social Affairs, Family Database (Dec. 2013 version). Retrieved February 22, 2014, from www.oecd.org/social/family/database.

(2013l). Table PF3.2.A, "Participation Rates in Formal Care and Pre-school for Children under Six, 2008." OECD Social Policy Division – Directorate of Employment, Labour and Social Affairs, Family Database (Dec. 2013 version). Retrieved February 22, 2014, from www.oecd.org/social/family/database.

(2013m). "Total Fertility Rates, 1970–2012," in *OECD Factbook 2013*. Retrieved February 22, 2014, from www.oecd-ilibrary.org/economics/oecd-factbook-2013/total-fertility-rates_factbook-2013-table9-en.

Office of Head Start, Administration for Children and Families, US Department of Health and Human Services (2012). "Early Head Start Services Snapshot (2011-2012)." Retrieved July 13, 2013, from http://eclkc.ohs.acf.hhs.gov/hslc/mr/psr/NATIONAL-EHS.PDF.

(2013). "History of Head Start." Retrieved July 13, 2013, from www.acf.hhs.gov/programs/ohs/about/history-of-head-start.

(2014). "Head Start Program Fact Sheets" for FY 2004 through FY 2013. Retrieved December 7, 2014, from http://eclkc.ohs.acf.hhs.gov/hslc/data/factsheets.

Olk, Thomas (2010). "Investing in Children? Changes in Policies Concerning Children and Families in European Countries," in Mimi Ajzenstadt (ed.), *Children, Gender and Families in Mediterranean Welfare States*. New York: Springer, 3–33.

Ondrich, Jan, and C. Katharina Spiess (1998). "Care of Children in a Low Fertility Setting: Transitions Between Home and Market Care for Pre-school Children in Germany," *Population Studies* 52(1): 35–48.

O'Reilly, Jacqueline, and Silke Bothfeld (2003). "Regulating Working-time Transitions in Germany," in Jacqueline O'Reilly (ed.), *Regulating Working-Time Transitions in Europe*. Cheltenham: Edward Elgar, 86–122.

Orloff, Ann Shola (1993). "Gender and the Social Rights of Citizenship: The Comparative Analysis of Gender Relations and Welfare States," *American Sociological Review* 58(3): 303–28.

(1996). "Gender in the Welfare State," *Annual Review of Sociology* 22: 21–78.

(2006). "From Maternalism to 'Employment for Self': State Policies to Promote Women's Employment across the Affluent Democracies," in Jonah Levy (ed.), *The State after Statism*. Cambridge, Mass.: Harvard University Press, 230–68.

(2009a). "Gendering the Comparative Analysis of Welfare States: An Unfinished Agenda," *Sociological Theory* 27(3): 317–43.

(2009b). "Should Feminists Aim for Gender Symmetry? Why a Dual-Earner/Dual-Caregiver Society Is Not Every Feminist's Utopia," in Janet C. Gornick and Marcia K. Meyers (eds.), *Gender Equality: Transforming Family Divisions of Labor*. London: Verso, 129–57.

Osawa, Mari (2002). "People in Irregular Modes of Employment: Are They Really Not Subject to Discrimination?" *Social Science Japan Journal* 4(2): 183–99.

(2003). "Japanese Government Approaches to Gender Equality since the mid-1990s," Wayne State University College of Urban, Labor and Metropolitan Affairs Occasional Paper Series, 9.

(2007a). "Livelihood Security System and Social Exclusion: The Male Breadwinner Model Revisited," in Ilse Lenz, Charlotte Ullrich and Barbara Fersch (eds.), *Gender Orders Unbound*, 277–301. Opladen, Germany; Farmington Hills, MI: Barbara Budrich, 2007.

(2007b). "Comparative Livelihood Security Systems from a Gender Perspective with a Focus on Japan," in Sylvia Walby, Heidi Gottfried, Karin Gottschall and Mari Osawa (eds.), *Gendering the Knowledge Economy: Comparative Perspectives*. New York: Palgrave MacMillan.

(2007c). *Gendai Nihon no Hoshō shisutemu (The Contemporary Japanese Livelihood Security System)*. Tokyo: Iwanami Shoten.

Ostner, Ilona (1998). "The Politics of Care Policies in Germany," in Jane Lewis (ed.), *Gender, Social Care, and Welfare State Restructuring in Europe*. Aldershot, Hants.: Ashgate.

(2010). "Farewell to the Family as We Know it: Family Policy Change in Germany," *German Policy Studies* 6(1): 211–44.

Palier, Bruno (2007). "The Politics of Reforms in Bismarckian Welfare Systems," the European Union Studies Association (EUSA) Biennial Conference, Montreal, Quebec, May 17–19. Retrieved May 21, 2013, from http://aei.pitt.edu/7994/1/palier-b-05i.pdf.

Pearce, Diana M. (1985). "Toil and Trouble: Women Workers and Unemployment Compensation," *Signs* 10(3): 439–59.

Pedersen, Susan (1993). *Family, Dependence, and the Origins of the Welfare State: Britain and France 1914–1945*. New York: Cambridge University Press.

Pekkanen, R. (2004). "After the Developmental State: Civil Society in Japan"*Journal of East Asian Studies* 4: 363–88.

Peng, Ito (2000). "Childcare Policies in Japan: Postwar Developments and Recent Reforms," in Thomas P. Boje and Arnlaug Leira (eds.), *Gender, Welfare State and the Market: Towards a New Division of Labour*. London: Routledge, 165–97.

(2002). "Social Care in Crisis: Gender, Demography, and Welfare State Restructuring in Japan," *Social Politics* Fall: 411–43.

(2004). "Postindustrial Pressures, Political Regime Shifts, and Social Policy Reform in Japan and South Korea," *Journal of East Asian Studies* 4(3): 389–425.

Périvier, Hélène (2003). "Emploi des femmes et charges familiales: repenser le congé parental en France à la lumière des expériences étrangères," Symposium on Women's Employment and Family Responsibilities, the OFCE, Observatoire français des conjonctures économiques, the French Economic Observatory, Paris. Retrieved May 31, 2012, from www.ofce.sciences-po.fr/pdf/revue/9-90.pdf.

(2004). "Emploi des mères et garde des jeunes enfants en Europe," *Revue de l'OFCE* 90(3): 225–58.

Pfau-Effinger, Birgit (1998). "Culture or Structure as Explanations for Differences in Part-Time Work in Germany, Finland and the Netherlands?" in Jacqueline O'Reilly and Collette Fagan (eds.), *Part-Time Prospects: An International Comparison of Part-Time Work in Europe, North America and the Pacific Rim*. New York: Routledge, 177–98.

Pierson, Paul (1995). "The Scope and Nature of Business Power: Employers and the American Welfare State, 1900–1935." Paper presented at the Annual Meeting of the American Political Science Association, Chicago, Ill., September.

(2001). *The New Politics of the Welfare State*. Oxford University Press.

(2004). *Politics in Time: History, Institutions, and Political Analysis*. Princeton University Press.

Pierson, Paul, and Theda Skocpol (2002). "Historical Institutionalism in Contemporary Political Science," in Ira Katznelson and Helen V. Milner (eds.), *Political Science: State of the Discipline*. New York: Norton, 693–721.

Pontusson, Jonas (1995). "From Comparative Public Policy to Political Economy: Putting Institutions in their Place and Taking Interest Seriously," *Comparative Political Studies* 28(1): 117–47.

Population Reference Bureau (2013). "2013 World Population Data Sheet." Retrieved February 17, 2014, from www.prb.org/pdf13/2013-population-data-sheet_eng.pdf.

Prud'homme, Nicole (2004, April 29). Quoted in "Travaux de la commission des affaires sociales du sénat," *Proceedings of the Social Affairs Committee of the Senate*. Retrieved May 31, 2012, from www.assmat.com/defaut.htm.

Rampell, Catherin (2012, December 17). "The 'Mommy Penalty,' Around the World." *New York Times*. Retrieved December 28, 2012, from http://economix.blogs.nytimes.com/2012/12/17/the-mommy-penalty-around-the-world.

Ray, Rebecca (2008). "A Detailed Look at Parental Leave Policies in 21 OECD Countries." Washington, DC: Center for Economic and Policy Research.

Raymo, James M. (2003). "Educational Attainment and the Transition to First Marriage among Japanese Women," *Demography* 40(1): 83–101.

Reid, T. R. (2010). *The Healing of America: A Global Quest for Better, Cheaper, and Fairer Health Care*. New York: Penguin Press.

Retherford, Robert D., and Naohiro Ogawa (2006). "Japan's Baby Bust," in Fred Harris (ed.), *The Baby Bust: Who Will Do the Work? Who Will Pay the Taxes?* Lanham: Rowman and Littlefield, 5–47.

Revillard, Anne (2006). "Work/Family Policy in France: From State Familialism to State Feminism?" *International Journal of Law, Policy and the Family* 20(2): 133–50.

Revue de l'OFCE 90(3) (2004). "Travail de femmes et inégalités." Paris: OFCE, Observatoire français des conjonctures économiques (the French Economic Observatory).

Rindfuss, Ronald R., Karen Benjamin Guzzo and S. Philip Morgan (2003). "The Changing Institutional Context of Low Fertility," *Population Research and Policy Review* 22: 411–38.

Ristau, Malte (2004). "Family Means Future: Guidelines of a Sustainable Family Policy." Document received from the BMFSFJ in July 2004.

Roberts, Glenda (2002). "Pinning Hopes on Angels: Reflections from an Aging Japan's Urban Landscape," in Roger Goodman (ed.), *Family and Social Policy in Japan: Anthropological Approaches.* Cambridge University Press, 54–91.

(2005). "Balancing Work and Life: Whose Work? Whose Life?" *Asian Perspective* 29(1): 175–211.

(2007). "Similar Outcomes, Different Paths: The Cross-National Transfer of Gendered Regulations of Employment," in Sylvia Walby, Heidi Gottfried, Karen Gottschalk and Maria Osawa (eds.), *Gendering the Knowledge Economy: Comparative Perspectives.* Basingstoke: Palgrave, 140–60.

Rosenbluth, Frances McCall, ed. (2007). *The Political Economy of Japan's Low Fertility.* Stanford University Press.

Rosenbluth, Frances McCall, and Michael F. Thies (2010). *Japan Transformed: Political Change and Economic Restructuring.* Princeton University Press.

Ruhm, Christopher J. (2011). "Policies to Assist Parents with Young Children," *The Future of Children* 21(2): 37–68.

Rürup, Bernd, and Sandra Gruescu (2003). *Nachhaltige Familienpolitik im Interesse einer aktiven Bevölkerungsentwicklung.* Gutachten im Auftrag des Bundesministeriums für Familie, Senioren, Frauen und Jugend.

Sainsbury, Diane (1994). *Gendering Welfare States.* London: Sage.

Saraceno, Chiara (1997). "Family Change, Family Policies and the Restructuring of Welfare," in Patrick Hennessy (ed.), *Family, Market and Community: Equity and Efficiency in Social Policy.* Paris: OECD Publications, 81–99.

Satō Hiroki and Takeishi Emiko (2008). *Hito o Ikasu Kigyō ga Nobiru: Jinji Senryaku toshite no Wāku Raifu Baransu (Companies that Make Full Use of People Grow: Work–Life Balance as a Human Resource Management Strategy).* Tokyo: Keisō Shobō.

Satō Hiroki, Osawa Mari and Charles Weathers (2001). "'Atypical' and 'Irregular' Labor in Contemporary Japan: The Authors Debate," *Social Science Japan Journal* 4(2): 219–23.

Schattschneider, E. E. (1960). *The Semi-Sovereign People: A Realist's View of Democracy in America.* New York: Holt, Rinehart and Winston.

Schmidt, Vivien A. (2002). "Does Discourse Matter in the Politics of Welfare State Adjustment?" *Comparative Political Studies* 35(2): 168–93.

(2008). "Discursive Institutionalism: The Explanatory Power of Ideas and Discourse," *Annual Review of Political Science* 11: 303–26.

Schönberg, Uta, and Johannes Ludsteck (2007). "Maternity Leave Legislation, Female Labor Supply, and the Family Wage Gap," IZA Discussion Paper 2699 (Forschungsinstitut zur Zukunft der Arbeit, Institute for the Study of Labor discussion paper series, March). Retrieved June 28, 2012, from http://ftp.iza.org/dp2699.pdf.

Schoppa, Leonard (2006). *Race for the Exits: Women, Firms, and the Unraveling of Japan's System of Social Protection.* Ithaca: Cornell University Press.

(2010a). "Exit, Voice, and Family Policy in Japan: Limited Changes Despite Broad Recognition of the Declining Fertility Problem," *Journal of European Social Policy* 20(5): 422–32.

(2010b). "Review of Welfare and Capitalism in Postwar Japan, by Margarita Estevez-Abe," *Journal for Japanese Studies* 36(1): 97–101.

Schulman, Karen, and Helen Blank (2012). "Downward Slide: State Child Care Assistance Policies 2012." National Women's Law Center. Retrieved December 8, 2012, from www.nwlc.org/sites/default/files/pdfs/NWLC2012_StateChildCare AssistanceReport.pdf.

Schultz, Vicki (2000). "Life's Work," *Columbia Law Review* 100(7): 1881–964.

Seelieb-Kaiser, Martin (1995). "The Development of Social Assistance and Unemployment Insurance in Germany and Japan," *Social Policy & Administration* 29(3): 269–93.

Seelieb-Kaiser, Martin, and Timo Fleckenstein (2009). "The Political Economy of Occupational Family Policies: Comparing Workplaces in Britain and Germany," *British Journal of Industrial Relations* 47(4): 741–64.

Seelieb-Kaiser, Martin, and Tuukka Toivonen (2011). "Between Reforms and Birthrates: Germany, Japan and Family Policy Discourse," *Social Politics* 18(3): 331–60.

Senior, Jennifer (2014). *All Joy and No Fun: The Paradox of Modern Parenthood.* New York: Harper Collins Publishers.

Shiota, Sakiko. 2000. *Nihon no shakai seisaku to jendaa: danjo byōdō no keizai kiban (Japan's Social Policy and Gender: Economic Basis of Gender Equality).* Tokyo: Nihon Hyouronsha.

Shirahase, Sawako (2002). "Women's Working Pattern and the Support to Working Mothers in Contemporary Japan," Working Paper Series (E). Tokyo: National Institute of Population and Social Security Research.

Siim, Birte (2000). *Gender and Citizenship: Politics and Agency in France, Britain and Denmark.* Cambridge University Press.

Skocpol, Theda (1992). *Protecting Soldiers and Mothers: The Political Origins of Social Policy in the United States.* Cambridge, Mass.: Belknap Press of Harvard University Press.

(1995). *Social Policy in the United States: Future Possibilities in Historical Perspective.* Princeton University Press.

(2000). *The Missing Middle: Working Families and the Future of American Social Policy.* New York: W. W. Norton.

Sleebos, Joëlle (2003). "Low Fertility Rates in OECD Countries: Facts and Policy Responses," OECD Labour Market and Social Policy Occasional Papers 15. Paris: OECD Publishing.

Smith, Steven (2002). "Privatization, Devolution, and the Welfare State," in Bo Rothstein and Sven Steinmo (eds.), *Restructuring the Welfare State: Political Institutions and Policy Change*. New York: Palgrave MacMillan, Chapter 4.

Song, Jiyeoun (2010). "Japan's Labor Market Reform after the Collapse of the Bubble Economy: Political Determinants of Regulatory Changes," *Asian Survey* 50(6): 1011–31.

Soskice, David (2005). "Varieties of Capitalism and Cross-National Gender Differences," *Social Politics* 12(2): 170–9.

Statistisches Bundesamt (German Federal Statistics Office) (2012). *Kindertagesbetreuung in Deutschland 2012 (Childcare in Germany 2012)*. Wiesbaden: Statistisches Bundesamt. Retrieved December 6, 2014, from https://www.destatis .de/DE/PresseService/Presse/Pressekonferenzen/2012/kindertagesbetreuung/ begleitmaterial_PDF.pdf?__blob=publicationFile.

Steiner, Viktor, and Katharina Wrohlich (2005). "Household Taxation, Income Splitting and Labor Supply Incentives – A Microsimulation Study for Germany," DIW Discussion Papers Abstract 421. *CESifo Economic Studies* 50(3): 541–68. Retrieved August 23, 2005, from www.fu-berlin.de/wifo/forschung/splitting.pdf.

Steinmo, Sven (1993). *Taxation and Democracy: Swedish, British and American Approaches to Financing the Modern State*. New Haven: Yale University Press.

   (2010). *The Evolution of Modern States: Sweden, Japan, and the United States*. Cambridge University Press.

Steinmo, Sven, Kathleen Thelen and Frank Longstreth (1992). *Structuring Politics: Historical Institutionalism in Comparative Analysis*. Cambridge University Press.

Stetson, Dorothy McBride, and Amy Mazur (1995). *Comparative State Feminism*. London: Sage Publishing.

Stone, Pamela (2007). *Opting Out? Why Women Really Quit Careers and Head Home*. Berkeley: University of California Press.

Streeck, Wolfgang, and Kathleen Thelen, eds. (2005). *Beyond Continuity: Institutional Change in Advanced Political Economies*. New York: Oxford University Press.

Strobel, Pierre (2004). "Les pouvoirs publics et la famille: l'état et les transformations de la famille," *Cahiers français* 322: 57–64.

Strohmeier, Klaus Peter (2002). "Family Policy – How Does it Work?" in Franz-Xaver Kaufmann, Anton Kuijsten, Hans-Joachim Schulze and Klaus Peter Strohmeier (eds.), *Family Life and Family Policies in Europe: Problems and Issues in Comparative Perspective*, Volume II. New York: Oxford University Press, 321–62.

Suleiman, Ezra N. (1974). *Politics, Power, and Bureaucracy in France: The Administrative Elite*. Princeton University Press.

Sundbye, Annamaria, and Ariane Hegewisch (2011). "Maternity, Paternity, and Adoption Leave in the United States." Institute for Women's Policy Research Fact Sheet A143. Retrieved December 6, 2014 from file:///C:/Users/boling/Downloads/A143_ updated.pdf.

Suzuki, Toru (2006). "Fertility Decline and Policy Development in Japan," *The Japanese Journal of Population* 4(1): 1–32.

Swiss Federal Statistical Office (2011). "Quality of Employment in Switzerland," Federal Department of Home Affairs, Neuchatel. Retrieved May 20, 2013, from www.bfs.admin.ch/bfs/portal/en/tools/search.html.

Takahara, Kanako (2010). "Kindergartens, Day Care Centers May Merge" (November 17). *Japan Times*. Retrieved June 14, 2013, from www.japantimes .co.jp/news/2010/11/17/reference/kindergartens-day-care-centers-may-merge/# .Ubsz8_nVDzg.

(2011a). "DPJ Withdraws Child Allowance Bill as Opposition Digs its Heels In" (March 31). *Japan Times*.

(2011b). "Preschool, Day Care Integration Plan Eases" (January 25). *Japan Times*.

Takeda, Hiroko (2005). *Political Economy of Reproduction in Japan*. New York / London: Routledge/Curzon.

Tamiya, Yuko, and Masato Shikata (2010). "Analysis of Time Use Surveys on Work and Care in Japan," in Debbie Budlender (ed.), *Time Use Studies and Unpaid Care Work*. New York: Routledge, 142–70.

Teschner, Julia (2000). "Conflicting Conceptions of Feminism in United Germany," in Anna Bull, Hanna Diamond and Rosalind Marsh (eds.), *Feminisms and Women's Movements in Contemporary Europe*. New York: MacMillan / St. Martin's Press, 194–210.

Thelen, Kathleen (2004). *How Institutions Evolve: The Political Economy of Skills in Germany, Britain, the United States, and Japan*. Cambridge University Press.

Thévenon, Olivier (2011). "Family Policies in OECD Countries: A Comparative Analysis," *Population and Development Review* 37(1): 57–87.

(2013). "Drivers of Female Labour Force Participation in the OECD," OECD Social, Employment and Migration Working Papers 145. Paris: OECD Publishing. Retrieved February 5, 2014, from http://dx.doi.org/10.1787/5k46cvrgnms6-en.

Tokyo Pregnancy Group (2011). "Maternity Leave in Japan." September 25, 2011, blogpost to Tokyo Pregnancy Group. Retrieved June 23, 2012, from http:// tokyopregnancygroup.blogspot.com/2011/09/maternity-leave-in-japan.html.

Torr, Berna Miller, and Susan E. Short (2004). "Second Births and the Second Shift: A Research Note on Gender Equity and Fertility," *Population and Development Review* 30(1): 109–30.

Toulemon, Laurent, Ariane Pailh and Clementine Rossier (2008). "France: High and Stable Fertility," *Demographic Research* 19: 503–55.

Tuttle, William M. (1995). "Rosie the Riveter and Her Latchkey Children: What Americans Can Learn about Child Day Care from the Second World War," *Child Welfare* 74(January/February): 92–114.

Ulrich, Ralf E. (2004, July 13). Interview, Institut für Bevölkerungsforschung und Sozialpolitik (Institute for Population Research), University of Bielefeld.

Uno, Kathleen S. (1999). *Passages to Modernity: Motherhood, Childhood, and Social Reform in Early Twentieth Century Japan*. Honolulu: University of Hawai'i Press.

Upham, Frank K. (1987). *Law and Social Change in Postwar Japan*. Cambridge, Mass.: Harvard University Press.

US Congress, Ways and Means Committee Prints (2004). *Green Book*, section 9 – Child care, Table 9–26, "Summary of Discretionary and Mandatory Child Care and Development Fund Expenditures, Fiscal Years 1995–2001," 108–16. Retrieved February 17, 2011, from http://frwebgate.access.gpo.gov/cgi-bin/getdoc .cgi?dbname=108_green_book&docid=f:wm006_09.pdf.

US White House, Office of Management and Budget (OMB) (2002). FY 2002 Budget, Table 22-4, "Tax Expenditures by Function." Retrieved June 13, 2005, from www.whitehouse.gov/omb/budget/fy2002/bud22_4.html.

Vienna Institute of Demography (2013). European Demographic Data Sheet 2012. Retrieved February 17, 2014, from www.oeaw.ac.at/vid/datasheet/download/ European_Demographic_Data_Sheet_2012.pdf.

Vogel, Suzanne (2013). *The Japanese Family in Transition: From the Professional Housewife Ideal to the Dilemmas of Choice*. New York: Rowman & Littlefield.

Vogt, Andrea, and Susanne Zwingel (2003). "Asking Fathers and Employers to Volunteer: A (De)Tour of Reconciliation Policy in Germany?" *Review of Policy Research* 20(3): 459–78.

Von Wahl, A. (2008). "From Family to Reconciliation Policy: How the Grand Coalition Reforms the German Welfare State," *German Politics and Society* 88(3): 25–49.

Waldfogel, Jane (2001). "Family and Medical Leave: Evidence from the 2000 Surveys," *Monthly Labor Review* 124(9): 17–23.

Weathers, Charles (2001). "Changing White-collar Workplaces and Female Temporary Workers in Japan," *Social Science Japan Journal* 4(2): 201–18.

(2003). "The Decentralization of Japan's Wage Setting System in Comparative Perspective," *Industrial Relations Journal* 34(2): 119–34.

(2004). "Temporary Workers, Women, and Labor Policymaking in Japan," *Japan Forum* 16(3): 423–47.

(2005). "In Search of Strategic Partners: Japan's Campaign for Equal Opportunity," *Social Science Japan Journal* 8(1): 69–89.

(2006). "Equal Opportunity for Japanese Women: What Progress?" *Japanese Economy* 33(4): 16–44.

Weldon, S. Laurel (2002). *Protest, Policy, and the Problem of Violence Against Women: A Cross-National Comparison*. University of Pittsburgh Press.

Wersig, Maria (2006, January 12–13). "Legal and Social Dimensions of the Male-breadwinner Model in Germany – Current Welfare-state Reforms and Gender Equality." Paper presented at the International Interdisciplinary Conference on "Equality and Diversity in Europe: Comparative Perspectives on Equality, Law and Politics." Helsinki, Finland. Retrieved May 21, 2013, from web.fu-berlin.de/ernaehrermodell/MaleBreadwinnerModelGermany.pdf.

White, Linda (2009). "Explaining Differences in Child Care Policy Development in France and the USA: Norms, Frames, Programmatic Ideas," *International Political Science Review* 30: 385–405.

Wilensky, Harold L. (1985). *Comparative Social Policy: Theories, Methods, Findings*. Berkeley: Institute of International Studies, University of California.

(1987). *Democratic Corporatism and Policy Linkages: The Interdependence of Industrial, Labor-market, Incomes, and Social Policies in Eight Countries*. Berkeley: Institute of International Studies, University of California.

Wiliarty, Sarah Elise (2011). *The CDU and the Politics of Gender in Germany: Bringing Women to the Party*. Cambridge University Press.

Williams, Fiona (1995). "Race/Ethnicity, Gender, and Class in Welfare States: A Framework for Comparative Analysis," *Social Politics* 2(2): 127–59.

Williams, Joan (2000). *Unbending Gender: Why Family and Work Conflict and What to Do About It*. New York: Oxford University Press.

(2005). "The Interaction of Courts and Legislatures in Creating Family-Responsive Workplaces," in *Working Time for Working Families: Europe and the United States*. Washington, DC: Friedrich Ebert Stiftung, Chapter 2.

Yamaguchi, Kazuo (2009). *Wāku Raifu Baransu: Jisshō to Seisaku Teigen (Work–Life Balance: Evidence and Policy Proposals)*. Tokyo: Nihon Keizai Hinbun Shuppansha.

Yamaguchi, Kazuo and Higuchi Yoshio (2008). *Ronsō: Nihon no Wāku Raifu Baransu (Debate: Work–Life Balance in Japan)*. Tokyo: Nihon Keizai Hinbun Shuppansha.

Yu, Wei-hsin (2002). "Jobs for Mothers: Married Women's Labor Force Reentry and Part-Time, Temporary Employment in Japan," *Sociological Forum* 17(3): 493–523.

Index